MW00668886

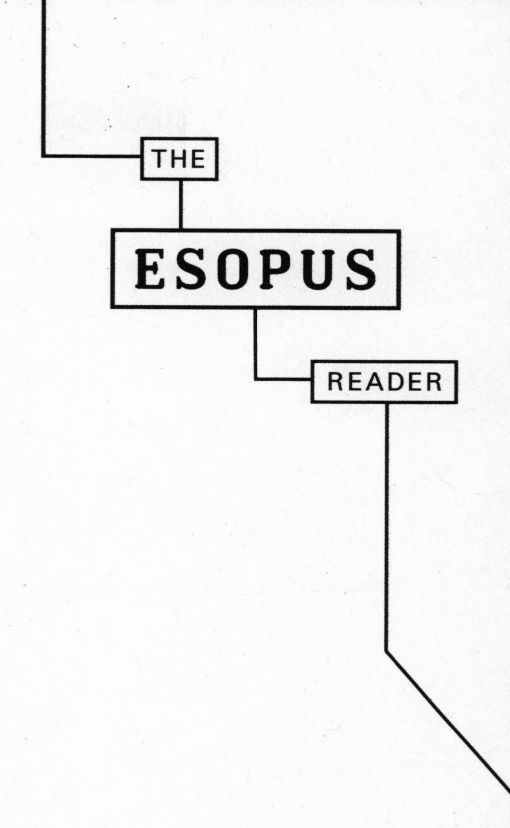

THE ESOPUS READER

THE ESOPUS READER

A COLLECTION OF WRITING
FROM *ESOPUS*, 2003–2018

EDITED BY TOD LIPPY

EB
ESOPUS BOOKS

Published in the United States by Esopus Books

Library of Congress Control Number: 2021921199

ISBN: 978-0-9899117-8-8

Printed and bound in Canada

This book was produced with support from the New York City Department of Cultural Affairs.

NYC Cultural Affairs

Contents

Introduction

BY TOD LIPPY

When I began to conceptualize the first issue of *Esopus* in the spring of 2003, one of the first people I reached out to was a young writer named Heather Larson. I'd met Heather, who was then working as an assistant editor at a New York City music magazine, through Edward McPherson, a friend of mine she had started dating. After spending a laughter-filled weekend with the two of them in upstate New York, I sensed she might be the perfect person to write about Jessica Lynch.

That name may not ring many bells now, but in the spring of 2003, Private Jessica Lynch's capture by Iraqi soldiers and her subsequent rescue—the first of an American P.O.W. since World War II, and the first ever of a female soldier—by U.S. Special Operations Forces had whipped up a media frenzy that laid bare the machinations of the corporate conglomerates running the major networks. News divisions not only pushed government-supplied propaganda about the rescue (some of it later challenged by Lynch herself), they also created unholy alliances with their parent companies' entertainment divisions. High-dollar book, television, and movie deals were dangled in exchange for the first exclusive interview with Lynch, who was still recovering from her injuries at Walter Reed Medical Center in Washington, D.C. This was exactly the type of commercially motivated mediation of content that had compelled me to create *Esopus*, which I envisioned as a forum for pure creative expression—free of advertising, profit-driven content, and any other filters that would dilute or corrupt its meaning.

I asked Heather if she would consider making a trip down to Lynch's hometown of Palestine, West Virginia, to "get the story on getting the story," and she agreed. Heather has a sardonic sense of humor and a razor-sharp intellect, but she also hails from a small town in the Midwest, and my gut told me that this combination might just be a perfect fit for the subject matter.

The resulting piece, "Nothing Personal," closes this collection. What I had originally imagined would be a witty takedown of big-time media mucking about in small-town America ended up being something very different, and much better: a witty, compassionate story about Heather's experiences with a group of locals she befriended on her journey. In fact, its authentic, personal tone embodied exactly what I hoped would set *Esopus* apart from more typical arts journals.

I have always been obsessed by process, so I made a point from the start to invite a broad range of creative professionals—few of whom had ever published any writing—to talk about their work in similarly personal terms for *Esopus*. In "Cuoca," the chef Jody Williams recounts in almost Proustian detail her early apprenticeship in a restaurant in Reggio Emilia, Italy; in "Haunted," the choreographer Christopher Wheeldon vividly relates the struggles he underwent to craft a series of dances for the New York City Ballet set to the music of atonal composer György Ligeti. In "Music at 6," the film composer Carter Burwell trains a critical but empathetic eye (and ear) on the work of musical composers creating scores for major news networks' coverage of the second Iraq War. Another composer, Anthony Cheung, shares the sense of liberation he feels when making use of the tools of contemporary musical composition in "New Colors." In "Light Unseen," the legendary lighting designer Jennifer Tipton offers a fervent manifesto arguing for theatrical lighting design to be viewed as an art form, and in "Paintings for Cash," the pseudonymous decor artist "Penelope" paints a fascinating—and disconcerting—behind-the-scenes picture of how mall art is made.

This exploration of process also pervades the interviews published in *Esopus* over the years with figures such as mathematician John Conway, playwright and filmmaker Kenneth Lonergan, game designer Raphael van Lierop, translator Ann Goldstein, soap-opera director Larry Auerbach, actor Lisa Kudrow, and director Michael Patrick King, all of which are reprinted here. The longest piece in this book, "Critical Conversations," sensitively compiled, edited, and sequenced by Danielle Spencer and Stephanie Adler Yuan, comprises a series of illuminating interviews with a cancer patient and the constellation of medical professionals—from administrative assistants to phlebotomists—who care for her.

One goal of *Esopus* from the very beginning was to promote the work of emerging and underrecognized artists, and nowhere were we able to fulfill this mission more successfully than with our "New Voices" series, which debuted short fiction by young writers whose work had never before been published. I came upon most of these stories by reading through hundreds of unsolicited submissions sent to our post-office box or, later on, emailed via a link on our website. I was fortunate, however, to also have advisory board members, including author Jim Shepard, who never hesitated to let me know when they had encountered the work of a student or young colleague they felt was worthy of consideration.

The first "New Voices" story we featured was by Lev AC Rosen, who also happened to be our first intern. At some point early in his tenure, Lev mentioned he was writing fiction and that he would soon be applying to schools for an M.F.A. in creative writing. I asked if he would contemplate writing something on spec for *Esopus*, and he came up with the impressive story "Painting," which we included in *Esopus 2*. Lev has since published four novels, one of which, *Camp*, will soon be an HBO Max film directed by Billy Porter. In fact, the majority of our "New Voices" alumni have gone on to illustrious careers as established authors with award-winning novels and short-story collections released by major publishers.

I believe *Esopus* served as a soft landing of sorts, affording young writers that all-important "published author" credit without forcing them to subject their early work to the raking light that might have accompanied publication in more traditional literary journals. The same is true of much of the nonfiction that appeared in *Esopus*, from the gripping recollections of four veterans who toured the front lines in Vietnam with a production of *The Fantasticks* ("Off-Off-Off Broadway") to "Obituary Birthday," Pamela A. Ivinski's fierce defense and forensic analysis of Kurt Cobain's lyrics. And then there's "Ten Rivers to Cross," an unforgettable piece by Edward McPherson (he ultimately married Heather, who now shares his last name), in which we get a front-row seat to his torturous experience—on assignment from *Esopus*—of watching the film *Mystic River* in theaters ten times over the course of one month.

Not all of the writing that appeared in *Esopus* was by emerging or previously unknown authors. One particular thrill for me was working with the remarkable writer Karl Ove Knausgaard, whose essay "On the Value of Literature" we presented in *Esopus 23* in the form of a 16-page removable pamphlet. Pulitzer Prize–winning playwright Stephen Adly Guirgis penned three memorable short scripts for *Esopus* ("The Sissy Monologues"), and we were fortunate to publish poetry by Chantal Bizzini, Nicole Sealey, and Jessica Rae Elsaesser; song lyrics by the artist and musician Lonnie Holley; and engaging essays by academics on subjects including the history of Ouija (Mitch Horowitz's "Spellbound"), changing perceptions of Nostradamus (Stéphane Gerson's "Searching for Nostradamus"), and the evolution of, and technology behind, ice cream truck music (Daniel T. Neely's "Soft Serve").

It's worth noting that *Esopus* was generally viewed as a primarily visual object (in a 2004 review in *The New York Times*, the late David Carr called it "a thing of lavish, eccentric beauty, less flipped through than stared at"). Nearly all of the work included here was accompanied by visuals when it first appeared in the publication (see the inside of this book's dust jacket for images of original spreads). But every one of these pieces is more than capable of standing on its own in this text-only format.

That was unfortunately not the case for many other written contributions to *Esopus*. Some were just too inextricably tied to their paired visual content. These include the introductions to installments of our "100 Frames" series—featuring stills from films like *Killer of Sheep*, *Tropical Malady*, *Blue Velvet*, and *Tulpan*—written by filmmakers, artists, and writers, among them Claire Denis, Gregory Crewdson, and Hamid Dabashi; and Michelle Elligott's revelatory essays accompanying each iteration of our "Modern Artifacts" series (all 18 since collected into the 2020 book of the same name). Another series, "Guarded Opinions," edited by Paul VanDeCarr, featured museum guards' unique perspectives on the artworks they oversee. Publishing these insightful commentaries without including the paintings and sculptures they were referencing didn't make good sense. Neither did reproducing the hundreds of written contributions from our readers commissioned for the various *Esopus* "subscriber invitationals." These submissions served as the basis for songs on our compilation CDs, or as inspiration for artists' projects, or, in one case, as source material for student medical illustrators. And the immediacy and power of the facsimile reproductions of archival material we presented of work from William Carlos Williams, Jessica B. Harris, Christopher Isherwood, Joey and Faith Soloway, Matthew Weiner, Suji Kwock Kim, Norman Lear, and Jennifer Moxley, among many others, would have been lost had the words alone been transcribed and typeset for this volume.

"Submission #790532," another *Esopus* contribution that was replete with visual material, opens this anthology. This compelling essay by the architect Michael Arad describes the initial conception of, and the long struggle to realize, his design for the 9/11 Memorial. In *Esopus 21*, it appeared alongside a number of his unrealized sketches and models for early designs of the memorial, as well as a full-size foldout replica of his winning submission to the competition. But ultimately, the power of "Submission #790532" comes from Michael's deeply considered prose. It is imbued with the same passion, candor, and clarity that resonate through every chapter in this book.

Tod Lippy
Brooklyn, January 2022

Submission #790532

BY MICHAEL ARAD

I.

It was a beautiful sunny day. My wife, Melanie, had left for work early, and I had our East Village apartment to myself while I shaved and got ready to go to the office. As I stood facing the bathroom mirror, I heard the announcer on NPR report that a plane had hit the World Trade Center. Assuming an accident had occurred, I crossed our apartment to take a look out our bedroom window: I saw a thin plume of smoke rising from what seemed like a small gash in the north face of one of the towers. I grabbed my camera and headed to the roof of our building for a better view. A couple of minutes later an airplane appeared, swerving sharply and flying fast. It crashed into the second tower, and a ball of flame and debris shot out and engulfed the towers.

Across the street, construction workers were erecting an apartment building. Standing on the steel beams, they screamed when the airplane crashed into the building, then watched in horror as the towers burned. I turned sharply, faced north, and stared at the Empire State Building, expecting another airplane to appear. I noticed people walking by on the sidewalks below and envied them their ignorance.

The prospect of witnessing an historic accident had brought me up to the roof. When it became clear to me that this had been a coordinated attack, my first fear was that there was more yet to come. I tried calling Melanie—the offices of her law firm, Sullivan and Cromwell, were just a few blocks from the World Trade Center—but couldn't get through. I jumped on my bicycle and headed downtown with the hope of finding her.

Along the way, I saw a city in distress. Most traffic was headed north, away from Lower Manhattan, while police and rescue vehicles were making their way south. For the most part, road traffic seemed to be fairly well controlled, but thousands of people were out on the streets, milling about, staring uncomprehendingly at the smoking towers. In the middle of Chinatown, my phone rang and I stopped. It was a friend from Atlanta with whom I had not spoken in years. She asked me what was going on in New York and wanted to know if I was okay. It was not the call I was waiting for. As I said goodbye and got back on my bicycle, I noticed two elderly Chinese women standing on a traffic median, smiling and posing for a picture with the towers behind them. I felt a sense of incredulity and anger—did they not understand what was going on?

By the time I got to Melanie's office on Broad Street, her building had been evacuated. Throngs of people had gathered in chatty clusters across the broad plaza at its base. There seemed to be little sense of urgency or comprehension: People were wondering if they would be let back into the building soon and were complaining about the inconvenience of it all. Somehow I found Melanie standing with some colleagues, and I insisted we leave at once. Her best friend, Briana, said she was staying because she had left her purse in the office. Some 20 minutes later, she found herself running away from an angry cloud of dust and debris that threatened to swallow up her and everyone else in its path.

We headed north on Water Street. Two of Melanie's coworkers joined us as we started walking home, hoping to find a way to Westchester and New Jersey, where they lived. The streets were covered in a confetti of burned paper. I stopped when I saw a charred photograph of a woman and her dog lying on the sidewalk right next to me. Melanie and I had a Rhodesian ridgeback named Ginger, and we had many pictures just like this one at home: a portrait of a beaming owner and a proud dog at a dog show. I carefully put the picture in my pocket. I hoped the woman was still alive, and I felt obliged to find a way to return the photo to her or her family.

By the time we got as far north as Fulton Street, a few short blocks from the World Trade Center, a sudden wave of panic inexplicably seemed to wash over the crowds of people who had been for the most part walking in a slow and orderly fashion. I could not see the towers from where we were because of the tight, narrow layout of the streets of Lower Manhattan, but that wave of panic was a ripple generated by the collapse of the first tower. As people screamed "It's falling!" I failed to comprehend what they meant. Only when we had made our way farther north and walked under the Brooklyn Bridge—where every lane was taken up by a river of pedestrians making their way back to Brooklyn—were we able to look back and see that only one tower still stood. By the time we walked past the Williamsburg Bridge along the East River Park, littered with the abandoned high heels of fleeing office workers, we heard a sickening creak and saw the second tower collapse. When I got home to the East Village, I went back up to our roof and stared in disbelief at the skyline. Where the towers once stood was a gray and yellow cloud of dust, slowly drifting toward Brooklyn.

We turned on the TV. Melanie went out to get some coffee and came back with beer, and we sat there in silence rewatching what we had just witnessed. First Avenue was jammed with cars heading north, and I went back out after a few minutes and helped a policeman barricade the right lane to keep it free for rescue vehicles. Melanie's colleagues, unable to find a way back to their suburban homes, came to our apartment and continued to try to contact their families. One started weeping with relief after speaking to his wife. Rumors of another attack in Chicago and the collapse of additional towers came and went, some true, some not.

Within a few hours the mass exodus through our neighborhood ended, and all of a sudden it was very quiet and empty. A police barricade was set up along 14th Street to prevent gawkers from entering, effectively cutting off our neighborhood from the rest of the world. As darkness set in, it felt eerily still with no cars or buses rolling by. Feeling a bit like an explorer in a forbidden city, I set out on a bicycle to see what was going on. More barricades had been erected to the south of us on Canal Street. I found my way closer to the World Trade Center site as I biked around TriBeCa and I encountered groups of people cheering the rescue and recovery workers at a checkpoint on the West Side Highway.

The next few days were similarly quiet. I remember eating a late breakfast with Melanie at Life Café in our neighborhood, and it was as if we were having brunch on a weekend in a placid, remote town. But the stench of the burning towers hung over everything. Most stores and restaurants were closed. Food wasn't being delivered to the local delis. We went to Beth Israel Hospital to donate blood but left when we saw the line of volunteers snaking around the block and were told that we should try again some other time. Impromptu shrines began to spring up at street corners and public squares: candles in jars, flowers, teddy bears. Thousands of "Have you seen..." flyers went up seemingly overnight.

It was in the late hours of the second or third night after the attack that I made my way to Washington Square Park along the deserted streets of downtown. There, by its iconic fountain, I found a group of people standing around the circle of water. Candles formed a ring at the edge of the fountain, and the six round pedestals within it held even more candles and flowers. No one said a word; a few couples held hands. Some people left and others came, and for the first time I felt a tremendous sense of community and belonging in New York. The attacks killed many—at the time the estimated toll was as high as 6,000—but they led those of us who survived to come together in a way that I believe most New Yorkers never would have expected. Standing there, in the darkness, as a part of this circle, I no longer felt alone in the face of death and destruction.

The photograph I had found seemed to demand my attention, and I thought that if I could find the proper authority figure, that person could return it to its rightful owner. That week, Melanie and I made our way to the 69th Regiment Armory building on Lexington Avenue; it had been set up as a command post for family members who were hoping against hope that their loved ones would still be found. I tried to give the picture to the police, but instead we were ushered into a great hall holding hundreds of grieving people and filled with thousands of missing-person flyers covering every available surface. Nobody inside would take the picture from us, and we left, saddened by the sight of so many people feeling such desperation.

On the fourth day after the attacks I decided I could leave Melanie at home and go back to work. Over the previous three days I had grown used to walking around with a mask over my nose and mouth because of the stench and smoke in our neighborhood. As I made my way to work in Midtown, I seemed to leave a war zone behind me. It was a block-by-block advance into "normal" terrain. Suddenly, I was surrounded by cars and people, and I was the only one wearing a face mask. I took it off, stuffed it in my pocket, and continued on my way. At the time I worked for the architectural firm Kohn Pedersen Fox (KPF), whose office was on 57th Street. I remembered how clearly one could see the Twin Towers from the intersection of 5th Avenue and 57th Street, and there I was, looking south—down that long urban corridor—and they were gone.

I found it impossible to concentrate on work. The tasks seemed pointless. I was then working on the design of the top third of what was planned to be the world's tallest tower, with hotel rooms surrounding an 11-story-high atrium, and topped with restaurants and bars at the building's apex. The structural engineer we were working with was Les Robertson, who had designed the innovative structure of the Twin Towers. At the office, people speculated about the death of the skyscraper.

The following week, I went to Coliseum Books and found an illustrated guide to dog breeds. I figured out that the dog in the picture was a wheaten terrier, and I called the American Kennel Club in Washington, D.C., asking for its help in tracking down its owners. The dog turned out to belong to two couples, and the AKC had their names but not their phone numbers. I got one of the numbers by calling 411 and gave it a try. It turned out to be that of the breeder who co-owned the dog, but he didn't keep it at home. He had the number for the other couple, who did—Ken and Toby Glotzer—but had no idea if they were okay. I placed a call to them with trepidation. When I found out that Ken, who had worked for Aon in the South Tower of the World Trade Center, was alive, I felt a surge of relief. Here was a person I didn't know and who I had feared was dead, and I found him alive! It seemed like a small victory, and a reason to be hopeful about things again. I got the news on the day before Rosh Hashanah, and although I am agnostic, I took at as a sign to start the Jewish New Year with hope.

When we met for dinner about a month later, Ken told me that he had been running late the morning of the attacks. He had stepped into the elevator at the ground floor but for some reason, it didn't go up. He and the other passengers were stuck inside for 40 minutes before they finally managed to force the doors open, finding the lobby transformed from order into chaos. They escaped the building before its collapse. Many of his colleagues were not as fortunate. As he recounted his story to me, it was clear that he felt guilt about his survival in the face of their deaths.

The year that followed was filled with sadness in New York. Everything seemed subdued. Restaurants were empty and businesses were closing left and right. Fear permeated everything, even routine activities like taking the subway. Many people found they had to pause and take stock of where their lives were heading; Melanie and I decided it was time to have kids.

That summer, I found myself on a forced hiatus from my job at KPF because my work visa had expired. What should have been a routine renewal was delayed because of huge 9/11–related backlogs at the Department of Homeland Security and the Immigration and Naturalization Service. I took the time off to study and undergo the lengthy and expensive process of taking my architectural registration exams.

One of my college roommates from Dartmouth had grown up in Forest Hills, Queens, and he had continued to volunteer with the local EMS when he returned to New York. His unit had lost one of its members during the attacks, and he asked me to think about designing a memorial they might be able to erect nearby. One night, we toured the station's dark parking lot filled with ambulances, but I felt no inkling of design direction. While this experience didn't lead to anything tangible, it prompted me to start thinking about how to respond to what I'd witnessed. Other factors propelled me as well: My hands were idle now that I was unemployed; I was also harboring a growing desire to come to terms with my feelings about the attacks as they receded backward in time.

I was initially uneasy with the idea of turning to design—an everyday tool for me—to address a tragedy of such magnitude, and I was uncomfortable witnessing the exuberance of some architects at the "opportunity" to design while the ashes still smoldered on the site. An exhibition of rebuilding proposals was quickly mounted at a Chelsea gallery specializing in the work of dozens of famous architects. It felt unseemly to me, and I refused to join friends who were going to see it. It seemed like it was happening too soon and without any acknowledgment of the loss of life that had taken place—just another beauty contest among the usual suspects. I remember one of the proposals called for towers with a giant assault rifle mounted onto one of them. Not all of the proposals at the show added insult to injury, but the fact that a few did was enough to sour me on the whole enterprise when I eventually saw the exhibit.

One day, while sitting at home, I decided to revisit some sketches I'd done the year before of two square voids carved into the surface of the Hudson River. It was an inexplicable vision, one that suggested a rupture in the fabric of our world. I imagined these voids remaining empty as water continuously poured into them. I tried to picture how such an image could be made real, and I came up with an idea for a fountain design that contained a hidden reservoir and pump. I sketched and sketched and finally solved the problem I had set up for myself, so I decided to build a model. I drew plans for all the pieces of this miniature fountain on my computer at home, and I bought some Plexiglas and tubing at Canal Plastics in Chinatown. I went to Bed Bath & Beyond and purchased a desktop fountain, breaking it open to remove the pump I needed. I then went to Awad Architectural Models in the Garment District and asked them if I could use their laser cutter for half an hour to cut up some of the Plexiglas pieces. I had gotten to know Jimmy Awad and his crew of model makers while working at KPF. Jimmy very generously agreed to help me. None of his employees were busy; recessions hurt model makers even more than architects. What I thought was going to be a 30-minute visit turned into two full days as one of Jimmy's employees, Edison Morales, sat down with me and kindly helped me assemble all the pieces that had been cut out of the thick Plexiglas sheets. Every joint had to be perfectly true and waterproofed in order for the fountain to work. As it became clear to me that it was going to take longer to build than I had expected, I realized how lucky I was to have Edison's enthusiastic help. Finally, after two full days of sanding and caulking and sealing, we were ready to fill our fountain with water and plug the pump into an outlet. Nothing happened. After a bit of a scramble and the straightening of a kink in a hose, the pump gurgled to life in the lower, hidden reservoir, and just like magic, the upper, visible reservoir started filling up. The water flooded the entire top of the fountain, and all of a sudden the two voids appeared as water began to flow over their edges. I'm not sure if everyone at the model shop understood why I was so excited and pleased with my little fountain, but I was thrilled to have built it. To conceive of an idea and then to actually see it realized—I knew only too well that architects could toil for years before getting to that point.

I thanked Edison profusely and took my fountain home with me. I carried it up to our building's roof, connecting it to an outlet in our apartment two stories below with a series of long extension cords snaking their way down the stairs. After filling it with several pitchers of water, I took some pictures of the model in the late-afternoon light with the reflection of the New York City skyline, in particular the Empire State Building, breaking on its surface, which was torn by the voids. I then proceeded to pack it up along with the chipboard model that preceded it and put them out of the way in a closet.

I went back to studying for the exams, and a few months later I heard from my immigration attorney that my visa had finally come through—I could go back to work! I called KPF and found out that the previous day the firm had just laid off eight employees, and as much as they would like to have me back, now was not the right time. Could I wait a bit? Not really. I began sending out dozens of letters and going to interviews. At some point I remember standing in a blistering wind in a line with hundreds of other applicants for city jobs. The line wound all the way around the municipal building and then halfway around again. I was applying for an advertised position with the architectural-design team of the New York City Housing Authority. It felt like a scene from a movie about the Great Depression, but it was my life in 2003.

With help from friends of friends of my parents, I got my foot in the door at a small production firm called Leclere Associates. It was very different than KPF, but it was a job I could learn from and earn from, and I dove into my new assignments. I was assigned to a project for a new store for the luxury brand Asprey at Trump Tower at the corner of 5th Avenue and 56th Street. The design architects for the project were from England, Norman Foster's firm, and we were the local firm helping to expedite the project. It was almost a perfect role reversal from my former position at KPF, where I had been part of the team designing a tower in Hong Kong.

II.

Despite many claims that a memorial at Ground Zero should have preceded and laid the groundwork for any other design at the site, the decision to rebuild the 10 million square feet of destroyed office space was made long before the memorial competition was even announced. The rebuilding efforts in Lower Manhattan became a free-form struggle for dominance between competing agencies, politicians, and developers. New York received federal funds for rebuilding, and the state set up the Lower Manhattan Development Corporation (LMDC), under the auspices of the Empire State Development Corporation, to receive and disburse these funds. Because the Republican establishment feared that a Democratic candidate would succeed Rudolph Giuliani at City Hall, the state, rather than the city, was given predominant control over the LMDC board. The fact that the site was owned by the Port Authority of New York and New Jersey, a quasi-public institution with little public oversight, only made more inevitable the endless clashes to come.

In July 2002, the Port Authority commissioned the architectural firm Beyer Blinder Belle to develop a straightforward initial massing proposal, delineating the location, height, and bulk of any new buildings on the site. What the firm put forward was immediately eviscerated by the press as bland and uninspired. The LMDC countered by inviting a host of famous architects—or as the press dubbed them, "starchitects"—to submit proposals, which led to a dazzling performance that some critics felt consisted of more flash than substance. Instead of a basic planning and programming effort that would form a foundation for more-developed designs down the road, fully "realized" designs were rendered, modeled, and exhibited to the public in December 2002 at the newly rebuilt Winter Garden at the World Financial Center. These highly specific designs ought to have included an "actual results may vary" disclaimer of the type accompanying the latest fad diet. I remember visiting the exhibition that winter to see the nine proposed master plans that the LMDC had selected for further development. As I walked through and looked at a plethora of drawings, models, and renderings, I could not have imagined that my own work would be shown there the following year.

In 2003, the jury that the LMDC had assembled under the direction of Governor Pataki had narrowed its selection to two finalists. One team, which named itself Think, and included Shigeru Ban, Frederic Schwartz, Ken Smith, and Rafael Viñoly, proposed three alternative visions for the site and was championing an idea for two enormous latticework towers with cultural amenities suspended high in the sky within them. The other design that garnered attention was Daniel Libeskind's. The fight between the two design teams became public and personal, with Viñoly's long-past association with the military junta in Argentina being raised by one side, and characterizations of Libeskind's proposal for the site as a "wailing wall"—with clear allusions to his Jewish background—being brought up by the other. Dignified it was not, and the triumphant smile on Libeskind's face that graced the front page of *The New York Times* after his design was selected indicated how off-topic the discourse over the direction of redevelopment at Ground Zero had become.

Libeskind's master plan bore a strong resemblance to the preliminary proposal by Beyer Blinder Belle. Excepting the aesthetic angular and frenetic veneer that Libeskind draped over his buildings, it adopted the same configuration of the five office towers. Compared with the other architects' proposals, such as Norman Foster's poetic "kissing towers," Libeskind's was the most developer-friendly: Five individual towers, sitting for the most part on separate sites, would allow the rebuilding to proceed incrementally and in accordance with a time line that would be determined by the developers' financial constraints and leasing opportunities. Libeskind's master plan also pushed the restored section of Fulton Street south of its original location in order to accommodate a deeper floor plate for the so-called Freedom Tower. As a result, the newly formed quadrant featured a sidewalk curb that was a mere 15 feet from the edge of what many had described as sacred ground: the hallowed footprints of the Twin Towers. This left very little leeway for the design of the memorial and made clear what was the most important criterion for the site's redevelopment.

Within a few months, a competition was announced for the development of a memorial at Ground Zero. The competition brief for the memorial was the first truly public and open step in the rebuilding process. Anybody could propose an idea, and the entry fee was a modest $25. More than 13,000 people registered online for the competition, and eventually 5,201 entries were submitted. The brief that was issued by the LMDC was formulated to fit within the parameters of every idiosyncratic ripple and fold of the Libeskind master plan—and to violate none of them. In plan, the shape of the site that was open to design proposals was a multisided irregular polygon; three separate pages of illustrations in the brief were dedicated solely to outlining the complex definition of the boundaries of the competition, and the document made it clear that the buildings and facades that delineated the memorial site were not part of the competition submission. The guidelines called for sinking parts of the site 30 and 70 feet below the level of the adjacent streets, with the large buildings that Libeskind had proposed spanning over the memorial site. Essentially, Libeskind had already designed a memorial, and the competition was a fig leaf of openness and transparency covering the acceptance of his design. It was as if the competitors were being asked to suggest which fabric swatch or wallpaper would fit best within the memorial that Libeskind had envisioned.

The memorial-design jury objected to these restrictive conditions and insisted that the following language be made part of the competition brief: "Design concepts that propose to exceed the illustrated memorial-site boundaries may be considered by the jury if, in collaboration with the LMDC, they are deemed feasible and consistent with the site plan objectives." In effect, a single sentence in a 38-page document said, "These are the rules. Disregard them if you wish; we still might be interested in your proposal."

Earlier that year I had sent in a proposal for a design for the 9/11 memorial at the Pentagon. It was the first design competition I had ever entered, and it turned out to be a learning experience. I spent about two days putting together my entry, and midway through the process I realized that I should have devoted much more time to the effort. My proposal was a series of irregularly spaced bands that created a memorial field whose grain echoed the direction of Flight 77 before its crash. Portions of this field of stone pavers would be raised and would form broad tablets upon which the names of the victims were to be inscribed. I imagined an open-ended design process that would involve the next of kin and allow them to participate in the selection of what text and images might be inscribed on an individual tablet. Some tablets might commemorate a single person, while others might group friends or family members together.

I felt the final presentation had clarity of intention, but the renderings were schematic black-and-white images derived from a basic three-dimensional model I had build in the computer-drafting program AutoCAD. In the age of digital simulations, juries and the public expect photorealistic images of prospective designs. Ideas are important, but compelling imagery, or as a cynic might argue, "eye candy," is essential. When I turned my attention to the competition for the World Trade Center site, I knew I would have to spend much more time on it than I had on the one for the Pentagon and that I would need help with the rendering.

III.

In the spring of 2003, I was hired as an assistant architect with the New York City Housing Authority. In my new position, I found myself working for Bogdan Pestka, whose police station in Alphabet City I had seen and admired the previous year. It was exciting to be working on projects like police stations and community centers in underserved parts of the city, and it was a welcome change from designing luxury hotels 12 time zones away. One of the greatest surprises for me with the job was how much free time I had. I was automatically enrolled in a union, DC 37, and I was prohibited from working more than eight hours a day unless it had been authorized by my supervisor. Any additional time I put in would result in overtime pay or added vacation days, and so it was rarely permitted. This short workday allowed me to spend time designing under my own direction.

I revisited my ideas of the voids in the Hudson River and started to ponder how I might be able to modify them for Ground Zero. Flooding the site was not an option, of course, but that notion of twin voids was important to me, and I sought a way to incorporate them into the design so that they could be experienced by visitors to the memorial. I remember looking at dramatic pictures of an abandoned quarry and being struck by the clear geometry of the absence left by the excavation, as well as by the sense of ruin and rebirth created by the rubble, mingling with large puddles and patches of vegetation.

I imagined a broad horizontal plaza punctuated by two large voids, each ringed by waterfalls that would cascade down a 30-foot drop to a reflecting pool below. At the center of each pool I placed another void, this one cut out of the surface of the water, from which another set of waterfalls would plunge into a seemingly bottomless abyss.

I pictured visitors walking up to the massive voids and staring into their depths, and then finding their way underground via a set of covered ramps that would lead them to the edge of the pools. There, behind the waterfalls, they could peer out across the surface of the water, contemplating the void at the center of each pool, which would remain empty despite the constant flow of water feeding into it. Standing at the water's edge, in a sheltered and removed spot—a place that was in the city, yet removed from it by a veil of falling water—they would come across the hundreds of names of the dead surrounding each pool as they took in the magnitude of the towers' footprints. I imagined a descent into a netherworld, a confrontation with death, and a return back up to the plaza and life. It was as if visitors were walking up to a line that separated the dead from the living, stopping at the banks of the River Styx, and then turning back to return to the world, transformed by the journey.

As I started drawing plans and sections for the memorial and exploring this idea of a descent into darkness that ends in an encounter with light, I was reminded of the Church of the Holy Sepulchre in Jerusalem, which I had visited many times. One part of the church is accessed by a set of stairs that descends deep into the bedrock, past stone walls upon which visitors have scrawled their names for centuries, and where the only illumination is from dozens of ornate hanging oil lamps. Jerusalem, where I grew up, is a remarkable city that is both modern and ancient, full of spaces like this that create strong and emotional connections with people. Some of these places could have been designed yesterday, a hundred years ago, or a thousand years ago: They embody the timeless and eternal qualities of shelter and community that have always been important to human civilization.

I wanted this memorial to have a similar effect. I envisioned it being the kind of place I would be drawn to if I were seeking solace and the opportunity for quiet introspection. It felt like the right way to mark this site and make clear its horrific history. It would be neither maudlin nor histrionic, but stoic and defiant. As I worked on the design, I was reminded of my feelings as I had wandered the city in the days following the attacks, recalling the sense of community and support I found late that night at Washington Square Park, when I ceased to feel like a stranger in the city and became for the first time a New Yorker and an American. I imagined that people could come by themselves to visit this memorial and not feel alone as they confronted the enormity of the death and devastation that had occurred here. Invoking a sense of unity was critical to me, and it allowed me to react positively and affirmatively to the hatred and evil that had led to this attack—not to move past it, but to move forward without a sense of fatalism and futility.

I started preparing my submission for the memorial competition early, some two weeks before the June 30, 2003, deadline. Assembling all the materials I would need to create a compelling presentation, I drew sections and plans, built a three-dimensional model on my computer, gathered photographs of the fountain model, and carefully composed the text describing my design intent. However, I knew I'd have to find a way to get arresting images of the proposal, and I did not have the rendering skills required.

Bruno Caballé, a former colleague from KPF, said he would try to help me despite the fact that he didn't care for the design. There were other complications, including the fact that the three-dimensional model I had built in AutoCAD was of no use in 3DMax, the program he used for digital renderings, but on the last possible night—Friday, June 27, 2003—Bruno modeled the memorial and produced two renderings for me. I left his apartment at two in the morning on Saturday, walking past revelers in the Meatpacking District, beaming: I had the images I had feared would never materialize. They were not perfect, but they were evocative, and I felt they made my design intent, whether one liked it or not, clear. I headed home to spend the rest of the night at my computer using Photoshop to add silhouettes of people into these images and assembling the various plans, sections, images, and text onto the 30-by-40-inch submission board that I would have to print and drop off with FedEx that Saturday afternoon in order to ensure delivery for Monday. I had foolishly decided to learn how to use a new piece of software, Adobe Illustrator, to create the final file, and the hours flew by like minutes as I struggled to pull together the different images and text blocks.

Later that morning, I saved the file and dashed off to meet another friend from KPF, Robert Jamieson, who had promised to help me print my submission at his office. Robert was training for the upcoming New York City Marathon and agreed to meet me early before a training run in Central Park. I was giddy with excitement at the prospect of finally being done with this project that had grown to consume me like a wildfire. I hadn't slept in 48 hours, and for the preceding two weeks, every minute of my free time had been dedicated to realizing this proposal. Melanie was six months pregnant, walking our two large dogs by herself, and understandably annoyed by my maniacal obsession. But now the end was finally in sight: I could send in my submission, knowing that I had done everything I wanted to do, putting everything I had into the effort. I had no expectation of success, but it was deeply important to me to see this through. It was my way of responding to the trauma I had felt—and to be honest, that I could still could not completely acknowledge—ever since the attacks.

Robert and I sat down at his desktop. He clicked open the file and sent it to the printer, and we walked over to see it slowly start to unspool from a large-format printer. About a quarter of the way through the process, the printer suddenly stopped. We tried again and again. I was growing more panicked by the moment. Robert, standing there in his running shorts, realized how much work and effort had gone into this and promised to stay in the office and keep trying while I hopped into a cab with a copy of the file and attempted to find a professional digital-printing house somewhere in the city. Every place I walked into or called was mobbed; dozens, if not hundreds, of other New Yorkers were working toward the same deadline. Despite everything Robert and I did that day, we could not get the file to print, and by three that afternoon it was clear that it was not going to happen. I had to go to a friend's wedding in Long Island, so I thanked Robert, went home, showered and shaved for the first time in many days, and headed out to the wedding with Melanie. I was so tired, and the stop-and-start traffic was moving very slowly on the Jericho Turnpike; Melanie yelled at me to wake up as I dozed off at the wheel, and we finally made it to the celebration. Considering the circumstances, I was remarkably upbeat. I accepted that I was not going to submit an entry, despite my best efforts, and I made the decision to move on.

When we got home late that night, I went onto the LMDC's website and discovered that they had changed their guidelines and would now accept deliveries of proposals via local courier services in New York on Monday. I decided to rebuild the file—which was an amalgam of many different images and bits of text—overnight, and early Sunday morning I headed to a Kinko's near our apartment. I was one of the first people there, and I handed my file to the employee behind the desk. Unbelievably, it printed without a hitch, and shortly thereafter I left with a rolled-up printout the size of a small poster under my arm. I dropped by the apartment and showed it to a relieved Melanie and her friend Briana. I rolled the print up again and headed to my office to mount it on a piece of foam board. Even this simple step seemed more difficult than usual, as I had to cross Fifth Avenue in the midst of a crowded obstacle course: that year's Gay Pride March. My friend Jonas Bronk, who went to Georgia Tech with me, met me at my office, and together we sprayed glue on the back of the print, carefully draped it on top of a piece of foam board, smoothed out the wrinkles, trimmed it, and wrapped the finished product in brown kraft paper. I called a courier service and scheduled a pickup early the following morning.

After sending off my submission, I forgot about it. It had been an intense effort, a way to reconnect with the autonomy of a creative process that was lacking in my day-to-day work life, and as with the fountain model I had built the previous year, now that I had completed my investigation, I could set the results aside and move on.

Our son, Nathaniel, was born on August 13, 2003. I could not have anticipated what a tremendous change he would bring to our lives. Melanie was lucky enough to be able to take a full year off from work, and the first few weeks were incredibly exhausting as we slept very little and struggled to adjust to a completely new life with a wonderful boy. One night, about six weeks after Nati was born, I was up late and decided to check my personal email—an account I didn't use very often. I found a cryptic message from a compliance officer at the LMDC informing me that a question had come up about my submission. My first thought was that my $25 check must have bounced. I had the late-night hours to ponder what could be the meaning of the email that asked me to respond to its sender only by email or at a specified phone number. I didn't want to entertain any hopes, but the thought that my submission might have been selected entered my mind.

After a series of emails and phone calls with the LMDC, I learned that I was one of eight finalists in the competition. I was sworn to secrecy and allowed to tell only my immediate family. Working with the landscape architect Peter Walker and consulting with friends, especially Doug Allen, a former professor of mine at Georgia Tech, I devoted the rest of the year to developing the design further for review by the jury before it made a final decision. One morning in January 2004, I heard on the radio that the jury had chosen a winner. Later that day, I received a call from an LMDC official asking me to come in and sign some papers: My design had been selected.

IV. Epilogue

Revisiting my journals, sketches, and the submission board from the period leading up to this moment brings a wry smile to my face. I had a sense of certainty and conviction about the memorial: In my mind's eye, it was complete, just waiting to be birthed.

That expectation turned out to be naive and misguided. After my design was selected, I entered a period filled with challenges. The jury that had chosen the winner of the competition was disbanded, and the LMDC, the client that had requested the jury's services, now seemed to view me as a nettlesome burden to be managed. Minders and managers were soon demanding changes to my design, and the process of death by a thousand paper cuts began. Some of the ramps that led below grade to the memorial pools were eliminated, others were reconfigured; finally, the ramps were eliminated entirely. The experience of a transformative journey for visitors—beginning at plaza level, descending into darkness, and moving toward a distant light beckoning them to the pools' edge, where they would encounter the names of the dead before finally ascending back to life and the city—was excised as though it were superfluous.

By the middle of 2006 I found myself nearly beaten by this process. I had been unsuccessful in defending what I thought was essential to the design and was seriously considering abandoning the project. I was angry and felt betrayed by a process that allowed "design collaborators" who had been foisted on me to alter the memorial in such fundamental ways. I knew that more than anything, they wanted me to give up and walk away, leaving them free rein to change the design as they wished.

At some point I found myself pleading with a jury member for help in staving off the design changes that were being pushed through over my objections. She told me that the jury had selected me, not my design. At first, I had no idea how to respond to this. I had focused so intensely on the specifics of each aspect—the dimensions separating each joint line, the geometry of each volume and path, the materiality of every surface—that it was real in my mind, and I had always imagined it was real in the minds of the jurors as well. Instead, I was told that the design I proposed signified less an idea to be realized than it did an emotional response—my emotional response. At first, I wasn't sure how to handle that responsibility.

But ultimately this involuntary free fall forced me to find a way to see what was integral to my original design of the memorial: its representation of the sense of social and civic engagement that I witnessed in the days that followed the attacks; the compassion and stoicism I saw in my fellow New Yorkers; and the sense of solidarity and humble wonder that imbued the lives of everyone in the city for that brief period of time. My challenge from that point forward was to find a new assemblage of forms and surfaces that would remain true to all of these ideas and emotions.

The two years that I spent generating design responses to the elimination of the memorial galleries showed me that the process I was engaged in wasn't linear—continuing further and further down the same avenue—but one in which I could return to the point of origin and chart another path to the same destination. I found a productive way to respond to multiple voices. I learned how to describe the design, and the process of telling others what I was trying to achieve quickly became a process of hearing what others wanted to see in this design themselves. I soon found allies, and the design became ours, not mine. I owe a tremendous debt to so many partners in this process—yet debt seems like the wrong word, because it marginalizes the inordinate role so many people played in realizing the memorial; it is theirs as much as it is mine.

I am incredibly proud of the memorial that we finally built. In it, I see absence made visible. The voids, hidden in plain sight, open up below you as you approach the parapets bearing the weight of the names of the dead. The experience captures a moment I experienced—and was compelled to convey to others—long ago. I have held on to it dearly ever since.

Three Poems

BY CHANTAL BIZZINI

SEPTEMBER

Fugitive silhouettes in the midst of spaces
crammed with signs, filled with paths
already lined with footprints, with marks
of passage.

Yet, the thought of the unknown seizes
the throat at the entrance of this avenue of lofty dreams, bright and raked
over…

these are only the surroundings, but we already imagine another journey,
a pleasant journey, because we remember some;

go forth gently, now,
in a multifarious thought, thus,
in times of war and love, with, in the spirit, beauty,
this thread broken with regret, always taken up again
through inquiry, a gentle question.

Barely reconnected outside, we can still attempt to close the distance
that separates us from it and ponder childish and ill at ease this deep shadow
that gets closer, solitary and graceful
in the winter sun's white clarity gilding the roofs, sketching
the chimneys of another time against the light,
belted with metal to support the
satellite antennae's white disks

and which deliver this sense of the ancient—only place
where I imagine we could live.

The cranes planted among the buildings
turn amidst the
midday sounds, car horns, displacements,
voices, crying children,
heated exchanges heard only
here, far from life, from this battle.
Reading, in this flood,
the turning movement of this crane,
the traces of rain
and the dusty constellations
of former skies
that the sharp light conjures on the panes,
from far away comes the certitude
of returning to what was begun,
of resuming speech
with and without words, of evoking
a place still unknown where these
signs might lead us,
reconciled perhaps
with this perpetual construction site,
this profound movement without which
life does not go on,
these strident echoes
which are the stuff of days;
in this instant, from afar,
the road is gashed with violence
and sound, I long to be there too;

continuous but slack thread, crossed with immaterial strands:
these footsteps to be deciphered and followed;
and then the impossibility is knotted in haste,
we must get out of here: there is no more emotion in these faraway voices

History is to be relived:
heavy path of what is and what shall be, thrust
into the edge of the forest where every step is decisive in the high
white building that no longer belongs to us.

Night gushes down like a waterfall
and open hearts receive its freshness,
while remaining on the black
facades of the facing buildings
some lighted windows
where hope was yesterday, impossible yielding
to sleep, a refusal and an attempt to prevail;
we will be thirsty all night,
turning our fevered bodies
until morning, while the heart
races at the overheard news
unable to pacify itself:
bird palpitating from its own song,
caged and restless from the morning
where the sumptuous and temporary red flower
unfurls, continuation of the thought,
clinging to the black and iron support
of the window,
flower at the threshold of vision that seizes
the first hours of the day
before entering into a renewed life;
constancy is the name of this flower nourished
with rain and gas, clinging
to the side, at the moment of passage,
lips that speak
of endurance, despite
the fragile opening out and the certain wilting.

INTO THE NIGHT

Nothing tonight but
this electric ribbon
tracing the coastline;
here and there a city appears a shining heap
and this twinkling
calls us beyond ourselves,
atom of another incandescent beauty;

sea night, sand night,
we can't see the waves anymore but we can hear
this noise;
over there,
a black curve, which is land, ringed in phosphorescence;
the night is not completely pinned to the horizon;

soon, the lights pulse with an uncertain existence,
outlining the contours of the shoreline;
and, between here and there, the night falls,
garlanded with life, now visible
and trembling.

THE DISENCHANTED CITY

Red-eye flights, skidding
cars, words, broken glass,
distant screams and catcalls...
a fog of laughter, slamming
doors...
is the night becoming silent and dark
in fever and discord and intensifying sounds?
In front, the wall, enclosed in sky,
is still dark, the noise from
telephones, car horns, ashcans and shattered windows,
the door rattles and, beyond the screams, whispers filled with pleading, bangs,
behind the nearest conversations,
the TV: its gigantic blue shadows
twitching all over the walls...
The city builds itself
through the arrangement of sounds,
ideal citadel, bristling with chained animals
and the flux of spirits that wakes up in heat and alcohol.

I saw you like this and
I lowered my eyes.

Later,
we would leave the house
where everything had been said, among the frail broken
flowers – that day's pink snow –
and the disfigured streets would open
to our wandering.

My joy had fallen at the tube's
edge, left waiting. Everyone spoke
an incomprehensible language.

The streets violently lurched,
decorated with absurd trees
and my anger grew, in waves.
We had to turn around, we did not see the park.

I know you now
always happy alone out of tune.

Barges
seem immobilized in the middle of the river,
the riverside offered its desolation
to our thoughts of the old world's
fall and despair's triumph,
but we still laughed
as we passed amidst the disorder of renovated ruins
and modern wreckage.

Translated by J. Bradford Anderson

From *Esopus 4* (2005)

For Emergency Use Only

BY ETHAN RUTHERFORD

It was in probably Montana when Alex popped a squat in the middle of the road and right there, with her pants down at her ankles, let it loose on the asphalt.

"Oh, come on," I said. "There's a bush like three feet away."

"What," she said. "You think someone's gonna come round the bend?" As she said this she made an arching motion toward the bend that just about put her off balance.

We'd been driving for days, just the two of us, and had seen no one.

Radio reports were vague. Explosions up and down the coast, heightened levels of toxicity. We'd spent the first few days on the road sweeping the dial for news, but the towns we passed through told us everything we needed to know: that the evacuation had begun, weeks ago, without us.

We'd driven through western Washington without seeing a soul. Our solitude was overwhelming. One road cut through a plateau, vast in all directions, dipped into a valley, and came back up. Always we expected to run into someone as the next stretch came into sight; always we saw nobody. Gas stations and roadside attractions ghosted by. We'd stopped pulling in. None of the pumps worked, and the *What You Are Seeing* maps, laminated and overlooking some vista or another, were like relics, signposts of the outdated.

At first, Alex said it was the vacation we'd always dreamed of—away from everybody and everything. We blew red lights, crossed the median on a whim, drove with our knees. We had relations on the abandoned steps of municipal buildings. Then our reality set in. She stopped talking and spent her time absently holding her hand out of the open window to surf the air, scanning the horizon intently for the parade of cars we assumed was just ahead.

I tried to keep her spirits up. But there's a limit to how many times you can say "Now entering the hamlet of Shitsville, population zero" and not get depressed about it.

On the third day we watched two hawks, faint in the distance, dive and swoop. We stopped the car and stood in the middle of the road, feeling a relief so intense it surprised us.

Why we were still alive was a confusion to both of us. From what we'd been led to believe we fully expected to be wiped out along with everyone else. The feeling in Seattle was that things were coming to a head, but instead of doing the hedonism thing, Alex and I had decided to get married.

Our friends thought we were kidding. They said, "You two?" They said, "I know these are stressful times, but..." They tried to ply us with drugs and sex and End Times manifestos, but we were undeterred.

We were on our honeymoon on the Olympic Peninsula when the first wave of aggression hit. A man knocked on the door of our Lovers' Cabin to tell us. He was a bundle of emotion, and the news lurched out of his mouth in fragments. Seattle had been the first hit. Buildings were burning. I asked if anyone had ever told him he looked like Peter Lorre. I don't know why I said it; it just came out. He stared at me, in disbelief, and shook his head.

"Bravo," Alex said, after he'd left.

"How am I supposed to respond to news like that?" I said.

We stayed on the peninsula because we didn't know what else to do. Every morning we walked to the beach and stared at the empty ocean, thinking maybe it was all just some hoax. We were looking for tidal waves, but the water was calm. Was the sky black with ash? Nope. Did we taste annihilation? We were still standing.

We couldn't wrap our minds around it. Things didn't look any different from where we were.

Three weeks passed. Every day we waited for something to signal us that now was the time. At the first flash, we were ready to hop in bed so our shadows—when they were found later, burned into the wall—would give some humorless archaeologist of the future something to think about. An iconic image—our present to the world. But, no flash.

Then one day we made our way down to the beach and saw ships as big as islands on the horizon. Gray and white. Bows cut like icebreakers, pointing toward us.

"They don't look like they're moving," I said.

"What's it going to take for you to realize the situation we're in?" Alex said.

We packed the car and started driving east, avoiding the cities, looking for someone who could tell us what we were supposed to do. Out the window, we would occasionally glimpse coils of dark smoke rising from the north or behind us. When we looped below Olympia, positive that it had been reduced to embers, the air smelled vaguely like burnt eggs. We had not planned for survival.

We drove and drove. Past tract houses and supermarkets, through endless farms and res land. These places were ghost towns to begin with, but completely empty they were welcoming.

We tried the phones. They didn't work. I picked up receivers anyway and dialed made-up numbers. Then my own number.

"Dumb luck," Alex said. We were standing in the middle of a tiny drive-through town, a strip of abandoned fast-food joints and gas stations.

"Maybe we've been chosen," I said. I scraped my sneaker on the asphalt, trying to kick out a rock that had lodged in the tread of my shoe.

"I think forgotten is more appropriate," she said.

As we drove east, Alex got quieter. Her melancholy filled the car. I did my best to be buoyant for the both of us.

"You really think we're going to be fine, don't you?" she said, rubbing her temples as if she had a headache, like even talking was too much.

"I do," I said.

She reached across the seat and patted my leg, firmly, then let her hand rest on my thigh. She exhaled through her nose until it seemed like she might collapse. It was a gesture she used for everything.

We'd taken a drive similar to this once, to celebrate our engagement, which was supposed to be momentous, but wasn't. It felt like nothing. It offered no relief. So we decided to leave the house. Our car broke down and we spent the weekend in a small town in northern Idaho. The whole place was western-themed—old boardwalks, saloons with swing doors, horse hitches, saddle stores. Not where I'd intended to spend a romantic couple of days.

"But forget Montana," she said. "*Look* at this place."

Our motel room had buffalo blankets. The bathroom had a basin and a wooden back scrub. The shower was planked. Alex left and returned with chaps. "Put them on!" she said. "Put them on."

We watched an elaborate gunfight on the main drag—cowboys in white versus cowboys in black—and then went to dinner. Our waitress was dressed like a dance-hall girl.

"What're you folks doin' in these parts?" she said when she brought our food.

"Horse done broke down," Alex said. She was beaming.

"Well, dangit," she said. "Y'all fit in just fine."

"Hear that, darling?" Alex said to me. "Time for you to take that long face and buck it up."

"I'm wearing chaps," I said.

"Not convincingly," she said.

"Well, y'all make a cute couple," the waitress said before sauntering over to the bar.

We drank from bottles marked XXX until it started to feel like it actually was 1850. Alex danced with some locals who knew how to lead. I felt tight and small and idiotic watching her. Someone broke a prop chair over someone else to some rousing whoops and we left. "How was the square-dancing?" I said. Her fingers were in my hair, and she took them out.

Our radio stopped picking up signals near the Dakota border. I spent an hour on the antenna before calling it quits.

"Mr. Fixit," Alex said. I pretended I didn't hear.

We drove in silence through the Black Hills, past empty houses set back from the road, and irrigation devices that were stock-still and loomed like iron insects over the flat soil. It was like moving across a painting. Every once in a while I would stop the car so Alex could just scream, at the top of her lungs, in the middle of wherever we were. I waited in the car.

Hours of road. We'd thought for sure we'd have seen people by now. I thought maybe they were there, in their houses, just watching us pass through. Finally, Alex said she couldn't take the quiet anymore and rummaged through the glove compartment. She found a cassette and popped it in. It was a mixtape I'd made for her birthday, before we were married. The first thing on it was an introduction I'd recorded in my bathroom, which wrapped up with a lousy reading of a love poem. I remember thinking it was all someone could say about two people. My voice sounded terrible. It was like I had never heard myself talk. We were both glad when the music started.

It was halfway through the tape, in the middle of a Merle Haggard song, when we crested a hill and pulled up alongside the first sign of life on the ground—a lonely car, left diagonally in the middle of the road. There were bullet holes through the windshield. We stopped. We got out. Here we were, staring at a shot-up car. There were no bodies.

Alex sat down. She reached up to her mouth and covered a quiet hiccup. When she pulled her hand away, a small string of saliva webbed her fingers. She looked at it. Even from where I was standing I could see it was pink.

"Oh Jesus," she said.

I helped her to the car and drove until we found a gas station. I tried the doors on the Quicky Mart. They were locked.

"He probably expected to be back," Alex said.

I used our little lug-nut loosener on the windows. Alex said she was feeling better but I grabbed all the first-aid stuff I could find and loaded it into the car. Then I went back for whatever canned food was left: Vienna Sausages, Pork-n-Tots, the kind of food no one ate. The kind of shit that people leave behind, even when they know they might starve. We climbed a lookout tower and spread our sleeping bags.

"What are we going to do?" Alex said. She said it like she wasn't upset, just exhausted.

"Keep driving," I said. "We'll find someone."

She looked at me and then cupped her hands, like she was holding something small she was trying to protect. "Optimism has its limits," she said quietly.

We looked west from the tower, from where we'd come. We didn't touch each other. I tried to remember the first few days of our honeymoon but all I could come up with was something she had said about how nice it was, finally, to be just us.

The sunset, when it came, was iridescent, red and then a deep brown, and very beautiful.

Abandoned cars appeared on the side of the road, each pointing in the direction we were driving. They dotted the landscape. "Does this mean we're going the right way or the wrong way?" I said. Alex shrugged.

After the first few we stopped counting. I would siphon whatever gas was left while Alex circled the vehicle slowly, closing doors and turning off hazard lights or turn signals. There were still no bodies, but there was a finality to the sound of those doors closing, like we were placing coins on the eyes of the dead, securing their vessel, giving proper burials in absentia. One of the cars had a child's safety seat in the back, and Alex lifted it out and fastened it on the drop seat between us, not bothering to explain herself.

We were both feeling sick. Wobbly in the morning, light-headed. Alex developed what looked like stretch marks at the base of her neck, striping her collarbone. After driving for hours, I would let loose of the steering wheel and skin would slough off in my fingers.

The incessant hum of our engine, working overtime in the heat, enfolded us.

We'd sometimes rifle through the empty cars, for something to do. We found photos, and empty bean cans. What I thought was a book turned out to be some lady's diary. I tried to read it but couldn't get past the first page, which had a drawing of a duck with the date in the corner. From a late-model Buick 6 Alex snatched a pair of reflective aviator sunglasses, which were at least four sizes too big and dipped down almost to her upper lip. Each time we stopped, it became harder and harder to get back in the car and continue with our driving.

When I started in on something, like wondering how things had gone so wrong, she would tilt her head toward me and stay mum, and I'd be talking to myself in her sunglasses.

"Well, I, for one, am glad we got married," I said.

She exhaled loudly.

"There's nothing wrong with being glad you're alive," I said.

There was a time, before all of this, when I think we would've done anything for each other. Everything about her made me feel seasick—her smell, her thighs, how she was so tall that most beds didn't fit right and she'd sleep diagonally. How she took her socks off and balled them up so they wouldn't get lost in the laundry. We'd just wanted a normal life. We convinced ourselves we could make one together, in the face of everything. All we thought we'd need was someone else; the rest wouldn't matter. We agreed on that point. It was real for us, genuine. We thought if we wanted it badly enough, we could create it. That when our time came, we'd be ready.

The drive dulled us. The abandoned cars dulled us. The unseen but known dulled us. Road after road dulled us. The immense sky and clear evenings dulled us. The small space inside our car dulled us. The pressure of no one dulled us.

We saw everything, but there was nothing to see. It was like being locked inside a museum and slowly realizing you're bored to tears.

We'd turned south and were somewhere in Texas when I looked at my hands and noticed abrasions. They weren't sore. I kept it to myself.

Alex, for her part, had become almost completely withdrawn. She had symptoms like morning sickness, but she was coughing up bile and blood in the morning. Her eyes were shot with minute streaks. I only saw them in the morning, before she got to her sunglasses. She was losing weight.

We'd both been having dreams. Alex called them Dead Dreams. Horrifying. My dreams were vivid, but nothing like the ones she described.

It was probably El Paso when I saw a car, heat-squiggled, in the distance. It was moving toward us. I was sure of it.

I nudged Alex. "I don't see it," she said.

"Take off your glasses," I said.

"There's nothing there," she said. She was squinting.

"You are such a fucking doubter," I said, louder than I meant to.

She collapsed back into her seat and returned to looking out the window. The car, which must've been going in the same direction we were, but faster, gradually faded over the curve of the road until all I saw was a shimmery puddle, the dead reflection of the asphalt.

We slept under the stars. It was so cold and quiet that before we succumbed to our nightly visions we imagined we heard footsteps, crunching gravel in the distance.

We woke up to a clear day and no wind. Neither of us was interested in motion anymore, but we couldn't think of anything else to do. We ached ourselves back into the car, I turned the engine, and we drove a slow circle back onto the road. Our food was almost gone, but neither of us was hungry.

After a few hours, Alex said we had to stop. She looked terrible. "What's with your hands?" she said.

"I think we should keep on," I said.

"We don't even know where we're going," she said. "We're not being chased. We've got nowhere in mind. Stop. I've had it."

I looked at her. She was pleading.

"Listen, just find a house. You can drop me off. I don't care."

"I can't believe you would say that," I told her. Nothing back.

We drove a few miles and passed a magnificent house, one out of an issue of *Southern Living*—columns, a large porch, hanging plants, wind chimes. "That one," Alex said.

I did a three-point turn, and we pulled off the road. Large elms canopied the driveway and the feeling as we approached was that we were returning to a house we'd lived in years ago.

I helped Alex up to one of the bedrooms. It was all I could do to get both of us up the stairs. The room was large, and one side was almost all windows, which faced away from the road and looked out over a large, sun-kissed grainy field. "I'm just going to stay here," she said and snugged under the covers. I watched until she fell asleep.

Alex remained in her room and I walked the halls, looking at family photos—baseball pictures, fishing trips, birthdays. The man of the house looked like Ernest Hemingway, like a fat, friendly uncle. I was transfixed just looking at him in these photos—at the texture of his gray beard, how he always seemed just about to smile. I stood there in the hall and then it was like he started to reach for me through the glass.

I woke up downstairs. There was blood on my shirt. I looked at my hands, red and rubbed almost raw, and it was like seeing them for the first time.

"What?" Alex said.

"Forget it," I said. "I'm going to see if there's any food."

Down in the kitchen a wreath of copper pots hung from the ceiling and ropes of garlic festooned the walls. I rifled the pantry and found nothing. I reached up for a garlic cluster and twisted it off but I lost it in my hand and it fell to the ground with a crispy thunk. I stood there for a moment before lifting my foot and stomping the cloves.

The television got no signal and there wasn't a radio, not that we could find, anywhere. We walked the property. In one of the barns there was a saddle in the center of the floor, neatly displayed, like someone had left it there on purpose. In one of the silos we found a concrete bunker—empty—but there was enough food there to last us awhile. There was also a shortwave that had been smashed, a rifle, and a small glass box protruding from the wall. The sign below it read FOR EMERGENCY USE ONLY: SONIC INVASION ALARM and inside the glass was a black lever.

"And it remains unpulled," Alex said.

"And it remains unpulled," I said.

We gave names to all the people in the photographs and assigned them rooms. We talked about Little League games and pie-eating contests. There was another woman, but the marriage recovered. And always, in every picture, the bearded father looked like he was about to speak some funny little truth that would put everything in perspective.

We spent our days napping in different rooms. When I wasn't with Alex, the house felt cavernous, but she'd made it clear that she wanted time alone. In the evenings, we would open whatever can sounded the least unappetizing and sit on the porch, looking out over the wheat field in back, watching as it rippled in the wind like some golden ocean.

We were so sick we didn't think about getting better. All we were concerned with was how to not make it worse. If I sat up too fast, eight thousand knives pricked my lower intestine. I was constantly parched. My eyes felt like they were drying out and would sink into my head if I was on my back for too long. Alex had nosebleeds like I'd never seen before, black blood trickling over her lips until she pinched it off. Her red stretch marks now striated her spine and inner thighs.

"I can't take this quiet," she said. "There's no one for miles. Not one sound. I feel extinct."

She went to bed and refused to leave. I tried to coax her out, but she had none of it.

"We're dying," she said. "On our own. And there's no one to see it."

"I'm here," I said. I told her the real tragedy was that we were isolating each other, and I found it unbearable.

"Cry a thousand tears," she said. "Start a river."

Days passed. We were out of things to say. I lay next to her in bed and listened to her irregular breathing, her chest heaves and her gulps of air. She dreamed with her whole body. When she woke up, she would look around the room slowly as if checking for something, and then, seeing me, would close her eyes again. I'd bandaged my hands, and every once in a while I would flop one over onto her, and she would take it and hold on.

One morning I woke up and she was gone. I inched my way around the room. I tried calling for her but the only thing that came out was a rattle that sounded like it came from behind me. I closed my eyes to feel the house, but felt nothing.

She was not in the kitchen. I scanned the field from the porch, but if she'd gone that way it had completely swallowed her up.

Our car was still outside. I sat in the driver's seat and rifled through the memento mori until I found her sunglasses and put them on. I saw the safety seat and was suddenly overcome with claustrophobia and as I stood to get out of the car the air began to pulse with a low-pitched wail. The shock of the siren, clear and piercing and close, buckled me. She knew it wouldn't be anything but sound, knew that no one was coming. And even if they were, what did we have to offer? We were just two people, sitting as far away from each other as possible. But what noise! It was like the earth was cracking open. It filled the sky. It was lovely and terrifying and I could feel it in my chest; it was full and alone and it moved right through me.

Going Solo: Creating The Long Dark

INTERVIEW WITH RAPHAEL VAN LIEROP

While visiting family during the holidays in 2015, I happened to glance over the shoulder of my 13-year-old nephew as he was engrossed in a video game on his computer, and I was immediately taken with what I saw on his display: a haunting winter landscape rendered in a distinctive, painterly way, dotted here and there with abandoned structures, snow-crusted pine trees, and the occasional bear, wolf, or deer. As he navigated through this eerily beautiful world, I asked, "Where are the enemy combatants?" He told me that there were none of these in *The Long Dark*, a remarkable first-person game that pits its users in a battle against only one foe: their own mortality. Players enter the game as the survivor of a plane crash in the frigid Canadian wilderness after a global geomagnetic disaster. They must count on their own ingenuity in order to survive, which means foraging for food and fuel, seeking shelter, monitoring constantly shifting weather conditions, and making use of whichever items (from crowbars to energy bars) they might happen to find along the way. *The Long Dark* represents the vision of Raphael van Lierop and his creative team at Hinterland, the Vancouver Island–based studio he founded in 2012 with the purpose of bringing this concept to life. I spoke with van Lierop in early 2016, and this interview, along with a series of visuals and a removable poster related to the game, appeared in *Esopus 23* that spring.

Tod Lippy: *How did you first get involved in gaming?*

Raphael van Lierop: I've been playing games for 30 years, basically, but never had thought of it as a career option until I'd already been working for a while. I did an English lit degree, and I really didn't have any firm career plans in mind. I'd always been into computers: My dad was a scientist, so I grew up around them and was always comfortable using them. I had one foot in the arts world and one foot in the technology world—in fact, I was paying my way through school by working at the university's computer lab. When I was doing my honors thesis, my adviser said, "You've got to make a choice—do you want to mess around with computers, or do you want to become an academic and focus on literature? You can't do both." As soon as somebody says, "You can't do that," I immediately try to figure out how I'm going to do it.

What was your first job out of university?

Even before I'd finished my degree I went to work as a technical writer at Matrox, a graphics-hardware company in Montreal, which is still around. You hear a lot about 3D graphics hardware in the context of the film industry—especially where special effects are concerned—but the industry is really driven by games. At Matrox, I was embedded in their engineering team and surrounded by these hard-core computer scientists and hardware engineers.

There were companies Matrox worked with that were using its 3D hardware for video-game development, and that's how I started learning about the game industry: "People actually get paid to make games—that's crazy!" Technical writing was a great way to pay the bills, but it's not very creative work. As I was exposed to more of these game projects, I started thinking, "Maybe this is something I should look into."

I embarked on this two-year process where I spent every spare moment reading everything I could get my hands on about game development. I would pin down and ask questions of anybody in the industry who would talk to me. I was doing everything I could to figure out how to break in, because it was—and still is—an extremely competitive industry. And I wasn't a programmer, not even really an artist. My "way in" turned out to be working on a project helping to North Americanize PlayStation 2 games that were coming to the original Xbox in 2000 or so. The Japanese developers would provide the literal translations—which of course would make no sense to a native English speaker—and I would turn them into something that a North American player could actually understand, something that would have a little bit of cultural nuance to it.

I was able to use that experience to get a job as a developer in Vancouver at Relic Entertainment. Back then, the Canadian game industry was really focused on Vancouver, and it was clear to me that if I wanted to break into this world I needed to "go West." My girlfriend at the time—she's now my wife—agreed to the move. I started as an assistant producer, basically the bottom rung of the production ladder—taking meeting minutes and ordering pizza for people—and over the years moved my way up to being a producer with my own team and my own projects. I got a chance to work with some fantastic people on some really good games. But I hit a wall—I was working in a creative field, but I wasn't truly in a creative role that felt fulfilling to me. I wasn't doing the designing or writing or lots of other things that in my heart I really wanted to do.

Around 2005 I had an opportunity to go work with a start-up developer, Radar, that was dealing with what is now called transmedia, which is basically coming up with intellectual property, or IP, that's designed from the ground up to be used in multiple ways—games, film, TV, you name it. I did that for two years and worked on a bunch of cool projects, but then, right around the time of the credit crisis, the company went out of business. It was kind of a mixed blessing, because it forced me to figure out what I was going to do next, and I ended up getting a job at Ubisoft Montreal—one of the best studios in the world—as a narrative director on the video game *Far Cry 3*. So my wife and I moved back east, but it proved to be challenging for us this second time around because we had young kids and it was just really hard for us to integrate into the city as Anglophones, etc. etc. After a little while, we returned to Vancouver. I went back to Relic, where I worked on something called *Space Marine*, a console action game in the *Warhammer 40,000* setting, which was a British tabletop game from the 1970s that has this strangely rabid following. Imagine heavy-metal album covers from the 1970s as an IP, and that's kind of what it was. It's very, very rich, and very deep and fascinating, but it's some of the nerdiest sci-fi you can imagine.

It was interesting to try to translate it into an action-game experience, because it had always been a real-time strategy game. It was all about figuring out how to take an aesthetic that had existed only on paper—in novels and rule books and things like that—and put the player in the middle of that world, make them feel its texture: What does it sound and feel like to be this hulking warrior in this weird, sci-fi fantasy setting? So it was pretty cool from that perspective.

One thing about *Space Marine*, though, was that it was literally one of the most violent games ever made. I mean, its tagline is something like, "In the grim darkness of the far future there is only war," and its sole premise is that there are all of these different alien races constantly at war with one another, trying to snuff each other out. So it's very grim and dark and depressing in a lot of ways, since you have no chance of winning; you're just prolonging the inevitable. I remember one evening when I was working on a build of the game at home after my kids were asleep, and my wife was kind of looking over my shoulder. She's not a gamer or anything, and at first she made polite comments about it, but later that evening, she said to me, "You know, you talk a lot about how much you care about your industry and your medium, and how you want to push interactive entertainment forward in all of these meaningful ways, and how important storytelling and emotion are—and I don't see any of you in that violent game." And she was right: There was really nothing in the game that was an expression of my creative values. I think I found values in the IP that I cared about—like bringing that world alive in a way that would be truthful to fans' expectations—but it didn't at all feel like the kind of experience I would happily show my kids when they were older, or talk about with people in a meaningful way.

Was this the moment you decided to begin work on The Long Dark*?*

It was definitely a reaction to finishing that game. You go through this kind of postpartum depression. It's such an intense process; you work on a game for two or three years, and when you're in the middle of it, going 100 miles an hour, you lose all perspective—it feels like it's the only thing that matters. And then it's out, and it's over and you don't know what to do with yourself. These junctures are always really powerful times for reflection for people who make video games, and for me particularly. You have that existential *what the hell am I doing with my life?* kind of moment.

I realized I needed either to do something different—something more truthful to my experience and my sensibilities—or I needed to leave the industry. Ironically, at around that time, I had all of these amazing job offers on much better projects with much better teams than I had any right to expect, especially having just shipped this incredibly violent game. These were projects that a year or two earlier I would have killed to work on, and yet I didn't feel excited about them at all. It helped me see that I was really ready for a change.

Right around that time I had lunch with my friend Jamie Chang, who runs a studio called Klei, whose games include *Don't Starve* and others that have been really successful. We had worked together at Relic—he was a programmer—and as we were reflecting on our career paths, he said, "You know, the only difference between you and me is that you've been searching for this credibility that you think you need in order to do the thing you really want to do, whereas I just went into a part of the industry where that doesn't matter. In the world of independent games, nobody gives a shit about the stuff you've worked on before." It was an interesting moment for me, because I realized that my concern that I needed to work on all of these big, triple-A titles—gain all of these credits—before I could do my own thing was probably unfounded.

All of these things put me in a frame of mind to do something different, and this happened to coincide with my wife and I deciding that we were pretty much done with living in the city. She had grown up on Vancouver Island, and it had always been in the back of our minds that we would end up there, so we just decided to do it. At first I did a bunch of consulting work for game studios to pay my bills while I incubated the idea of *The Long Dark* in the background, for probably about a year, before things started to come together.

From what I understand, the development of The Long Dark *is related directly to your founding of Hinterland Studio.*

Hinterland Studio and *The Long Dark* are all wrapped up in my decision to no longer be a part of the mainstream industry. I didn't want to make that kind of game. My wife and I didn't want to be in the city; we wanted to raise our family in the "hinterlands." Everything's connected, right? So that's how it all started. And we're really lucky to have the Canada Media Fund, a government program created specifically to promote Canadian film, TV, and interactive industries, so we were able to get some money to build a prototype. It was a loan, essentially, but it allowed me to hire my first team members, and that's when things really started.

How did you find collaborators?

Most of the team, then and now, are people with a story similar to mine: They either left the mainstream blockbuster industry for the reasons I did or they decided they wanted to live here. My initial hire was my technical director, Alan Lawrance, who had been at a studio called Volition for 16 years—he'd basically grown up there—and he had been involved in several really big franchises. He and his wife decided that they didn't want to be tied down to a specific city for work, and he was senior enough to be able to work anywhere. So he reached out to me about Vancouver Island. Our original conversation had nothing to do with *The Long Dark*, which at that point nobody knew about. He was just interested in learning more about the island and our decision to move here. But as we continued to talk about why someone might choose to relocate here with a family, we discovered that we had lots of shared values around quality of life and the kinds of things we might want to create, and I realized he was exactly who I needed to get started with this. I pitched him on the idea of joining the project, and he agreed, and that was really the start.

For the first year we had a small team of four or five people. We built a prototype, we got it to a place where we felt we were ready to talk about it, and then we pitched it on Kickstarter to see if there might be any interest out there in playing a niche, artistic survival-experience game. We got great feedback and lots of press attention, and people supported the idea really enthusiastically, so we started to think, "Maybe we've really got something here."

Did you feel it was important to get this feedback before you went ahead with development?

Well, we knew we were doing something outside of the mainstream—we never approached it from the standpoint of making a game within an existing genre. Our initial thought behind it was, "What's the experience we want to have?" So the next step was to see if we could find people who were interested in that kind of experience too. I had no expectations whatsoever. I still feel like I somehow have to qualify that, to say to people, "You know, we started out with this really niche thing but somehow it managed to resonate with this substantial audience." In the end it's proven to be really popular, which probably just tells you how ready the gaming audience is to try something fresh.

Can you talk about how you came up with the concept for the game in the first place?

I've always been interested in the idea of wilderness survival as an experience. There weren't really any games that were solely focused on that when I first started thinking about this. Back then, when you talked about survival games, you were talking about zombies. You were talking about "action survival," not about what survival is at its core: making smart choices in very challenging scenarios, conserving your resources, keeping your wits about you.

It's funny: We've ended up a part of a "survivalist" genre that kind of grew up around us when we were working on the game. There's *DayZ*, *Rust*, and many other games that have come out over the past two or three years that form this genre that didn't exist before. But I don't think we approached it conceptually in that way. It was always more about making a game that explores this postdisaster, northern Canadian wilderness setting, and more specifically, that considers the notion of survival in the most essential sense: that of managing your overall "condition." How cold, tired, thirsty, or hungry you are—those became the mechanics that drove the whole experience of wanting to look for more things, for needing to explore. That was really at the core of everything.

Were there any other games that you found to be influential to the development of The Long Dark?

A few games have really resonated with me throughout the years. One was *Fallout 3*, which I played so much when I was starting to think about doing my own thing. It struck me how compelling it was to just move through the world and uncover what felt like all of these artifacts from an abandoned place and time. For me, the combat of the game, and a lot of the mechanics, were almost secondary to that. I just enjoyed wandering. I remember when it first came out it had a "level cap," which means that you grind through the mechanics and increase your character's skill level until you max out and can't get any more rewards for playing. Several months after the game came out they increased the level cap, but I didn't even care. I'd already invested over 100 hours just exploring the world without getting any of the game-play rewards, which seemed really superficial to my experience. I was so happy to just wander around and was loving this feeling of being in this world and being able to see things on the horizon that were interesting to me and checking them out. You know, that whole psychology of urban exploration: "There's a building over there that's broken down, and I probably shouldn't go into it, but I'm going to anyway, to see what I find." And every time you go up to a locker or desk or whatever, you're hopeful you're going to find something that will help you survive a little bit longer. One of the most significant questions that came out of that for me was, could I make a game that was almost purely about that experience—that *feeling*. Strip away all the other stuff—take away combat, take away skills, take away mechanics—and just make it about the aesthetics and the emotion of exploring an abandoned space that generates that *I just need to go a little bit further* feeling. That was one of the major influences on the mechanics of *The Long Dark*.

A Ukrainian first-person-shooter game called *Stalker* inspired me too. We named one of our modes after it as a sort of homage. The game is set in a fictionalized post-Chernobyl exclusion zone, where these weird portals into other dimensions exist. And there are bounty hunters, called stalkers, who go and search for artifacts that appeared because of the disaster. When you enter this zone as a player, you encounter other stalkers and there's conflict and that sort of thing.

Does it bear any relation to the Tarkovsky film of the same name?

Actually, both the game and Tarkovsky's film are based on a Russian novel called *Roadside Picnic*, although the two offer obviously very different interpretations. But the game really struck me because it provided one of the most atmospheric experiences I've ever had as a player. The team behind it actually went to the Chernobyl site and took photos: They built their world based on the real world, so it has a feeling of intense verisimilitude.

Stalker and *Fallout 3* inspired a lot of thinking about *The Long Dark*, which is meant to offer, more than anything else, an experience of being immersed in a world, and being allowed to soak up its atmosphere—the wind, the snow, what the structures look and feel like. And it's something we try to push forward as we continue to develop the game—how to communicate more and more of that sense of place.

Despite what seems to be a trend in the mainstream gaming industry toward an increasingly photorealistic visual experience, the visuals in The Long Dark *are much more stylized, even impressionistic. Can you talk a litte bit more about that choice?*

The practical side is that an independent game really needs a look to help it stand out in the marketplace. The art direction of every game I've ever been involved with is always concerned with defining a style that is strong enough for someone to be able to identify the game from one screenshot. Another thing is, the photorealistic approach to graphics is very expensive. Making the content for it is very time-consuming—with a small team and a small budget, you can take your money only so far. So do you want to make a small, extremely detailed world, or do you want to have a broader, more stylized world? Creatively speaking, the challenge becomes how to make something simplistic look beautiful—almost like an abstraction. That becomes the style, and the fact that it's simpler doesn't detract from the experience but actually gives it a unique identity.

How are these visuals actually created? For instance, what was the process for coming up with the cabin interior that serves as "home base" for players?

That's actually the first interior we ever made in the game. For a long time we called it "the safe house." It was the place where you start the game, and where you keep your gear, so it had to feel cozy and protected compared to everything else. Lots of times in games you'll use concept art, but it's only meant to be a visual inspiration to the team. Our goal with *The Long Dark*, though, was always to make the game look like it was moving concept art. So with this cabin, which was literally the only interior location we had in the early stages, we started with a piece of concept art that we iterated with an artist to get the right look—the right color combinations, the right lighting, the right position of all the different pieces of furniture—to communicate the vibe of the space. We worked with all of those bits and pieces to get the look exactly where we wanted it to be in 2D; then our goal was to recreate that as closely as possible in 3D. All the assets you see there—the chairs, the bed, the window, all the objects on the shelves—each one is a 3D object crafted by hand. The textures on everything you see in the game have all been hand-painted.

This is fairly unusual in this day and age, and it kind of goes back to your question about photorealism. Most games that are highly photorealistic will use photo references for texture. So they'll take a picture of something and then they'll map that directly into the game on the object itself, so it ends up with a texture that has been taken from the real world. So for, let's say, a gravel road, you would go and take a whole bunch of photos of paved roads and then turn those into textures in 3D. But in our case, everything is painted by individual artists, which is part of what gives it its unique look. It's very handcrafted in a way that a lot of games aren't anymore.

To me, it inspires a confidence in the vision of the people behind the game, which in turn allows me to enter into it as a player in a more complete way.

Having worked on some large-scale, big-budget productions that were really pursuing high-end graphics, I feel like photorealism is not a particularly interesting challenge. I mentioned starting out my career in the graphics-card industry, which is driven by this belief that what people need to feel immersed in a world is for it to look like the real world. I don't think that's true—Pixar's success, for instance, comes from their understanding that it's more about style than realism. There are some fantastically beautiful games out there, many of which are extremely realistic, and that's great, but I care more about creating an interesting experience people will become immersed in. And that has very little to do with what it actually looks like. It has a lot more to do with how it feels, which has to do with many other things beyond just what you see on-screen. For instance, the audio experience is in a lot of ways just as important as the visuals, if not more so. I think that's the reason we've put so much effort into the soundscapes in the game.

How are these soundscapes constructed?

Some of our audio is taken from libraries, but the majority of it is stuff that we recorded ourselves, either in Foley sessions or out in the world. For instance, a lot of our wind sounds were recorded in the wintertime on a frozen lake out near Edmonton. We have a very sophisticated audio system for this scale of game; there is a lot of detail in the soundscape. For example, the sounds that you hear when you move around the world change depending on what you have in your inventory: If I'm carrying a bunch of water with me, I'll hear that water sloshing around when I'm walking through the world. If I've got a rifle slung over my shoulder and I'm wearing a nylon ski jacket, I'll hear different sounds when I move than when I'm wearing a wool sweater. These are the kinds of details that probably only my audio director, Glenn Jamison, would ever notice—like how the sound of snow crunching under your feet changes based on the kind of footwear you have. It's really subtle stuff, but I do believe that, as an overall experience, it definitely reinforces that feeling of *presence* in the world. And even if only one out of every hundred people notices, it pays off.

How did you go about assembling The Long Dark*'s creative team over the past several years?*

When we started, I knew I wasn't going to be able to recruit the people I needed locally—I was really the only one here. *[laughs]* At that point, I didn't want to have a very big team anyway, and what really mattered was finding talented people who were motivated by the same things I was. I believed at the time, and it's been proven true since, that there were people out there who wanted to make great games but didn't necessarily want to live in the city or work in the established studio system. Over time, the team has grown—we're over 20 people now—and more than half work out of the studio on Vancouver Island.

I've never asked anyone to move here—I've been really careful about that, because I remember moving my family around a lot for work, and it didn't always work out, which can be a real drag. But the people who have moved here did so in large part for quality-of-life reasons. My user-interface artist, Warren Heise—who was at BioWare for more than 10 years working on the game *Dragon Age*—is hugely into the outdoors and a big hiker, and he just wanted to be on an island where there are mountains and trails. And, actually, he fell in love with the game from that perspective, as an outdoors person.

Where are the other team members located, and how does the creative process work?

The rest of us are distributed between Vancouver, Edmonton, and the United States. We work mainly using Skype or Basecamp, and a little bit of email, and we've managed to create a set of processes using tools that allow us to work effectively even though we're not all together. The challenges have become more pronounced as we've grown: How do you build a team culture when half the team is here and the other half is spread all over the place? How do you make sure the people who aren't here feel fully incorporated into the process? However successful we end up being, I'm pretty sure there will always be a certain component of the team that is not here in the studio. The most important thing is working with really, really great people, and I would never want to say no to someone great just because they live in a different city.

How important was research for The Long Dark, *whether related to wilderness survival or just certain aspects of the human body and its limits?*

Years ago, I worked on a World War II strategy game called *Company of Heroes*. World War II history fans are some of the pickiest players you'll ever meet. So we had to do a ton of research for every aspect of the game, from the color and cut of uniforms to the design of weapons and vehicles. What that project taught me was that you have to embrace either realism or authenticity—they're not the same thing. What a game needs, in my view, is authenticity; realism can limit the creation of mechanics designed to promote and enhance a compelling player experience.

A good example is the way we chose to deal with starvation in *The Long Dark*. In reality, starvation is not a concern on a really short-term timescale. You could survive for weeks without eating. But that timescale is not interesting in the context of a game, right? Starvation and food management need to become a problem you care about over the 10 or 20 hours of a typical game-play cycle. So we tweak it to be relevant to the experience we've created. We do have people in our community who are really bothered by that. And I love that they approach it from that perspective, but we always have to remind them that we'll support realism where it serves the player experience; however, when it contradicts that experience we'll break those rules. *The Long Dark* is not about creating a truly realistic survival experience, and the truth is that 99.9 percent of our players never have been, and never will be, in such a scenario.

I think the sense of realism comes into play in the level of detail we try to reach by simulating certain choices. So in addition to having to worry about how cold, tired, or hungry you are, we put these little moments in there where you have to make very specific choices. "Oh shit, I'm stuck in this little house in the middle of the blizzard and I don't want to go outside to get snow to melt for drinking water because there are wolves out there. I'm going to take water out of the toilet, make it potable by boiling it, and drink that instead." These are the kinds of things that the mechanics of the game support that make it feel realistic even though under the hood it's just a bunch of numbers. It's playing on the sense of realism but being very selective about the kinds of choices you have to make in a survival situation.

"Independent" is a label that can be applied at this point to virtually any creative enterprise, from filmmaking to music. Could you possibly define it in terms of Hinterland's relationship to the larger world of game developing and publishing?

We're both a developer and a publisher, because we self-publish. We are not owned by anyone else. We fund all of our work, we control our IP, and we own all of our content, so we're not beholden to anyone but our community. There's a lot of discussion about "indie" games in our industry, and it feels a bit like a meaningless label to me. We're an independent studio creating an artistic experience that we wouldn't be able to make if we were owned or funded by someone else. I think that's the only way in which being "independent" really matters: Do you ultimately call the shots?

You cited some feedback you'd received from players about the starvation issue; I was wondering if you could discuss the role community feedback plays for you and the studio. Do you feel this type of response has a different impact in the independent arena than it does in the mainstream game industry?

The community is so much more important to what we do here than it is for a publisher-run studio or a large-scale production house. Especially because of how we're funded: We're in multiple early-access-style programs, which essentially means we have an incomplete version of the game that's live right now that you can buy—kind of like how *Minecraft* was originally funded. I think we're one of the only games, if not the only one, that is on all three early access platforms: Steam on PC, which is kind of like the iTunes of games, Game Preview on Xbox One, and GOG [Good Old Games].

Our game and our company have grown up around this development model, and it's one in which we iterate really, really often, and publicly. We take community feedback in all forms—what players have to say, what we see in the metrics and analytics—and we use this feedback to validate decisions we've made. We're quite careful about the way we interact with our community and the way we talk about how it's involved with the game, because there are other projects that are in this early access model that have lost their way. You can imagine: We have 675,000 players now. You don't hear from all of them, but you hear from a lot of them. *[laughs]* How do you make one game satisfying for a cross-section of people from all over the world—we've been purchased in over 150 countries, and the game is played in over 40 languages—working from entirely different contexts, all looking for different things?

What often happens is that developers find themselves being influenced by a vocal minority, and then the project gets pulled in different directions. Then other people react badly to that, and suddenly it seems as if there is no vision behind the project. So we've been always really careful to say to our community, "This is our game, and we have a clear vision of where it's going, but we want you guys to be a part of the process of vetting the decisions we're making. We also want to hear what you think about mechanics, about tuning, and we want you to tell us what you like and don't like, and we'll use all of this as another data point for our decision making."

But we're never going to put something in the game or change a mechanic just because we have a bunch of people complaining about it. We're very, very fortunate to have a community that's really open to that. We get a lot of support from them, and we know we have a huge responsibility to them, and I think that's partly why it works so well: They give us their trust, but we work twice as hard to earn it. As long as we stay true to our vision and produce a high-quality experience, they will continue to trust us and support our exploration in making the game, which in many ways is analogous to the experience of the game itself: You don't always know where you're going to end up.

You will be launching a new mode for The Long Dark *this year; can you talk about that a bit?*

We're preparing the first installment of our story mode, or what we call our narrative experience. When we originally conceived of the game, and when we pitched it on Kickstarter, it was meant to be a narrative experience more than a sandbox experience. And we decided to bring the game to early access platforms so we could use the community feedback to help tune and polish and tighten the core mechanics that the story mode would then be layered on top of, because nobody wants to play-test a half-completed story. We were going to take three or four months to gather the data, finish up the story mode, and then launch that first installment. What we didn't anticipate was that the game would blow up.

That reaction has convinced us to invest a lot more of our time and resources in creating an experience that we are passionate about, and we really want it to be excellent. You know, I've been making games for 15 years, and I've seen, and worked on, a lot of projects that were good, but I feel that we have something now that is very special and quite rare—it's connecting with people in ways that we couldn't have anticipated, and when we do launch this thing we want it to be as groundbreaking as it can possibly be. Because of this success with early access, we have the resources to continue developing the game and don't have to push it out until we're ready. We've said that we're going to launch our first episode next spring, and that's what we're focused on right now.

Can you offer any details?

The narrative that will be layered on top of the core mechanics will include other survivors, two playable characters, and a whole story line. And that's just the beginning. What we hope to be able to do is a whole year of seasons. Season 2 would take place in the spring, so that it would be an entirely different environment with a different game-play focus, and we'll advance the narrative along with it. The grand vision for the game is for players to experience a full year of *The Long Dark*: what was it like to live the year after the lights went out, the first year of the "quiet apocalypse."

And we have aspirations beyond that. We've had a lot of interest in the IP from people outside of games who would like to work with us on things like films and TV series. We're trying, though, to be really disciplined and not get too distracted. I've seen how much the film business always seems like such a big draw for game developers, and I don't really know why that is. I think maybe it comes from a lack of confidence in our medium—maybe we don't feel it is as respected as film is, and so we're always looking to the film industry for validation.

I love film, but I think we can offer a level of experience you can't have in a film. Game design is a more challenging medium, and I don't think we've even hit our stride yet as to how far we can push it. But I do think film is an exciting way to reach more people. And having worked in the transmedia space, I really appreciate the fact that when I really, really love a world, I want to watch it on TV and read books and articles about it and discuss it with my friends, and I want to get wrapped up in the fiction and know about the characters and speculate on story and plot threads—I want to make it a part of my life, you know? So it would be great to reach people whose entry point may not be the game. It might be a novel, or a web show, or who knows. Hopefully there's something compelling enough beyond the game we've created in this wintry northern Canadian landscape, something about the aesthetics, the theme, the setup, that allows us to have this cohesive IP that can be expressed through all of these different media by playing to the strength of each. Once you create something you're really excited about, you just want to share it with as many people as you can.

Why do you think people want to play a game that essentially forces them to confront their own mortality?

It touches on a few different things. Blockbuster games have become similar to big-budget superhero films: really formulaic, made with the sole goal of getting as many people as possible to see them. Games have become way too easy; they're more about being taken on an amusement-park ride that involves little or no threat to your success than they are about offering an experience that players can in some way drive, or be truly challenged by. So in the last five years there's been a little bit of a push in the independent-game space to bring some challenge back to players. That's one reason our game resonates with so many people, because there's this permadeath aspect to it that makes your choices feel like they have a lot more meaning. When you die, you lose everything, and you have to start again from scratch, which adds some weight to those decisions.

But more than that, I think people really connect with the theme of vulnerability. One thing those big action games have become great at is delivering a fantasy of being a powerful warrior who can overcome all odds. In a way, that's what games have always been, right? One of the things about *The Long Dark* is that it's the exact opposite of that. It's putting you into a scenario where you know you're going to fail; you know you're going to die. How can you prolong that and make good choices that will sustain you as long as possible? Can you face that mortality? Can you come to terms with the fact that you're a tiny speck in this vast majestic nature that's completely neutral about whether you live or die?

Talk about realism!

[laughs] People often talk about *The Long Dark* as if it's a horror game. And I always find that really interesting, because I don't think about it in those terms at all. But some people feel as uncomfortable and intimidated by it as they would a more traditional survivalist or horror game, because they feel that fear. Other people find it poetic. They love walking through the world and listening to the wind and looking at the sunset: "I know that eventually I'm going to die, but while I'm here, I'm going to soak it up." But I do think it comes down to that feeling of snatching one more day from the jaws of death, even though you know you're going to eventually fail. It's kind of this affirmation of life, you know? You can look at it either as fatalism or as giving you a reason to fight to live. You either roll over and die, or you fight. And the game is asking you to fight. Not with guns, but with choices, with decisions, and by not giving up.

Off-Off-Off Broadway

BY RICK HOLEN, JOE MAURO, JOHN NUTT, AND BOB SEVRA

John Nutt: In 1969–70, the American military in Vietnam assembled a group of 11 soldiers, myself included, and one female civilian employee to put together a production of the musical *The Fantasticks*. Traveling by truck, helicopter, and C-130 air transport, we entertained troops throughout the war zone. After the tour was over, we returned to our original military companies. I lost all contact with the other troupe members; in fact, in the ensuing years I told the stories so many times to my family and friends that the tour seemed more mythic than real.

Not long ago, I ran across an invitation to a reunion I had received more than 10 years earlier. It had a phone number for Rick Holen, who had played the part of The Mute in the musical. The number still worked, and I was quickly reconnected to the past. Rick, as it turned out, had been trying to make a documentary film about our experience and the CMTS, or Command Military Touring Shows.

Rick Holen: Throughout American military history, music has been used to bolster troop morale. The fife and drum were used in the American Revolution; the Civil War and the Spanish American War had their brass bands. During World War I, Irving Berlin brought contemporary music to the rear areas, as did Glenn Miller and his band (not to mention many other stars of stage and screen) during World War II. The Korean conflict featured appearances by Bob Hope, Marilyn Monroe, George Jessel, and Joe E. Brown.

Vietnam was a little different. While Army Special Services in Saigon brought over movie stars like John Wayne, Martha Raye, and Roy Rogers and Dale Evans, and Bob Hope staged an annual Christmas show, these appearances were only for the handful of rear areas where it was safe enough for them to appear. So the military decided to try something else: assemble groups of trained GIs that could defend themselves if they needed to and yet use their musical, acting, and entertainment experience to take the war away from the men in the field for a couple of hours.

The first group of American soldiers to tour frontline areas was called the Black Patches. The unit was put together in 1966 by a group of career military officers and enlisted men. They performed mainly covers of popular music, although they were known for some off-color original tunes that lampooned various members of the office staff back in Saigon. The group not only played for the troops in the field, they also performed at many hospitals, where they felt they were needed the most. The Command Military Touring Shows really began with this group. After the success of the Black Patches, there were 118 other groups that toured Vietnam from 1966 to 1971. Many units were folk, soul, country, and rock bands. A group of GIs from Special Services first put together a revue called *The Maniactors*, followed by a number of other small-scale musicals, from *You're a Good Man, Charlie Brown* to *Stop the World—I Want to Get Off* (and even some one-act plays, like Beckett's *Krapp's Last Tape*). All in all, 580 men and women took part in these CMTS productions.

Joe Mauro: I arrived at Cam Ranh Bay, Vietnam, on February 6, 1969, with no assignment to any unit. I had been warned to take anything but the First Air Cavalry Division. Of course, the following day, I found out I had been assigned to the First Air Cav list and would be stationed in Phuoc Vinh. Just my luck: Everyone talked about how the Vietcong loved to come out of the mountains and mortar the troops. Eventually, our unit relocated to Bien Hoa, and I was assigned to Special Services, with a hooch and a phone line. We had no commanding officer, so being an E-5, I was put in charge.

Before I left for Vietnam, a friend had given me the number of someone to contact should I get to a phone. His name was Brad Arrington. Brad was a fixture in Saigon and was responsible for many of the military shows that were put together to entertain the troops in the field. I phoned Brad, and we became fast and close friends. In the course of our working together I threw a lot of ideas out to him and never once did he say it couldn't be done. My first undertaking was to stage a talent show in Saigon. We put out a notice through the army distribution network, and the guys arrived, all of them vying for a chance to get out and perform. After that show, we put together a number of groups, rehearsed them, and sent them out into the field to perform.

Nutt: I arrived in Vietnam on July 4, 1969. I was stationed in Saigon, working as a personnel clerk in an army intelligence unit housed in an old French compound near the edge of the city. One day not long after my arrival, my office phone rang. It was a call from a college friend working for a general at army headquarters in Long Binh who had responsibility for troop entertainment. He asked if I wanted to stage-manage a production of *The Fantasticks*. My friend and I had both been involved in theater at Dartmouth—he had always been onstage performing, while I was always behind the curtain stage-managing, set-building, or doing the lighting, so his question made sense. When I got his invitation to do some theater, I thought I had lost touch with the tenuous hold on reality I was maintaining in those first months in Vietnam. After the initial shock, I realized this would mean as much as two months away from my unit, and I jumped at the chance.

Bob Sevra: I was drafted in the fall of 1968, the first year the draft stopped giving student deferments for more than one year of graduate work. Trying to make some use of this new "brainy" influx, the army gave an accelerated "language aptitude test" to all those new grad students in the hopes of finding Americans they could quickly train to be Vietnamese interpreters. I was one of the first group of 30 to go through the program—nine months stateside. Of course, since it was the army, we didn't learn the language worth a damn; and besides, by the time we got to Nam, most of the natives had learned English—or French, which was my second language.

The day after I landed in Saigon, I reported to 4th Psy Ops, not having any idea what my job would be, or where I might be going. The first sergeant told us new guys that some sort of inspector general was expected in the next day or two, and we rookies should just go back to the hotel we were assigned to and keep out of sight. While the others checked out the town and the bars, I found my way to Special Services, just to see if I might find something that would keep me out of the war.

Mauro: A fellow named Jay Kerr was assigned to the entertainment division of Special Services in Bien Hoa. He had known the late Clark Gesner, the creator of *You're a Good Man, Charlie Brown*, and somehow he convinced him to give us the rights to produce it in Vietnam (this was its first staging off of Broadway, as far as I know). I played Schroeder, and we hit the trails, performing anywhere and everywhere.

Because of the success of the production, Brad and I had a conversation about staging *The Fantasticks*. There was a civilian female in the Special Services office with a voice that both of us thought was ideal for the female lead. We felt the show would be perfect because it didn't rely on props and many of the other trappings of large productions.

Notices were sent out for auditions, and I quickly realized that we had a hell of a lot of creative talent going to waste in a country they shouldn't have been in in the first place.

Holen: My theater experience was rather limited compared with the rest of the cast. Many of them had majored in theater or music performance in college—some even had M.F.A. degrees. Most of us had been drafted right out of college, but we all had one thing in common: We hated the military and wanted nothing more than to live through the experience and get back to working in the theater—and living in the world.

I had played a role in *The Fantasticks* in summer stock when I was on leave from the air force. Later that summer, on July 4, 1969, I left for Vietnam. One day I got lost in Saigon, which was very easy to do, and I passed by the Army Special Services Compound. There was a banner that read "Auditions for *The Fantasticks*." I pulled my jeep over, and after chaining the steering wheel with a paddle lock—it wouldn't have been there when I got back, otherwise—I ran in and filled out a form and walked into the audition. It felt like a typical theater audition you would find in New York.

Sevra: I had always been a singer and an actor. Years before, when I first heard a recording of *The Fantasticks*, it had been my dream to someday play the character of El Gallo. (Also, from the first time I saw her picture on the album cover and heard her sing, I fell in love with The Girl from the original show, Rita Gardner. As luck would have it, she was cast as my love interest in a musical at the Barter Theatre in Abingdon, Virginia, in 1973, and we've been together ever since.)

As it turns out, the day I walked into Special Services, they were auditioning and casting for the touring production of *The Fantasticks*. I couldn't believe my luck when I was told I'd gotten the part of El Gallo.

Nutt: When I approached the rehearsal hall, I was greeted by the sound of a piano and the lyrics "Try to remember the kind of September..." booming down a small alley in a humble neighborhood of Saigon. I met some of the performers and in short order was informed that my budget was $50 and a jeep. The vehicle was necessary, I was told, because I was going to have to steal practically everything I needed.

Mauro: I directed the production—and the egos of some of the finest voices I have ever encountered. I had played Matt in college, and, like most of the cast, was very familiar with the show. In two weeks, working day and night, *The Fantasticks* was ready to go. Brad did all of the scheduling. I was coming up on the end of my tour of duty, so I only went out on tour for a couple of shows before heading home.

Holen: *The Fantasticks* was written in 1960 by Tom Jones and Harvey L. Schmidt and was performed at the Sullivan Street Playhouse in New York City for 42 years. The story, whicih was based loosely on a turn-of-the-century French play called *Les Romanesques*, is about two fathers who want their son and daughter to fall in love and marry, so they decide to use reverse psychology to make it happen by forbidding them to see each other. Eventually the children fall in love, but when they find out about the fathers' plot, they each go off on their own to experience the world. Ultimately, of course, the lovers are reunited. As Joe mentioned, the musical was chosen because the cast was small and production requirements were minimal. We used just an electric piano, basic stage lighting, and hand props.

I expected we would rehearse for a couple of weeks and then perform the musical in Saigon for two or three weekends—that would be it. Little did I know that I would be transferred from the air force to the army's 1st Log Command for two and a half months and tour all over Vietnam for three shows a day, putting myself into countless situations where I ran the risk of getting my ass shot off.

Nutt: Our troupe consisted of eight performers, a musical director/pianist, a stage manager (that was me), a prop man, and most amazingly, a piano tuner who not only tuned but also rebuilt many of the pianos we used. Later, I found out that a number of the military commanders had requested that our troupe perform for them in order to get their pianos tuned!

Holen: A number of times during the tour we were called out of the field because of heavy combat, so we would pack up the set and props and fly back to Saigon. The army would billet us at the Metropole Hotel, a small, run-down place that had been built during the French occupation of Vietnam. The walls were very thick concrete because the Vietnamese were trying to kill as many Frenchmen as they could. Bomb blasts had been commonplace in Saigon in the previous 100 years: The Vietnamese fought the Chinese, the Japanese, the French, and finally the Americans. (The Vietnamese call our conflict the American War, which of course they won hands down.)

The Metropole's lobby was made into a military dayroom. It had about five pool tables, leather-covered sofas, and a small bar. Black Label, the only American-made beer in Vietnam, could be purchased for 25 cents a can. The tin was so thick that a "church key" can opener was needed to open it. The lobby had been moved to a side street that had sandbags stacked at the entrance, with a Vietnamese ARVN (Army of the Republic of Vietnam) troop standing guard. He generally was sleeping or eating some Vietnamese food.

One time while we were billeted at the Metropole, we were all in one room on the second floor when we heard a big explosion go off right beneath us. I rushed to the window and was immediately grabbed by someone who pulled me to the floor. I said, "What the fuck did you do that for?" "Snipers, you idiot," was the response. The VC would often set off explosions just to see if they could flush out targets after the sapper charge went off. As it turned out, the bomb had taken out the entire dayroom, including the five or six GIs playing pool at the time of the explosion. I never went back into it.

Nutt: We got around Vietnam primarily by flying in C-130 or C-123 air transports, CH-47 Chinook helicopters (also called "shithooks"), Huey helicopters, and occasionally large troop-transport trucks. One particularly vivid incident I recall was when a CH-47 Chinook crew member decided to use our large box of costumes and props as a landing marker. As it hit the ground, the box popped open and the contents started to fly out. I jumped out and threw myself on top of the box to protect it, and the helicopter landed about two feet from my head.

Holen: Vietnam was carved up into military zones. IV Corps was in the South, and I Corps was up near the DMZ on the northern border of Vietnam. We often had to fly from one location to the other because there were no roads between bases. We would wind up stuck for hours on some remote flight line, waiting for a cargo plane to pick us up to fly to another performance.

Sometimes we would fly in choppers, and often I would look down into the jungle and see little green tracer rounds coming up at us. The chopper door gunners would just laugh at them, like they were bumblebees. We didn't think it was so funny. We knew we were being watched from the tree lines wherever we landed. Even in Saigon, I would see people following us as we walked around the city. There were rumors that any VC or North Vietnamese Army soldier who killed an entertainer would get a $1,500 bounty. I don't know if that was true or not, but it was a little unnerving.

Nutt: The places we performed tended to be unusual. In one location, we set up the stage in a boxing ring. Everything was going well until the electric piano our musician was using started to receive radio communications from B-52 pilots flying overhead. The musician turned off the power to the piano and the performers sang a cappella after that. Another time, we set up in a large movie theater and several hundred mud-covered marines walked in carrying weapons. As soon as the music started, almost all of them rushed out in a kind of stampede—apparently, they had expected a movie. A few soldiers remained, though—they moved up to the front and watched the whole show.

Holen: We played at Freedom Hill, which was a Marine Corps base near the DMZ. It was a large tent that was used normally as a chow hall. We set up for the show, and the tent was just packed with hard-core jarhead marines (and I mean that as a "mark of honor and high respect"). We had stage lights, so they turned off the regular lights. Halfway through the show, about 12 troops entered with their steel helmets and weapons. They had just come off a patrol. In the low light, it looked like they had dark mud all over their uniforms. As the two lovers started to sing "Soon It's Gonna Rain," I noticed that two or three of the troops right down in front—just a few feet away from the edge of the stage—suddenly had tears running down their face. At the end of the show, the house lights were turned on, and I could see that it wasn't mud on their uniforms; it was blood—a lot of it. It turned out they had just been in a firefight and lost many of their brothers.

Nutt: At one point we played in a large amphitheater in Cam Ranh Bay. The theater was right off the beach, and a huge wind blew across the theater from the audience's side toward the stage. I ran a spotlight behind the audience that night and discovered from that perspective that the wind was so strong no one in the audience could hear any music at all; to them, it was just a mime show.

Holen: We had performed a number of times at Long Binh army base because it was one of the largest bases in Vietnam. The army used it as a storage area for most of the war materials brought into Saigon Harbor. They had pallets of Black Label that went on for what seemed like miles. (A Vietnamese kid told me that they didn't run out of Black Label beer in Vietnam until 1978. The Vietnamese not only drank the beer, they used the cans as house-building materials. They would flatten them out and weld them together into sheets for walls and roofs.) One night we performed at an outside movie theater there. It was nothing more than five sheets of plywood painted white with a small stage. The seats were long two-by-eight-foot boards. In the middle of the first act, I turned upstage for only a moment, and when I turned back around, everyone in the audience was gone. Then I heard a series of mortar rounds going off one after another, each round coming closer to the stage. There was a bunker off stage right, and I ran to the doorway. It was crammed full of people, like a can of sardines. As the sixth round exploded, I asked, "Room for one more?" From deep inside the bunker, someone yelled, "Fuck no!" I ran back and jumped under the electrical field generator as the last round exploded about 20 feet away. Someone later explained that Special Services had plastered flyers all over the base giving the place and time for the performance, and the VC had used the movie screen as a focus point for rockets and mortars.

After the attack, the audience demanded that we pick up where we had left off. We did, and they loved the show.

Holen: Not all the venues we played were so primitive. We performed at the Bob Hope Theater in Da Nang. It was a large movie theater, with maybe 500 seats—the stage even had a grand curtain. I had to use the bathroom, so I asked this very tall jarhead marine where the john was. He looked down at me and said, "You mean *the head*?" I shrank like a small spider, and he pointed stage right. As I went into the bathroom, I noticed a small gold star on the door. I sat down on the flush toilet and saw a brass placard on the wall that read, "Ann-Margret shit here Dec. 23, 1968."

Nutt: For me, the most memorable event was a show we put on in a bar that was part of a Special Forces camp on the Cambodian border. The GIs had strung up a rope to divide the bar into two sections. Roped off in the back section was a group of Montagnard soldiers. They were a native people who lived in a nearby village and fought on the same side as the Americans. They couldn't have understood a word of the lyrics, but they appeared completely mesmerized by the performance. In the meantime, the Special Forces troops in the front completely ignored us, drinking at the bar with their backs turned.

When the show was over we were invited to the sergeant major's hooch for some serious drinking. As we were all getting pretty plastered, the sergeant major leaped up and announced that we had to see the Cambodian border, which was not far away. By this time it was getting dark, and we were a bit wobbly from the alcohol as we started across a small field to a tree line in the distance. After a few steps, the sergeant major yelled, "Walk where I walk!" We asked why, and then he yelled, "Land mines!" So we threaded our way to the tree line, walking in his footsteps as carefully as we could. Once there, we could look down into a valley, which he said was the Ho Chi Minh Trail, and across the valley was Cambodia.

The next day, the troupe was invited to visit the Montagnard village, which was a beautiful group of thatched-roof houses built on stilts. The houses were built with a very fragrant wood; the whole area had a wonderful perfumed smell as a result. The chief of the village invited us into his house, and we all sat around drinking rice wine out of a large vat that had many long, reedlike straws. Water was poured in at the top, and then over the course of many days it made its way to the bottom, by which point it had fermented. As we drank from the bottom of the vat through the long reed straws, the level dropped and was measured by refilling the vat with water—it was a kind of drinking game. Needless to say, we all got pretty drunk downing rice wine by the quart.

Holen: One time we were performing for a transportation unit at a service club at Long Binh. There were about 200 troops watching the performance. Right in the middle of the second act, I heard the sound of something rolling across the floor. Looking down, I saw that a green pineapple grenade had rolled upstage. My first instinct was to jump on it to save the rest of the cast. But then I noticed that there was no smoke coming out of the top of it—it was a fake. The soldier who threw the grenade was sitting with his feet resting on the stage. One of the cast members, who had attended the High School of Performing Arts in New York City and was trained as a comedian, picked up the fake grenade, broke character, and asked the soldier, "Do you want to be in show business?" The guy answered, "No!" The actor responded, "Then get your boots off the stage!"

Holen: After one performance, we had loaded the costumes, lights, and props on a deuce-and-a-half truck and were headed back to Saigon for the night. When we got about a mile out of the main gate at Long Binh, we could see a long green line coming out of the bush to our right. A convoy that was less than a half mile in front of us was being hit with a large machine gun. There were about 10 vehicles in the convoy, and they were really getting hit hard. We could see that they weren't even returning fire because they were pinned down by the massive amount of fire they were receiving. Our tracer rounds were red in color and the VC rounds were green, so we knew what was going on. I was sitting in the middle of the cab, and I told the driver, "Fuck this—let's go back to Long Binh." So he turned around and we went back. Our lead actress stayed with the nurses at the 24th EVAC hospital.

We ended up at the replacement battalion with no sheets, pillows, or blankets. As we walked into the hooch, we could see long, thick strings hanging from the rafters. I thought they were light pull switches until someone turned on the lights: They were rats' tails. Everyone took a lower bunk and tried to get some sleep. Back in Saigon, we found out we all had lice from sleeping on very dirty mattresses.

That next day we drove past the convoy that had been hit the night before. All that was left were burned-out hulks of armed personnel carriers and deuce-and-a-half trucks. We didn't know how many guys had been killed or wounded. The only thing I could think was, "Christ, that could have been us!" And it would have been if we had left five minutes earlier.

Holen: We played every hospital and aid station in Vietnam. There was one night performance at an aid station out in the bush. These were places where, if the injuries weren't serious enough to put the injured into a hospital unit, they would take the individual off the line and stitch him up. As soon as the wounds healed, they would send him right back out. I would say there were about 100 guys in the audience. We played on another movie-screen setup. There was a movie after our performance. Once our show began, a blue cloud of smoke started to rise above the audience. It wasn't normal smoke; it was pot. It got more intense as the play continued, and we could tell the troops were beginning to lose interest in our little musical. At the end of Act I, one of the lead characters, lying on a small box at the front edge of the stage, reaches his hand out to the audience as he pretends to die. One of the troops put a pot pipe into his right hand. We knew we'd never make it through Act II, so we just ended the show at that point. As we were striking the set, the movie started: John Wayne's *The Green Berets*.

At one hospital we performed for a large number of very badly wounded troops. A majority of the audience sitting closest to the stage were soldiers who could not be transported to a navy hospital ship or to a stateside hospital. Some were burn patients; others were still in their bed with tubes attached. A number of them were in wheelchairs. We knew this was a big event for them, so we set up and did our show with as much energy and professionalism as we could muster. During the show, one of the fellows in a wheelchair turned gray, and his head just fell forward. A nurse rushed to him, put a towel over his head, and wheeled him out. I am pretty certain he had just died.

One time we were at another hospital on the coast overlooking the South China Sea. We had set up in what looked like a dining hall or large room. On one side of the stage, double doors led into the ER, and on the other side of the stage, the outer door led to the Dustoff chopper pad. We started the show, and in the middle of Act II, five or six ER people rushed by the front of the stage and out the swinging door leading to the chopper pad. Seconds later, two or three litters were rushed by the front of the stage carrying guys, moaning and screaming, with their guts hanging out. We just continued as if nothing had happened—this was war and we had a job to do.

Sevra: As far as the tour itself, my memories are faded at best. I do remember feeling a bit apprehensive as to how this very delicate, innocent show would go over with a bunch of grunts, just out of the field and looking for booze and hookers and dope. In a few places, it took the audience a while to figure out what it was they were seeing. But in almost every case, they'd slowly warm to it, and by the end, they'd be cheering. I'll never forget one guy. He was a great big old first sergeant who could have snapped me in half like a toothpick, and he nervously, almost reluctantly, came up to me after a show and said, "Man, I ain't never seen no thee-ay-ter before. That...that...that was *good*!" I think that was one of the best reviews I've ever gotten, and certainly one I'll always remember.

Nutt: Personally, I thought the choice of material was kind of odd, but at the same time, many people really liked it. I think for the audiences, the show provided a complete break with reality. Everyone wanted to get back to "the world" and away from Vietnam, and for a few hours, the play had that effect.

Holen: The GIs seemed to be transported to another plane of existence during the performances. The play lasted only about an hour and a half, but for that short period of time, we felt that we could put at least a temporary stop to the death and devastation, the boredom and total terror of war. The audiences would sometimes give us a standing ovation for five minutes. That is the magic of theater.

Mauro: For both the performers and the audiences, these shows were like an oasis in the desert. It was truly gratifying to be able to get GIs out of a combat situation by putting them in a show for a month or two. And I know the troops who saw the shows viewed them as a welcome relief from the absurd world that all of us had been thrown into at that time. Everyone could relax, unwind, and get lost in the moment. I wonder, too, if these performances didn't help all of us to stay focused on our ultimate goal: getting out of that hellhole in one piece—and with all our marbles.

The Sissy Monologues (#1)

BY STEPHEN ADLY GUIRGIS

Dear Sissy—

Last year i told you i didn't give a fuck about coming home for the holidays, and, i really believed i didn't give a fuck, but i guess i did give a fuck kinda, mostly cuz i wanted to see you. Actually, only because i wanted to see you. But this year, Sissy—this year i truly don't give a fuck at all, and that's as true as true can be —at least for right now it is, and, prolly for forever, Sissy... Time changes things, Sissy. There's lots of good-looking girls up here in new york. Girls who like me and want to know things about me and hang out with me and have sex with me and think i'm funny and good looking and different. Last night a girl baked me an actual Christmas pie and brought it over. I put it on top of the fridge and told her that i was full, but thank you so much, and i'll eat it for breakfast. She wanted to hang out, but i told her i had to go somewhere, and i pretended to look for my keys till she left. This girl's really pretty, Sissy—really pretty—maybe even prettier than you if someone other than me was looking. When she finally left my place, I opened up this bottle of Kentucky Moonstar Bourbon and started drinking from the bottle. I lit a candle and smoked cigarettes, sitting indian style on my kitchen floor staring up at the top of my fridge—staring up at that fuckin pie till the cigarettes burned my fingers one after the other. She's really pretty, Sissy, really pretty. And that pie? That fuckin pie—it's everything anybody would ever want a pie to be. It really is. It really, truly looks like one hell of a perfect—and i mean perfect—looking fuckin pie... I hope you have a not-bad christmas, Sissy. I hope your Dodge doesn't stall, and that if you have some new boyfriend, that he gets you something nice that makes you think you're happy. I hope your family is doing good. I hope your dad takes the doctor's advice. I hope your mom's ham tastes like how i think it will. I got the day off. I'm going to do nothing Christmas-y today. I'm going to smoke a joint and go to the movies, and go to the movies again, and walk around Times Square and wait for the day to be night and then over... Over... I'll tell you one more thing, Sissy: about two hours ago, at 4 in the morning, in the middle of lost in you, my phone rang two times. My whole heart just jumped outta my balls and bounced off the linoleum floor and into the living room. For a split second i could smell you, and picture you in that red flannel shirt with your hair pulled back a little too tight and that cute kinda tense expression on your perfect, perfect face. I could see you smiling that smile, and I could feel what it would feel like to kiss your round, puffy lips again and collapse into your whole self with my whole self and I could remember what your pillow smelled like exactly. Then the phone stopped ringing. And then nothing. Just me. Just me and the floor and an ashtray, and a half-empty bottle of bourbon, and that perfectly red and round and crusty fuckin perfect holiday pie on the top of my fridge... And, Sissy—Sweet Sissy—the saddest, saddest thing i ever, ever, ever felt in my entire life was the fact that i just knew. I knew it wasn't you...and that it'll prolly never be. Merry Christmas, Sissy. I wish you the world.

Music at 6

BY CARTER BURWELL

***Music makes a people gentle.*—Gustave Flaubert**

On April 19, 1995, I was in my studio, writing music for the film *Fear*. To fight the cabin fever that results from being locked in a room with a film for 16 hours a day, week after week, I had the television tuned to CNN.

On this day the regular rhythm of news coverage was interrupted by the report of a large explosion in Oklahoma City. The first reports, accompanied by confused video images of smoke rising from the city, told little more than that. The passing hours added only a small amount of information—a building destroyed, many people dead—but added a great deal of window dressing. There was a special computer-generated graphic that introduced the video footage, and a somber musical theme. I wondered how these were developed. I pictured a windowless room full of designers and composers with a producer standing in the middle screaming "More pathos!"

On September 11, 2001, my encounter with breaking news was very different. My wife and I live a few blocks from the World Trade Center site, and we experienced that day at street level. It wasn't until later that we saw the television package that had been developed, and the disjunction between the reality we'd seen and the packaged version was so great we still haven't really been able to watch that coverage—not only because of the violence it presents, but also because of the window dressing and what it says about the motives of the presenters.

It is now 2003 and we seem to be winding down from a war in Iraq, a war that was extensively covered and extensively packaged. Each network and cable news organization came up with its own "war" music, most but not all of it of the rally-round-the-flag variety, and this again raised questions: Where does this music come from? What is it intended to do? And why do Americans seem to want their news presented as a marriage of music and drama—as melodrama?

It is 1914, and the unmistakable cadence of military drums and a fanfare of brass announce the arrival of the war news. On a screen of light embellished in gold ornament, you watch the machinery of war go about its timeless business, the spectacle and drama of each moment driven home by rhythms and melodies familiar from previous reports. It's news of the First World War, courtesy of the Pathé Weekly newsreel.

The live music for these newsreels varied from theater to theater—sometimes only a pianist performed it, sometimes an organist playing a device like the Fotoplayer Style 50, a 21-foot-long music machine capable of simulating everything from a 20-piece band to horses' hooves, crackling flames and 75 mm cannon fire. In big-city movie palaces the presentations might be accompanied by 60-to-100-piece symphony orchestras. The actual notes played varied as well, since the film distributors didn't provide scores specific to each newsreel. The theater's musical director had to go to sources such as popular songs and classical music to find material appropriate to each news story.

To ease the burden, publishers offered digests of music categorized by dramatic need, such as the *Sam Fox Moving Picture Music Volume* (1913, composed by J. S. Zamecnik, a student of Dvořák) or the *Kinobibliothek* (1919, by Giuseppe Becce). As the newsreel played, the musicians could simply turn to page 11 for "War" music (*Sam Fox* offers three varieties) or page 17 for "Hurry" music (four flavors).

"Marches are the most abused compositions for newsreel accompaniment. Any time a leader cannot decide just what music to choose, the easiest way out is generally found by taking any old march and playing it through."
—Erno Rapee, 1925, musical director of the Capitol and Roxy Theaters in Manhattan

I haven't been able to find a date that establishes the origin of the town crier, but this seems an obvious early example of the use of music in the broadcasting of news. The crier's handbell served both to gather an audience and focus its attention, and I suppose the difference in tone and ringing pattern between the famous bell of Antonio Pucci and that of any other 14th-century crier served what we might now call a "branding" function.

Written news was often the basis for the town crier's announcements, and its market value was established in Venice in the next century when the government sponsored readings of *avvisi* for the general public, price of admission one *gazeta*. It is from this tradition that we get the word "gazette."

It's a good bet that the news the Venetian Republic gave the gazeta audience reflected well on the republic and somewhat less well on its enemies, the Turks. Despite efforts at impartiality, whether in the 16th or the 21st century, we cannot understand news without considering the interests of the parties involved in making, distributing, and receiving it. Newsreels were produced and distributed by well-capitalized corporations such as Pathé and Time, Inc., which may have been impartial with regard to any one story, but which depended on the stability of the capital markets to exist, and thus could not be impartial in the face of any war that involved territories where they did business.

***"It is to the mutual reinforcement of an ideological demand ('to see life as it is') and the economic demand to make it a source of profit that cinema owes its being."*—Jean-Louis Comolli**

In the 1930s, newsreels became "talkies" and began to include prerecorded music, putting a lot of pianists and organists out of work but creating jobs for composers who could write music specifically for each film. When the newsreel industry finally died at the end of the 1950s, many of its makers joined its killer, television. TV, like radio, was subject to more government regulation than the film industry—the belief being that when a limited number of broadcasters use a public resource (the electromagnetic spectrum), they have an obligation to the public. As early as 1941, both the Federal Communications Commission and the National Association of Broadcasters were making it clear that radio and television newscasts could not be "editorial." Perhaps it was in reaction to this expectation of objectivity that there was much less use of music in television news than in newsreels.

The first nightly network newscast was that of Douglas Edwards on CBS-TV in 1948, but affiliate stations generally thought news unattractive to their audiences. It was only in 1963 that CBS and then NBC found enough interest to expand the newscast from 15 to 30 minutes, and President Kennedy's assassination that year established the role of network news as a place of common comfort, as well as information, for the country.

***"I wanted production elements that would 'say' ABC News over and over again, on radio as well as television, creating a kind of Pavlovian brand recognition. This led to the opening fanfare of drums and trumpets that is used to this day to introduce every news program, and to the signing—ABC Moscow, ABC London, and so on—in uniform graphics."*—Roone Arledge, president of ABC News from 1977 to 1998**

If music was present at all, it was only at the very start and end of the newscast, and it served primarily the same branding function as theme songs did on serials and sitcoms; unlike its role in newsreels, it didn't score the news. As studies of viewing patterns revealed that televisions often remained on when Americans weren't watching, music was asked once again to serve the function of the town crier's bell: to gather the audience.

***"It's what we refer to as the 'kitchen mix,' which draws the viewer from the kitchen (or now their computers) to the TV....These notes come in and the theory is that people go, 'Oh, here comes the news—I better pay attention.'"*—Gary Anderson, composer and executive vice president of Score Productions, which has been responsible for most of ABC's news music, as well as the original CNN music package**

At the same time that the public was increasingly turning to television for news, the '60s brought a growing sense of civic responsibility among journalists who were discovering that much of the information they received from their government about the war in Vietnam—which they had traditionally presented without additional perspective—was false. By 1968, CBS News was airing special reports like "The Vietcong" or "Hanoi," which are startling to watch today. There is no music over the opening or closing or anywhere else in these pieces, and since the footage was largely shot without sound, there is a pervasive sense of quiet and, at least to someone listening in 2003, what must be called seriousness.

"Conventional practice has made an anchor of background music, such that it dictates what the viewer's response to the images ought to be. Remove it from a scene whose emotional content is not explicit and you risk confronting the audience with an image they might fail to interpret."*—Claudia Gorbman, from *Unheard Melodies: Narrative Film Music

To create the drama of a breaking news story for his broadcast of *The War of the Worlds* in 1938, Orson Welles used music to score the story negatively. The broadcast begins with a live concert—"We now take you to the Meridian Room in the Hotel Park Plaza in downtown New York, where you will be entertained by the music of Ramón Raquello and his orchestra"—which is then repeatedly interrupted as news of the alien attack breaks in. "Ladies and gentlemen, we interrupt our program of dance music to bring you a special bulletin from the Intercontinental Radio News..." Music is used to establish a "comfort level" for the audience, which is then subverted.

While in the instance of this fiction the question of "comfort" may seem trivial, its place in actual news broadcasting is far from it. A force for both the psychological stability of the individual and the cohesion of society, news reports frame fragments of often terrifying information so that they seem to be in some sense "under control"—familiar music, familiar graphics, familiar faces all make a scary world seem manageable. This is certainly what the public wants, and would it do any good to show us how truly out of control the world is? If we are to function, the world needs to seem ordered—but it helps to remember who is defining this order for us.

***"There's definitely a difference [in] the way America portrays news. If you turn on the BBC or something like that it's very low-key and underplayed, and we tend to overplay a lot of things and that's just the way it is.... Music now is just so in-your-face all the time on TV in general....It's really changed—I don't know if for the better or not.*—Michael Karp, composer of Iraq War music for NBC, CNBC, and MSNBC**

Post-structuralist literary theory holds that the meaning of the written word is diffuse, endlessly contingent on a web of equally diffuse meanings. But how much more is this true of a filmed image? And how much more still of music? When news is presented visually, every effort is made to constrain an image's meaning. Newspapers give captions to their photographs, a practice Roland Barthes describes as *ancrage*, an attempt to anchor meaning, and this is surely what is being attempted with titles, voice-over, and music in newsreels and television.

Even though broadcasters may consider music to be simply "announcing" the news rather than "underscoring" it, it is impossible to confine the meaning of music. Its significance spreads and shifts uncontrollably with changes in context—the context of its presentation, the context of the viewer's state of mind.

Lalo Schifrin may have been asked to score the tarring of a dusty road in the film *Cool Hand Luke*, but that didn't prevent ABC News from appropriating the same piece of music to announce its evening news during the '60s. To the folks at ABC, it wasn't about work gangs or the failure to communicate; it was about breathless urgency. But there's no way to know what it meant to the audience.

"This couple comes up to me. 'Mr. Anderson, we saw that you were involved in the music for "Nightline." We wanted to thank you. We wish that we had

***met you earlier. We used the music at our wedding, but we couldn't get a version without Ted Koppel's voice on it.'"*—Gary Anderson**

As it happens, the *Cool Hand Luke* theme partook—unintentionally, I'm sure—of cliché number one in the news music business: the rhythm of the teletype. While this cliché is kept alive by news organizations around the globe, every composer I spoke to for this piece had made a conscious effort to get as far away from it as possible. The teletype rhythm as a symbol of news had one major benefit over music: much less semantic baggage. It wasn't in a major or a minor key. It had no melody that would color the broadcast as either uplifting or somber. As we entered the Age of Branding, however, it also had one shortcoming: it could not be copyrighted. It is the simple sound of a machine doing its job.

***"The lead instrument conundrum. News is serious and electric guitars are sporty, and in spite of the fact that Fox News has been doing a lot more sporty rock things, and some, particularly cable, networks have tried to introduce more contemporary sounds, brass is the sound of the important news."*—Cynthia Daniels, engineer at Score Productions**

The two loudest instrument groups in the Western orchestra are the brass and drums, so it should come as no surprise that they have both served for centuries as long-distance communications devices, not only in the West but all around the world. Before metals could be worked to form brass instruments, animal horns were used for the same purpose—shofar in the Middle East, conch shell in the Pacific, ox horn in medieval Europe. By the 9th century horns had become associated in Europe with the military and nobility, and that association is still with us today, simultaneously renewed and enshrined in such pieces as Aaron Copland's "Fanfare for the Common Man." Brass and drums represent cliché number two of news music, and we haven't gotten far from it since the first newsreels.

***"If you go into countries where this is not in the culture, it still is ingrained in them. When we do CNN Español the last thing they want is Latin music. They want Aaron Copland. And we give it to them."*—Gary Anderson**

War reporting is an ancient tradition of journalism, and it represents the crux of many of journalism's challenges. Wars always generate propaganda, a word we get from the Vatican's 18th-century efforts to propagate the faith, and journalists are always keen to distinguish between their work—providing information—and propaganda. At the same time, a war is traditionally a sport in which you cheer for the home team, regardless of the facts. Whether your side is right or wrong, you'd still rather not have your family or friends killed in battle.

For this reason, there's often a thin line between a German newscast from the '30s and Leni Riefenstahl's *Triumph of the Will*, or between an American newscast of the '40s and Frank Capra's *Why We Fight*. The differences are actually more in form than content—the propaganda films bring all the art of master filmmakers to bear on the propagation of the "faith," while the broadcasters simply don't have the talent, the time or the resources to shoot, edit, write and score the news that well.

Advances in technology in the second half of the 20th century have allowed shooting, editing, and scoring to happen many times faster than before. Writing, however—injecting an intelligent point of view into the news process—has not kept up with technology, and many reporters from the age of film, when it took at least a day to process and transport the footage of the Vietnam War, bemoan the speed with which live or almost-live video can make it onto the air without any vetting or interpretation by a real journalist.

***"We did music for a special on the hunt for Osama bin Laden, finished the music at around 7:15, messengered it over to ABC here in New York and at eight o'clock watched it on the television set. That's about the closest we've gotten to a deadline."*—Gary Anderson**

Every composer I spoke with felt that NBC erected a milestone in the use of music for news in 1985 when it hired John Williams—the composer who wrote the scores for the Lucas and Spielberg films that defined American commercial cinema in the last quarter of the 20th century—to write a set of themes for NBC News. The package of orchestral music he created was called "The Mission," and the network is still mining it almost 20 years later. While the central melody is often carried in brass voices, it was much more highly developed than anything that had been written for news previously—and probably since. Written in the self-ennobling Richard Strauss mode, its orchestral colors, countermelodies, thematic variation, and development create a much richer musical experience, and a much more diverse palette of moods and emotions, than any news music before. It had to have been a very expensive proposition to commission someone like Williams, but the effect it had, at least on the composers working in this field, was to make television news, and by extension, its music, seem like serious business, worthy of respect—an honorable, if you will, mission.

***"The other networks, they always go for that John Williams, big, grand music, but our music is always pointedly more aggressive. I feel the sound of Fox News Channel has branded us more than the look has. It's rock influenced, for sure. We try to keep the sound and look younger and hipper than what our competition is.*—Richard O'Brien, vice president and creative director of Fox News, quoted in *The Philadelphia Inquirer*, March 30, 2003**

Television news music is delivered by a composer in the form of a "package," of which "The Mission" is one example. A package consists of many—sometimes more than 100—different "cues," short pieces of music that presents the thematic material with a certain feel, duration, and purpose. A feel might be "funky" or "somber," durations are typically very short, between 10 and 30 seconds, and purposes include a "teaser" to announce an upcoming show, or an "open" to start it. Four feels each performed for four durations and for four purposes would generate 64 cues. The numbers add up. All the networks commission exclusive packages from composers such as Peter Fish (CBS) or Michael Karp (NBC) or from music production companies that represent teams of composers, such as Score Productions (ABC). But generic packages, generally known as "libraries," can be licensed by anyone who can do without proprietary themes, and there is much of this music in local news.

***"Something as simple as a one-hour special may get 60 cues, of which they might use 12. We have to give them the choice as best we can. Because you're not scoring anything—you have no idea what the images are going to be—basically, it breaks down into four moods: a generic, everyday, neutral mood; one that's a little bit more dramatic; one that's lighter; and they always ask for somber—we don't use the word 'funereal,' but it's really for that purpose, when they do have bad news. It's not used very often."*—Gary Anderson**

***"The package for the Gulf War was maybe 14 or 16 cuts, because basically there's tragedy and there's blood-and-guts. But if you do something for 'The Early Show' you have to do tragedy, blood-and-guts, general news, sports, Christmas, Easter, Thanksgiving, Election Day, and what I call 'dead Pope music,' for when the Pope finally dies."*—Peter Fish, composer for *CBS Evening News, Face The Nation, The Early Show*, the CBS Iraq war coverage, and others**

And so we come to the American news coverage of this year's war in Iraq. It's important to note that there was a great divide between the tone of war coverage here and of it everywhere else in the world. In a striking return to the melodramatic traditions of the newsreel, American television invested every piece of war news—down to the titles and graphics—with an overwhelming amount of emotional context. Special music packages for the war were commissioned by each of the broadcast and cable networks. Who made these calls, and how was the assignment described to the composers?

***"For the Iraq War it would be the director of the program, Eric Shapiro, who is both the director of the evening news and director of special event programming [at CBS]. I did the last Gulf War for him in '91, so this was the 'once-every-ten-years-we're-going-to-do-a-war' call."*—Peter Fish**

***"On the Iraq War, the direction [from ABC] was: 'Serious but not down, somber or morbid. Serious but uplifting.' They also veered away from 'military' or 'martial.' Again and again the words are 'serious,' 'powerful,' 'uplifting.'"*—Gary Anderson**

***"They said, 'It looks like there's going to be a war and we could use a good theme...big but not overpowering.' They always want that kind of classy signature sound that NBC seems to have over many of the other networks."* —Michael Karp**

The increasing use of screen real estate for graphics and various informational "crawls" and displays, as well as the use of propulsive music and sound effects, has prompted many people to liken today's war coverage to video games. The comparison completely ignores the most distinguishing characteristic of these games: interactivity. Although our television screens may be so crammed with information that we feel as if we're piloting a jet, we are as much on autopilot as ever. The better simile is sports. Two adversaries meet on the field of honor. Instant replay, interviews with coaches and players, color commentary and the complete absence of relevance are all pleasantly familiar from sports coverage. (It's worth noting that Score Productions, which did themes for ABC's *Wide World of Sports* and *Monday Night Football*, got into the news-music business when Roone Arledge, who ran ABC Sports from 1968 to 1986, took charge of the network's news division in 1977.) The Iraq War was, of course, a rematch, and it was inevitable that some aspects of the coverage would relate to the '91 Gulf War.

"The creative brief in the first [Gulf War] had more to do with the conflict of cultures and ideologies—it was the Islamic or Arabic East versus the West, and so the conflict was set in those tones. The second time it was more like they were trying to promote the war the same way they would promote **Terminator 3*—it was like 'Battle of the Megaheroes.' So the first time, what I delivered was vaguely militaristic and vaguely Arabic, simultaneously. And the second time it was just Techno Ali vs. Frazier-IV, 'we're going to knock the crap out of them'–testosterone driven, big punch music."*—Peter Fish**

Score Productions can chart the musical pedigree of ABC's Gulf War music back even further. In 1979 ABC put on a special 15-minute nightly report on the Iranian hostage crisis following the news at 11:30, and despite doubts that news could compete with Johnny Carson at that hour, it went on to become *Nightline*. The variation on the ABC *World News Tonight* theme which was done for the Iranian hostage report became the theme for *Nightline*.

***"[The request was] can you expand upon the library that we did in '91, an extension of something we had done at the last minute for the Iranian hostage report. That sound, because the directors and producers were the same, drifted into the '91 package for the Middle East conflict—I think that's what it was called—and then that was brushed up a little bit and updated [for 2003]. I never got instructions that 'we want music to be gung ho'; nobody has ever said that to me."*—Gary Anderson**

Even if we agree that it's impossible to write music that is only "serious and uplifting" and is nothing else, it is hard to avoid the impression that much of the music for the coverage of this Gulf War strove to make one "feel good" about the war. This is particularly true for CBS and Fox, which invoked contemporary rhythm tracks to give an undeniable air of excitement to the proceedings. Clearly the networks had come to the conclusion that this was what the public wanted.

"Going back 10 years ago, one of the networks we were working with did in fact take what came to be known as the 'Drums of War' from a generic library—not something we had supplied them—and then actually pulled it off the network because it was too 'gung ho.' Cut to the chase, 10 years later, that kind of thing did get on the air. I don't personally agree with it. As a viewer I don't really appreciate that kind of thing. I want the music that we supply and we create to do what it's supposed to do. It's supposed

***to draw the viewer in, give them an identifying factor, so they know what network and what show is on the television whether they're looking at the screen or not, and you're not editorializing. You're not trying to have the music express an opinion as to whether this is right or wrong. It's not a movie."*—Gary Anderson**

***"There certainly couldn't be any greater opponent of this war than me. Nonetheless, I have my job to do. But I believe the general mood of this country at this point in time is 'We're going to go kick some Arab ass,' and I don't think they need my music to tell them that."*—Peter Fish**

While the music packages that were developed for the war included more solemn pieces with more deliberate tempos, those did not typically introduce the war news. Of course, if the war had not gone well for the U.S. we would probably have heard them. It goes without saying that no war goes well for everyone, and there were obviously people dying on all sides, but this rarely became the focus of the coverage or set the mood of the music.

NBC even found a way to suck all the musical and emotional depth out of John Williams's "The Mission" by simply looping the opening measure of drums, creating a vapid bit of martial vamping. In the face of this kind of editorial recontextualizing, one can hardly blame the composers for the way their music was used.

***"You do what you're asked. We try to give the client what they're looking for in their music. You never have control over what's going to be used, of course."*—Gary Anderson**

***"You give them the music, you hope for the best. I give up the minute I hand in the material—officially give up."*—Peter Fish**

***"They could take some of the celebratory, uplifting [music] from the many heroic stories where that kind of music is appropriate and just stick it on top of a picture of the general of the day...and there you have it—you've got heroic branding on top of a war. Ultimately you can't control how they're going to use it."*—Cynthia Daniels**

As John Leonard, television critic and ex-editor of *The New York Times Book Review*, noted after the first Gulf War, the American public wanted to "feel good about itself—it hadn't for a while." Is it the responsibility of the news media to make us feel good about ourselves? Inevitably the current system of using advertising to pay for news, and pricing that advertising time according to the number of viewers, results in a competition to attract viewers. But advertisers are not driven simply by audience size. When CBS presented prime-time specials on the first Gulf War they got better ratings than the entertainment shows they had replaced. Still, CBS canceled them because they couldn't sell the ad time. Advertisers were afraid their product might end up following a shot of dead bodies.

We want to feel good about ourselves, the advertisers want us to feel good about their products, the producers want the advertisers to feel good about their news shows, the state wants the producers to feel good about its government. Someone has to compose the music for all this good feeling.

Leonard comes to the conclusion that "media should stand in a quasi-adversarial relationship to the government because the government lies to us." In my opinion this skirts the issue. The media should stand in a quasi-adversarial relationship to us, the viewers, because we lie to ourselves. On television, though, it's hard to see how this could happen.

The unmistakable cadence of military drums and a fanfare of brass announce the arrival of the war news. On a screen of light embellished in gold ornament you watch the machinery of war go about its timeless business, the spectacle and drama of each moment driven home by rhythms and melodies familiar from previous reports. It's news of today's war, the same on every channel.

From *Esopus 13* (2009)

How to Win in Reno

BY KELLY SANDOVAL

If they're drinking bourbon with their orange juice, they won't be tipping. You learn that the first time you work graveyard and discover that some of the regulars never go home. You learn it then because no one will teach you; after the first night of following nervously behind one of the more experienced girls, you're on your own. If you run into a problem, improvise. Wandering out of your section to ask for help is the quickest way to get accused of poaching. That's not a reputation you can afford.

Other things you can't afford: rent, your son's day-care bill, new brakes for your car. Your day job as a receptionist doesn't pay for these things, so nights find you in tights, tap pants, and three-and-a-half-inch heels. At the end of your shift, when you have to peel your tights from your bleeding feet, you wonder if you might have been better off trying to get a job as a stripper. You think the tips might be better, and maybe they spend less time on their feet. But you got this job just by fitting into the uniform; strippers have to know how to move.

You learn how to move. The heels are the easy part. What's difficult is balancing a tray laden with drinks on one arm while navigating the maze of the slots. That's one of the tricks they use to keep patrons in, like the artificial twilight, the lack of clocks, and you. At first you feel guilty bringing people free drinks while they feed the slots with their next month's rent, their pawned engagement rings, their Social Security checks. But then you discover that if they're spending all they have, your tips are going into the slots as well, so you waste as little time on them as you can.

Your time is limited, and your section is busy, so you have to figure out when someone is worth lingering over and laughing with, and when it's better to leave the drinks and go. The best customers are tourists in their late twenties, the sort that come in loud, laughing groups and aren't gambling to save themselves. Foreigners are hit-or-miss. Half the time they're convinced you're a prostitute and either keep their eyes lowered and their tips minimal or put you in the position of deciding whether it's worth calling a bouncer. Bouncers, like bartenders, are to be befriended.

A year and this is all you know, so when they tell you there's a new girl and they want you to train her, it all fills your throat and you find yourself gagging on the words. You don't like to think of yourself as part of this place. The girl is small and fragile-looking, with mild doe eyes that fix on you with apparent trust. She's the sort that starts and quits, all in a week. She wasn't born in Reno, you can tell that by the way her attention keeps darting away from you every time one of the slots goes off in an explosion of sirens and flashing neon. She smiles at all the wrong customers and gets lost when you send her on a solo trip to the bar.

What you want to do is treat her gently, the way you treated your son when he took his first wavering steps into your arms. You swept him up into the air and tried not to think that his walking meant he was learning to walk away from you. You're reminded of him when you watch her, awkward in high heels and smiling at everyone, as if the world has never given her reason to think of a smile as currency. You know that can't be the case, because she's here, and no one spends their nights helping drunks get drunker to fulfill a childhood dream. She's either less delicate than she looks, or she's an idiot. Either way, you don't have the energy to play the encouraging guide you wanted when you were her. You have tips to make, and it's easier to just write her off as one more pretty, stupid girl who won't make it past tomorrow.

Then she spills a drink on a man's shoes, and you have to grab her arm to keep her from darting off. You know her pretty brown eyes welling up with contrite tears are probably your only chance at getting a tip out of him tonight. She sniffles and stutters through her apology, but he laughs and pushes a crisp twenty into her fluttering, hopeless fingers. You watch her try to smile, try to thank him while still apologizing. She's so small in that moment that when you guide her away you reach for her hand, as if to lead her safely across a street.

You don't have friends here, because girls here aren't friendly. You aren't friendly. But you sit next to her on your shared break and watch in confusion when she bursts into tears again, crying on her peanut butter and jelly sandwich. Half the girls spend their breaks doing lines of coke, and she's got a sandwich and a Hostess fruit pie in a brown paper bag. It's enough to make you laugh, and you don't get many chances to really laugh, so when she raises her head, looking wounded by your smile, you ask her what's wrong.

It turns out that everything's wrong, so maybe she has a right to be wearing the uniform after all. She's coming out of a four-year relationship, with a 4-year-old to show for it. She's 22 since January, and until she arrived here and couldn't find work, she hadn't even thought of going to college. She's in Reno because she heard the stories about wedding rings thrown in the Truckee River, and she likes the idea of this being the place that women start fresh. You're about to tell her that people don't come here for divorces anymore, but it turns out she was never married anyway, so that's alright. She says she's got a friend watching her kid tonight, but doesn't know about tomorrow. She says she won thirty bucks on the slots before work, and she's hoping it's a sign that she'll get lucky here.

As you listen to her you realize that she'll make it past tomorrow. The casino already has her wrapped in gossamer strands of neon, and she won't be allowed to stop showing up. This is a girl whose eyes keep jumping to jackpot sirens; she'll get off her shift and every tip she's made will go right back in the slots. She'll go home to her kid with nothing to show for tonight but bloody feet and some cowboy's number. She'll even dial it, because she's new to Reno. She likes their boots and doesn't know that cowboys never tip.

You start to tell her everything you thought when you first saw her, everything you learned in your year. Tips about bartenders and foreigners come easy, but being a successful cocktail waitress won't do her any good, because she thinks there's such a thing as luck in Reno, and she thinks maybe she has it. You try your best. You start telling her stories. You tell her about the guy who was still coming in until about a month ago, loud and demanding and at the tables until the sun rose. He shot himself in the parking lot, you say. It happens a lot. You tell her there's a reason there's a pawn shop catty-corner from every casino. You tell her people don't win.

And she tells you she heard on the radio that a woman won big just last night, some maid at the Nugget. You know the maid will be living in a trailer in Sun Valley again before the year is out, but she's smiling around her fruit pie. She's such a little thing, already overflowing with dreams and desperation. There's no room left in her for your warnings.

So you tell her about Mamma Mia's; they've got rows of cots and not much more, but she can leave her kid there from 8 p.m. to 7 a.m., and that's more reliable than some friend she thinks she can trust. You lead her back to the floor, and you tell her everything you can remember. You tell her that rich men tip well when they're alone, but not when they're with their wives, that barbacks will make her drinks if the bartenders are busy. You catch her wandering gaze and tell her again that cowboys are a waste of time, so she should stop smiling at them already. You make her memorize the gerrymandered borders of her section, and you tell her the other girls will not be kind if she crosses them. And at the end of the night, while she stands wavering between the dollar slots and the tables, you try to warn her. Try to tell her there are other jobs, better jobs. But she's already gone.

So you find your boss and tell him you won't be coming in again.

He says he'll leave your spot open. One week, just in case. Then he smiles, and it's a smile that knows you haven't paid the power bill for two months now, and if you don't pay it this time, they'll turn it off again.

You think you should tell him that you've seen enough of what this place does to people. You think you should ask him if he's ashamed to meet his own gaze in the mirror. You are. You think about your power bill. You don't say anything. Just in case.

Paintings for Cash

BY "PENELOPE"

When I was in art school, I had such romantic notions about art that I never even imagined being able to make a living at it. But I've been lucky: I've had solo shows in galleries around the country, have received a number of commissions, and have even on occasion been given money for work before I started painting it. The pay is decent and the hours are amazing.

There is one catch: I paint pictures that people use to decorate their homes—decor art. Some of them are actually beautiful, though, in their own way.

Right after I graduated from art school 13 years ago, I came across a classified ad in the local paper for an "artist's assistant." I bought one of those huge fake-leather portfolios, filled it with my best drawing and printmaking work, and took the bus to a dirty old warehouse on the other side of town. My "interview" consisted of a thin, pleasant man holding up one painting after another, asking, "Can you paint like this?" The whole thing was pretty much a formality, as all new artists were given a two-week trial period. You were hired only if you could learn fast and prove your talent.

This company, which will go unnamed, is one of many that employ artists to imitate the style of top-selling paintings in the decor-art market. They sell the work at trade shows to hotels, restaurant chains, corporate offices, and mall galleries. The company represented a seedy, nasty side of the art world that I hadn't known existed.

It was a job.

Their warehouse was a small, raw industrial space suffused with paint and polyurethane fumes and dust. The artists—a bunch of kids like me, fresh out of art school—were "in the back," making six bucks an hour, and the salespeople, like the guy who had interviewed me, were "up front." It was always us versus them. They had a showroom with stacks of paintings on tables and a few tiny offices. Our work spaces were pretty cramped too, especially in the summer. Only three studios within the raw space had air-conditioning. In the winter, people tended to spread out into the unused space to take advantage of one overhead heater. We threatened to call OSHA all the time—it was thrilling to imagine the bosses being fined for not providing us with a safe, comfortable work space. I vaguely recall someone from the agency actually paying a visit once while I was there. After I'd been there about two years, the company moved.

The new warehouse was huge in comparison, not to mention well lit and clean. Artists no longer had to share easels, and there was a spray booth for toxic media. Even the guy who cleaned the borders of the paintings had his own space—quite a change. But although there were fewer tangible things to complain about, there was no getting rid of the resentment that we were making peanuts compared to the money that was coming in from sales of our paintings in the gallery out front.

I started out, like everyone else, assisting the successful in-house artists and learning the tricks of the trade, like how to paint fast, or how to use layering to make it look as if you'd labored a week over a painting that in fact took 45 minutes. Everyone worked on heavy paper that had been screen-printed with solid colors, cutting out the need for underpainting. A lot of us used brayers, which are small hand rollers employed in printmaking to spread ink. Rolling instead of brushing paint allowed for a quick application of color and made blending easy. I remember my friend Danny joking, "I'm a painter, not a roller!" This was the early '90s, so we were told to use lots of gold leaf, "jewel tones," and geometric patterns. Everyone got very excited about TEXTURE.

Eventually I was asked by the bosses if I could create work "in the style of" an artist with one of their biggest competitors. I'd seen this artist's embellished prints in person at a national chain gallery. They were delicate, impressionistic still lifes, landscapes, and figurative works, employing generous amounts of gold leaf and plenty of TEXTURE. The serigraphs alone sold for a few thousand dollars each. I was flattered and excited about the idea of a promotion, since some artists never got beyond the position of assistant. But I was anxious about making sure the work paid homage without being a direct copy.

I created a pseudonym, Penelope Valdez, to protect my own name and copyright—I'd been warned by another artist early on that any name I signed to the work would remain the property of the company once I'd left—and began work. The first paintings skirted dangerously close to being direct copies, but soon they took on a life of their own. The company gave me a private studio in the new warehouse and I got a raise—even health insurance! The perks were nice, but they didn't really quell that little voice in my head asking me how long

I wanted to be a schlock artist. I starting collecting my college transcripts, took the GRE, and decided to look for graduate programs in urban planning—a "real career." I never thought that I might still be doing the same thing 10 years later.

I left the company after three years. As it so happened, one of the front-office salesmen had quit around the same time. He knew all the buyers and offered to become Penelope's representative. I figured I could continue painting on the side to help pay for school. He wanted to distinguish the new work from the old and suggested that I switch to working on canvas. I also changed Penelope's last name, because, as expected, other artists at the company I'd left were still churning out paintings under my old pseudonym.

During this period, I was paid up front for each painting. This is rare in the art world, where you usually have to leave your work with dealers on a consignment basis, especially when you're just starting out. I never asked where they were sold, partly because I didn't want my rep to worry that I'd cut him out of the deal and go to the galleries directly. I knew that he was making the same amount per painting that I was, and that the gallery sold them for four times what I was paid. Even so, it was way more money than I'd ever thought I'd make as an artist, which made postponing grad school easier to do.

Actually, there was another reason why I didn't ask where the paintings were sold: As sad as it sounds, I really didn't care where they went. I was putting minimal time and energy into the work because I didn't have to stand up and represent it myself. It was easy, but ultimately not very gratifying. I was essentially trading the paintings for cash.

After about a year of working exclusively with him, I started to make my own gallery connections. To my surprise, I found that as soon as I started repping myself (even though I was still using a pseudonym), I began to devote more time to each painting. I researched other artwork for inspiration and created a book full of clippings from magazines for reference. I even built a website—just like a real artist.

These days, I work with a handful of galleries directly. Art in this decorative genre does well in resort towns, vacation spots where people have second homes, and areas where travelers shop for art instead of souvenirs. I've been contacted several times by people who want to represent me in a particular town. If it seems like a good fit, I pack up some paintings and they send me a contract spelling out the financial details: Typically, these types of galleries ask what your price is and double it for retail. I don't get paid up front anymore, though. It's always on consignment. From my experience, these gallerists are very good at connecting their customers with the type of art they're looking for. Every once in a while, I'll be asked to do a commissioned piece for a client, in a specific color palette or at an exact size. But usually I just send them the last 5 to 10 paintings that I've made and they hang them up.

The paintings are always the same subject matter and created in the same style, but each one is slightly different in terms of color and composition. Needless to say, it can be a monotonous job. I have to look at each new painting as a puzzle to solve, and find a way to make it interesting. Sometimes everything comes together easily and the results, if I don't think about them too much, are quite nice. The best ones are usually those I paint the fastest (and often, the last one I finish when I'm on a roll).

In my free time, I make art that is—certainly compared to what I do for a living—nonmarketable. I'm so fickle I can't settle on a medium or a style, so my work is all over the place. I've done paintings and drawings (for a few years I created landscapes that were just as decorative as the Penelope pieces, but for a more sophisticated audience). I've sewn collage landscapes made up of vintage thrift-store pillowcases. I've even worked out in the name of art: For a show a couple of years ago, I made a series of ink drawings by attaching two Chinese brushes to a light-tension spring grip, which I used to tone my right forearm. My husband, who's also an artist, and I collaborated a couple of years ago on some top-secret guerrilla mini-installations that he photographed. Most recently, I've been involved in a collective that tackles more conceptually oriented projects, for which we tend to poke a little fun at traditional ideas about fine art. We've worked in media ranging from mosaic to papier-mâché to sound.

Every once in a while, I'll attend openings "in character" as Penelope. In some ways, I view these (I've only been to three in the past 10 years) as a kind of performance art. At them, people are always very complimentary and tend to notice details that I was unaware of when I was creating the work. My only job is to come up with answers to questions like "What inspired this painting?" or "Did you intend to collage this birdcage upside down next to this chair?" I worry that people will be disappointed if I'm too frank about my process, so I always end up talking in technical terms about the work. (Luckily, most people really don't expect a fruit-and-flowers painting to be deep or emotionally driven.)

Needless to say, I'm conflicted about what I do for a living. Sometimes I'm embarrassed, but other times I'm proud—it tends to depend on the audience and how I think they'll perceive it. I do feel guilty about selling art to people who imagine their piece being created by a person who believed in what she was doing, but that guilt is diluted by the fact that galleries take on the responsibility of "lying" to the customers.

I was once interviewed for an article in the local paper of a town where I'd just had a show, but despite my attempts to spice things up, my answers were deemed so dry that none of them were quoted. The reporter ended up interviewing the gallery owner, who talked about how she had discovered me. Most of the article focused on the sales generated by the show. Obviously, I'm no actress. I guess the only time I'm successful at playing the role of the artist is when I'm alone in my studio, working on a painting.

Not It Anymore

INTERVIEW WITH LISA KUDROW AND MICHAEL PATRICK KING

Lisa Kudrow and Michael Patrick King have each left indelible marks on television: Kudrow for her winning portrayal of the character Phoebe Buffay on hit NBC sitcom *Friends* (1994–2004), and King as a writer, director, and eventual co-executive producer on the HBO series *Sex in the City* (1998–2004). But perhaps their most remarkable contribution to TV is something they conceived of and worked on together: the short-lived HBO series *The Comeback*, which ran for only 13 episodes in the summer of 2005. The show revolves around the unforgettable character of Valerie Cherish (played brilliantly by Kudrow), a faded sitcom actress so determined to regain her celebrity she agrees to be the subject of a reality show documenting her return to television (playing the thankless role of "Aunt Sassy" on a sitcom called *Room and Bored*). A penetrating and often brutal satire of reality TV, sitcoms, and show business in general, *The Comeback* received three Emmy nominations, including best actress for Kudrow and best director for King, despite being canceled after only one season. [Four years after this interview appeared in *Esopus 15*, the series was renewed for a second season by HBO.]

***Tod Lippy:** Lisa, didn't the character of Valerie Cherish originate with a sketch you did when you were part of the Groundlings comedy troupe in L.A.?*

Lisa Kudrow: It was actually a character monologue: an actress on a talk show who was phony and self-serving. That was it.

Michael Patrick King: An unnamed Valerie...

LK: I called her "Your Favorite Actress on a Talk Show." She talked about how she hadn't worked in a while, and it was all just spin, spin, spin. It wasn't much appreciated there because my sensibility didn't always translate to a big sketch-comedy context. *[laughs]* But that character was really just like a grain of sand compared to what Valerie is in *The Comeback*. When you take an idea like that to Michael Patrick King, he whips it into this gorgeous character.

Let's talk about that process a bit. My understanding is you both knew each other before you worked together on this...

MPK: My friend John Stark was at the Groundlings, so I had seen Lisa do things there, and I was aware of her very unique energy. I once saw her do a sketch as Audrey Hepburn on a fishing show, which was not an accurate Audrey Hepburn, but that wasn't the point: It was the most absurdly brilliant idea. And of course I had a crush on Lisa because it's impossible not to. Later on, we were both working on the Culver lot—Lisa was on *Mad About You* and I was running my first show—a failed sitcom with Shelley Long that I had been brought in to fix, and as it turns out, you can't fix stuff sometimes—and Lisa and I would get together and complain about showbiz.

LK: I don't think I was complaining. I think I was thrilled at this point.

MPK: I'm not saying we were bitching—it was more funny. Like—"what's going to happen to me today?"

LK: Right. "What a brutal business this is." We had heard tell of it...

MPK: And then, years after that, we had the complete opposite of that relationship. We were in this weird grown-up show business relationship at the Golden Globes at our separate tables every year.

LK: I would literally have to move out of the way so that all of the *Sex and the City* people could get up to receive the awards they beat *Friends* out for every year. *[laughs]*

MPK: It was this amazing and strange knew-each-other-in-different-time-periods thing. We had always had an emotional connection, and now we were playing these other parts. Then one day Lisa called me up and said, "Let's have lunch," and we went to the Beverly Hills Hotel.

LK: Actually, our agents called each other.

MPK: Oh, the agents called! That's right—we were both done with our respective shows, and they wanted to get the two of us together. And at lunch, Lisa said, "I have this idea..."

LK: No, the first thing was—

MPK: I don't remember.

LK: You don't remember! *[both laugh]* We sat down, and we looked at each other and said, "So, it's good to see you...." And Michael said, "I have to tell you, I really don't see myself doing a sitcom, and I don't really see you in this, like, shiny multi-camera thing." And I said, "No, I really don't have an interest in doing another show. The only thing I could ever see myself doing"—and then I started telling him this very vague, not-at-all-fleshed-out idea of an actress who is so desperate to be in the limelight that she agrees to be in a reality show called *The Comeback*. And we sat there for four hours.

MPK: Once we started talking, it literally just flew, didn't it?

LK: Oh my God, I think we pitched it two weeks later. It was ridiculously fast.

Who did you pitch it to?

MPK: Well, we knew it was going to HBO because that was where I had some heat and power, and everybody wanted Lisa at that time. I'm not kidding you—everybody wanted Lisa. The idea that she was returning to television a year after *Friends* was a big deal. So we pitched it to Carolyn Strauss at HBO. I think the thing that made her laugh the hardest—and I knew it would—was the idea that in the pilot, Mark, her husband, is noisily defecating during Valerie's personal video diary. *[both laugh]* In the meeting, Lisa actually did the video diary improv—it wasn't scripted yet—and I would make these farting noises, and Carolyn laughed. I'm telling you, from then on, we just railroaded it down their throats.

So you hadn't written a pilot script at this point?

MPK: No, we wanted the idea to be bought first. It was hard for HBO, quite frankly—all egos aside—to get it.

LK: No, they didn't get it. I think they actually said it out loud at one point: "You know what, we don't fully get it, but go ahead."

MPK: It was hard for them not to say yes to us, because we were bound and determined.

LK: And you were Michael Patrick King.

MPK: Well, I had come off of a hit, and Lisa had come off a hit, so it was hard for them to say no. And Carolyn has a great sense of humor, so she understood the dark stuff. But I don't think they understood the whole concept.

LK: It's very hard to describe.

MPK: And then when we wrote the pilot, we had a blast.

Can you talk about your writing process a bit?

MPK: Lisa is a brilliant, brilliant writer. Brilliant and also ruthless. She's not at all indulgent. As we were writing the pilot, she would be cutting things as they were coming out of her mouth: "No, we don't need that." It's this fantastic stuff, and I'm typing it, and before she even finished the sentence, she'd say, "No, it's too long, we don't need that either." We always knew the Valerie stuff was going to be funny, but then we came up with the idea of the sitcom, *Room and Bored*, that Valerie gets the "Aunt Sassy" part on, and things really took off.

The crucial thing Lisa contributed to the pilot—in addition to everything else—is something I would never have come up with on my own. It's a small but significant idea: the water leak in the house that Valerie ignores after being warned about it by her housekeeper. Lisa kept saying from that scientist part of her brain, "There's a leak in the wall that she's ignoring because of her career." What was so smart about it was that it was the beginning of the germ of the idea that if you pay too much attention to show business, your personal life will collapse out from under you. You will literally gut your home. It's very subtle, and it's only there on a kind of subliminal writing level. But the thought that Lisa, underneath it all, put into the series was that this choice would destroy Valerie's house. And she's more than happy to have her home destroyed, because she cares more about her career.

LK: Right, so even when the wall in her house is in shambles, the thing that breaks her heart is the fact that her pictures from showbiz have been damaged.

MPK: The things she cherishes the most. That reminds me of that whole other idea we had there—Mark gets one little spot on the wall for his Rotary Club plaque. *[both laugh]* So anyway, yes, we wrote the pilot together, and when it was finished, we were very happy with it. It's unlike any other pilot you've ever seen because it's just Valerie talking to the camera for the whole first section. And I remember that people couldn't figure out if it was funny.

LK: Right.

MPK: And then when Lisa read it at the table, everybody laughed.

LK: That was during the auditions for the other actors. That was the first time anyone at HBO had heard it. And they were pretty happy.

MPK: Up until then, there was this vague concern: "Is it going to be funny?" And that's because it's not written "jokey." It's all character stuff, like all of the weird Valerie pauses and stuttering. When we were actually shooting the series and Lisa was on a break, we'd ask her to come into the writing room—she was there a lot, considering the fact that she basically never left the camera—and it was my job to type in every vocal tic and grammatical mistake while Lisa went on a run, speaking as Valerie. I would make sure it came out exactly as Lisa said it, down to the stuttering and the dashes. I was like a Nazi in there—

It sounds almost like you were taking dictation.

MPK: We actually looked into getting a court stenographer, because I wanted the dialogue exactly as it was pouring out of Lisa. It was too expensive, though. And then, part of Lisa's brilliance as an actor was that she was able to commit it to memory—almost like Morse code. She would use all of these mannerisms as anchors, and they would get her right back into character. As an actress, she paid very close attention to the writing.

LK: Most of the time. *[laughs]*

This series aims its satirical sights at two television genres: One, of course, is the sitcom, which we'll talk about more in a moment. The other is reality TV. I remember reading somewhere that you had gotten hold of some bootleg tapes of raw footage from one of the reality shows, and that these ended up being your "way in" to the unusual format of the series.

MPK: That's right, and we had even hired a couple of writers who had worked on reality shows as well. Those tapes gave us access to the boringness of unedited reality-show footage, and we fell in love with the idea that the actual story was in the stuff that Valerie thought would be cut from the final series because of that boringness. What interested us, a lot, was this kind of Stockholm syndrome situation with Valerie and Jane, the producer of the reality show. We knew that Lisa was going to be on camera, and we wanted to find ways to show the cracks in her performance versus the real thoughts she was having while being constantly filmed. We came up with the idea of "leaking" people from the outside—Jane, the cameramen, the sound guy—into the frame. This was important, because we didn't just want to do a parody of a reality show; we wanted to put in the foreground the behind-the-scenes manipulation and the cruelty. Once we realized we could use this unedited-footage approach, it just became really interesting to us, because then you can see everybody that is in the show. But it was that boringness—the endless hours of unmanipulated footage—that we thought would be interesting to show. That's why we started each episode with the color bars.

It essentially allows the viewer to become an editor, which turns the experience of watching these episodes into a very suspense-filled exercise. You're constantly thinking, "Are they going to use that line they just tricked her into saying in the final show? Are they going to squeeze in that humiliating fall she just took?" It makes you kind of squeamish as a viewer, but it also allows you to take a more active role, at least conceptually.

MPK: Right. The macro thought for us was that this footage maybe represented the very first assembly of a junior editor that would then be given to the other editors. Even the way it starts, with that annoying, alienating color-bar sound. I have to say, we really knew what we were doing in terms of what we wanted people to feel.

I would imagine, though, that this must have presented enormous challenges as far as narrative exposition is concerned, since Valerie is virtually never off camera.

MPK: It was very tricky. I don't think there's ever been a show on television where another character doesn't say at some point, "Boy, she's in a bad mood today..." There was never a moment of exposition behind the scenes, because Valerie was hyperaware of everything, and she never left the camera. So as a writing team, we had to figure out how to have everything happen in front of the camera, with her always somewhere in the frame. It was a big puzzle, and it cost us a lot of figuring-out time.

LK: That's why it was so important for Michael to direct the pilot and the second episode. And he would have done more if there were time, but he had to do everything else.

MPK: When you're running a show you usually get to do the first two, because at that point the scripts are caught up. And then if you're lucky, you get to do one in the middle—I did the red-carpet episode—and then the final one. But the idea was that she was always the center, and then the camera will swing too far in one direction or the other and you catch the writers, for instance, glaring at her. Jimmy Burrows, the TV director, who plays himself in several episodes, said to me, "You're running six cameras at once, I don't know what the hell you're doing." We had a lot of cameras going, to get the sitcom, the backstage, the handheld. It was a really interesting puzzle.

Did you create storyboards?

MPK: Ever since doing *Sex and the City*, which was a very expensive film show, I have always done storyboards. But then when we worked with great guest directors, like Greg Mottola and Michael Lehmann, there was never a storyboard approval. They had to be creative and figure out their own way to do it within this very specific landscape that we had already set up. It had to be about the stories happening behind her, behind her, behind her. Like an Escher print, almost. The unraveling behind her that she can't see. But you see it. You almost see the fuse being lit over her head.

One of the most amazing moments along those lines is in the second-to-last episode, when Jane offers to speak with the writers about giving Valerie more lines in order to promote the about-to-premiere reality show. In the foreground, Valerie sits with her hairdresser, Mickey, while we can just barely make out Jane and the two writers, Paulie G. and Tom, out of focus in the background. While Jane and the writers are engaged in this intense shouting match, Valerie is extolling the virtues of Mickey's heirloom tomatoes. It's so layered, because we—and, of course, Valerie and Mickey—are hearing what's going on, but Valerie is desperately trying to distract us, and herself, from what is being said. It's an important moment, because it manages to pack so much information—about character and story—into the frame.

MPK: You know, it's so great to hear you say it's important, because we thought it was hilarious. It was so alive. We were giggling all the time and laughing. You know what I mean? Even though the gravitas was there, we thought it was really funny. At the start, people said it was too harsh, and I said to Lisa at one point, "This is a documentary. Everything I'm writing, I know for a fact is true, true, true."

Michael, you worked as a writer on Murphy Brown, Cybill, *and a number of other shows, and Lisa, obviously you had your many years on* Friends *and on other sitcoms before that. How did you conceive of* Room and Bored, *the sitcom in the series? And how did you come up with the scene from* I'm It!, *Valerie's sitcom from the late 1980s/early 1990s featured in episode four?*

MPK: I didn't direct episode four, but I did direct the *I'm It!* section—I was like, "No, I'm in there. I know this world." I love that *I'm It!* scene with her, when they're doing that crass Tracy/Hepburn–esque thing and she closes the guy's tie in the file drawer. "Oh, come *here*, you!" How many times have you seen that on TV? That crazy, multi-camera coverage when she goes to the door, and the camera goes with her, and then that fake, awful pathos moment when they finally kiss.

And what I love about it is Valerie watching it. This was her peak. She's actually convinced herself that that was a Sam and Diane moment. And she looks over at Mickey, and he gives her that beaming look. That's the dream—that's what sitcoms are. Her hair, the suit, the fake office set, the sight gags—

LK: It seems like at a certain point in television history, that's all you needed: people who looked a certain way and were able to memorize lines.

And a pumped-up studio audience.

MPK: Yeah. And I have to tell you this, having been in many development meetings with actresses that I wound up not working with who thought they were going to be sitcom stars. There is one thing that every actress always says: "I'm really good with physical comedy."

That's a line given to Valerie in the show.

MPK: That's the line used by every actress who is insecure about an innate comic rhythm. You would never hear Lisa say that—in fact, you'd hear Lisa say the opposite.

LK: "I want stunt pay." *[laughs]*

MPK: But they all say that. So for us to put that *I'm It!* shtick with the computer keyboard and the tie getting caught in the file drawer—it was important, because that's what paraded around in television as comedy for a while.

LK: Also, women couldn't be flawed in the way that men are, because it was seen as insulting. You were putting them down. They always had to be—

MPK: Cute but flummoxed.

LK: Right. It wasn't sexist; it was overcompensating for sexism. But that essentially meant that the female characters in these shows couldn't even be interesting.

MPK: So, yeah, we decided to include that scene from *I'm It!* to show her heyday, and also as an excuse for her to trap Gigi, the new writer, in her dressing room for a writers' meeting. "I'm going to get this girl on my side."

LK: Right, I need someone in that room writing for me.

MPK: "Aunt Sassy's bitch," in the other writers' words.

Speaking of Aunt Sassy, can you talk about coming up with Room and Bored? *It's so perfectly rendered—and perfectly awful—that it feels like something you might catch on the WB.*

MPK: Or the CW, or maybe even Fox at one point. What we took from all of those kinds of shows was the colors of the set, the design, the surfboards on the wall. I mean, come on! *[both laugh]* And I think there's a little bit of the *Friends* set in there—that brightly colored stuff. We decided to set the sitcom in California and put in the fake ocean backdrop. Most important, of course, was the sex. Because that's what replaced that corporate vibe in sitcoms from the 1980s and early 1990s, like what you see in the *I'm It!* scene we wrote. Now it's all about partial nudity, the audience oohing and aahing when they kiss—shit like that.

We worked hard on the dialogue and setups for *Room and Bored*, to the point where "I don't need to see that!"—Valerie's signature line—

The "clam," as you referred to it in one interview...

MPK and **LK:** The clam!

LK: That's what Michael kept saying: "We've got to have that clam." And I didn't know what he was talking about.

MPK: I'm going to brag now. "Clam" is a term Peter Tolan and I came up with when we were working on *Murphy Brown*. [Show creator] Diane English asked us to read a bunch of spec scripts, and I said to Peter, "Have you noticed that every script has a line like, 'I came back from lunch and got sick—I must have had bad clams.'" And he said, "Yeah, there must be a lot of bad clams out there." So we decided that any recurring joke that can be found in pop culture's lint drawer is a clam. The current clam, by the way, is "Wait for it...!" Anyway, the original clam we had in there for Aunt Sassy after she opens the door and finds the two kids making out was, "Why don't you two get a room?" And then Lisa and I thought we could do better than that: "We have to come up with our own clam, something that sounds like a sitcom line." And we came up with "I don't need to *see* that!"

LK: "Note to self—"

MPK: Right. "Note to self: I don't need to *see* that!" Right. "Note to self" was the clam.

LK: It was a clam and a hook. *[laughs]*

MPK: With an extender! But yeah, we both know that whole sitcom world really well. And then we had such fun casting it. And we had rehearsals with the kids where we wrote entire scenes that never aired so that they had a better sense of what they were doing.

LK: I want to say one thing, though, because I would hate to have any confusion about what we did on *The Comeback* and my feelings about *Friends*. None of this was informed by *Friends*—that was a really great experience, and [show creators] Marta Kauffman and David Crane were always generous and collaborative with the actors. I'm not sure what happened in the writers' room. I think we all know that there was some tension, and that maybe they felt a little differently about the actors. I knew that stuff existed, and always felt like, on other shows especially, there is this tension between the actors and the writers. The actors are getting all the attention and accolades, and the writers are just told,

"Stay in your room and write this stuff for me. And by the way, where is it? Why isn't it ready?" I think writers get a little, well, sad about that.

MPK: Having not been around *Friends*, and having no awareness at all of what that writing room was like, my experience has been very different. I have been in a couple of writing rooms—not *Murphy Brown*'s, by the way, because that was like the Harvard of sitcoms. But before and after that, I'd been involved with shows where—I'm just going to go on the record here—the writers hated the actresses. They just hated them. There was something about an actress of a certain age—at least in the rooms I was in—that bugged people.

These were just male writers, or female writers also?

MPK: Well, there's a fine line. The writers that I thought were most lethal were guys. And then it would get down to a more specific complaint, like "She can't do my jokes." This often happened at sitcoms where somebody wound up in charge who wasn't, for some reason, a comedy person. "The joke was good." "No, she couldn't do it." It was a constant war. This led to one of my favorite scenes in *The Comeback*, the cookie "rape" scene, where Valerie stops by the writers' room late at night with cookies, and they're making brutal fun of her. In my writing rooms, I've never allowed that to happen. It's just not good. I believe you have to be in love with the people you're writing for.

LK: It's worth mentioning that it always gets more tense when the show's not a big hit. *Sex and the City* was at the top, and *Friends* was at the top, so everyone was pretty happy. But when all of these egos—and it's not like writers don't have them too—start getting a little nervous and threatened and scared, I think there's no more dangerous an animal than a writer. *[laughs]*

MPK: And then there is the split between the two types of writers, which is embodied in *The Comeback*: Tom, who is the sycophant who will literally bend over backward because he has a house in Toluca Lake and a wife and kids and wants a career, and Paulie G., who's probably truly gifted but is stuck in a cul-de-sac, tied to his writing partner, and ultimately, to Valerie Cherish.

LK: It's a case of the artist being paired with "Get along to go along."

MPK: And I actually understand all of those people. I understand Paulie, I understand Tom, and I understand Valerie. It was an interesting kind of lethal combination—a death pact.

LK: Also, it's worth mentioning that the writers who worked on *The Comeback* had experiences in many other writers' rooms, and none of this seemed foreign to them. In fact, it made all the sense in the world to them.

Valerie Cherish has got to be one of the most memorable and complex characters ever to appear on television. She has a funny line early on in the series when she chastises Chris, one of the younger actors on Room and Bored, *for "playing to the camera," but the irony is that Valerie is always playing to the camera and is always desperate to come off well, even if it means throwing someone else under the bus in the process. I'm reminded particularly of the scene in the Palm Springs episode when she is recognized by the gay couple on the street who are huge fans of hers. When Jane presents them with release forms to sign, the younger guy declines nervously because he isn't out to his family, but Valerie is so desperate to have a scene with adoring fans in the show that she convinces him to sign it anyway—in the guise, of course, of encouraging him to be true to himself.*

MPK: But also in that Palm Springs episode is the only moment when she chooses Mark over showbiz. That's our big "Valerie gets it" moment. *[laughs]* I just started thinking about another scene in that episode, when Mark and Valerie, who've both taken sleeping pills because the people in the room next door are having an all-night party, wake up and realize they've missed their chance to get the good chairs by the pool. The film crew knocks on their door, and Valerie with her crazy raccoon-smeared makeup opens the blinds, and you see Mark's bare ass as he's sleeping on the bed behind her. *[both laugh]* That's the balance I love. That we actually have that crazy mania, and then at the end of the episode, she puts those sunglasses on, not letting the audience see her eyes, and says, basically, "I choose Mark." She chooses Mark's need to hear the Cheap Trick song over her need to be on a reality show. It's the beginning of a turn.

Lisa, your portrayal of Valerie not only brings out the humor we talked about earlier but also imbues her with a humanity that makes her at times feel almost like a character in a tragedy. Alessandra Stanley in The New York Times *called the series "the saddest comedy on television," and she's right. I couldn't watch more than three episodes at a time—it's really draining, as hilariously funny as it is at the same time.*

LK: Especially those first two episodes.

MPK: I think Lisa's performance is like no other performance I've ever seen before. In terms of the complicated layers that you're not being told you're experiencing, but you are subliminally feeling.

It's interesting how the viewer's relationship to the character of Valerie constantly changes. At one moment you feel sorry for her, then a scene later you're exasperated with her, then she does something that makes you really revile her. And then, before you know it, you love her for some hilarious insight she offers.

MPK: What you just said, that's everything. That's what we became fascinated by. That you could actually portray a human being in the midst of doing a comedy reality show. A character who is so complicated and so changeable that you change while you're watching her.

In the "Valerie Demands Dignity" episode, Valerie becomes anxious after she sees an Entertainment Weekly *cover story with the headline "Is Reality TV Dying?" She starts to worry that the only way the show will be a hit is if she humiliates herself. She has a great line: "People do not want to see Valerie Cherish brutalized!" Of course, that's exactly what they want to see—and more to the point, it's what we're witnessing constantly in the series. One minute we see her crawling up the aisle of a plane experiencing intense turbulence, the next she gets dog poop in her hair, then in another scene she falls and scrapes her knee while trying to make it to an interview with a* TV Guide *reporter. It's horrifying but also hilarious. Again, I think that probably has to do more with your performance, Lisa, than anything else.*

LK: Thank you for the nod to it possibly being about a performance, but no, it's the idea of a person thinking they're in control of something as random and chaotic as life. That's always hilarious to me. And then on top of that, working with manipulative producers on a reality show with a very definite agenda, and thinking you can somehow control that. That's really funny to me.

MPK: Right, like whenever she gives the "time-out" sign with her hands to Jane and the film crew. Even in this tornado, she has to have a moment where she's saying no, even if it's clear that she has absolutely no power.

LK: She's also living in another time. She hasn't caught up to the fact that there's no such thing as propriety anymore. The ironic thing is that people have seen so much reality TV that the show might be received a little bit differently now. When we did this, it was, like, season two of *The Amazing Race*. To me, that was the height of humiliation—vomiting and crying on TV—

MPK: Or eating bugs on *I'm a Celebrity, Get Me Out of Here!*

LK: We felt the show had to be brutal, because one of the things we were trying to shine a little light onto, even if it's in a subtle way, is that even though these people who sign on to these shows are human beings, they've essentially decided to become brands—that's the big word now. And by doing that, they're actually throwing away their humanity, you know? It's as if that's not important. What's important is, how much can you get paid to show up at a party? I see interviews with reality stars who say things like, "I don't like what's happening to my character." It's their name, their husband, their child, their address—that's not a character, that's you. *[laughs]*

Reality TV has certainly become more extreme since the show was shot. The stakes have gotten so ridiculously high that you end up with situations like that of the couple in California who staged the "runaway balloon" hoax with their six-year-old son, who then vomited on two different morning news shows after his parents asked him to lie about it.

MPK: Well, of course, Valerie had a double vomit.

That scene, which occurs in the second-to-last episode, when Valerie finally gut punches a drunk Paulie G., is worth an entire interview on its own.

MPK: That's the one moment where Lisa and I almost came to blows. She was fully on board with the vomiting, wearing the cupcake costume, everything—and then when we were filming it, every time we did a take, some innate actress-survival-Darwinian skill *[Kudrow laughs]* would make her turn her mouth away from the camera.

Lisa, you didn't want to be filmed actually vomiting?

LK: I really thought no one would want to see that. *[laughs]*

MPK: She wasn't opposed to the vomiting, but she didn't want it to be shown. You know, you see the vomit hit the floor as she turns away from the camera. And I kept saying to David Steinberg, the director for that episode, "I didn't see the vomit come out of her mouth." And I would keep coming out onto the set and saying, "Lisa, I didn't see the vomit." She's in a giant cupcake with a cherry on her head, and every time she did it she would still turn her face away and vomit. I came back in again and she glared at me and said, "You're here *again*? You're brave!" And I said, "I'm here to represent Lisa Kudrow the writer. She's on board with the vomit coming out of Lisa Kudrow the actress's mouth."

What did you say to that, Lisa?

LK: "You're a sadist!"

MPK: She was also saying "Shit. Fuck. Shit. Fuck!" And then I walked away, and in the next take she directed her head right toward that camera and vomited.

And I was delighted.

Lisa, do you think it could be that it's easier to write a scene in which someone humiliates themself than to actually play it?

LK: I didn't feel humiliated—that wasn't it. I just didn't feel like anyone should be subjected to watching vomit come out of anyone's mouth. It's too vulgar, or at least that's what I thought. Since that happened, of course, all I see on TV are people vomiting from the front.

MPK: Listen, Snooki got punched in the face on *Jersey Shore* and it became a hit because of it. I saw Khloé Kardashian give her sister a Brazilian bikini wax and they pixilated her blistered vagina. Pixelated her vagina! The difference between *Kourtney & Khloé Take Miami* and *The Comeback* is that in the former, somebody cut away the humanity and the humiliation from the show that ended up on the air, and we didn't cut away from it.

I could actually see a scenario where Valerie would consider the Brazilian, because that's where we are now. It's good reality-show stuff.

LK: Yeah. *[As Valerie:]* "You gotta be flexible..." *[laughs]*

MPK: I could see a scene where Mickey says, "Red, that's going too far," and she says, "Well, Mickey, I'm competing with Khloé. They got very big numbers for that. And Jane, you're not going to see it, right? You're going to pixelate it?"

LK: She can rationalize anything.

MPK: "If you're not going to see it, can't I just keep a thong on? Can't we fake it?" *[both laugh]*

Jane, the producer, is such a seminal figure in the whole structure of the show. As with Valerie, the viewer's feelings about her constantly shift. She's cold and clearly manipulative, but there are times when it's clear she's actually moved by something Valerie has said or done—in a few instances, the camera even catches her tearing up. It gives the viewer the chance to hold out a bit of hope that the "nice" side of Jane will prevail when the reality show is finally put together.

LK: Well, you know, the truth of these shows is that the producer just shoots it and then hands in the material. It's someone else who's doing the assembling. But Jane does "guide" Valerie—

MPK: She's very canny. "Oh, you don't want to do that, Valerie? Okay, I'll just call Ben Silver, the studio exec, and tell him you're not on board." Or when Valerie asks Jane to turn off the camera, and she says, "No, we can't." Just the idea of saying "no" to Valerie creates an energy that's going to make for good reality TV. You see Valerie swallowing and trying to figure it out: "What am I going to do with a 'no'?" Jane was really important, because she was the fire stoker, and Valerie needed a push and a pull. And the fact that she was a woman was important, too.

There's that wonderful scene between them near the end of the last episode, after Valerie's Leno *appearance, when Jane spontaneously hugs Valerie. I read somewhere that was an undirected move on actress Laura Silverman's part.*

MPK: Right, when Valerie's so excited about getting picked up, and Jane just jumps across and gives her hug. That line of yours is the one improvised line in the series, Lisa. Valerie says, "Well, look at that. She just cracked open." That breaks my heart.

We actually wrote that part with Laura Silverman in mind, because we wanted someone who was a "nonactress actress." That was very important for Jane, Mickey, and Mark. Those three characters needed to be completely believable, "real" people. We kept saying, "We want Mickey to be eccentric; we don't want an eccentric actor."

How did you find Robert Michael Morris, who plays Mickey in the series?

LK: Michael knew him.

MPK: He was my college theater teacher. Michael would write these incredibly emotional Christmas letters every year and send them out: "Well, I've got melanoma again, but they froze it." And I started telling Lisa about Michael. We wrote the part with him in mind, and then we saw a lot of actors for Mickey. We had to audition everybody, and we had to see how each would work with Lisa. But when Michael came in, it was a reality. And he brought Lisa a little fake diamond necklace.

LK: Which I wore every day. It was good luck.

The relationship between Mickey and Valerie is almost like a comic version of the one between Petra and her assistant, Marlene, in Fassbinder's The Bitter Tears of Petra von Kant*: basically a sadomasochistic dance. Valerie tends to put Mickey through hell, but he still adores her, and she depends on him, too. Michael, I think in one interview you called him "Valerie's airbag."*

MPK: It's an interesting dynamic in that he annoys her, but he also buoys her up. Without him, she wouldn't be able to make it, because he's almost mirroring back the person she wants to be—or the person she was. It's a case of the star and the sycophant. And then there is another complicated level that's only briefly alluded to in the show, and that is that he's eating the shit because he needs the health insurance. You know what I mean? He needs the job, so he's not quite just a victim; he's also pushing her to continue, because there's not another job for him in all of Hollywood. There just isn't. Not with that hairdo he does for her, or those big curlers. They're both keeping each other's heyday alive.

Perhaps they get along so well because they're both so self-deluded. There is a very funny scene in which Mickey is mortified when one of the young actors on Room and Bored *offers to set him up with a male friend of hers: He can't understand how anyone would guess he were gay.*

MPK: He's from a different time. They both are. And they're both from the end of that time, so now they're living in this different context. He's thinking that because he hasn't said it, it doesn't exist. And she's thinking she's a star because she has a hairdresser who follows her around town.

LK: I love the look on the face of Dan Bucatinsky, who plays Valerie's publicist, when Mickey announces he's going to come out—"Come out of what?" *[laughs]*

MPK: He's just another great deluded character.

One of my favorite characters in The Comeback *is Juna [played by Malin Akerman], the young actress in the sitcom with Valerie. She's adorable, sweet, a little naive—*

MPK: She's true.

LK: Right, and everything is going her way. She doesn't have to fight for anything.

MPK: She's a golden child. It was really important to us in the writing that Juna be good—

LK: So that you're not allowed to hate her.

Is she there to serve as a reminder to Valerie of what she can never be?

MPK: Well, she represents the effortlessness with which some people move through life, versus the struggling so many others have to undergo. Making Juna a nice person was important, because you know, show business isn't all snarky. Every now and then there is someone who is lovely and wonderful and who does come to your chocolate-fountain party. And that created another level of struggle for Valerie, because she couldn't write her off. She's in a beauty pageant with someone who actually is Miss Congeniality. I love Juna, and Malin Akerman was flawless.

LK: She was.

Mark, Valerie's husband, is the most "centered" character on the show, which might have to do with the fact that he's the only one not in show business. Can you talk about how you came up with him? Was there any real-life referent?

MPK: Lisa, you should talk first about Mark and Valerie as husband and wife, and how important that was.

LK: Well, I thought it was important not only that he be a good guy, but that he be successful. It's important that she's not doing any of this because she needs the money. This quest of hers has nothing to do with her having to pay a mortgage. And he's this guy who's only mildly interested in what she's doing. As long as whatever it is she's doing doesn't interfere too much with his life, it's going to be okay.

MPK: He also gives her complete permission to be, I would say, a "lazy wife." Do you know what I mean? She always orders out for dinner, and he's fine with it. There's a very Beverly Hills aspect to it all.

LK: But I also like that they each have their independence. She sees them as sort of a modern couple. Yes, he doesn't insist that she cook. But she is the one who prepares his lunch and takes care of him and makes sure he's not too put out. Like arranging car pools for his daughter, Franchesca, when she goes to New York. The key was that Mark couldn't be needy. A little selfish at times, but not needy.

MPK: It was another interesting part to cast, and there weren't a lot of options.

LK: Well, at first we thought he should be a lot older. She just married this very successful guy, and it's not a love thing.

MPK: But then we wanted to have someone who thought of her as a catch, and someone she actually could catch, because she's a genius about surviving. She saw the career dip and suddenly she was married to a guy who has money, and who also sees her still as a star. Damian Young came in many times when I was casting *Sex and the City*, and he was always too complicated for any of the one-off guys we would have on that show. He was too interesting to be the idiot, and he was too handsome to be the ugly guy, and he was too real to do a cartoon turn. So we were thinking, "Who's handsome, and yet real? Who's appropriate, and who's dry?" That was the most important thing. He needed to be dry. Effortless. Present. Valerie was such a hummingbird, so we wanted a low vibe from the husband so that together as a couple they're tolerable. And then Damian read and we all loved him.

The other thing that's really important about their relationship is that she sexes it up for him. She might not cook, but she likes to wear those tight-fitting dresses. So when they put her in that baggy Aunt Sassy tracksuit, it really is a humiliation.

One of the reality cameras is mounted on the ceiling in their bedroom, and they seem to be making relatively frequent trips into the bathroom to have sex—one of these off-camera episodes ends up being featured as a voice-over at the end of one episode.

MPK: We wanted to make sure that there was a sex vibe to Valerie, because she was being categorized by others as not sexual. She has a sex life, and the tragedy is that, because of her age, on sitcoms, she's basically dead, which explains all the terrible jokes about Aunt Sassy's "big beaver" coat. There is a vital woman there who is being desexualized because of what the network says is sexy.

Speaking of the network, I was curious if all of the unidentified people—and there are quite a few—at the table readings for Room and Bored *were meant to be from the show's network.*

MPK: They're network executives, junior executives, studio execs. Everyone who is paid to be there to laugh too loud when something is working, and give too many notes when it isn't.

This is typical for any kind of television series?

MPK: Not for a filmed show. It's unique to a show like *Room and Bored*, when there is an actual sound that's supposed to come out of an audience that registers whether it's funny or not. For sitcoms that I've been on—*Cybill, Good Advice, Good Sports*—there's always someone there from the network to laugh at the good parts and to give you notes when there are no laughs.

LK: For a big, big hit, those table reads are not as populated, because there aren't really notes.

MPK: Right. On season three of *Friends*, it's really hard to give Marta Kauffman and David Crane a note, because it's like, "Oh, don't worry, we'll fix that." But there's a lot of worry when you're starting a new sitcom that network people are going to make you do something that won't necessarily be good for the show.

LK: You haven't yet had a chance to prove that you can fix a problem.

MPK: And the other thing is, everybody wants to make sure that it works, because everybody's livelihood is tied to it. So it made perfect sense that those first couple of episodes of *Room and Bored* would be greatly populated, because the show is starting and people are like, "We got this thing on the air, now let's move forward."

The second or third episode on any sitcom is brutal, because you work a long time on the pilot, and then suddenly, you're like, "Oh, this is really it." Even on *The Comeback*. When we were filming the Palm Springs episode, I was editing the third episode. There's that scene near the end where Valerie goes to the Ivy to meet Juna, and she's just sitting at the table waiting for Juna, who's late. Valerie awkwardly eats a piece of bread, checks her watch—it goes on for what feels like forever—and I had a moment of complete panic. Lisa talked me off the ledge. She said, "No, it's exactly what it's supposed to be. Sometimes it should be inert and it should be about nothing. It's enough." But I started to get the vapors! Even I didn't know if that was enough.

LK: It was enough.

MPK: Lisa was standing outside at the Parker Palm Springs with her hair in a towel, and she said to me, "It's exactly what we wanted it to be." I mean, thank God you have a partner in those situations.

LK: But the thing was, when the network saw that third episode, they loved it. Remember?

MPK: Right, they were like, "Oh, *this* is what it's about."

Yet another aspect of the series that was really pitch-perfect was your employment of all of those product-placement moments, particularly in the Palm Springs episode, where Valerie and Mark are given a Lincoln Navigator but are then accompanied on the trip by a public-relations flack from the car company who keeps insisting they insert "the Navigator" into every comment they make about the car.

MPK: At around that time I began noticing this on reality shows. You know, you're watching *Top Chef* and you're thinking, "Why I am looking at the stove?" "Why are there all of these shots of the Tupperware?"

LK: But we'd also hear stories from people working on scripted shows, where it was like, "Oh God, we have to figure out how to work in this product because they're going to underwrite a lot of the budget."

Did you ever have to deal with this issue on any of the other shows you've been involved with?

MPK: When *Sex and the City* was on HBO there was never any product placement. As a matter of fact, people said to me, "Trojan must have given you a lot of money," since we had a shot, for example, of Samantha opening her cabinet and grabbing the rubbers. I said, "No, not at all, I just wanted the most instantly recognizable condom." I just don't like it on a show when people are drinking fake Diet Coke, you know? With the fake swirls of color on the can? One of the great joys of writing *Sex and the City* came in knowing I could actually write, "She's on the runway in a Gucci outfit," as opposed to, "She's on the runway in a Fafoofoo from Paris outfit." Which makes everything seem so fake to me. Same thing on sitcoms: When people are drinking swirly colas, it drives me crazy. But since *Sex and the City*, product placement has become a big deal. It's a huge revenue stream on reality shows, which is why we used it. Even in the second episode, Valerie is given a huge basket of hair product for Mickey to use before the upfronts.

That's one of the few times Valerie won't give in to the demands of Jane and the show.

MPK: I said to Lisa when we were filming it, "Do not say 'no' right away. Take as long as you possibly can before saying it." It's great—you can see the wheels turning, you see every thought—"Am I going to get yelled at?" "Will this damage me in some way?" Her head is practically vibrating! And then she finally says, "No. No. Sorry." But it's the longest pause ever. So all of this came from reality shows, not from anyone telling me to put anything in. We were ahead of the curve on that one.

Not only on that one. I read somewhere that you two were amazed to find Madonna sporting Valerie's hairstyle after the show aired.

LK: Oh, we couldn't believe that!

MPK: We couldn't believe it. We were flattered, because—

LK: How could you not be?

MPK: Madonna was trying to work it as retro style, but Valerie was wearing it without thinking it was retro, it was just style. *[both laugh]* If we were still on the air, that would be a great moment for Valerie: "Madonna stole my hair. She stole my hair. I was first."

Do you think this show could have been made for network television?

LK: No.

MPK: No. It apparently couldn't even be made for HBO. It is too complicated. Also, the nightmare of cutting to a commercial in the middle of raw footage would have destroyed the tension we were trying to create, which would usually break near the end when we would use all that really great music to close the show. That was the only salve we gave the audience; you get to see a slightly more polished end.

LK: Right, like you were actually watching a TV show!

MPK: But up until then there is no music, no credits, no break. We wouldn't have been able to do it.

LK: No, and also the pacing...

MPK: Right, the timing was important. A half-hour show on network TV is now 20 minutes when you factor in commercials, and that extra 10 minutes is the stuff that makes you love Valerie. The character stuff, and the luxury of watching paint dry. The non-energy of not moving it along was basically the antidote to a network show.

And I'm guessing it was probably also important to have the option of showing nudity and using swear words, for instance, which heightened the "raw footage" feel.

MPK: Well, I'll tell you that even in the simplest, simplest edit, a network would have told us that Mark could never say that he and Valerie had tried cocaine—which is a significant, significant part of their backstory. I know we would have gotten a note about that on network TV. And the other, much more general note we would have gotten—the ultimate network note about a female character—would have been: "Is she likable?" You would have heard it from everyone. "Is she likable?" "Do we like her?" "Is she likable?" "Will the audience like her?" And that question can't exist for a character like Valerie Cherish, because the answer is "yes," "no," "yes," "yes," "no..."

LK: And just off the page, it's "no."

MPK: So there you go. Without Lisa's performance, off the page, it's "no." Because there's no energy, no sadness behind the eyes, no investment. Like when she really loses herself dancing during Juna's concert at the Viper Room. The one moment she actually forgets about the camera. And what did we do? As she comes back to earth, she sees Mark dancing with another woman.

Valerie calls it "dirty dancing."

MPK: Right. It's the only moment she lets go, and all hell breaks loose. *[both laugh]*

So now for the big question: Why do you think this show only lasted one season on HBO?

MPK: I have theories.

LK: I do too.

MPK: First of all, you have to understand that it was the greatest mystery and disconnect for Lisa and me. It wasn't even like we had the normal emotional infrastructure that happens when something gets canceled. It's almost like we were in a Jean-Paul Sartre play—"I don't understand anything that's happening." The direct evolutionary line that I can draw, having worked at HBO before, is that their MO is "quality, not ratings." They're not in the ratings game, they're in the quality game. The only manifestation of quality at the beginning of a series is critical response. So if *The New York Times* says that *The Comeback* is a significant, important new type of television series, that puts you on a track that is quotable—and comforting to a show-business machine. And I think our first wave of critical responses—with the exception of, as I like to say, "the Pulitzer Prize–winning Tom Shales of *The Washington Post*," who really got it—didn't include enough snobby quotes. And I do say snobby, because there were plenty "Lisa Kudrow is a genius" comments.

LK: But they all came back later and wrote more favorable pieces—

MPK: They all turned around.

It's funny you mention that, because when I was doing research, I was fascinated to find that reviews of the series when it was airing were generally much less enthusiastic than later reviews of the DVD. And these came from the same publications. What does that say to you?

MPK: I know what it says. People have so little faith that there is an actual method to the madness. When they saw the first or second episode, they thought, "They can't keep this up—this is so off the track I'm not even sure there's a thought behind it." Angela Tarantino was our publicist at HBO, and after I showed her the pilot, she said to me, "Uh, it's really good. We're going to have to educate them as to how to talk about this." And we never accomplished that, as much as we tried. The reality was that out of the gate, people had never seen anything like this character before. It's like in life, where you only really start to understand someone's sense of humor after you've gotten to know them for a period of time. So at first, people were kind of stunned, and then by the final episode, they got it.

LK: In my mind, people weren't going to "get it" until some point well into the second season. To me, that's why we were at HBO, because that's where you can do that. I mean, all of their biggest hits were shows that for the first couple of episodes or even seasons you kind of went, "Wait, what is this? How do I even categorize this?" I think it's the same with anything new and different. Conan got horrible reviews when he first started on *Late Night*. But that's who he was, and he didn't go anywhere, and then everyone went, "Oh, okay, we get it!" That's what I was expecting, and it actually took off even more than I ever expected it to in the first season.

MPK: Also, Lisa was not Phoebe.

LK: And you weren't delivering *Sex and the City*.

MPK: It was kind of a bait-and-switch situation, because people thought that they were in for the greatest, funniest, sexiest show, because that was our brand.

LK: Something else was happening. HBO had just come off of *Sex and the City*, and everyone was still waiting for the next season of *The Sopranos*, and the network had done a few industry series—*Entourage* and *Unscripted*, the George Clooney show—which weren't reviewed well at all. People were starting to wonder aloud about what HBO was doing with all these "inside-industry" shows, and then *The Comeback* came out. So I think it was HBO's turn to get a little flack.

How far into the series were you when you found out it wouldn't be renewed?

MPK: We didn't find out until the series was over. I remember going into HBO—I actually dragged Lisa in with me—right before we shot the Palm Springs episode. I said to them "I'm going to be very bold right now and tell you the truth: It's going to turn around, and if you pick us up now, there will be fuel behind this. If you say there will be a second season of *The Comeback* right now, everything will change. Lisa will get nominated for an Emmy"—which she did anyway, although my feeling is she would have won if it had been renewed. I even said, "Get us off Sunday. Create a new night: Monday. Call it 'Monday, Monday' and play The Mamas and The Papas song, make it kind of sad. 'You think your boss is bad? Here's Valerie Cherish.'"

LK: *[laughs]* Right, I forgot about that—that was great!

MPK: Lower the expectations. Make it an off-Broadway night. Stop trying to make it be Carrie Bradshaw and Mr. Big in Paris. It can't be that, yet or ever...

that took six years to build. Put it on Monday—"Rainy Days and Mondays" as the theme song—go with a darker, sadder vibe, and let it find a small audience.

But for some reason they didn't buy it. I could have gone in there and pitched the second season like crazy: This is what we're going to do—you'll love it. We'll never paint ourselves into a corner—it's Lisa and me. But it didn't happen.

LK: There were other powers at work that we don't know about, obviously. The quality was there, the ratings were actually fine for a first-season show. It had done better, as I recall, than *Entourage* in its first season. So essentially, there wasn't anything where you could definitely say, "Here's why." And what I heard later from people who were at HBO at the time was that they went back and forth every day on whether it was going to get picked up or not.

Do you think the critique of the TV industry was off-putting to some people?

LK: I do. The interesting thing to me was that artists—writers, directors, actors—loved it and could not believe it had been canceled. Executives and business types would look at me and say, "Wow, yeah, I guess it was just too brutal." Or "I guess it wasn't funny enough." Or "I guess the ratings weren't good enough." But it was funny to see how those two different types responded to the cancellation. The executives had to justify it: "It can't have been wrong, because they did it." *[laughs]*

MPK: I've gotten some "We shoulda" calls since then. I loved it when *Entertainment Weekly* named it one of the top 10 shows of the decade. *Newsweek* called it one of the 10 funniest comedies of the decade, but *Entertainment Weekly* called it one of the top 10 shows of the decade. *The Sopranos* was number 1, and we were number 10. It was a nice validation, as were the three Emmy nominations.

LK: What I'm noticing also is that it seems to be gaining popularity with college-age kids.

MPK: It is truly an original, and I have to tell you that we had such a great time on this, and we were a great team. And to this day, we still call each other up and say, "What if Valerie did this? Or that? Should we?"

LK: We might not be done.

Lisa, you've been working on the terrific Web Therapy *series on the Internet—would you consider something along those lines?*

LK: I don't know. We talk about what it could be, but you know, we don't own it. *[laughs]*

MPK: It's a very interesting situation, because the idea of Valerie in the world is like a creative wellspring. It never goes away. The idea of an unsatisfied person who's not going gently into that good night represents an endless opportunity for comedy—and tragedy.

Would you two be willing talk a little bit about some of the ideas you had for the second season if the show had been renewed?

MPK: Well, off the top of my head, we thought that Valerie's fame would give her more power. And that she would therefore probably get rid of Paulie G. and promote Gigi to the showrunner—and then Gigi would become a monster. And I can tell you that Mickey was going to get bad porcelain veneers. And leave his boyfriend for a young man. And we had a great idea for a drifting-away Mark.

At the close of the final episode, when Valerie is signing the vomit bags with her likeness on them in the Leno *parking lot, you see Mark suddenly realizing what this newfound fame is going to do to Valerie, and by extension, to their relationship.*

LK: Right.

MPK: We always thought about doing an episode where we get to see Valerie and Mark's wedding. We decided they had a ski wedding, and she wore a white parka.

LK: In Aspen!

MPK: They got married on the slopes. It was completely correct for her. Just a photo of them on skis getting married.

LK: And we really wanted to introduce the character of her father, who is this grumpy guy. The kind of person who would trip and then blame her.

MPK: That's what my father did. At my sister's wedding, he tripped on his own feet walking her down the aisle and he looked over at her and said: "Jesus *Christ*, Ellen." *[both laugh]* So we thought he would be a fun and painful character. But the second season was really going to be about the rise of Valerie's power. And how, even with power, the ambition just starts to destroy her.

LK: It would never be enough. Even if she ends up in a movie with Nicole Kidman, she's still not going to be invited to the same parties.

MPK: The reason that we had absolute confidence that we could continue doing *The Comeback* was that Valerie would never be satisfied with what she had. Celebrity is a race against time. I'm sure even Nicole Kidman has days where she says, "What happened?" The spotlight will not stay on you, whoever you are.

And our übersophisticated thought was that Valerie would eventually gain some sort of awareness about this, but to what level, we weren't sure. We even talked about her leaving Hollywood and going to a different city.

LK: We wanted her to go to New York.

MPK: Right. Here's the thing about the character of Valerie: I can say to myself, "What is the worst, most tragic situation I can think of?" And then I put Valerie in it, and I immediately start thinking about what she would say that would make me laugh. It's the same with every bad situation you can think of: If you put Valerie Cherish in it, and think about her trying to get her head around it, it's funny.

Notes for a Young Alchemist

BY JULIA DRAKE

The year you're born, Master Niels Henrik Ångström, one of the last living men to turn tin into gold, slips outside his local grocery store and cracks his head open on the sidewalk. Alongside the announcement of his death, the newspaper runs a photograph of his spilled groceries, oranges and onions scattered beneath the bumpers of parked cars. The world mourns. His obituary, above the fold and epically long, declares that he was "that rare and sparkling interloper between science and art, whose work was a fairy tale come to life...a visionary who reminded us of the importance of wonder."

According to your mother, you cried the whole week after he died, though, admittedly, that may have been the colic.

In high school, you're pretty good at chemistry, plus the smartest girl in the class sits next to you and never covers her answers. You like lab, but you love your teacher: tall with ginger-silver hair and dressed in short-sleeved button-downs patterned with trout, with handsome crow's-feet and hands as big as paddles. He looks less like a chemist and more like a wildlife researcher, and perhaps this is why you're drawn to him. You've always liked the outdoors. Plus he can light dollar bills on fire without reducing them to ash, and he can make potassium iodide explode into enormous marshmallows, ones even bigger than your sheltie, Juniper.

He likes you best too, more than even the smartest girl. You stay after school to help him deep-clean the lab, and one afternoon he says "watch," and mixes lead nitrate and potassium iodide together in a flask. Before your very eyes the chemicals react to form a golden solution—not gold, just the illusion of it, but nevertheless the sparkle snags at your heart. He hands you the stirring rod and when you stir, the liquid becomes a glittering blizzard. He tells you that you have a terrifically light touch, that the solution shines more when you stir. About a week later the two of you are drinking Cokes in the dark, blinds pulled so as to protect a photosensitive experiment, and he mentions that you remind him of his daughter—same smile, he says. You ask her name, her age, and he stands up and wipes his palms on his khakis. "She died in a bicycle accident," he says, pulling the blinds up and spoiling the experiment with light. "Eight years old."

The Coke turns syrupy in your mouth. You don't speak of her again, and he continues to let you help after school, telling you to think of the lab as one big sandbox. When it comes time to apply to college, he recommends the Ångström School for the Alchemical Arts and in the same breath reveals he has some sway with the board. He'd be happy to make a phone call, he says; he's never had a student so enormously talented.

The school emerges from the woods of a small New England town, woods the Masters encourage you to lose yourself in as you seek spiritual enlightenment. There's a taco joint and a Vietnamese restaurant and one pub called Au79, which everyone refers to, naturally, as Oh-69 (try your hardest not to be overly critical—these are your *people*, after all). A mile or so down the road there are a few husks of defunct factories and a sprawling abandoned insane asylum—only a matter of time, you assume.

Alchemical *Arts*, the Masters remind you during orientation, are not a hard science but something murkier and ineffable. Oh, sure, there are roots in chemistry, but achieving gold requires a kind of "loosening of the soul" that few people are actually capable of. But that's why you're here and not at MIT hammering away at your Ph.D.—we should say, though, that those hammerers might make great providers later in life; the great irony is there's not a lot of money in alchemy, hahaha! A collective chuckle fills the room, but you feel a tug, an unspoken kinship with the undesirable hammerers. Keep this quiet. Sense you should be ashamed, that you should project a holier-than-thou attitude of Alchemy or Bust. Of course, the Masters continue, there's a great debate about whether this "loosening of the soul" can in fact be taught. They clear their throats and there's a collective plummeting of stomachs; the temperature of the room drops. A competitive edge kicks you in the stomach, sharp and fetal.

That first night you and your fellow students gather for beers at Oh-69. Everyone has such a juicy origin story, each one irritatingly told: This one talks about apprenticing with the great Master Fjorlief Beurling but insists on referring to him as simply "Fjorlief"; this one has synesthesia and insists that "sight is nothing more than a construct." Internships in Scandinavia, names on papers, works already published. What have you ever done, with your two parents and

Juniper and your beloved chemistry teacher? The night devolves into a debate over the merits of alchemy itself: arcane, chemical advances good for science, will probably save lives someday (*how?* You do not ask). Ångström > Shakespeare, etc., etc. Keep your mouth shut. You're only here because you look like a dead girl on a bicycle.

When everyone has moved on to the who-will-fuck-whom portion of the evening, the boy across the bar plays his trump card, hoarded until the perfect moment: "I didn't want to advertise, but I'm *actually* a descendant of Tesla." Roll your eyes, and as you do, make eye contact with one bespectacled boy across the room. An ally. A *muscular* ally. Smile big, your stomach starting to bubble, your crotch heated over low flame.

The lab is underground, temperature-controlled, protected from sunlight. The equipment looks like a jungle gym: Master Salcedo, your lab instructor, has set up an apparatus of shapely flasks connected by whirligigs of tubes and rubber bladders and shiny copper coils. The rounded sides of enormous alembics give way to distillation pipes, creating slides for melted liquids; thin glass tubes bulge in the middle like pythons mid-digestion. Before class starts, tap a glass chamber with the ring you wear on your fourth finger, right hand, and when the glass speaks back to you with a clean, high ping, realize you've never seen such beautiful objects in your whole life. Wish you could be zapped with a shrink ray and scramble inside these instruments. Better yet, that you could transmute into metal itself and luge through these vessels as you change from solid to vapor to liquid, on your way to something gold.

Master Salcedo has blond hair and fabulous shoes, ice-blue eyes, and a slight Spanish accent. She's got an impressive résumé—she's the youngest woman ever to achieve gold (supposedly less radiant than Ångström's, but still), and her new project involves farming rubies. Rumor has it she's in the market for a research assistant. The competitive edge is kicking, wanting, hungry.

None of you is shooting for actual gold just yet. Instead, the philosophy behind the school is to develop an understanding of reactions through following old recipes of former Masters. At best you'll develop something special of your own in the process; at worst you'll be a third-rate ape. Either way, the school gets paid. Task: Create the Elixir of Thorngal to understand the complex interactions between sophic mercury, Doves of Diana, and luna moth wings. Easy enough—you've got a recipe right in front of you—but as you begin, your mind grows unable to focus on the object in front of you, instead perceiving only its edges. Begin to think of this condition as Slippery Mind: as though your brain and the work you must do are repellent magnets, forever dancing around each other. In private, start slapping yourself in the face, the same way your father used to bang on the snowy television. Wonder how on earth that insane asylum went out of business.

On the rare occasion you can concentrate, you are plagued by the voice of a pesky juvenile, who insists on narrating everything you're doing: "I'm crushing moth wings! I'm pouring moth wings into an alembic! I'm creating the Elixir of Thorngal!" *as* you're doing it, thus distracting you from the actual creation and wrecking your results. The moth wings float on top of the mixture like silty coffee. The Fellow Eye-Roller's solution shines the color of opals. He receives praise and a pat on the shoulder from Master Salcedo; her hand lingers a little too long on the roundness of his shoulder. Bitch. Stupid smart bitch.

Amateur hour continued: The following month you blow up a flask. You've zoned out, transfixed by the fire's light and the quick shifts of the solution's color—so pretty, green as dandelion stems—when you feel the glass start to crackle in your hand. You know it will explode the second before it does, and you drop it just as the boiling liquid overheats and sends shards of glass singing across the room. Your classmates hit the floor and a shrieking scream erupts that you realize is your own, and as you cover your eyes you understand that this noise, this *caterwauling*, is your plane-crash scream, your caught-in-a-bombing scream, your gang-raped-and-on-your-way-to-a-violent-end scream. The sound of your own terror, you think; you can recognize it now. Your tuition dollars at work.

At Oh-69 that night, *Actually* a Descendant of Tesla mentions a study published in a fly-by-night journal that shows a correlation between lab accidents and lunar cycles.

"And I think we know what they mean by *lunar cycles*," he says. Pour your beer straight into his crotch and walk home shaking and alone, terrified and powerful.

After the Beer Incident, the Fellow Eye-Roller forges a bond with you over your shared hatred of *Actually* a Descendant of Tesla. He likes that you gave him "what for." Report to each other the things that he's said in class, or how he claims to have already locked up the position as Master Salcedo's lab assistant. Stroll through the woods together, which you hadn't explored yet, despite the Masters' urgings. Yeah, yeah, meditations and spiritual purification are critical to the process, "loosening the soul," blah, blah, fucking blah. As far as you can tell, all anyone is doing in these woods is hooking up and getting high off stolen bee venom.

In the woods, your mutual hostility blooms into lust that feels a lot like love. Confess, in one of these early walks, the words erupting from you like a frog's tongue, that you're not sure what you're doing here, that dumping that beer in that guy's lap wasn't you, that you're not sure where this violence comes from, that your chemistry teacher only liked you because—

He'll cut you off with a kiss, which seems romantic at the time.

What does Loren's Tincture matter compared to this, the poetry of two bodies together, the feeling of bubbles in your blood? Besides, your boyfriend is a very good young alchemist and perhaps sex has undiscovered osmotic properties. And let's not forget he is very muscular: bonus! Ångström himself spoke of the transformative power of love, and God knows volumes have been written about his beloved Mara, who reportedly blew on all his hot food before serving it to him. You bomb a few more labs and are energized by how little you care. And why should you; you're the next incarnation of Mara! You're not an alchemist, but you're something better, you're a goddamned muse! Focus: Think about fucking him every second of every day, including when you are fucking him. Tend ferociously to his needs. Nights, let him leave the bedroom light on so he can work. Sometimes you wake up, the fluorescents wreaking havoc on your circadian rhythms, the stacks of paper next to him growing taller and taller, and you're overcome by a sudden desire to smash his head in with your bedside lamp.

The violence continues to come in contractions, bolts of ambition and hate so thick they scare you. Memorize the Fenske equation, Rauolt's law, Dalton's law, the properties of reflux. Alone, you know how important these are to your future career. Fuck that dead girl on a bicycle; fuck Tesla; fuck your idiot boyfriend—there will be an equation named after you someday, ME; you can see the shapes and numbers swirling before your eyes. Or you'll name it Mara's equation and finally give that woman her due—you're doing this for her now, you're in this together! Solidarity! Womenfolk! If you close your eyes you can see it, molten and red-hot, poured from an iron flask into a cooling pan and turning into a brilliant element of your own making, something better than gold—the aurora borealis, perhaps, turned solid. Why not? Why not you?

But more often than not, you gaze out the window and imagine life as something else, anything else, a florist maybe, Tuesday morning, the tulip guy late again, that rat bastard.

Weeks pass. There is weather. In lab, you develop headaches from sneaking glances at others' solutions. Everyone else's looks better, shinier. Master Salcedo tells you over and over that in order to succeed you must love the process and not the result, but mother of God, the process is so boring: melting and waiting and chopping and adding and waiting, distillation one, remelting and rewaiting, sneaking a glance, hating Tesla, distillation two, your face full of acne, your stomach growling. The routine just makes you sad and bored, and how can you enjoy that? This is the process they tell you to love: everything you think has the potential to be brilliant congeals in an ugly way, stuck to the bottom of a flask like lard.

Find yourself flummoxed by the concept of talent. Did you ever have it? Is it still there somewhere inside of you, singular and shiny and hard as a marble? In a moment of desperation, make an appointment to meet with Master Salcedo. Her office is ten thousand degrees and she's drinking hot, hot tea that smells like pine trees. She offers you some, which you immediately regret accepting. The gangplank of her desk stretches between you. You should have prepared something to say. How have you prepared nothing to say?

"What can I do for you?" she asks. She's open and inviting, but even before you speak to her, you sense that the two of you will miss each other slightly, your conversation a broken seat belt. You miss your chemistry teacher with a fierceness that you didn't know existed. Her question, admittedly, is a good one. What do you want from this woman, really? For her to hand you a talent marble and say, Here, take this, swallow?

You wind up talking about her childhood in Madrid, her tailor father and her schoolteacher mother, but how she sensed in her core that *this* was the life she wanted. You mention crying over Ångström's death as a baby and she chuckles. A moment of hope: Perhaps the two of you might have the relationship you had with chemistry teacher after all. You'll grow to love pine-tree tea and she'll loan you her shoes and teach you how to walk in high heels. "Truthfully," she says, sipping her tea, "it made a big difference in my work when I considered that no one cared what I was doing. Gold already exists in our universe. What does it matter if I make my own. Why care at all?" She shrugs. "Liberating, no? To let go of the caring?"

"Liberating," you agree. (*I care,* says a tiny voice inside you, a feeble rodent of a thing.)

Your body recedes under a puffy jacket, which you wear even as the cold weather starts to lift. You cannot remember the last time you shaved. You bet Mara shaved, even when she was exhausted from cutting the crusts off Ångström's sandwiches. Not that shaving really matters, since your boyfriend does not seem to recognize you as a muse. In fact he complains that you are too affectionate and says he prefers the crusts *on*, Jesus. Once, over egg salad, attempt to talk to him about how much you miss your chemistry teacher—though perhaps, you say now, there was just some strange Oedipal drama being played out between the two of you. Sigh. Maybe there are some people in the world we just *click* with, you say, but where are they and how do we find them, and is it okay if we find them because of our Oedipus complexes? He gets a kind of glazed expression and then snaps back in, saying, "Sorry, sorry, I just remembered I have to take something to the post office."

A shame that despite how little work you do, you're not even at the bottom of the barrel. *That* would be an honorific you could jump into and splash around in. Instead you're middle of the road and it's Deirdre DeMarco, who now sports a permanent frown and bags under her eyes so big they'll have to be checked on her next flight home. Deirdre DeMarco, a failure so enviously obvious. Deirdre DeMarco, who in spite of it all works with a stoic commitment and talks about her solutions as though she "gave birth to them." Deirdre DeMarco, who'd never conduct secret and exhaustive research into nearby florist shops that are hiring for the summer. Who'd never make a call to Cheryl's in the next town over, past the insane asylum, and set up an interview, sweat pouring from her armpits, her heart pumping like a jackhammer.

Imagine it: Cheryl will have a green apron and friendly moles, eleven on the right side of her face alone. You'll bike to the shop every day, giving the finger to the insane asylum as you cruise past. You'll grow tan and muscular and deft with dried lavender. You will finally have finished products, objects you can hold: prom corsages and floral crowns and wedding bouquets, all artfully accessorized with twigs and pussy willows and yellow billy balls. On exceptionally hot days, you'll jump naked in the green river that runs behind her shop. Maybe you'll move to the Pacific Northwest. You've always thought you might like it there.

And of course, *of course*, right when you've been buoyed along by this dream, you'll have your breakthrough. You're working with gold seed for the first time in lab and your interview is in two days; you heat and distill your sophic mercury while practicing answers to potential interview questions. Outside the lab, it's sunny and you're struck by what seems like the very dumb idea that maybe your solution could do with a little sunshine (in fact, you are inspired by the memory of an off-brand orange juice commercial that regrettably states "Everyone Needs a Little D!" but you leave this out later when you recount the story). So you carry your flask outside and hold it up to the sun for ten minutes, smiling stupidly.

When you return to the lab the following morning, the gold seed and the mercury have sprouted into a tiny silver forest. Crystalline branches and leaves stretch to scrape the bulbed edge of the glass; when you turn the flask in your hands, the branches glitter slightly, as though they are fake snowy pines in a Christmas diorama. It's not gold, but it's *something*. Look around the room: The alchemical forest is in your flask and no one else's. Double check. That thing of beauty? In your flask, and no one else's. You can hardly believe it. Is this what they mean when they say "loosening the soul"—allowing yourself to blunder upon something wondrous and claim it as genius, the thing you were intending all along?

Smile. Laugh. You are on your way. You are on your motherfucking, arbitrary way.

Of course, this so-called way means years of work of cleaning out tubes and breaking them in frustration and cutting yourself by accident, of gaining and losing the same twenty pounds, of suffering through bad relationships and ending good ones for no reason. Often you will look back on this moment with the sunlight and you will hate it for its simplicity, even when you recognize it as the seed of all things good in your life. Every other success (and there will be a few, your career will not be without success) will fail to measure up—you will learn to find a certain pleasure in the work, but nothing will ever feel as good as the thing that came to you like a gift. You will lay your head on your desk and a million failed ideas will percolate around you, a constellation of zits forming on your forehead, your husband pissed off about something, kids at home with the babysitter, breakfast for dinner *again*?

But for now, the breakthrough will be enough to sustain you; enough to make you choose instead of flounder. Master Salcedo will want to know if you've given any thought to your summer plans. She's looking for a research assistant. Breaking up with Cheryl is harder than breaking up with your boyfriend. Cheryl:

the one that got away, the ghost life that you will always dream of, never sure if your excitement over a life among flowers was an eject button or what was right (an eject button, you'll think firmly, in order to get by). Put your work first; channel the violence that runs through you into something useful. Start to get it, the long nights spent in the lab, the tired feeling of being on your feet all day, the handfuls of granola eaten for dinner. Try to hold on to your first day walking into the lab and imagining a shrunken life inside flasks: how badly you wanted that! It's worth it, you tell yourself, for the glimmer you sometimes think you see hidden in a normal solution.

From *Esopus 7* (2006)

Spellbound

BY MITCH HOROWITZ

Ouija. For some, the rectangular board evokes memories of late-night sleepover parties, shrieks of laughter, and toy shelves brimming with Magic Eight Balls, Frisbees, and Barbie dolls.

For others, Ouija boards—known more generally as talking boards or spirit boards—have darker associations. Stories abound of fearsome entities making threats, dire predictions, and even physical assaults on innocent users after a night of Ouija experimentation.

And the fantastic claims don't stop there: Pulitzer Prize–winning poet James Merrill vowed until his death in 1995 that his most celebrated work was written with the use of a homemade Ouija board.

For my part, I first discovered the mysterious workings of Ouija nearly 20 years ago during a typically freezing-cold winter on eastern Long Island. While heaters clanked and hummed within the institutional-white walls of my college dormitory, friends allayed boredom with a Parker Brothers Ouija board.

As is often the case with Ouija, one young woman became the ringleader of board readings. She reprised the role of spirit medium that had characteristically fallen to women in past eras, when the respectable clergy was a male-only affair. Under the gaze of her dark eyes—which others said gave them chills—the late-night Ouija sessions came into vogue.

Most of my evenings were given over to editing the college newspaper, but I often arrived home at the dorm to frightening stories: The board, one night, kept spelling out the name "Seth," which my friends associated with evil (probably connecting it with the malevolent Egyptian god Set, who is seen as a Satan prototype). When asked, "Who's Seth?" the board directed its attention to a member of the group and repeatedly replied: "Ask Carlos." A visibly shaken Carlos began breathing heavily and refused to answer.

Consumed as I was with exposing scandals within the campus food service,

I never took the opportunity to sit in on these séances—a move I came to regard with a mixture of relief and regret. The idea that a mass-produced game board and its plastic pointer could display some occult faculty, or could tap into a user's subconscious, got under my skin.

And I wasn't alone: In its heyday, Ouija outsold Monopoly. Ouija boards have sharply declined in popularity since the 1960s and '70s, when you could find one in nearly every toy-cluttered basement. But they remain among the most peculiar consumer items in American history. Indeed, controversy endures to this day over their origin. To get a better sense of what Ouija boards are—and where they came from—requires going back to an era in which even an American president dabbled in talking to the dead.

Spiritualism Triumphant

Today, it is difficult to imagine the popularity enjoyed by the movement called Spiritualism in the 19th century, when table rapping, séances, medium trances, and other forms of contacting the "other side" were practiced by an estimated 10 percent of the American population. It began in 1848 when the teenage sisters Kate and Margaret Fox introduced "spirit rapping" to a lonely hamlet in upstate New York called Hydesville. While every age and culture had known hauntings, Spiritualism appeared to foster actual communication with the beyond. Within a few years, people from every walk of life took seriously the contention that one could talk to the dead.

For many, Spiritualism seemed to extend the hope of reaching loved ones, and perhaps easing the pain of losing a child to one of the diseases of the day. The allure of immortality or of feeling oneself lifted beyond workaday realities attracted others. For others still, spirit counsels became a way to cope with anxiety about the future, providing otherworldly advice in matters of health, love, or money.

According to newspaper accounts of the era, President Abraham Lincoln hosted a séance in the White House—though more as a good-humored parlor game than as a serious spiritual inquiry. Yet at least one vividly rendered Spiritualist memoir places a trance medium in the private quarters of the White House, advising the president and Mrs. Lincoln just after the outbreak of the Civil War.

Making Contact

In this atmosphere of ghostly knocks and pleas to hidden forces, 19th-century occultists began looking for easier ways to communicate with the beyond. And in the best American fashion, they took a do-it-yourself approach to the matter. Their homespun efforts at contacting the spirit world led toward something we call Ouija—but not until they worked through several other methods.

One involved a form of table rapping in which questioners solicited spirit knocks when letters of the alphabet were called out, thus spelling a word. This was, however, a tedious and time-consuming exercise. A faster means was "automatic writing," in which spirit beings could communicate through the pen of a channeler; some complained, however, that this produced many pages of unclear or meandering prose.

One invention directly prefigured the heart-shaped pointer that moves around the Ouija board. The planchette—French for "little plank"—was a three-legged writing tool with a hole at the top for the insertion of a pencil. The planchette was designed for one person or more to rest their fingers on it and allow it to "glide" across a page, writing out a spirit message. The device originated in Europe in the early 1850s; by 1860 commercially manufactured planchettes were advertised in America.

Two other items from the 1850s are direct forebears of Ouija: "dial plates" and alphabet paste boards. In 1853 a Connecticut Spiritualist invented the Spiritual Telegraph Dial, a roulette-like wheel with letters and numerals around its circumference. Dial plates came in various forms, sometimes of a complex variety. Some were rigged to tables to respond to "spirit tilts," while others were presumably guided—like a planchette—by the hands of questioners.

Alphabet boards further simplified matters. In use as early as 1852, these talking-board precursors allowed seekers to point to a letter as a means of prompting a spirit rap, thereby quickly spelling a word. It was, perhaps, the easiest method yet. And it was only a matter of time until inventors and entrepreneurs began to see the possibilities.

Baltimore Oracles

More than 150 years after the dawn of the Spiritualist era, contention endures today over who created Ouija. The conventional history of American toy manufacturing credits a Baltimore businessman named William Fuld. Fuld was said to have invented Ouija around 1890. So it is repeated online and in books of trivia, reference works, and "ask me" columns in newspapers. For many decades, the manufacturer itself—first Fuld's company and later the toy giant Parker Brothers—insinuated as much by running the words "William Fuld

Talking Board Set" across the top of every board.

The conventional history is wrong.

The patent for a "Ouija or Egyptian luck-board" was filed on May 28, 1890, by Baltimore resident and patent attorney Elijah H. Bond, who assigned the rights to two city businessmen, Charles W. Kennard and William H. A. Maupin. The patent was granted on February 10, 1891, and so was born the Ouija-brand talking board.

The first patent reveals a familiarly oblong board, with the alphabet running in double rows across the top, and numbers in a single row along the bottom. The sun and moon, marked respectively by the words "yes" and "no," adorn the upper left and right corners, while the words "Good bye" appear at the bottom center. Later instructions, and the illustrations accompanying them, prescribed an expressly social, even flirtatious, experience: Two parties, preferably a man and woman, were to balance the board between them on their knees, placing their fingers lightly upon the planchette. (Subsequent instructions read, "It draws the two people using it into close companionship and weaves about them a feeling of mysterious isolation.") In an age of buttoned-up morals, it was a tempting dalliance.

True Origins

The Kennard Novelty Company of Baltimore employed a teenaged varnisher who helped run shop operations, and this was William Fuld. By 1892, however, Charles W. Kennard's partners removed him from the company amid financial disputes, and a new patent—this time for an improved pointer, or planchette—was filed by 19-year-old Fuld. In years to come, it was Fuld who would take over the novelty firm and affix his name to every board.

Inventor's credit sometimes goes to an E.C. Reichie, identified variously as a Maryland cabinetmaker or coffin maker. This theory was popularized by a now-defunct Baltimore business monthly called *Warfield's*, which ran a richly detailed—and at points, one suspects, richly imagined—history of Ouija boards in 1990. The article opens with a misspelled E.C. "Reiche" as the board's inventor, and calls him a coffin maker with an interest in the afterlife—a name and a claim that have been repeated and circulated ever since.

Yet this figure appears virtually nowhere else in Ouija history, including on the first patent. His name came up during a period of patent litigation about 30 years after Ouija's inception. A 1920 account in *New York World* magazine—widely disseminated that year in the popular weekly *The Literary Digest*—

reports that one of Ouija's early investors told a judge that E.C. Reichie had invented the board. But no reference to an E.C. Reichie, be he a cabinetmaker or coffin maker, appears in the court transcript, according to Ouija historian and talking-board manufacturer Robert Murch.

Ultimately, Reichie's role—or whether Reichie existed at all—may be moot, at least in terms of the board's invention. Talking boards of a homemade variety were already a popular craze among Spiritualists by the mid-1880s. At his online Museum of Talking Boards, Ouija collector and chronicler Eugene Orlando posts an 1886 article from the *New-York Daily Tribune* (as reprinted that year in a Spiritualist monthly, *The Carrier Dove*) describing the breathless excitement around the newfangled alphabet board and its message indicator. "I know of whole communities that are wild over the 'talking board,'" says a man in the article. This was a full four years before the first Ouija patent was filed. Obviously Bond, Kennard, and their associates were capitalizing on an invention—not conceiving one.

And what of the name Ouija? At times pronounced "wee-JA" and at others "wee-GEE," its origin may never be known. Kennard at one time claimed it was Egyptian for "good luck" (it isn't). Fuld later said it was simply a marriage of the French and German words for "yes." One early investor claimed the board spelled out its own name. As with other aspects of Ouija history, the board seems determined to withhold a few secrets of its own.

Ancient Ouija?

Another oft-repeated, but misleading, claim is that Ouija, or talking boards, have ancient roots. In a typical example, Frank Gaynor's 1953 *Dictionary of Mysticism* states that primeval boards of different shapes and sizes "were used in the 6th century before Christ." In a wide range of books and articles, everyone from Pythagoras to the Mongols to the ancient Egyptians is said to have possessed Ouija-like devices. But the claims rarely withstand scrutiny.

Chronicler-curator Orlando points out that the primary reference to Ouija existing in the premodern world appears in a passage from Lewis Spence's 1920 *Encyclopedia of Occultism*—which is repeated in Nandor Fodor's popular 1934 *Encyclopedia of Psychic Science*. The Fodor passage reads, in part: "As an invention it is very old. It was in use in the days of Pythagoras, about 540 B.C. According to a French historical account of the philosopher's life, his sect held frequent séances or circles at which 'a mystic table, moving on wheels, moved towards signs, which the philosopher and his pupil Philolaus, interpreted to the audience.'" It is, Orlando points out, "the one recurring quote found in almost every academic article on the Ouija board." But the story presents two problems: The source of the French historical account is never identified, and the Pythagorean scribe Philolaus was not a contemporary of Pythagoras, but rather was born 20 years after his death.

It is also worth keeping in mind that we know precious little today about Pythagoras and his school. No writings by Pythagoras survive, and the historical record depends upon later works, some of which were written centuries after his death. Hence, commentators on occult topics are sometimes tempted to project backward onto Pythagoras all sorts of arcane practices, Ouija and modern numerology among them.

Still other writers—when they are not repeating claims like the one above—tend to misread ancient historical accounts and mistake other divinatory tools, such as pendulum dishes, for Ouija boards. Oracles were rich and varied from culture to culture—from Germanic runes to Greek Delphic rites—but the prevailing literature on oracular traditions supports no suggestion that talking boards, as we know them, were in use before the Spiritualist era.

Ouija Boom

After William Fuld took the reins of Ouija manufacturing in America, business was brisk, if not always happy. Fuld formed a quickly shattered business alliance with his brother Isaac, which landed the two in court battles for nearly 20 years. Isaac was eventually found to have violated an injunction against creating a competing board, called the Oriole, after being forced from the family business in 1901. The two brothers would never speak again. Ouija, and anything that looked directly like it, was firmly in the hands of William Fuld.

By 1920, the board was so well known that artist Norman Rockwell painted a send-up of a couple using one—the woman dreamy and credulous, the man fixing her with a cloying grin—for a cover of *The Saturday Evening Post*. For Fuld, though, everything was strictly business. "Believe in the Ouija board?" he once told a reporter. "I should say not. I'm no spiritualist. I'm a Presbyterian—been one ever since I was so high." In 1920, the *Baltimore Sun* reported that Fuld, by his own "conservative estimate," had pocketed more than $1 million from sales.

Whatever satisfaction Fuld's success may have brought him was soon lost: On February 26, 1927, he fell to his death from the roof of his Baltimore factory. The 54-year-old manufacturer was supervising the replacement of a flagpole when an iron support bar he held gave way, and he fell backward three stories.

Fuld's children took over his business and generally prospered. While sales dipped and rose, and competing boards came and went, only the Ouija brand endured. And by the 1940s, Ouija was experiencing a new surge in popularity.

Historically, séances and other Spiritualist methods proliferate during times of war. Spiritualism had seen its last great explosion of interest in the period around World War I, when parents yearned to contact children lost to the battle- field carnage. During World War II, many anxious families turned to Ouija. In a 1944 article titled "The Ouija Comes Back," *The New York Times* reported that one New York City department store alone sold 50,000 Ouija boards in a five-month period.

American toy manufacturers were taking notice. Some attempted knockoff products. But Parker Brothers developed bigger plans. In a move that would place a carryover from the age of Spiritualism into playrooms all across America, the toy giant bought the rights for an undisclosed sum in 1966. The Fuld family was out of the picture, and Ouija was about to achieve its biggest success ever.

The following year, Parker Brothers is reported to have sold more than two million Ouija boards, topping sales of its most popular game, Monopoly. The occult boom that began in the late 1960s, with astrologers adorning the cover of *Time* magazine and witchcraft becoming a fast-growing "new" religion, fueled the board's sales for the following decades. A Parker spokesperson says the company has sold over 10 million boards since 1967.

The '60s and '70s also saw the rise of Ouija as a product of the youth culture. Ouija circles sprang up in college dormitories, and the board emerged as a fad among adolescents, for whom its ritual of secret messages and intimate communications became a form of rebellion. One youthful experimenter recalls an enticing atmosphere of danger and intrigue—"like shoplifting or taking drugs"—that allowed her and a girlfriend to bond together over Ouija sessions. Sociologists suggested that Ouija sessions were a way for young people to project, and work through, their own fears. But many claimed that the verisimilitude of the communications was reason enough to return to the board.

Ouija Today

While officials at Parker Brothers (now a division of Hasbro) would not get into the ebb and flow of sales, there's little question that Ouija's popularity has declined precipitously in recent years. In 1999, the company brought an era to an end when it discontinued the vintage Fuld design and switched to a smaller, glow-in-the-dark version of the board. In consumer manufacturing, the redesign of a classic product often signals an effort to reverse falling sales. Listed at $19.95, Ouija costs about 60 percent more than standards like Monopoly and Scrabble, which further suggests that it has become something of a specialty item.

In a far remove from the days when Ouija led Parker Brothers' lineup, the product now seems more like a corporate stepchild. The Ouija Game ("ages 8 to Adult") merits barely a mention on Hasbro's website. The company posts no official history for Ouija, as it does for its other storied products. And the claims from the original 1960s box—"Weird and mysterious. Surpasses, in its unique results, mind reading, clairvoyance and second sight"—have been significantly toned down. Given the negative attention the board sometimes attracts—from both frightened users and religionists who smell a whiff of Satan's doings—Ouija, its sales likely on the wane, may be a product that Hasbro would just as soon forget.

And yet...Ouija receives more customer reviews—by turns written in tones of outrage, fear, delight, or ridicule—than any other "toy" for sale on Amazon (280 at last count). What other game so polarizes opinion among those who dismiss it as a childish plaything and those who condemn or extol it as a portal to the other side? As it did decades ago in *The Exorcist*, Ouija figures into the recent fright films *What Lies Beneath* and *White Noise*. And it sustains an urban mythology that continues to make it a household name in the early 21st century. There would seem little doubt that Ouija—as it has arisen time and again—awaits a revival in the future. But what makes this game board and its molded plastic pointer so resilient in our culture, and, some might add, in our nightmares?

An Occult Splendor?

Among the first things one notices when looking into Ouija is its vast, and sometimes authentically frightening, history of stories. Claims abound from users who felt they had experienced the presence of malevolent entities during Ouija sessions, sometimes even describing being physically harassed by unseen forces. A typical story line might involve communication that is at first reassuring and even useful—a lost object perhaps recovered—but that eventually gives way to threatening or terrorizing messages. Hugh Lynn Cayce, son of the American psychic Edgar Cayce, cautioned that his research found Ouija boards to be among the most "dangerous doorways to the unconscious."

For their part, Ouija enthusiasts note that teachings such as the inspirational "Seth material," channeled by Jane Roberts, first came through a Ouija board.

Other channeled writings, such as an early 20th-century series of novels and poems by Patience Worth, a disembodied spirit, and a posthumous "novel" by Mark Twain (pulled from the shelves after a legal outcry from the writer's estate), have reputedly come through the board. Such works, however, have rarely attracted enduring readerships. Poets Sylvia Plath and Ted Hughes wrote haunting and dark passages about their experiences with Ouija, but none attain the level of their best work.

So, can anything of lasting value be attributed to the board—this mysterious object that has, in one form or another, been with us for nearly 120 years? The answer is yes, and it has stared us in the face for so long that we have nearly forgotten it is there.

In 1977, the American poet James Merrill published—and won the Pulitzer Prize for—a poetry collection that included an epic poem that recounted his experience, with his partner David Jackson, of using a Ouija board from 1955 to 1974. This work, *The Book of Ephraim,* was later combined with two other Ouija-inspired long poems and published in 1982 as *The Changing Light at Sandover*. "Many readers," wrote critic Judith Moffett in her penetrating study titled *James Merrill*, "may well feel they have been waiting for this trilogy all their lives."

First using a manufactured board and then a homemade one—with a teacup in the place of a planchette—Merrill and Jackson encounter a world of spirit "patrons" who recount to them a sprawling and profoundly involving creation myth. It is poetry steeped in the epic tradition, in which myriad characters—from W.H. Auden to lost friends and family members and a Greek muse and interlocutor called Ephraim—walk on- and offstage. The voices of Merrill, Jackson, and those that emerge from the teacup and board offer theories of reincarnation, worldly advice, and painfully poignant reflections on the passing of life and ever-hovering presence of death.

The Changing Light at Sandover gives life to a new mythology of world creation, destruction, resurrection, and the vast, unknowable mechanizations of God Biology (GOD B, in the words of the Ouija board) and those mysterious figures who enact his will: bat-winged creatures who, in their cosmological laboratory, reconstruct departed souls for new life on earth. And yet we are never far from the human, grounding voice of Merrill, joking about the selection of new wallpaper in his Stonington, Connecticut, home; or from the moving council of voices from the board, urging: In life, one must stand for something.

"It is common knowledge—and glaringly obvious in the poems, though not taken seriously by his critics—that these three works, and their final compilation, were based on conversations...through a Ouija board," wrote John Chambers in his outstanding analysis of Merrill in the Summer 1997 issue of *The Anomalist*.

Critic Harold Bloom, in a departure from others who sidestep the question of the work's source, calls the first of the *Sandover* poems "an occult splendor." Indeed, it is not difficult to argue that, in literary terms, *The Changing Light at Sandover* is a masterpiece—perhaps *the* masterpiece—of occult experimentation. In some respects, it is like an unintended response to Mary Shelley's *Frankenstein*, in which not one man acting alone, but two acting and thinking together, pierce the veil of life's inner and cosmic mysteries—and live not only to tell, but to teach.

One wonders, then, why the work is so little known and read within a spiritual subculture that embraces other channeled works, such as the Ouija-received "Seth material," the automatic writing of *A Course in Miracles*, or the currently popular Abraham Hicks–channeled readings. *The Changing Light at Sandover* ought to be evidence that something, be it inner or outer, is available through this kind of communication, however rare. It is up to the reader to find out what.

Voices Within?

Of course, the Merrill case prompts the question of whether the Ouija board channels something from beyond or merely reflects the ideas found in one's subconscious. After all, who but a poetic genius like James Merrill could have recorded channeled passages of such literary grace and epic dimension? Plainly put, this wasn't Joe Schmoe at the board.

In a 1970 book on psychical phenomena, *ESP, Seers & Psychics*, researcher and skeptic Milbourne Christopher announces—a tad too triumphantly, perhaps—that if you effectively blindfold a board's user and rearrange the order of letters, communication ceases. A believable enough claim, but what does it really tell us? In 1915, a specialist in abnormal psychology proposed the same test to the channeled entity called Patience Worth, who, through a St. Louis housewife named Pearl Curran, had produced a remarkable range of novels, plays, and poems—some of them hugely ambitious in scale and written in a Middle English dialect that Curran (who didn't finish high school) would have had no means of knowing.

As reported in Irving Litvag's 1972 study, *Singer in the Shadows*, Patience Worth responded to the request that Curran be blindfolded in her typically inimitable fashion: "I be aset athin the throb o' her. Aye, and doth thee to take then the lute awhither that she see not, think ye then she may to set up musics for the hear o' thee?" In other words, how can you remove the instrument and expect music?

Some authorities in psychical research support the contention that Ouija is a tool of our subconscious. For years J.B. Rhine, the veritable dean of psychical research in America, worked with his wife, Louisa Rhine, a trained biologist and well-regarded researcher in her own right, to bring scientific rigor to the study of psychical phenomena. Responding to the occult fads of the day, Louisa wrote an item on Ouija boards and automatic writing adapted in the winter 1970 newsletter of the American Society for Psychical Research. Whatever messages come through the board, she maintained, are a product of the user's subconscious—not any metaphysical force: "In several ways the very nature of automatic writing and the Ouija board makes them particularly open to misunderstanding. For one thing, because [such communications] are unconscious, the person does not get the feeling of his own involvement. Instead, it seems to him that some personality outside of himself is responsible. In addition, and possibly because of this, the material is usually cast in a form as if originating from another intelligence."

For his part, Merrill took a subtler view of the matter. "If it's still yourself that you're drawing upon," he said, "then that self is much stranger and freer and more far-seeking than the one you thought you knew." And at another point: "If the spirits aren't external, how astonishing the mediums become!"

To Ouija or Not to Ouija

As I was preparing for this article, I began to revisit notes I had made months earlier. These presented me with several questions. Among them: Should I be practicing with the Ouija board myself, testing its occult powers in person? Just at this time, I received an email, impeccably and even mysteriously timed, warning me off Ouija boards. The sender, whom I didn't know, told in sensitive and vivid tones of her family's harrowing experiences with a board.

As my exchange with the sender continued, however, my relatively few lines of response elicited pages and pages of material, each progressively more pedantic and judgmental in tone, reading—or projecting—multiple levels into what little I had written in reply (most of which was in appreciation). And so I wondered: In terms of the influences to which we open ourselves, how do we sort out the fine from the coarse, allowing in communications that are useful and generative, rather than those that become simply depleting?

Ouija is intriguing, interesting, even oddly magnetic: A survey of users in the

2001 *International Journal of Parapsychology* found that half "felt a compulsion to use it." But in a culture filled with possibilities, and in a modern life of limited time and energy, is Ouija really the place to search? Clearly, for James Merrill, it was. But there exists a deeper intuition than what comes through a board, or through any outer object—one that answers that kind of question for every clear-thinking person. For me, the answer was no.

It was time to pack up my antique Ouija board in its box and return to what I found most lasting on the journey: The work of Merrill, who passed through the uses of this instrument and, in so doing, created a body of art that perhaps justifies the tumultuous, serpentine history from which Ouija has come.

Three Poems

BY NICOLE SEALEY

UNFRAMED

Handle this body. Spoil it
with oils. Let the residue
corrode, ruin it. I have no
finish, no fragile edge. (On
what scrap of me have we
not made desire paths, so
tried as to bury ourselves
therein?) I beg: spare me
gloved hands, monuments
to nothing. I mean to die a
relief against every wall.

AND

Withstand pandemonium
and scandalous
nightstands
commanding candlelight

and
quicksand

and zinfandel
clandestine land mines
candy handfuls
and contraband

and
handmade

commandments
and merchandise
secondhand husbands
philandering

and
landless

and vandal
bandwagons slandered
and branded
handwritten reprimands

and
meander

on an island
landscaped with chandeliers
abandon handcuffs
standstills

and
backhands

notwithstanding
thousands of oleanders
and dandelions
handpicked

and
sandalwood

and mandrake
and random demands
the bystander
wanders

in
wonderland.

UNFURNISHED

Something was said and she felt
a certain way about said something
                                        certain only
that there was no mistaking the feeling
she felt—the sound empty makes inside
            a vacant house.

Cuoca

BY JODY WILLIAMS

On the morning of November 5, 1989, when there were 80 cents to every thousand lira and there was a smoking section on Alitalia, I arrived at Malpensa airport in Milan. Anxious on the flight over, I had scoured the pages of my pocket-size Italian dictionary. I remember managing to learn the word *mele* for apple, but with my inconsistent pronunciation I could have been saying either pig (*maiale*) or honey (*miele*). My knowledge of Italian food, culture, and history was about as extensive as my familiarity with the language.

I moved to Italy to learn how to cook. I had been trying to teach myself for several years beforehand. Just out of college I answered an ad for a steward at the Clift Hotel in San Francisco. My first lowly task at this five-star establishment was to climb up a ladder, jump into a shiny 50-gallon steam kettle, and clean out its lurid contents with a shovel. If it was a veal stock that had been left to simmer overnight, I would be shoveling an unctuous mix of bones, onions, celery, and carrots into the morning garbage. My stay there was relatively short and filled with similarly menial jobs, but it was long enough for me to realize I was finally in my element.

Soon after, I left for New York City to gain some experience as a line cook. I picked up skills quickly; it was the first thing I ever enjoyed studying, maybe because it came to me effortlessly. That is not to say, however, that it was easy. One chef hired me without realizing I was two inches too short to reach his precious copper pots hanging above the stove. I didn't realize this either—until dinnertime. Desperate for a quick solution, I hunted around the kitchen until I found a dirty gray brick in the prep room that I could hide under the stove and use as a step. I worked all evening next to the *poissonnier*, Max, who eventually asked why I was standing on the chef's sharpening stone. The next day I brought a piece of a wooden two-by-four, which I carried around in my pocket for a year.

That particular restaurant proved to be a good starting point for my culinary education. The food, though spectacular, was contrived and complicated. Possessed with a desire to "reimagine" fish and fowl, the chef forced salmon and asparagus into great pyramids and whipped fresh basil leaves into a foamy essence that bathed sea scallops hiding in nests of fried potatoes. He was always immaculately dressed. He tied his ankle-length apron at the waist around his starched white chef's jacket, knotted the apron strings on the side, then tucked them into the apron so they would not escape into sauces or drag across plates. He rarely smiled and never said good morning or good night to the staff. An hour prior to dinner, the chef would check everyone's station, and if he found something under par, like mealy tomato concasse or an insipid sauce, into the garbage it would go. This would send a cook into a panic, scrambling to start over. We served a "family meal" for the staff but no one had time to enjoy it, and during dinner service not a word was spoken. Each day was a test of endurance, both physical and emotional. I'm sure I wasn't the only one to break down and cry in the walk-in box.

A friend of a friend knew a chef who was seeking two cooks to help her prepare five dinners at five different restaurants from Milan to Rome. The purpose of the tour was to promote American food exports—in other words, cornflakes—and the sponsor was an Italian grocery store chain called Coop Italia. One of these dinners was at Caffè Arti e Mestieri, a restaurant located in the historical center of Reggio Emilia, where we were to prepare a five-course American-themed dinner for 150 people. We arrived there early one morning, our translator in tow, to begin preparing the dinner.

It was here that I first met Enzo, the restaurant's chef, standing in his kitchen. By the end of that day, he had invited me to return to Italy and be his *cuoca*, the Italian word for a cook. When I asked him what I would do, he offered one word: "Cook." He spoke very little English. There were few details provided other than that he would pick me up at the airport when I arrived in Milan. I dared myself to go and we shook hands. I returned home to New York to sublet my apartment and quit my job. Sure enough, when I came out of the Malpensa airport a few weeks later, Enzo and the proprietors of Caffè Arti e Mestieri were waiting for me in a white Volvo station wagon. The four of them chain-smoked all the way back to the restaurant as we sped through the foggy Italian countryside at 110 miles per hour.

On my first day, two young cooks shepherded me into the kitchen. They changed into kitchen whites, donning floppy cotton toques and tying old tablecloths around their waists for aprons. (We never were so thrifty at home.) I tied on my tablecloth and quietly followed the cooks through their morning chores.

Enzo's rectangular kitchen had a gleaming 14-foot line consisting of an oven, a fryer, eight gas burners, a *piastra* (griddle), and a pasta boiler. In front of this line rested an eight-foot-long stainless-steel island with refrigeration below and shelves built above for storing and drying pasta. A cocktail bar and espresso machine stood on the other side of the island. At one end of the kitchen, *prosciutto di Parma* was sliced and appetizers were made, and on the other, dishes were washed and dried. The dinners we prepared left the kitchen in a dumbwaiter for the dining room on the second floor. A deep prep-sink, which I spent a lot of time huddled over, cleaning artichokes and fish, anchored one corner. The kitchen was contemporary and beautifully designed, but still, there was something peculiar about it—something I couldn't quite place.

When I first met Enzo, he was in his late 30s. He had long hair that fell almost to his waist. In the kitchen he either tied it back into a ponytail or twisted it up into a bun and held it there with a pencil. Six feet tall, he would gain and lose the same extra 50 pounds all year long. When he was not dressed in kitchen whites and a tablecloth, he was wearing flamboyant silk shirts and alligator shoes. He loved to tease everyone. He had a special song to irritate the waiters from Naples—something about missing shoes and barking dogs. Once, he stuffed Rosie, the dishwasher, into the dumbwaiter and sent her upstairs. If he knew you did not like spiders, he would find you a spider. He was jovial and friendly and a natural cook.

We made bread by hand first thing in the morning and then again later in the afternoon. Out would come a weathered six-by-three-foot pine board that lay across the center island. First, Enzo would turn out the raised dough from a huge oiled bowl onto the board and begin kneading. The mass of dough was the color of raw almonds, and the pungent yeast added to the air's already aromatic mix of *brodo di carne*, coffee, and dried rosemary. Next, he rolled it into thick ropes and with a straight-edged knife cut these into two-inch pieces. "*Pane*," he would always announce, as if it were an invitation to come play. We would stop whatever we were doing and race to the pine board. We stood, one on each side of him, tying the pieces of dough into soft-knotted rolls. We kept time to the cadence of his knife as it tapped and scraped at the board. A third cook would grab the *pane* and arrange them in baking trays. What first struck me about our bread-making was the tranquility it bestowed upon the kitchen. I could hear Enzo's raspy breath as he worked the dough to a supple shine. When we finished, I would fill the bowl with a new sponge starter, cover it with a cloth, and leave it to rest for dinner.

One day, it finally struck me what was so odd about this kitchen (besides the fact that the chef was smoking): It had no walk-in refrigerators to store food, no food processors to prepare mayonnaise, no industrial mixers to make bread or pasta. Other than the basic equipment I described, it was "unplugged"—a sort of acoustic version of an American restaurant kitchen. It was here that I learned how extremely gratifying and sensual it is to cook by hand. You are guided by all of your senses, rather than by machines, and the food you make maintains its integrity and flavor. It grounds you in the task.

Often, the morning calm was interrupted by a shrill bell announcing a delivery at the gate, which opened onto Via Emilia San Pietro, the main street in Reggio Emilia, originally built by the Romans. Bicyclists swarmed over the cobblestones, rain or shine, and parked their bikes in perfect rows of 50 under the portico. I would greet many of our produce suppliers here on the garden path leading to the restaurant. Ivy grew up the facade of the Caffè Arti and jasmine climbed its fences. In the winter, the deliverymen stacked wooden crates of local squash, thorny artichokes, cabbage, radicchio, and oranges in the cellar; in the summer, there were farm-fresh tomatoes, zucchini, fava beans, peaches, and melons. Foraged greens, like wild nettles, arugula, or dandelions, were marched into the kitchen and quickly deposited into the sink to be washed for that day's preparations.

The deliverymen on occasion would bring things I had never seen, such as tiny wild strawberries, pungent white truffles, and porcini mushrooms, which came in rainy seasons and then again in dry. Within a few seasons I could tell which mushrooms grew under pine trees and which flourished under oaks. It was in Enzo's vegetable garden, in nearby San Michele della Fossa, where I learned how to pick basil and trim zucchini blossoms correctly. I remember the fresh, green smell of warm tomatoes picked in the afternoon sun and the rich, dank aroma of potatoes pulled from the cool earth. I would not feel confident cooking Italian food without having experienced so many gardens and markets from one season to the next.

I had grown up in suburbia, where outdoor markets were a rarity and processed food was the norm. My mother's cooking did not reflect the seasons. Only our holiday dinners had a hint of seasonality: There was pumpkin for Thanksgiving, chestnuts for Christmas, asparagus for Easter, and watermelon for the Fourth of July. By contrast, Italy was all about local farm-fresh food and the artisans who, for generations, cured meats and made cheese, honey, olive oil, and vinegar. It was neither a trendy nor a radical idea; it was just the way it was—equal parts tradition and culture. In New York, half the work is finding good food and the other half is finding people who want to eat it. Reggio Emilia, like everywhere else in Italy, comprised a whole community of people truly involved with the food they were producing, buying, cooking, and consuming.

Often I would bicycle out to the countryside and visit these artisans. One of the first of many doors that beckoned me to knock was that of a small *caseificio* which produced Parmigiano Reggiano. The father-and-son team showed me how they made *grana*. They stood in the cheese barn in front of a brilliant copper kettle, catching the coagulated milk in cheesecloth. The collected curd was divided into fourths and placed in weighted molds to squeeze out the excess moisture, then marked with production numbers. After a salt bath, the aging began, and 24 months later, it might make the grade of the Consorzio, which sets the standards and controls the quality of cheese-making in the area. (For example, only local milk can be used to make Parmigiano Reggiano.) This technique had remained basically unchanged since the 14th century.

There is no better inspiration than being hands-on and knee-deep at the source. The barn air was cool and smelled like cut grass and sweet cow dung. I can remember being distracted by a half-dozen kittens playing under the table, waiting for the excess fresh cheese to be cut from the molds and thrown to the floor. Upstairs, the mother and daughter separated the milk and cream and made butter. All of us drank bowls of hot coffee and milk. The unpasteurized milk still had its thick cap of cream, and chunks floated on the surface and melted into pools of butter in my coffee. We tore up pieces of day-old bread to soak up the coffee. When I realized it was nearly eight in the morning, I headed back, already exhausted, to start my day at the restaurant.

Part of the joy I find in cooking is in the physical challenge it offers. Farms and kitchens alike test your strength and endurance. In New York, the adrenaline rush starts in the early morning with the first cup of coffee and a run through the crowded greenmarket. With one arm I cradle a flat of heirloom tomatoes topped by another flat of local strawberries, while with the other hand I use my cell phone to reach my fishmonger. I am surprised to see squash blossoms in the market and I think of stuffing them with crab for dinner. "Is it too late to get crabmeat today?" He promises to get the crab on the late truck. I take the squash blossoms and one bunch of lavender and hope for the best.

When I get back to my kitchen the intensity builds. Within an hour, all 12 burners and two ovens will be working. It takes two of us to lift a five-gallon pot of octopus onto the stove to boil. One oven toasts pine nuts while the other bakes two flourless chocolate cakes. We have a hundred things to be done at once and the clock is ticking. The noise and the temperature rise simultaneously. I pitch in to help clean three cases of artichokes that we will braise in white wine and anchovies. Each outer leaf has to be pulled off one by one until the tender yellow leaves are visible. Then we trim the stems with a potato peeler and scoop out the choke. Ten minutes into the chore the first fish delivery arrives, and I divert my attention to the two soggy boxes the driver dropped on my kitchen floor. I smell the pine nuts browning and shout over to the dishwasher to pull them out of the oven. By ten o'clock all 150 artichokes are braising in the oven and I have a second cup of coffee. Potatoes we boiled earlier have been riced and cooled for gnocchi. A couple of handfuls of flour, salt, and nutmeg is all that I've added, and I mix the ingredients and pinch the mix into balls against a wooden paddle. I don't look down while my hands do the job; instead, I concentrate on the pace of my cooks and the pots on the stove. I now have seven hours left until the first dinner reservation. The rush to dinner is always a challenge fraught with successes and failures. However, when the outcome is a perfect suckling pig, caramel colored and crackling, or compliments for a bowl of fresh peaches roasted in amaretto, I experience a sense of accomplishment that makes it all worthwhile.

At Caffè Arti, we worked a split shift called *spezzato* that entailed resting in the afternoons and working in the mornings and evenings for lunch and dinner. Between three and five p.m., Gabriella, an ample blonde woman in her 50s, would take down the pine board and make the pasta. She was highly animated and filled with good humor. She would curtsy when Enzo entered the kitchen, then poke him in the rear end with her rolling pin. Each had an obscene nickname for the other, and they enjoyed insulting each other's cooking. I spent maybe a hundred afternoons seated on the counter watching her. Every day she would turn out by hand yards of *pasta sfoglia* for tagliatelle and hundreds of *tortelli* filled with spinach and ricotta. In the beginning she would only let me break the eggs, which were speckled with soil and feathers and never refrigerated. They sat out on the counter in flats of 30 ready to be turned into pasta, frittatas, or zabaglione. The large yolks were the color of saffron.

Gabriella started by pushing three kilos of flour into a mound with a well large enough to hold 30 eggs. With two fingers, she stirred the pool of eggs clockwise slowly and deliberately, letting the yolks gradually break and mix with the flour until the two ingredients were combined. At this point, she divided the pasta into three bright-yellow portions and one by one began kneading each piece with the palms of her thick hands. She would rise up on her toes and come down on the pasta with all her might, folding it over and over on itself until it was warm and supple. She rubbed the pasta with olive oil to protect the surface from air as it rested. Then, using a three-foot-long wooden *mattarello*, she rolled each piece into enormous, paper-thin round sheets to be dried on white cloths and then cut. The tagliatelle sat drying on wooden trays in the center of the kitchen. Enzo would drop each order into the boiling salted water and minutes later toss it with butter and coarsely grated Parmesan cheese. During the month of November, shaved white truffles from the nearby Appennine Mountains would be added.

I learned something much more important than technique from Gabriella and Enzo. Their warm, easygoing personalities contributed to a nurturing environment, and a nurturing environment made for excellent cooks. We shared more than the clipped hellos and how-are-yous, "Yes, chef" and "No, chef." Enzo's kitchen was purged of formality and ripe with pleasure and kindness. It is no good, I realized, to respect the food but disrespect the cooks.

The restaurant opened its doors to guests at eight o'clock, so every evening at seven the waiters would go about setting a table in the dining room for our "family meal." Bottles of water and baskets of bread awaited the entire staff of 12. We mixed wine into our water and called it a *bevanda*. Depending on the season, we would start with prosciutto and butter or a salad of green tomatoes and basil. Then we would pass around bowls of broken-ravioli gratin with Parmesan or a green risotto of chives and marjoram. Sometimes we would make frittatas with zucchini and mint, or roast chickens in the oven with potatoes and fennel seeds. A bowl of pears, apples, or grapes ended each meal, and we ate the fruit with a knife and a fork. The rules were simple: Each cook made a dish for the table and the waiters cleared and served espressos. The meal nearly always fortified and relaxed us.

These family meals were my first eating experiences in Italy, but I also had the good fortune to be a dinner guest in other people's homes. Enzo's eldest sister would fry rabbit on Sunday. She separated each rabbit with a cleaver into small pieces and rubbed them with a coarse salt flavored with herbs and garlic. These pieces rested in the salt mix for a day. To prepare the dinner she would dredge the rabbit in flour (including their livers and kidneys) and add whole branches of rosemary and garlic to be fried together in her outdoor kitchen in a heavy pot of hot oil. The fried rabbit was served on brown paper and accompanied by a salad of sliced fennel and olives; we drank bottles of chilled Lambrusco.

I prefer to make dishes that have a story to them. Many I've learned to cook at their source, either through imitation or simply by listening. Italy has a strong tradition of passing along recipes verbally. Almost everyone likes to talk about the food of his or her city or from his or her mother. Once, at the fish market near the Ponte di Rialto in Venice, I asked a signora how to prepare the *palombo*, which is a little shark. We were standing in front of a stall that had live sea scallops, tiny shrimp, and fresh red rockfish for sale. She seemed so pleased that I had asked, she rattled off three different recipes. My favorite was also the simplest: The *palombo* is boiled with potatoes, onions, and celery in salted water until tender and served cold with chopped parsley, extra virgin olive oil, and fresh lemon. I have yet to make this dish, *palombo e patate lesse*, but when I do, I will remember the congenial signora holding her bag of clementines in one hand while demonstrating with the other how to chop the potatoes and pour the oil. I will also remember the rising tide washing away the gray stones of one of Italy's most beautiful markets.

At some point during my three years at Caffè Arti e Mestieri, I ceased to be an apprentice. I became restless. I dreamed about another challenge—to move to Rome and learn Roman cuisine from the Romans. When I finally left Reggio Emilia, it was an emotional departure. I spent the next two and a half years working all over Rome. I started at a hotel on the Spanish Steps, then moved to a splendid *ristorante* on Via Veneto, and ended up at a trattoria hidden in an alley at Campo de' Fiori. I eventually began to outgrow my jobs in Rome as well. I wanted more challenges and opportunities. For an American woman who wanted to be a chef, it meant a return to New York City.

This new challenge brought me home, and in the ensuing years, it has been my quest to personalize the lessons I learned in Italy. The aim is simple: to continue to honor the seasons, nurture my cooks with the same soulful decorum, and keep a balance in cooking between authenticity and spontaneity. This is the most creative and fulfilling part of my experiences. It is also the most difficult. I got my first chef's job out of *The New York Times*. It was at an eccentric downtown wine bar that wanted to turn itself into a great restaurant. I thought I could do it. At first I had no written menu, so the waiters had to recite at the table the five things I made for dinner. The kitchen had no walk-in boxes, so I felt right at home shopping every day and starting over the next. I would put a veal breast in a slow oven with some rosemary, garlic, and white wine and pray it would be edible by dinner. Basically, I let the things I saw and ate in Italy guide me in the kitchen. That first year, the voices and imaginations of Enzo and Gabriella never left me.

Today I have a little kitchen in Greenwich Village. It is rectangular with a 14-foot line that includes two ovens, a three-foot-long grill, 10 gas burners, a pasta boiler, a fryer, and an 18-inch bain-marie. In front of the line stands an island with refrigeration below and shelves above to dry pasta. The dinners we prepare are carried by hand up the stairs to the dining room on the first floor. In one corner, dishes are washed and dried, in the other, prosciutto is sliced and appetizers are made. The ceiling is painted celestial blue. On the tiled wall hangs a list I scribbled at an early age of every exotic thing I wanted to learn to make one day.

The kitchen is a little peculiar. You won't find the latest bells and whistles, just an old-fashioned pine board for making pasta and a large mortar and pestle. It's a crowded space, filled with five cooks all dressed in white jackets, aprons, and floppy cotton toques, waiting for me to tell them what we will make for dinner today.

Found in Translation

INTERVIEW WITH ANN GOLDSTEIN

Based in New York City, Ann Goldstein has translated works by, among others, Primo Levi, Pier Paolo Pasolini, Elena Ferrante, Jhumpa Lahiri, and Alessandro Baricco, and she is the editor of *The Complete Works of Primo Levi* in English. Goldstein, who was the head copy editor at *The New Yorker* for 30 years, is the recipient of a Guggenheim fellowship and awards from the Italian Ministry of Foreign Affairs and the American Academy of Arts and Letters. In 2016, her translation of Elena Ferrante's *The Story of the Lost Child* was shortlisted for the Man Booker International Prize. Goldstein sat down for an interview with *Esopus* in late 2016 that was published the following spring in *Esopus 24*; the issue also included facsimile reproductions of three drafts of her translation of Levi's short story "Hydrogen."

Tod Lippy: *How and when did you first come to learn Italian?*

Ann Goldstein: I had always wanted to read Dante in Italian, and in 1986 I convinced some other people working at *The New Yorker* that they, too, wanted to read Dante in Italian. My colleague Mary Norris, who was then studying Greek at Columbia, had a classmate who was the daughter of Maristella Lorch, a well-known Italian professor there. As it turns out, there were two daughters, and for a year we had an Italian class with one of the daughters, at *The New Yorker* offices, in which we mostly studied grammar. Then, the next year, the other daughter came, and we started reading Dante. Eventually we read the entire *Divine Comedy*. We continued the Italian class for quite a long time, and then it became a conversation class, and we would go out to dinner, with a teacher, and talk. The class stopped for a while, but we've actually revived it again.

It's amusing to me that a world-renowned translator of Italian literature would still be taking Italian lessons.

Well, you know, you can always learn something else. We have a teacher, an Italian, and we all talk, and just to have the language in your ear for an hour or so is something—it's really good.

Do you spend a lot of time in Italy?

No, not enough time. I try to go twice a year, but I haven't been that successful lately.

Your first work of translation was the Aldo Buzzi story "Chekhov in Sondrio," in 1992. How did that come about?

Buzzi was a friend of the artist Saul Steinberg—they studied architecture together in Milan—and Steinberg sent Bob Gottlieb, who was at that point the editor of *The New Yorker*, a book by Buzzi. Gottlieb wanted to write Steinberg a note, so he gave me the book, since he knew I was studying Italian, and said, "Just read enough to be able to give me something nice to say." I read the book—it was quite short—and I really liked it, so I thought, "I'll just try to translate it." And I did, and then Bob published it in the magazine. That was kind of amazing. It's a very literary piece about Russia and Italy—a strange piece, but a wonderful one.

So you were hooked?

Yes, I really liked the process of translation: of finding a more intimate relationship with the language. And then, I don't exactly remember the sequence of things, I translated other Buzzi stories—they're not exactly stories but more memoirs, or little essays—for Dan Menaker [an editor], who had just gone to Random House, and they were published, with "Chekhov in Sondrio," as *Journey to the Land of the Flies*. But the next book I translated was *Petrolio*, by Pier Paolo Pasolini.

Even for Pasolini aficionados, Petrolio *is considered a hugely challenging read—from my understanding, it was unfinished, and cobbled together from a series of notes and letters that Pasolini had written before he was murdered.*

Yes, that's right. And it, too, is kind of an amazing book, absolutely different from the Buzzi.

And so relevant to the end of his life.

Exactly. Several years ago, an Italian writer called Emanuele Trevi wrote a book about *Petrolio*, titled *Qualcosa di scritto [Something Written]*, which is the title of certain sections of *Petrolio*. Trevi worked at the Pasolini Foundation, in Rome, for Laura Betti, and so he wrote this combination coming-of-age memoir, literary analysis of *Petrolio*, and exploration of sadomasochism. For example, Trevi goes to Greece and visits Eleusis because the Eleusinian Mysteries have a role in Pasolini's book. I translated the Trevi book, but unfortunately it was published only in England.

What a challenge for an early translation.

Yes, I worked on it for about three years. I knew very little about Pasolini beforehand, but I obviously learned quite a lot.

You're neither an Italian scholar nor a specialist in Italian literature; do you think there are certain advantages to approaching translation from that particular angle?

I never really know. I mean, experience is usually an advantage. *[laughs]* It's probably in some ways an advantage not to be an academic, but I don't think it's an advantage that there are a lot of things I haven't read. I've read Dante, and a little Boccaccio, and a little of this and that, but I haven't really studied all of these things, so I would say that I'm sorry that I don't have that background. The other thing that I don't have is the cultural background—I've never lived in Italy for more than four months at a time, and so I think that's something of a disadvantage. I mean, I have other advantages—I think working in English as a copy editor is an advantage. It's a useful skill when it comes to translating.

Can you talk about that a little bit more?

I think that being focused on words to that degree—especially in the weird, specialized system of copyediting we have here at *The New Yorker*, which is to some extent like line editing—is helpful. It's very intensive. Our idea is that we're trying to make the writer sound as much like him- or herself as possible, and in translation you're trying to do the same thing. You're trying to bring this voice into English as closely as possible. In a talk about translation I've given recently, I offer the example of five different translations I've done of five different writers: It demonstrates how different they are not only in Italian but also in English. I think it works—at least, that's the idea:

> ***My Brilliant Friend*** (Elena Ferrante, 2012)
> "Although his features were very similar to Stefano's, the same eyes, same nose, same mouth; although his body, as he grew, was taking the same form, the large head, legs slightly short in relation to the torso; although in his gaze and in his

gestures he manifested the same mildness, I felt in him a total absence of the determination that was concealed in every cell of Stefano's body, and that in the end, I thought, reduced his courtesy to a sort of hiding place from which to jump out unexpectedly."

Mr. Gwyn (Alessandro Baricco, 2012)
"She went to Jasper Gwyn's studio on the Underground, but she always got out one stop earlier, to walk a little before going in. On the street, she turned the key over and over in her hand. And that was her way of starting work."

The Street Kids (Pier Paolo Pasolini, 1955)
"Riccetto felt a gnawing inside, right in the middle, and decided to skip out on them all: he left through the empty church, but at the door he ran into his godfather, who said: 'Hey, where you going?' 'Home,' said Riccetto. 'I'm hungry.' 'You're coming to my house, you bastard,' his godfather shouted after him, 'there's the lunch.' But Riccetto paid no attention and ran off over the sun-baked asphalt. All Rome was a single roar: only up on the hill was there silence, but it was charged like a mine."

The Periodic Table (Primo Levi, 1975)
"From the little I know of my forebears they resemble these gases. They were not all physically inert, because that was not granted to them: rather, they were, or had to be, fairly active, in order to earn a living and because of a dominant morality according to which 'if you don't work you don't eat'; but inert they undoubtedly were in their depths, inclined to disinterested speculation, witty conversation, elegant, pedantic, and gratuitous discussion."

In Other Words (Jhumpa Lahiri, 2015)
"I realize that in spite of the limitations the horizon is boundless. Reading in another language implies a perpetual state of growth, possibility. I know that my work, as a reader, as an apprentice of the language, will never end."

Why do you feel being an academic could be a disadvantage for a translator?

I think in some cases academics tend to approach things from a particular point of view—whether historical or linguistic or theoretical or something else—which means that they are sometimes trying to satisfy requirements beyond those of conveying a piece of writing from one language to another, and that can get in the way of the writing. Not to say that I'm a great writer, but people underestimate the fact that a translator has to be a good writer in his or her own language, and I think that's not necessarily the strong point of academics.

You talk about translating Primo Levi and the "dauntingness" of dealing, for instance, with the scientific terms that he often uses in his prose. Are there other specific issues you find particularly challenging when translating from Italian into English?

There are a number of things that are hard about it—that make trouble, I guess I should say. For one, Italian has gender, so the sentence structure is usually much more flexible. The verbs contain the pronouns—and a lot of information, actually, including the tense, the pronoun, the number—so they can move around the sentence to an extent that verbs can't in English. The modifiers have to stay with their nouns, so sometimes, with a complicated Italian sentence, you have to break it up, because although in Italian its parts go together, in English you just can't squeeze them in. And Italian sustains repetitions more easily than English. So you can use the same word a bunch of times in an Italian text, where in English it sounds awkward. Also, Italian has all those suffixes that change the nuance of a word: for example, *la strada* (the big street) and *la stradina* (the little street). If you keep saying "the big street" in English it sounds a little funny. A little childish. Those are a few of the difficulties.

You mentioned gender, and pardon the reductive nature of this question, but do you feel that being a female translator changes your relationship to the author depending on his or her gender?

I just think of it as writing. Every sentence—or even every word—is something that you have to figure out. So no, I've never actually thought of it as gendered. I think there are writers you feel closer to than others, but I don't know that it's a question of gender, although perhaps in the case of Ferrante it did help that I am female. And then there are, of course, little places where gender is an issue—in the beginning of *My Brilliant Friend*, someone who'd read my translation said to me, "In the original the name of the person is never mentioned in that passage—yet you mention it." The reason I had for doing that was I had to somehow indicate that it was a female speaking, because in the Italian you already knew that. So there are lots of little things like that you have to slip in.

So readers give you a lot of feedback on your translations?

Oh, people do. You'd be surprised.

In a recent interview, you mentioned—speaking specifically about translating Giacomo Leopardi's Zibaldone*—that in the process of translation, "you are so inside this person's mind, inside his thoughts." Can that be overwhelming, or even oppressive?*

Zibaldone is a philosophical tome. It really is his thoughts, his ruminations about everything; it's not, you know, "I looked out the window and saw this or that." It's about his reading, about his theories of language; he copies down quotations from different writers. So in that case you really are almost literally inside his head—his mind.

But is it similar when you're working on something that's not that intensely philosophical or ruminative?

You are still in the person's head. You want to be in his or her head. When you're working in a writer's language, you really have to be in his mind.

You've said before you sometimes like to toggle between two translations at once.

I do, actually. I think it started as a necessity because I had too much work. *[laughs]* But then I convinced myself that it was actually a good thing because sometimes one person's use of a word reinforces, or lets you into, somebody else's use of the word. Or you just see different ways that people use words. There are different writing states. So yes, I've decided it's helpful. You can still be immersed in one person's mind even if then you go and get immersed in somebody else's mind. I think that they reinforce rather than detract from one another. Anyway, that's my idea.

Can you walk us through your process for a typical translation?

I do a first draft very quickly. I may look up words, but I wouldn't stop to figure out complex stuff. I really just want to get through it. Then, in the second draft, I try to solve the major problems. And then I often do something that I've since discovered a lot of translators do, and probably writers, too: putting a choice of different words into the draft that I can pick from—or use as starting points—later on. And sometimes I put the Italian in, just to remind myself of the original wording. But in that second draft I try to solve a lot of those things, especially the larger issues. And then third draft, fourth draft, fifth draft, maybe. I just keep refining.

What are your specific translation tools?

I use a lot of different dictionaries. When I started, obviously, there wasn't the Internet, but now there's an incredible amount of stuff online. Endless numbers of regular dictionaries, because, you know, different dictionaries say different things. Then there are dialect dictionaries, which are very useful in Italian. There are some slang dictionaries, although the online ones are not that great. There's also a site called Word Reference, which has a discussion forum, so sometimes you can find stuff there. I've never actually joined it, or asked a question, but I suppose I could. Apart from words, you can also find a lot of information on the Internet—it was very helpful, for example, with the scientific terms in Primo Levi. And then I have people whom I consult.

Italian people?

Yes, usually Italian.

So with that first draft, are you literally typing as you read? And if that's the case, do you often not know how a particular novel or story is going to end?

Well, that depends. Usually I would have read the book first. But lately that's not been the case. For example, the Elena Ferrante books were on such a tight schedule: You know, she was just finishing writing them and they had to be translated in a pretty short turnaround time. The last three Ferrante novels I translated as I read. It's kind of an interesting way to translate. It's much more like you're in real time with what's happening in the book. You're much more with the character, I would say, in an interesting way. I don't know that it has an effect on the translation, because ultimately of course you're still going to go back and read it many times, but for the first draft, I think there's something exciting about that approach. You also go pretty quickly because you want to find out what happens. *[laughs]* But sometimes you want to go more slowly, if only to make sure you've fully understood something.

And when you translate without reading the book first, does it mean there's more recalibration in later drafts once you realize where the story is heading?

That's always true. But another thing about the Ferrante books is that when the first one came out I hadn't read the final one. So I don't know if I would have done some things differently or not. The *Zibaldone* is the opposite example, in which there were so many concepts that were set—certain words were meant to be translated certain ways. But then, when the editors went over everything at the end, they sometimes changed their minds and redid the whole. But that was a scholarly project.

A kid recently told me that there are programs that will tell you how you translated a word in every instance in a book. I mean, I guess you could do that yourself, but it would be pretty tedious. And I don't know, I feel that somehow you're probably losing something—the way some people say that something is lost when you write on a computer.

How do you type your drafts, by the way?

On the computer. And then I print them out after maybe the third draft. And I do a read on paper, because you see a lot of things on paper that you don't see on a computer screen.

That sounds like a New Yorker *copy editor speaking.*

Yes, I guess so. Because we still do work on paper.

How long, generally, does it take you to translate one page?

I actually just noticed with something I'm working on now—a new translation of Italo Calvino's *The Baron in the Trees*—that even on the first draft it's five pages in an hour. Something like that. Pretty slow. Maybe that's especially slow.

Do you find that you're always drawn to one particular character?

If there's a first-person narrator, I think it's almost impossible to not have some feeling about being that person. When you read a book, it's the same thing. I'm always convinced by the first-person narrator: I just take that point of view, somehow. I guess if there's not a first person, there's probably some character I identify with. But I don't think it's relevant to the process of translation.

From what I understand you've never had any direct interaction, even via email, with Elena Ferrante. You've also translated a number of works by dead authors; does it somehow seem like the same thing?

Yes, in a way. I guess there is a difference in the fact that the dead author can't read the translation, whereas the living author can. I think that Ferrante did read my first translation, and maybe some of the other early ones, so I had a feeling that somebody was looking at what I was doing who cared about how it came out. I believe that Ferrante reads English, so I presume she knows whether she liked it or not. I probably could have emailed her directly. But it's true, I never would have worked *with* her closely in any case. With the later books, she's been more accessible—and who knows what will happen now?

Are you confident that Anita Raja is the real Ferrante?

I have no idea. I don't know. No one has said anything—confirmed or denied, not the publishers nor Raja herself. I've never known who Ferrante was—as far as I know, no one does, except for the publishers.

It seems like such an elegant way to deal with literary celebrity on some level.

I know. But people are now saying, "Well, she gave all these interviews; therefore she's already compromised." Or the fact that she's now published *Frantumaglia*, a collection of letters, essays, and interviews. But that feels like hairsplitting, in a not-useful way. In a *gotcha* way.

You talk about "not wanting to be there" for some of the more intense scenes in her books. Does dealing with unpleasant or disturbing passages in prose make the translation process harder?

It means, at least for me, that I can't go over it too many times in a row. I have to get up and walk away from it. That's also true of some of Levi—especially the concentration-camp passages, of course. These kinds of things are upsetting, so it's hard to stay with them on that level of having to get the words—the sense of them, of the whole passage—right. But if it's uncomfortable in the original, of course it should be uncomfortable in English. You have to put up with it, as the translator who has to read it a hundred times. You try to get it right, however distressing. But it can be hard.

I'm also thinking of those incredibly intense sexual scenes in Petrolio, *in which he describes each partner's genitalia in such insane detail.*

Yes. That was difficult, in many ways. *[laughs]* And it was so early, so I didn't have much experience translating sex scenes into English—which I have since come to have many experiences with. People accuse me of being "proper" in my translations of these kinds of scenes, but, the Italians, at least in the books I've translated, don't use a lot of slangy or really "dirty" words. They're graphic but they're very particular: The body parts are the body parts. And in the Pasolini, in a way, that's at least partly the point. It's meant to be brutal, and there's a kind of brutality in just using the physical, plain words.

Do you think one must have a good intuition about others—to be a "people person," in a sense—to understand and translate what they're trying to communicate as authors?

I don't know. When I worked on *Petrolio*, as I already mentioned, I read a lot about Pasolini. I looked at many of the movies, I read the earlier novels, I read several biographies. I read a lot about him. So in that case I really studied him, partly because I really wanted to know him. And honestly I became a little obsessed with him, which is easy to do. And because that book is so weird and fragmentary, I wanted to at least imagine that I knew something about the personality of the writer. It was sort of the opposite with Ferrante. In her case, there was really nothing to go on. Normally I don't try to find out about the writer. It's really about the text.

It must be odd on some level to become the voice of Ferrante not only to all English-language readers of the book but also in a very public way.

I'm careful to say, "I'm not Ferrante, and I can hardly speak for her, but I can speak about her books." So yes, I guess I'm a voice of the books. And it's completely strange; it's not anything that in a million years I thought I would ever be or do. So it's an odd role. I started doing it, I think, because I felt an obligation to the books. I thought, especially with the earlier, lesser-known ones, that they were really wonderful books, and that she was a great writer, and I wanted to promote her work. And people like to talk about her books, which is also really interesting. So I felt some responsibility to them—not to mention to the publishers, of course.

I guess one silver lining is that quite a bit of attention has been brought to translators and translating.

I think that's an important element. It means that translation becomes important. People now pay attention to the fact that books are translated—that there is not only the author but another person behind the book they are reading—so it's good for all translators. Even in the past few years, translation has gotten a lot more attention, so I'm thrilled about that. Translators should be recognized.

You've also done a fair amount of editing of other translators' work for books like The Complete Works of Primo Levi. *Did you find that the "voices" of Levi were very different depending on the translator?*

I don't think they were that different, but I had certain criteria of what I might call faithfulness to the text, so when they were different, I tried to make them less so.

There's the copy editor coming through!

Yes, exactly. I guess I tried to make everybody sound like me. *[laughs]* But seriously, as far as I can tell, I think it worked pretty well.

Is it easier to copyedit translations than it is to copyedit English-language authors?

It depends, but, generally speaking, copyediting translations is more difficult. There are different kinds of problems that you run into. You come upon things where you're not sure if there's an issue with the translation or if there's something weird in the original. And sometimes, of course, you have to give up something that's weird in the original because it's just *too* weird in English. Then, there's the whole question of slang, or dialect—that's the worst example.

Have you translated much dialect?

No. Ferrante doesn't write in dialect, thank goodness. But Pasolini's *Ragazzi di vita [The Street Kids]* has a lot of dialect—and in fact it's not even exactly Roman dialect; it's Pasolini's version of Roman dialect. That was hard. I asked a lot of people about it—including a lot of Romans. But I didn't translate it into a dialect or accent in English. There really isn't an equivalent. My solution was to try to make the parts in dialect—which were mostly dialogue—"slangier." But that's a really hard issue. There are people who have theories about it. I don't know, it seemed to me that a reader would be put off by a line of dialogue spoken by a street kid in Rome that came out in, say, a Southern accent. The BBC did a dramatization of the Neapolitan novels. Someone wrote a play based on each of the novels, and it was decided to use North of England accents for the little girls. To me, that's weird—it sounded weird.

Has someone purchased the film rights for Ferrante's novels?

Yes, an Italian film company in combination with RAI is doing a TV series, eight parts for each book. I believe they're trying to co-produce it in English. But I don't know who is going to direct or produce. A very good Italian novelist and screenwriter, Francesco Piccolo, is doing the screenplay. And I think that Ferrante has some kind of say in it.

You've mentioned never wanting to translate poetry; you said elsewhere that prose is "more grounded."

There might be different ways to translate a prose sentence, but, basically, there's only one meaning there. I probably shouldn't say something like that. But it seems to me that, however unstraightforward it may be, it's still straightforward: It's one unit, somehow. The sentence is grounded in a paragraph, and it has a definite grammatical, syntactical relationship to the sentences around it. In a poem, the words could have many relationships to the words around them. And even if you were to do a literal translation of a poem, you might not have the right literary translation. Whereas in prose I think you can feel a little more confident that the words are part of a whole, somehow.

I believe you claimed in an earlier interview that a translator is like an actor interpreting a role, or a performer singing a piece of music.

That's actually a quote from Cesare Garboli, from an essay of his, which Domenico Scarpa and I included in the book *In un'altra lingua* (Einaudi, 2016). It's worth quoting in full: "To translate is to be an actor. The same attitude, the same condition of the spirit that leads us, institutionally, to perform, to create theater, to physically breathe the life of another. And, as it happens in the theater, there are amateur translators, professionals, touring companies, repertory groups. There is the commercial cooperative that translates mystery books, or the one signed up for the latest best seller. There is the refined translator and the colloquial, the lead and the walk-on. And there is, finally, the translator of genius: the great actor. He is the actor who has understood that, to be a great actor, it's enough to believe blindly in one's own lines, nothing else is needed."

Methods of Rest

BY VIVIEN SHOTWELL

1. You may find it helpful to write down your anxieties at bedtime.

—Dr. Joseph Kershner, Kershner's Guide to Insomnia, *p. 24*

I DO NOT HAVE TO THINK ABOUT

money, the fish, Peter Moss, sanitation, the environment, losing my virginity, death, death of parents and/or siblings and/or children, never having children, dying alone, dying young, sleep, Peter, Proust, being HAPPY, overeating, spiders

until the morning. GOD DAMN IT.

2. Count backwards?*—Peter Moss*

100...99...98...97...96...92...9998...9996...9995...5...66...63...4...
3...
2...

3. Keep a little port on your nightstand, sweet pea. It put Grandpa right out.*—Grandma*

Port comes from Portugal. Port is a fortified wine. This means it is wine that has been fortified with the addition of brandy. The effect of this is to kill the yeast in the partly fermented wine, which produces a rich, strong, sweet flavor. Because the wine hasn't fully fermented, there are still natural sugars present which result in retained sweetness. I have no tolerance for port. I am a sweet pea. I am a vegetable child-woman of refined natural sugars. I am *saturated* with sweetness. My skin is a honeycomb. My pores ooze nectar. When I walk barefoot I leave a golden trail of stickiness and the insects get caught, blissful, incapacitated, drunk.

My brain is a nauseated sponge. My yeast has been murdered, half-fermented. I am fortified with fluff. I am all filled up.

4. Embrace your fears. Let yourself realize they have no hold on you.

—Ilsabeth Anderson, disgraced high school drama teacher

An embrace. The subject lies in bed, naked, asleep, face and hands gummy with syrup and melted ice cream. The bed is strikingly reminiscent of a late-18th-century chamber pot. Carl, the morbid, lice-ridden custodian, is mopping the floor, which is similarly coated in syrup and ice cream.

Spiders are pouring from a faucet above the subject's head, covering her completely. They are small and tickly, just babies, but there are thousands of them and they are each highly poisonous. She will probably die. Nothing can be done—the plumbing is Carl's responsibility, and at the moment he is concentrating on the floor. He cannot attend to two things at once. The spiders continue to fall, unchecked, and the air fills with the hissing of their innumerable legs. The subject does not wake up. The spiders scramble around and bite her. Some are squashed. Others take shelter in her nose and ears, and the subject dreams she has a sinus infection.

Before her, in a large rectangular tank above the dresser, goldfish float motionless in the viscous blue-green water, gently reproachful, like capsized kayaks.

5. Warm milk?*—Peter*

I am not a two-year-old, Peter.

6. Establish bedtime rituals. Avoid becoming excited or emotionally upset before retiring.*—Kershner, p. 23*

The ritual will commence with three promenades clockwise around the room and four promenades in the counterclockwise direction, for a total of seven. Barefoot: It is essential for the body to be grounded. We will ignore, for the moment, the question of the mind. The body must be made heavy and ponderous, the lungs like sacks of barley, the calves like sand, the feet like boulders. This will create a sense of dullness and deep relaxation.

Following the promenades, a restorative glass of freshly squeezed grapefruit juice will be taken from a seated position. (Music, William Byrd's *Mass for Three Voices*, provides a soothing, melancholic underlay.) The moment is then ripe for four saltines—no more—with a contemplative pause of at least ten seconds between each. Thus nourished, the refreshed insomniac will continue on to the evening's reading: one page, at minimum, of Marcel Proust's monumental autobiographical masterpiece *À la recherche du temps perdu.*

7. Tell yourself the story of tomorrow, like we used to do when you were little. Remember? It always made you so calm.—*Mother*

THE STORY OF TOMORROW

Tomorrow, of course, begins at midnight. I lie awake, in my hated bed, for an hour or so, having spent the last hour or so of yesterday in a similar predicament. My bed is narrow and oppressive, with a creaky, bumpy mattress, and it is too short. Or else I am too long. I am too long for many things. My feet dangle over the end of it, cold, and laboriously I consider putting on a pair of socks. The sheets are of the palest blue and could use washing. There are two pillows—one flat, the other fat—which I alternate. The duvet, which I have had since I was seven, is sparsely feathered. I am wearing a sexy red nightgown. I have a teddy bear, Lily Emmeline Pia Fortuna, and I am not ashamed of her.

Around two thirty I heave up my body and turn on the light. My eyes clench like retreating sea anemones. I press the heels of my hands against them. When I have had enough of that, I visit the bathroom, where the light is harsh and the toilet seat is freezing; forgetting, until it is too late, that I am not supposed to glance in the mirror. I have visions of what I will look like to my grandchildren. If I have grandchildren.

I return to the bedroom, look at the bed, turn off the light, and arrange myself on my back with my hands folded lightly across my chest. I have developed a crafty theory, in the bluish space between the bathroom and the bed, that by playing dead I will be able to trick myself into oblivion.

Rank failure. I am not so easily self-deceived. The air is cluttered and stuffy, and something buzzes through the wall. My thoughts are like termites. Blood pounds in my brain. I flee the bed and roll around on the floor, bruising my back on a stapler.

This sort of thing cannot go on forever. It can't. Salvation comes secretly, without warning or prelude; sleep disguised as indifference, the abandoned child of despair. There are no dreams. At eight fifteen I find myself back in my nest with my body the wrong way round and Lily languishing in the empty wastepaper basket beside me. I leave the bed and draw the blind. The tender grayish light makes everything look pathetic and small. There are papers everywhere, clothes, a brown apple core, wilting plants, grimy water glasses. The fish is still dead. I tap the bowl.

Listening to the radio—there has been a plane crash—I get dressed, and softly groan with weariness. Sarah Marie, my pretty, well-adjusted roommate, is in the shower, and though I am greasy and itchy I do not feel like waiting for her to be done. I would have to talk to her, and she would have to ask me how I slept.

I am forgetting something, but as usual I cannot determine what it is. I poke around. The radio people speak in grave, mournful voices. They do not know much of anything yet, but they must fill the time. They are waiting for official word. They talk to witnesses, who are shocked and inarticulate, and to aviation experts, who are measured and manly. They repeat what they have said before.

I find a blueberry muffin in my sock drawer and eat it. I have given up coffee, and it makes me physically anguished.

Outside, the air is cold but the sun is glorious. Soon (agony) it is night.

8. Relax, sweetie. Listen to my voice.—*Yvette Zientek, hypnotherapist*

She says that I am on a plane to Ireland. It is all very pleasant. The passengers are courteous, the flight attendants handsome and obliging. I am traveling first-class.

We land, as expected, on time—and without, of course, crashing—and a dapper chauffeur picks me up to take me to the country. Everything is taken care of. The car is comfortable. I am comfortable. Light filters down. We drive through forests and fields, where there are lambs and so forth, and then we go up the long driveway to the manor where I am staying. She gives no explanation for how I am supposed to pay for any of this. The chauffeur takes my bags inside while I, *already feeling sleepy*, decide to take a turn about the grounds.

She has a good voice for this sort of stuff, smooth but not too smooth, with a faint accent. (French? Swiss?) Her eyes, which should be attractive, come off as weirdly reptilian, and her skin is poor. She was the only one I could find.

I have found my way to a small walled garden over-brimming with deliciously scented flowers. She cannot know that I have always been fascinated by walled gardens, that I used to long to have one of my very own—that when I was nine I went so far as to set up a cardboard box in the living room with all the potted geraniums we owned. I have told her almost nothing about myself. It must be a common fantasy for intense young women with chronic sleep disorders. That, or she is hiding something. I wonder if she's an agent of my mother's. But then she would also know that deliciously scented flowers only give me allergic reactions.

In the corner of the garden, she tells me liquidly, is a hammock, gently swinging in the shade. I lie down in it, etc.

9. What you need is a sweetheart. Somebody big enough to hold you.
—Grandma

Peat, characteristic fuel source of Ireland, is formed from the partially decomposed remains of plants and animals that have accumulated in oxygen-poor freshwater environments such as swamps and bogs. The deposits consist of sphagnum moss, sedges, reeds, fish, and spiders. Total decay is inhibited by acidic conditions and a general lack of nutrients. This is what makes peat so good at preserving corpses. Heavy and absorbent, intensely protective, it cradles them for thousands of years, cushioning their limbs, matting their death-furrowed brows, so that even though they will never wake they will never truly dissolve.

10. You could always sleep with me, you know, if you're so uncomfortable. It's a futon.*—Peter Hattauer Moss*

The thing about you, Moss, is that you are the opposite of a calming influence. You are, in fact, disruptive. Mr. Coffee Roaster, Mr. Fix-it—telling me you've never met anyone more self-absorbed, never in your life witnessed such unhappiness, such insecurity, such inertia.

And as to Proust: Contrary to what you may think, I am an extremely well-read virgin, and there is no reason for me to prove it to you or to anybody. I have read things so beautifully wrought they would make you want to hurl yourself into an arctic crevasse. I have, Pierrot, spent entire nights reading, in bed, at the desk, on the floor, while the hours shed like snakeskin around me. Books that made me burn and laugh, while the rest of creation was dreaming. So there is no great emptiness, no reason to resurrect my tottering high school French to read in the original the exquisite prose of your darling asthmatic genius. JE NE COMPRENDS PAS LE FRANÇAIS.JE SUIS FATIGUÉE.

11. Look, if you need anything, I'm yours. Okay? No questions asked. Even if it's four in the morning.*—Peter H. Moss, knight of the round table*

The virgin, weeping, calls at two. She says that her lungs are suffocating her and she is afraid she will lose her mind.

He says he will come.

She pulls on some clothes from the pile on the floor and creeps downstairs to wait in the doorway. She does not want him to have to come inside. She is thinking now that she would not like to see him after all, that it sends the wrong message, that she'll be all right on her own, but if she goes back to bed he'll ring the bell and wake Sarah Marie, who must be up at five thirty for her new job at the bakery and does not appreciate being tired.

The sobbing virgin swoons into the doorway. Her eyelid throbs, as if possessed. She can feel herself beginning to slide down the wall.

She lets go; she can't help it—slips, sighing, all the way to the ground. Across the street, a woman is going through the trash. For a moment they regard each other, and then the virgin closes her eyes.

12. Coffee, honey, is the devil incarnate.—*Trish Bauer, certified homeopath*

Coffee is the world's most popular beverage. As a natural commodity it is second only to oil. More than 400 billion cups are consumed each year. It comes from Colombia, India, Guatemala, Indonesia, Uganda, Ethiopia, Mexico, and Vietnam. It is made from berries, not beans. Under extremes of heat they double in size and pass through a range of luminous earth tones, from green to yellow to red to black. The heat releases steam, borne with them from the corners of the earth, and if you like you can stand under the hot white stream and know that you are breathing Ethiopian rain, Indian rivers.

When the temperature is right, the beans begin to hiss and pop. There is a first crack and a second crack. That is how you know they are ready to be dropped.

13. Are you all right?

She is being carried up the stairs.

"Hey," she says.

"I thought you were dead," he mutters, panting. She is neither small nor light, and the apartment is three flights up. Her feet keep catching on the railing. She wonders if she has been drugged.

The door, thankfully, is not locked. He carries her inside, into her room, and sets her on the bed. "I don't know what's wrong with me," she says, watching his hands as he slips off her shoes in the dark.

He sits beside her. "This mattress is awful," he says.

She says, "The sheets are dirty."

He kisses her neck.

"I need a shower," she whispers.

14. Eliminate clutter. The sleeping area is for two things only; anything else will serve as a distraction and a hindrance to both.—*Kershner, p. 4*

It is mortifying, after a long and empty sleep, to wake groggy and parched in the middle of a raucously sunny afternoon and discover that you have been living in squalor—particularly when that squalor has been seen by someone else, someone you needed to impress, to please, who is now, from the sound of it, grinding his own delectable forbidden coffee in your seedy kitchenette. It is excruciating, absolutely, to recognize the voice of your chatty little roommate, already back from work, asking him about his schooling and home life and religious practices, none of which are exactly conventional, and to hear him respond, as only he can, like she is his best friend in the world.

Later she will tell you, demurely, that he has an interesting scar. You will not answer.

You yawn and stretch, kicking off the duvet to examine your knees. In the next room, your roommate and your prince have lapsed into silence. Through the walls come sifting the sweet smells of fresh coffee and crepes, the faint, industrious tinklings of fork on plate, spoon in cup.

You shake your head and slap at your cheeks. You smooth your hair. You press your hands between your knees, in fists. You tell yourself: Now, now it's time, past time, to get up—to awake—

15. Let me tell you what I loved about you.—*P.*

I'd rather you not.

"You have eyes like the flaking gold leaf on a moss-covered Buddhist statue."

My eyes are shortsighted and brown.

"Your have hair like maple syrup in the morning. You have freckles, moles, and dimples. Your smile makes me tingle."

Please, Mr. Moss.

"You don't have any expectations."

I expect that when I am seventy I will be disappointed. I expect that I will go for long walks with an old dog. I expect that my bones will become riddled with holes and shiver like sandstone. I expect that my dreams will evaporate. I expect that I will never sleep again.

"You catch the sun on bare, freckled shoulders. You draw the light like you draw my touch."

The freckles are from old burns. I was a red, peeling child. My mother did not know about sunscreen.

"You don't believe me."

I don't.

"Lie with me."

I did.

"Lie with me."

I *am*.

16. Roses always bloom in other places.—*Ilsabeth Anderson*

On the day after The Story of Tomorrow, I remember what I forgot. I am lying on a hot, windy beach with my mother and Petey. There are goldfish strewn along the shoreline—debris, I believe, of the tragic plane crash. Ice cream clots my hair. Mother has purchased two dozen white wilting hyacinths and laid them spitefully in the sand by my face. Petey, resourceful Mr. Moss, has brought along his portable solar-powered espresso machine. Espresso and flower-bowers all around. Magnificent scents.

At the moment of my remembering Mother and P. are sweetly dozing on either side of me. I am awake. Salt in the air.

I prop myself on my elbows. "Hey!" I say. "Hey!"

Mum and Moss shift and sigh but don't wake up. I laugh exultantly, as though I've just discovered a great scientific formula, and shake their yielding, sun-baked shoulders. "Hey! You guys! It's not my fault. It's just the way I am. There's nothing I can do."

They don't answer. They're still asleep. But I'm awake. The sky is blue and hot. I sneeze and sneeze and watch the simmering sand-caked fish being guzzled by gulls.

Light Unseen

BY JENNIFER TIPTON

I was walking up the aisle of the City Center theater in New York City after catching the bunch of flowers thrown to me from the stage of one of Paul Taylor's 50th anniversary performances when I was stopped by a woman in the audience who said, "It's so wonderful that you technicians are honored in this way." In the excitement of that moment, it felt like a slap in the face. On another occasion I worked closely with choreographer Trisha Brown, musician Dave Douglas, and painter Terry Winters in the making of the three jazz pieces that constitute *El Trilogy*. The review in *The New York Times* mentioned specifically the three "artists" involved, leaving the lighting out of the creative process entirely. Is it really true that the critics, the writers, and the audience do not notice the light and its effect—the way that light allows us to see what is on the stage in very special ways? Having dealt with slights like these throughout my life, I swore to find a way to communicate the fact that lighting the stage is an art, and to do my best to explain why and how.

The first definition of "art" in *Merriam-Webster Dictionary* is "a skill acquired by experience or study." The last is "the conscious use of skill and creative imagination especially in the production of aesthetic objects." Certainly what we see on the stage must be considered an aesthetic object. What are the elements that combine to contribute to what we see, and how we see? For most of recent history, the art of painting has been an attempt to re-create light on a two-dimensional surface. It is interesting to me that in the 20th century, as abstract painters searched for ways other than light to give form to the shapes on their canvases, the technology for controlling light on a stage became increasingly sophisticated, making it more possible to use it onstage as an artistic medium. Perhaps by offering the example of an artist making a painting we can see how putting light onstage is comparable to applying paint to a canvas. There is, of course, one major way in which these two things differ. The painter works alone;

the lighting designer works in collaboration with a director/choreographer, a set designer, a sound designer, and a costume designer—as well as with the performers themselves. Each of these people is an artist in his or her own right, and each contributes immensely to the perception of the production as a whole. For this reason I often call the art of theater a "dirty art," whereas the art of painting is quite "pure."

A painter employs line and color on a flat surface. The way the arrangement is shaped, its proportions, and the relationship of one part to the whole create the composition of the painting, and this composition helps the viewer's eye move from place to place in the painting to find the focal point or the main object. The equivalent of line to a lighting designer is direction—the line of the light in the air. A piece that I have lit that makes the use of line very apparent is *In the Upper Room* (1986), choreographed by Twyla Tharp. *In the Upper Room* needs smoke in the air so that the dancers can exit and enter from upstage—in other words, so they can appear and disappear into the smoky background. A by-product of the smoke is that the lines of light reveal themselves very clearly and dramatically. Because the light in the piece is so visible, it has often brought me awards, but the truth is that my light always has such precise and controlled lines, and it always points to the place where one should look. There is just no smoke to reveal it.

Like the painter, the lighting designer uses direction and color to guide the viewer's eye. An additional element available to the lighting designer is intensity. In a San Francisco Opera production of Janáček's *Jenufa*, directed by Francesca Zambello, we shone a very bright light through the windows during a scene that takes place in the middle of the night to portray Jenufa's derangement and sense of impending doom (the death of her baby). The daytime scenes were not as bright. This poetic use of intensity helped the audience feel the extreme emotion of the moment. At the end of Act Three, the brightness was once again repeated—this time indoors, not coming from outside—to echo the earlier moment of high emotion. But this time the emotion was happiness, not despair.

By manipulating direction, intensity, and color, the lighting designer controls light and shade, weight and substance, and the sense of foreground and background that is so important to the way we see what we see on a stage. Like pigments on canvas, the use of colors onstage can give the audience a sense of the emotional content of a scene or let them know what time of day is being enacted. Often, colors can just be relished for their lusciousness—the "taste in the mouth" through the eyes. In a Santa Fe Opera production of Berlioz's *Beatrice and Benedict* (2004) directed by Tim Albery, with a set designed by Antony McDonald, I chose to use color in an abstract way. The floor of the set was a bright yellow. The director asked me if I could make it another color. I selected a deep but bright purple filter for backlight that made the floor an orangey purple. The first act of the opera takes place from dawn to dusk. We created a beautiful sunset by using red light from the front and yellow light from the back. The colors in Act Two, a night scene, were a dark blue frontlight and the deep purple backlight. The challenge was to find a good color for "white" light for the day and for the night. Light with no filter worked very well for the daytime, and a cool lavender worked well for night.

The lighting designer calibrates all of these elements to make a work of art. If there is too much highlighted detail onstage then the audience's eye is not able to take it in, organize it, and thereby understand the information intended. If the lighting is not well composed, the audience has to take time to look at and process each thing on the stage when it should be looking at only one element—the important element. The moment to begin paying attention to the action passes very quickly; half the scene may go by before you find yourself focusing on the dialogue, and then you are totally lost because you missed the beginning. Shakespeare, for example, created a new language for each play. It is very important that audience members listen carefully in the beginning of his plays so they can grasp this language early on and understand the rest of the play. Light, by focusing visual attention, can help guide the audience into paying aural attention.

Our looking is organized in time as well as in space. How quickly do we go from one scene to the next; how much time do we spend enjoying the scene, taking in the details, before we are ready to listen? Light can establish the rhythm of a production by determining how we perceive both real time and stage time. Light is the music of the eye, and the "rules" for composition in light-time are very similar to those in music: Statement of theme(s), development of themes, theme and variation, beginning, middle, and end (one must be able to remember the beginning of a piece when one gets to the end). The lighting can make time seem to pass quickly or make it feel relentlessly slow, allowing a particular action to burst forth suddenly with great speed and force. Transitions, which always threaten to interrupt the continuity of a production, can be made to seem very quick with the proper lighting. In a 2004 production of the Restoration play *The Provok'd Wife* directed by Mark Wing-Davey at the American Repertory Theater in Cambridge, Massachusetts, there were many scenes, and much scenery to be moved between each of them. Mark is a master at focusing attention away from the moving scenery so that transitions happen without our being aware of it, but if the transitions in the play had not been totally supported by the light, the production would have felt endless. The trick is to make the audience look here while the set is moving over there. By guiding the focus of the audience from place to place and by controlling the timing of this ever-changing focus, the lighting designer determines the dynamics of the production.

To be a lighting designer, one must accept the fact that few people will notice what you do. I have always said that 99.44 percent of the audience will not see the lighting, but 100 percent of the audience will be affected by it. I had hoped that my art would change that in some small way, but light seems to be too transparent, too ephemeral. We look through it to see the dance or the play, not really noting that there is a person who controls our perception by shaping it and giving it meaning and context.

A friend of mine keeps recommending me for an honorary degree at a well-known college, and she keeps being told, "We don't give those to technicians." Now that my work is approaching its final years, I am dismayed to find that I am still thought of as a technician, and I must admit that having produced a lifetime of creative work that exists virtually unseen by the audience is disturbing. My wish for all lighting designers everywhere, young and old, is that this perception will change.

From *Esopus 3* (2004)

The Sissy Monologues (#2)

BY STEPHEN ADLY GUIRGIS

Dear Sissy—

I know i said i wasn't gonna write you anymore, and, i'm not going to—believe me, i got plenny to occupy me up here in new york—plenny—but Jessica Lindsay called me up last week and told me something about seeing you and Johnny Bassner together by the river down there, ok? And, Sissy, even though it's not my business to care anymore about what you do or who you do it with—i just gotta say—and i pray you already know it's the truth—that Johnny Bassner is a fuckin dickhead scumbag clown-headed bitch-ass blank slate motherfucker with no personality—and if it's true what Jessica told me—which, i'm trying hard to let myself not believe it—but, Sissy, if it is true, and if you're going out with him cuz you actually want to—and not because you're trying to get over me or because you wanna hurt me or prove something to yourself or something—if you're with that fuckin cocky rich wannabe pretty-boy dickwad cuz you like him or something—then, well, all i can say is that i'm glad i don't live there no more because either they've clearly put something in the water supply down there that turns people fuckin retarded, or, i just made up an idea of you that was never really the truth at all—and if that sounds harsh, it's cuz it IS harsh, and if i sound angry, it's cuz i AM, even though i know i don't have the right to be—which just makes me angrier—and i know you don't respond well to anger, but, i need my anger—it's a survival mechanism, Sissy, because the truth is that after i got off the phone from hearing about you and Johnny Bassner, i cried so hard and so deep and so hopelessly and uncontrollably that in retrospect, it gave me insight as to how God prolly gave man anger as a way to take pity on him, cuz if we were forced to feel the full depths of what's really underneath it, it would shatter our frail mental compositions like champagne flutes against granite concrete. I'm not saying this to make you feel guilty or weird, i'm just saying it because it's true. And i'll tell you something else—and again, i say it only cuz it's true: i had sex recently—not the girl with the pie, someone else. and it only happened cuz, well, i guess i had given up hope, but anyway, i met this girl and everything about her was great—i'm not saying this to make you feel jealous, it was just a fact, and anyway, one night she came over and we ended up in bed. and, at first, it was great, and i was thinking; "wow, this is great, i shoulda done this months ago"—and it was great, the physical part—and then that part ended and we finished kissing and acting all; "wow, we just fucked and shit and it was real good and stuff," and then we lit cigarettes, and then...it got quiet...and not the good kind... and it stayed that way till she got the hint and left...and then it got worse... Sissy, i know i messed up with you and that maybe you don't want to hear this, but, i miss you so much it's hard to breathe sometimes, and i wish you were here to be with me, cuz i ain't been able to get that quiet outta my ears since that night with that girl. And i don't wanna haveta believe that sex is just sex and that all we are is a bunch of smelly horny animals hurling our limbs and libidos at each other just to noise up that awful quiet from time to time. And i guess what i just wanna say is that i hope—even though i can't stand the idea of it—that if you and fuckin Johnny Bassner have sex—or if you've already had it—that it doesn't come with that awful quiet afterwards. i hope you just enjoy it, and then fall asleep with your head under the pillow like how you like it... Just please, Sissy, if you can, don't do it by the river—i need the river to stay ours—even if we can't never have it again. I need one thing—other than how much i love you—to remain simple and the same. Best to your Dad and Mom, i hope they're well...

Ten Rivers to Cross

BY EDWARD McPHERSON

One of the best-reviewed films of 2003, *Mystic River* arrived with all the public preliminaries—the antic bouts of hucksterism and hand-wringing—that attend an Important Movie. Clint Eastwood produced, directed, and wrote the score for the film, whose story was adapted by Brian Helgeland (*L.A. Confidential*) from the Dennis Lehane best-selling noir. Eastwood received a long Lillian Ross love letter in *The New Yorker* five months before the film opened; critic David Denby pronounced that it was "as close as we are likely to come on the screen to the spirit of Greek tragedy (and closer, I think, than Arthur Miller has come on the stage)."

Far and wide, the film was judged brave and unflinching, a dark, cathartic tragedy, the sort of difficult but worthwhile film-going experience that demands from its audience sobriety, attention, and a kind of psychic grit. So when *Esopus* asked me to see *Mystic River* ten times over a short span and record the fallout, I thought it sounded like a lark. If one were going to see a movie that many times, this seemed the perfect choice: a complex, compelling—perhaps even ennobling—study that would accrue rich layers of meaning with every ticket I bought.

And so I saw it alone, I saw it with friends, I saw it in Dallas, I saw it in New York, I saw it late, I saw it early, I saw it on the weekend, I saw it during work, I saw it after coffee, I saw it after beer, I saw it with popcorn, I saw it without, and at each screening, I took notes.

But before going further, I should dispatch with the plot.

MYSTIC RIVER: THE PLOT

[WARNING: CONTAINS SPOILERS]

After a slow, simple score plays over slow, simple credits, we open on two guys sitting on a ramshackle balcony, drinking beer, radio on, talking Red Sox baseball ("If he gets on base twice, I'll paint your porch," etc.). Three kids appear, scamper around to the front of the house, and start playing street hockey. The goalie, Dave, knocks the ball down a storm drain. Game over. The redheaded ringleader muses about the possibility of "borrowing" a car, then decides to scratch his name into a square of wet cement. This ringleader, Jimmy, and his friend Sean (who didn't want to steal the car) write their names. Before the goalie, Dave, can finish his, two men pull up in a sedan. The driver, who sports a trench coat, badge, and handcuffs, curses the boys and orders Dave to get in the car—they're going to tell his mother what he was up to. Dave gets in, and the silent man in the passenger seat turns around and puts his hand on the back of his seat, flashing the signet ring of some Catholic order. We see Dave look out the back window at his friends, who stand there as the car slowly drives off.

A quick succession of shots: the two boys telling their fathers what happened; Dave in a dark cellar begging for mercy as the priest-man enters (the cross around his neck glowing ominously in the half-light); Dave running frantically through the woods. Then we open on a crowd milling in front of a town house as the "I'll paint your porch" dad says, "Looks like damaged goods to me." We see Dave's shadow come to the window; his two pals peer up at him (Jimmy stands there while Sean musters a weak two-fingered wave); then Dave is drawn away by his mother. Fade out.

Twenty-five years later, Tim Robbins walks his son down the same fateful street. We learn he is Dave Boyle, the molested boy, still haunted by his ordeal; when he sees his name half-scratched in the sidewalk, he flashes back to the horror. It turns out he still lives in the neighborhood, as does Sean Penn—Jimmy Markum, the no-longer-redheaded tough who runs a corner store. The boy named Sean has grown up to be Kevin Bacon, a homicide detective with the Massachusetts State Police, whose pregnant wife left him six months ago, gave birth, and periodically calls but says nothing—then hangs up. (So as not to confuse the two Seans—one real, one fictional—I will stick to using the actors' names. Minor players, however, will go by the names of their characters.) Kevin Bacon works with a partner, Sergeant Laurence Fishburne, who makes bad jokes. Sean Penn has a spunky 19-year-old daughter, Katie; she has a star-crossed lover named Brendan whom her father hates; Brendan looks out for his mute brother, known as "Silent Ray." Katie goes out barhopping with her girlfriends on the eve of her sister's first communion and never comes home.

That night, Tim Robbins sees her in a bar and stares. He returns home at 3 a.m. with a gash across his chest and tells his wife, Celeste (Marcia Gay Harden) that a mugger tried to knife him. He then "went off" on the mugger, he explains, bashing his head against the sidewalk, possibly killing him. The next morning, Sean Penn learns that Katie is missing; a 9-1-1 phone call reports a bloody car abandoned in the neighborhood: Kevin Bacon and Laurence Fishburne are dispatched to investigate; the car turns out to be Katie's; Sean Penn discovers the detectives discovering the car, then breaks into the crime scene with the aid of one of three wild leather-clad siblings named the Savage brothers. The police find Katie's body—clubbed and shot—in an old bear cage in a park. Sean grimaces and howls as he and a red-faced Savage brother, thrashing out of control, are wrestled to the ground by a squadron of police.

The rest of the film is framed as a mystery: What happened to Katie? All signs point to hangdog Tim Robbins, who despite being a good, gentle father (he plays Wiffle ball with his son and walks him to school), still suffers from his four-day-long molestation. He tells his son creepy bedtime stories about "the boy who escaped from wolves;" he also watches vampire movies, gives his wife long speeches about the beauty of being undead, refers to himself as "an animal of of the dusk," and says things like "I can't trust my mind," "Dave's dead," "I don't know who came out of that cellar, but it sure as shit wasn't Dave," and—in reference to vampirism—"Once it's in you, it stays." Furthermore, his mugger-slasher story doesn't wash: No body has turned up.

In the course of their detective work, Kevin Bacon and Laurence Fishburne uncover a tangled web. Sean Penn used to run a robbery gang with the Savage brothers and a guy named "Just Ray" Harris, who happens to be the father of Brendan, Katie's boyfriend. The gun that killed Katie was used years ago in a liquor store holdup, the main suspect for which was Just Ray. After Just Ray got busted by the cops, he finked on Sean, who went to prison for two years, during which time his wife (Katie's mother) died of cancer. When Sean got out of prison, he bumped off Just Ray, though few people, apparently, know that; he sends $500 a month to the Harris family, who assume their patriarch ran out on them and lives in Brooklyn. Sean remarried and had two girls with Laura Linney, who is Marcia Gay Harden's cousin.

Tim Robbins has a mangled hand and a car full of blood. Eventually, her husband's behavior convinces Marcia Gay Harden that he killed Katie, which she confesses to Sean Penn. The Savage brothers are dispatched, and they persuade Tim Robbins to get into their car. (The sequence explicitly recalls the childhood abduction, with a matching turnaround from the front-seated Savage and a parting shot of Tim Robbins's head through the rear window). Sean Penn and the Savages get Tim drunk at a waterside dive, behind which Sean confronts a vomiting Tim. Tim tells Sean that his mugger story was untrue; he was actually out hunting pedophiles, one of whom he killed. Sean doesn't believe him.

As that is going on, Kevin Bacon and Laurence Fishburne are rushing to the house of boyfriend Brendan Harris—they have been tipped off by a late-breaking clue (listening to the curiously overlooked 9-1-1 tape, they notice the caller makes a revealing slipup). While the detectives are en route, Brendan realizes his father's old gun has been removed from its hiding place; he confronts his mute brother, Silent Ray, and his brother's friend John—they are the killers, he says! Brendan throws his brother across the room and kicks John's face in. John draws the gun to kill Brendan, but before he can shoot, Kevin and Laurence arrive to save the day. Back on the waterfront, Sean Penn threatens to knife Tim Robbins if he doesn't confess to Katie's murder, then knifes him when he confesses, and then shoots him. The screen goes white with the muzzle blast.

The whiteout fades into a shot of a colorless sky—it is morning. Kevin Bacon finds Sean Penn sitting drunk on the curb where their (now dead) boyhoood pal was abducted. He tells him Silent Ray and his chum confessed to the murder: They stopped Katie's car on the street with the intention of scaring whoever was inside—then the guy went off. Wounded, Katie ran into the park, where the two boys killed her so as not to get in trouble. It also turns out the body of a known child molester has been found in the woods, and Marcia Gay Harden is worried about her husband. Kevin asks Sean when he last saw Dave, and with boozy gravitas Sean responds, "That was 25 years ago, going up this street in the back of that car." (They stand in the same pose as they did 25 years ago as another flashback plays.) Kevin replies, "Sometimes I think all three of us got in that car," that in reality they are just "11-year-old boys locked in a cellar imagining our lives if we had escaped." Sean staggers down the street and says that maybe Kevin is right. Then Kevin's cell phone rings: It's his estranged wife, who—after he apologizes—finally speaks to him. Kevin learns their daughter's name, and his wife agrees to come home. We fade out.

Enter a marching band—it's a neighborhood parade. Inside his house, Sean Penn confesses to Laura Linney that he killed the wrong man. She asks to feel his heart and makes a speech about how well the girls slept last night, because they have a strong father. She admits Marcia Gay Harden called the house yesterday, worried about Dave, but she did nothing, because a daddy's love is never wrong. She then pins Sean to the bed, saying, "We'll never be weak"—he is a "king" who could "rule this town." She wants to have sex, after which they will take the girls down to the parade, because "Katie would like that."

Outside, the gang's all there: the Savages, Kevin Bacon (who stands with his wife and baby), and Marcia Gay Harden, who frantically scurries along the sidelines, trying to get her son—who is riding on a float with his baseball team—to notice her. He doesn't. She shoots a worried glance at Kevin, who shoots a finger-gun salute at Sean Penn—bang! Sean responds with a palms-out shrug as the camera glides past three boys' names etched on the sidewalk, then out and over the Mystic River.

THE FIRST TIME
Saturday, December 27, 2003
AMC Theaters Glen Lakes 8
9456 North Central Expressway
Dallas, Texas
12:30 p.m.

Home for the holidays on an overcast, drizzly day, I escape a drowsy post-Christmas household by conning my constitutionally antsy father to go see a movie with me. There is a preview, something to do with the Rock, but I am distracted by a tray of jalapeño nachos. Then the movie begins.

My notepad out but not open, I am more interested in savoring the film this first time around than in taking notes; I am ready to begin my journey, which I don't view as a test of endurance, but as a kind of tragic feast. (Imagine *King Lear*, ten times in a row; if not that, then at least Arthur Miller.)

But many things bother me right away, not the least of which is the dialogue. For all its celebrated authenticity, *Mystic River* serves up some truly stilted speech. Having perchance killed that mugger, a still-bleeding Tim Robbins informs his wife, "Makes you feel alone, hurting somebody." Sean Penn, mulling over the loss of his daughter, says aloud, at night, to no one, "I know in my soul I contributed to your death, but I don't know how." Is it necessary to say he is contemplating the lights of a distant city?

But melodramatic excess is hardly the extent of the speech crime. The men in the film are given to odd flights of lingo, as if they were aging hipsters instead of the rugged Boston blue-collars we're repeatedly reminded they are. To wit, Sean Penn to Tim Robbins: "Just stay here for a minute, if that's cool." "Yeah,

Jimmy, it's cool." And then there's the exchange between Penn and one of his employees about how Penn seems to loathe the lovable Brendan: "You look at him like you're two steps away from slicing off his nose and feeding it to him." "Naw, really?" "Straight up."

The most flagrant offender, however, is Police Sergeant Laurence Fishburne, Kevin Bacon's minority partner in the timeworn tradition of Mel and Danny (*Lethal Weapon*), Nick and Eddie (*48 Hours*), and Huck and Jim. Here he is named—pause for effect—Whitey Powers. Puffy, and sporting an incongruous soul patch, Whitey offers his partner wit ("The girl just wants to bed you—she don't want to wed you!"), wisdom ("[A daughter dead at] Nineteen. Fuck, man—he's in for a world of hurt."), and more than a little street cred ("Yeah, I dig that."). He makes Bill Clinton sex jokes, and when he lusts after a woman, he offers the highest praise: "She makes gay guys rethink their orientation, if you know what I mean." Sadly, we think we do.

Other thoughts, in no order. The direction is almost always prominently on display. The camera swoops in and out (and frequently up, when dignity is called for); there are uninspired echoes of Coppola and Scorsese, especially as a First Communion is intercut with a crime scene investigation; and the big finale—the muzzle-blast-to-sky whiteout—feels cheap, like a distracting bit of theater. But perhaps the most heavy-handed episode comes first, during the molestation, when the compression of the story (a flash here, a flash there, now Dave's damaged goods!) is obnoxious in its coy readability.

Take, for example, the abductor who turns awkwardly in the passenger seat seemingly for the sole purpose of placing his giant ring—dramatically, ridiculously—in the center of the screen. We are just getting, in screenwriting parlance, "plot points." (Though one wonders that we have come so far that "priest" is now shorthand for "sexual predator.") In fact, despite the thorny narrative, the film bends over backwards to be easily understood: Every speech is laughably helpful, every action insistently emblematic. Even the Boston accents—yes, everyone gets one—are a nuisance, particularly as they seem to come and go. The least predictable element is the music, which is oddly triumphant at times—however, just as that might become interesting, it dips minor.

I am surprised that Tim Robbins is able to walk his son unwittingly down the street on which he was abducted: He blithely reminisces about how he and his boyhood friends used to play here, how they lost countless balls down that very storm drain. It isn't until he sees his name half-scratched in the sidewalk that he—remembering what happened—turns gruff and wants to head home.

I am bothered greatly by Kevin Bacon's wife; she-who-calls-but-says-nothing is beyond ludicrous—particularly as all we ever see of her is her strangely wrinkled mouth.

I am shocked to learn who killed Katie; then I'm confused. I see Sean Penn's meaty, well-telegraphed line coming a mile away—the last time he saw Dave? "That was 25 years ago, going up this street in the back of that car"—but I don't really catch Kevin Bacon's final bit about them all being boys locked in a cellar imagining their own lives. I know it's supposed to be deep, but I smell a rat. The final phone call from "The Mouth," and its subsequent reconciliation with Kevin Bacon, couldn't be more strangely motivated: All he had to do was say he was sorry? Furthermore, he is suddenly giddy, vigilante injustice be damned (by now, we presume Penn has staggered his way to a stop sign or something).

The parade—send in the band and everybody's jaunty!—feels like the kind of atonal hallucination David Lynch would concoct, as does Laura Linney's sudden, nasty turn as a vindictive sex kitten. That is when things truly get weird. Sean has just confessed to killing his good pal, her cousin's husband, and all Laura wants to do is talk dirty about his "heaaaaaaart" and plot their takeover of the neighborhood. Bringing up a dead daughter is a strange—but not entirely inappropriate, given their curiously charged relationship—way to get Sean in the mood.

The movie wants to be a flinty film noir, and it fails, despite tireless champion David Denby's assertion that "*Mystic River*, with its gray, everyday light, is a work of art in a way that, say, *The Big Sleep* and *Out of the Past*, which were shaped as melodrama and shot in glamorous chiaroscuro, were not." By pitting *Mystic River*'s "realism" (now there's a category for you) against noir flair, Denby shoots himself in the foot. These films all flagrantly withhold key information; armchair detectives please go home—figuring out whodunit is hardly the point. The facts can be sketchy, the motivations dizzy, the plot Byzantine—but only if the tale rides on something, and for noir that something is style. Nihilism served with bad accents? That's California politics.

I leave feeling muddled and annoyed. My father dislikes the movie. At the credits, the audience gets up immediately.

THE SECOND TIME
Sunday, January 11, 2004
Loews 84th Street
2310 Broadway
New York, New York
6:15 p.m.

A freezing winter day. Some friends have tickets to the matinee ballet at Lincoln Center. After George Balanchine's *Prodigal Son*—with its genuine pathos and tragedy—I find I have a deep reluctance to endure the vain trifles of *Mystic River*. My girlfriend begs off, my friends beg off. I head up Broadway alone.

The theater is half full. An older crowd, a sticky floor. At the very last minute, a preppy thirty-something couple sits directly in front of me. He of the well-coiffed hair and itchy turtleneck eats three-quarters of her buttered popcorn and repeatedly bangs his seat into my knee. There is one preview; the rest is ads.

The couple is quite tickled by the cartoonishly (then viciously) hot-blooded Savage brothers—sweaty and pudgy in their leather jackets and gold chains—which only reinforces a nagging suspicion from my Dallas viewing. The movie, for all its blue-collar flag-waving, is deeply condescending to its characters. (A.O. Scott, writing in *The New York Times*, lauds the milieu as "tribal.") The affluent might unilaterally be scum—there are overt anti-yuppie, anti-lawyer, anti-BMW, anti-Starbucks nods throughout, which might be fine to those of us who, as the movie celebrates, prefer our coffee from Dunkin' Donuts—but the poor are likewise typecast, for we will know the downtrodden if not by their sinuous tattoos, then by their drinking (solitary, in the dark), their moles (Sean Penn wears a constellation of them, including an enormous precancerous-looking slug on his throat), and their names, which are particularly off-putting not only for their ubiquity but for their lack of imagination ("Silent Ray," "Just Ray," the Savage brothers). Sean Penn's first wife was a fiery Latina who, he points out, was "regal, like a lot of Latin woman are." (It is a strange moment made stranger by the fact that Sean has taken the opportunity to speak of his ex-wife's regality in front of his current wife and the policemen who just showed him his daughter's bloody corpse.) Brendan's mom is a run-down harpy who entertains company in a brutally formfitting pale-blue satin nightgown with pink trim.

On the second time around, it is painfully clear how manipulative the movie is. It reads essentially the same way it did the first time. Although I'm privy to the surprise ending, there is still no pleasure to be had in untangling the mystery: There are no passed-over clues, no Hitchcock-like web of double meanings, of motivations misunderstood. It looks as if Tim Robbins did it, until it doesn't. We are relentlessly made to suspect him, and, as we lack any evidence to the contrary, we do. We are meant to be terrified by him (when he watches Katie in the bar, the camera creeps in on his face, which is lit an eerie green; when he breaks down telling Marcia Gay Harden about his abduction—for what seems to be the first time—horror music plays), and we are meant to pity him (when not delivering his sinister rants, he averts his gaze and sticks out his chin). In the end, it isn't Tim who is shot as Sean Penn fires into the camera—it is we, the audience, who take it right between the eyes. Are we supposed to feel remorse? Indictment? We followed the ellipses in the prelude and got the story right; when the film cuts from Tim leering to Tim bleeding, we assume some causality. Shame on us. The real killers, it turns out, had only three scenes.

Other notes. When the priest turns to face Dave in the car, someone in the audience murmurs, "Shit." Today, Katie bothers me to no end. She is meant to be peppy, vivacious—so that we shake our heads, "Such a shame: so young, so bright!"—but her enthusiasm borders on the pathological. Oversexed with her father—"Hi, you!" as she kisses his nose and hangs on his neck, inches away from a sloppy make-out session—she is nothing but trouble. Furthermore, she has the facial expressions of an animatronic toy. Perhaps she dies for her overacting.

As for Marcia Gay Harden, she could not be more mousy, more beat-down. She is all quiver and shiver, shuffling about and looking at the floor. She obviously didn't get the memo that everyone loves a parade, and in the final scene she is so pathetic that we laugh at her (she, a widow!). She also talks like a Muppet. Her funniest line: "But Daaaaave, I don't think anything."

There is intense product placement. The choice of this generation is clearly Coke, not Pepsi—up to and including such corporate offshoots as Dasani water, which gets an illuminated vending machine, and Sprite, which figures prominently in a joke and for which Tim Robbins asks by name. In the background, an old lady's TV plays a Ronco infomercial. Samuel Adams posters stand out in every liquor store, but Tim Robbins drinks Harpoon, and Sean Penn favors Miller High Life (he also stocks his pantry with multiple shelves of Jell-O). When you want to get your pal sloshed, so you can knife him, reach for the Wild Turkey.

Somewhere up front a cell phone plays "Für Elise"; in my row a woman shouts, "Turn it off!" As the case mounts against poor Tim, there are lots of sighs. When Brendan kicks his brother's friend John in the face—repeatedly—there are loud intakes of breath. (There are quieter gasps when John brandishes the gun.) As the death scene unfolds on the waterfront, the discomfort is audible—people exhale, squirm, rustle their clothes. Tim's forced confession strikes me as regrettably eloquent—he rambles convincingly about a "dream of lost youth"—which certainly doesn't help his case with Sean.

The haphazard ending irks me. Tragedy could have been averted two hours ago if only Kevin Bacon had bothered to listen to the 9-1-1 tape. Despite the knotted history—in which Silent Ray kills the daughter of the man who killed his father—the murder is an accident, the participants' connection pure coincidence. As Kevin Bacon puts it, "If this Markum thing's random…then shit."

Even given such randomness, the de facto motive—lost in the shuffle of last-minute theatrics—is absurd. The gun goes off and two boys—so as not to "get in trouble"—hunt their victim down, beat her to a pulp with a hockey stick, then shoot her execution-style in the back of the head. (Which oddly recalls Katie's dumb joke to Brendan about what her father would do if he found him kissing her: "Shoot you, then kill you.") At its best, the film hopes to illustrate how senseless violence can lead flawed men to commit tragic acts—the sour surprise being the ill-fated coincidence that sets such bleak gears turning. But Katie's murder makes no sense even as a random act, and there are no tragic consequences of Sean's poor behavior, other than a mean look from Kevin Bacon.

Which brings us to *Mystic River*'s other muddled claim, that these men are stunted by history, that they are, as Kevin Bacon asserts at the end, still boys locked in a cellar—which has given reviewers license to spout a lot of mumbo jumbo about the inescapability of the past, its dogged hold on the present, how one vile act can arrest the hands of time. Phooey. In the prologue, each boy's character is perfectly formed; they are little men, just waiting to grow into their Hollywood bodies, long before the irrevocable incident ever takes place. The abducted boy, Dave—doughier and dorkier than the rest, already the butt of the joke (who has to play goalie, natch)—grows up to be a sacrificial lamb. The good kid with the well-developed sense of justice—which makes him reluctant to steal cars, and who is named Sean Divine, I might add—grows up to be a cop. And the redheaded daredevil in his junior-size leather jacket, "the hard case" who picks on Dave, grows up to kill him. It's not the past they're trapped by, but cliché. And so boys will be boys, even if they're men, making the film play less like Greek tragedy and more like an after-school special on hazing.

As we filter out of the theater into the cold, we form pockets of explanation.

THE THIRD TIME
Thursday, January 29, 2004
Loews 34th Street
312 West 34th Street
New York, New York
6:45 p.m.

Two days ago the film picked up six Academy Award nominations: Best Actor (Sean Penn), Best Supporting Actor (Tim Robbins), Best Supporting Actress (Marcia Gay Harden), Best Director, Best Adapted Screenplay, and Best Picture. Sean Penn and Tim Robbins have already taken home a Golden Globe each. It is a shame to see the best performance in the film, Tom Guiry as Brendan Harris, go unrecognized.

My guess is that this might be Sean's year. I can see the screen at the Kodak Theater on February 29: insert a scene of operatic Oscar-clip grief, as the police wrestle a grieving father to the ground and the camera soars above them—the Crane Shot of Anguish, we'll call it—as the music swells. Perfect.

An alternate clip: Sean's unregenerate stagger down the street in the harsh light of morning, bottle in his hand, brushing a friend's death off his conscience.

Should Tim Robbins need a clip, I suggest the one of him spinning yarns about "the boy who escaped from wolves," his face looming large in the dark, filling the screen like a sad-sack Mount Rushmore.

As for Marcia Gay Harden: either sponging blood or scurrying at the parade, though I really doubt it.

Perhaps the accolades account for the 60-odd people in the early evening audience, a good number for a snowy midtown Thursday. I have slipped away from work, where I am on a tight deadline for another story. I have had all month to see the movie, but having procrastinated I now am staring down a busy wedding weekend punctuated by as many two-and-a-half-hour dips into the Mystic River as a body can stand. I feel like a polar bear. Furthermore, I have been ducking my *Esopus* editor, avoiding calls and e-mails, which now has riddled our friendship with guilt—entirely my fault. Is this an exercise in masochism or sadism?

The stadium seats are nice here, at an inexplicable $8.99 price.

Having rushed straight from the office, I am starving. Hemingway wrote that the best way to understand Cézanne is to look at his paintings hungry. Not so with *Mystic River*, where the stomach's hollowness only finds its twin on the screen. Once again, just as the movie begins, latecomers sit in front of me. Today they're in hoods.

Dave's miraculous escape from the dungeon continues to bug me. While his cozy bedtime stories about boys and wolves—sure to unnerve even the sleepiest child—feature flashbacks to spell out the already overt psychology, we never learn how Dave actually broke free. The elision of something so potentially dramatic—and the glib segue from him running through the woods to "looks like damaged goods to me"—flaunts Eastwood's willingness to sacrifice character for narrative pace. It is skywriting as storytelling.

I am proud: I spot my first continuity error. In Sean Penn's early scene with his employee, the coffee mug on his desk changes its orientation slightly between shots.

When Marcia Gay Harden attends to Robbins's wound, the woman behind me scoffs, "In the kitchen sink?" as Marcia Gay wrings out the bloody rag over a sink of dirty dishes.

Another thought: Why would the boys call in their own crime to 9-1-1, especially when they show no subsequent remorse?

Most of the Boston accents start strong out of the gate and falter, unless there's an *r* to be dropped on the last word. Also, I lived in Boston once, and I recall bumping into at least one person who didn't have an accent.

Why does Laurence Fishburne deliver a cup of cafeteria coffee to the newly bereft Sean Penn with the line, "Fresh brewed." Is it a lame joke? Sick taunting? From the get-go, Laurence does not like Sean.

Sean Penn has the same microwave as I do. Nice.

For the first time, two people walk out of the movie.

Today there is markedly more laughing at Marcia Gay Harden.

If Katie is only 19—and everyone knows everyone else in the neighborhood, as is clearly indicated—how can she be drinking beer in the bar? And why in the world would she and her friends choose to frequent the same old-man dive as her dad's friends? What Boston teenager picks the VFW over Lansdowne Street?

Strange: I can hear the whir of the projector.

Marcia Gay Harden is always trembling—someone find her a coat!

Poor Tim Robbins, always getting put in the backs of cars—with pedophiles, with the state police, with the Savage brothers. His vampire speech prompts cries of "What?"

I notice that after he rushes in and grabs the gun out of young John's hands, Kevin Bacon has an enormous self-congratulatory smirk on his face. He is strangely satisfied amid the devastation. The same goes for his giddiness upon hearing his wife is coming home. He has a gift for skating above tragedy on his own self-involvement.

I tire of the score's thoughtful bass line. We get it: It's serious.

As the truth comes out about the killers, there are a few sighs in the audience—of annoyance, not catharsis.

Two more people walk out as Laura Linney talks about her husband's big heart.

Eastwood frequently shoots from below, looking up at his characters, monumentalizing them; he uses moving aerial shots to evoke "mood of place," or something like that. (Else he's just showing off his helicopter budget.)

It is hard not to laugh at the final tableau: spider-woman Laura Linney aggressively cheerful at the parade, clapping psychotically for the benefit of poor Marcia Gay Harden, the victim of an unforeseen plot twist so pathetic her son doesn't even want to look at her. Sean Penn emerges and, after gripping two of the Savage brothers, gives his wife a postcoital nod. She smiles. Now that Kevin Bacon has The Mouth back in his life, Laurence Fishburne is nowhere to be seen. And as we skim out over the river, somewhere below is a watery Tim Robbins, looking sad. Overheard as I leave the theater: "What a silly movie." Then, "Man, my ass is asleep."

THE FOURTH TIME
Friday, January 30, 2004
City Cinemas Village East
181–189 Second Avenue
New York, New York
10:10 p.m.

Remarkably, I have talked my altogether healthier girlfriend—who typically watches a movie once and is done with it—into coming along. There are about 35 people in the beautiful old theater, which boasts an ornate dome and a hanging chandelier. There are no pre-preview advertisements, only bebop jazz. Then, with six minutes before showtime, a rush of 50-odd people comes in. Perhaps I have never noticed: Why do moviegoers cut it so close in the East Village?

There is a clutch of NYU freshmen behind us who are loudly infatuated with their own wit. When I find out they are seniors, I am embarrassed.

At the movies, I tend to discover new levels of misanthropy. I love seeing movies on my TV's decidedly not flat 26-inch screen perched on a dresser, an experience that might be sans surround-sound but is also sans consumptives, talkers, smelly feet, big hair, and punks with laser pointers. That said, it's like watching in a vacuum. Movies are at best a private, interior event undertaken in public—we enjoy watching the movie and each other. So in some way, I'm glad the kids are there.

We are sitting in the balcony and it's an interesting vantage point; looking down at the screen, the figures are not so heroic.

Random thoughts. Why do the molesters drive away at a sinister four miles per hour—for the entire block? My girlfriend also thinks the daughter is in love with Daddy Penn. And what drunk 19-year-old girl, when it comes time to choose a jukebox anthem to which to dance on the bar, goes with a brassy up-tempo jazz number? (Perhaps she knew it likely was written by Clint Eastwood.)

This time, as Katie and Brendan chat in her car, I notice through the windshield a blurry Tim Robbins walking by—unrecognizable but for his clothes and his gait. Was there a deleted scene with him in Sean Penn's store?

I doze off for a while, waking to Tim Robbins talking about vampires. I decide to nap some more.

I'm wondering what Dave does for a living. Laurence says he is "marginally employed," but we never find out how.

My girlfriend notices something brilliant: Katie, dead on a slab in the funeral home, is breathing. Her neck twitches; then, when Sean Penn lays a dress over her white-sheeted body, you see her chest heave up and down, up and down, up and down. She's not even trying to hide it.

When John gets kicked to the face, the woman to my right ducks and covers her face.

After Tim Robbins gets shot, a (Greek) chorus pipes up on the score, lots of deep male voices to accentuate the tragedy.

An audience member laughs at the final flashback of the molesters driving away with little Tim Robbins ("That was 25 years ago, going up this street in the back of that car..."); perhaps the same woman snorts at Laura Linney's "You could rule this town."

As people gather their belongings at the movie's end, they spin theories about who knew what when. The NYU girl behind us is wearing a deep frown; her friends try to console her. What right does the movie have to make her feel this way? It's not her fault; the deck is so laughably stacked against Tim Robbins. If you knew a guy who liked to tell weird bedtime stories, leer at soon-to-be-dead girls, draw vampire analogies with himself, lie to everyone, and confess to murders—you'd probably knife him too. It's not that I mind being tricked; that's why we go to the movies, that's the point: to invest these limited, overpaid vessels of flesh and blood with our dreams, to make them over as our better—and our worse—selves. (And we in the seats are willing to do tremendous narrative work to ease that delusion—it's more fun to play along!) But we want to be tricked with grace and with an honesty of sorts: We trust there to be a point, even if it is that there is no point. Otherwise, our faith has been abused—Godzilla comes out of left field to crush Bambi—and all we can do is laugh.

Overheard on the way out:

Girl #1: "Wait, I'm confused. So the two boys ran into her by accident?"

Guy #1: "Yeah, I know. That didn't make sense. It would have made sense if they killed her on purpose."

Guy #2: "No, it wouldn't have. Nothing made sense. I told you we should have gone to *Big Fish*."

THE FIFTH TIME
Saturday, January 31, 2004
Loews Kips Bay
570 Second Avenue
New York, New York
11:40 a.m.

Eleven hours ago, I was in a different theater, watching the same movie. I am at a morning show, as I have a wedding in the afternoon. Who goes to a movie at 11:40? About 45 people, mainly in their 30s and 40s. The theater sells chicken fingers, which smell great, though I stick with the food I smuggled in. I am treated to 20 minutes of previews. Once this viewing is over, I will be halfway there.

Young Sean Penn can't even wave to his raped pal?

Perhaps Tim Robbins's worst acting comes when he is "startled" by Sean Penn. Stepping out onto a porch, he lights a match, an unseen Sean says, "Hey, Dave," there is a beat, then he throws not the match but the matchbook.

My favorite line in the movie is delivered by none other than the inimitable Eli Wallach, appearing in a cameo as the owner of Loony Liquors. Talking about a robbery, Wallach says it was "scarier than a glass of milk."

I feel bad for the two guys in front of me whispering back and forth, trying to figure things out. I want to tell them it's no use. We are doomed to be Marcia Gay Harden, abandoning Tim Robbins, condemning him, then feeling sorry for it.

Those who sit all the way through the credits are an interesting bunch, I imagine. I'm out as soon as I see river.

THE SIXTH TIME
Sunday, February 1, 2004
UA East 85th Street
1629 First Avenue
New York, New York
4:00 p.m.

I am on the Upper East Side, in a dingy basement theater with a single screen. (The show is scheduled to let out in time for Super Bowl burgers at a friend's house nearby). The place is packed with more than 150 silver foxes, almost all of whom—curiouser and curiouser—are munching popcorn. The ads compete with the white noise of crunched kernels. I notice this theater, owned by Regal Entertainment, plays slight variations of some of the ones I have been getting at Loews. The previews are the same, however: the epic stories of Troy and the Alamo (coming this Christmas!), a dreadful-looking Robert Redford movie, and so forth.

It occurs to me that *Mystic River* is the kind of movie about which my mom would complain, "Why do they have to use such language?" And what's scarier than a glass of milk is that for once I agree with her. The cursing seems cheap, a too-easy indicator of the characters' hardscrabble lives—behold, says Clint, the tough talk of the violent classes. For lack of a better idea, I buy some caffeine and devote today's showing to documenting the language.

An unscientific tally: Number of uses of "fuck," or a variation thereof, in the course of two hours and 15 minutes: 63. (Roughly an F-bomb dropped every two minutes and nine seconds.)

Even more offensive are the 197 blatantly (though at times creatively) dropped *r*'s—from a range of words including "sewer," "bar," "car," "far," (as well as multiple "car"-"bar" combos and the delightfully lilting phrase: "What we got on the car so far?"), "mugger," "shower," "over," "Markum," "cruiser," "killer," "cellar," "parkway," "here," "Sergeant," "paper," "father," "collector," "remember," and "never." The math on that comes to one *r* lost every 41 seconds. The worst part is that they miss a few.

I am no longer sure what the father means when he says of little Dave: "Looks like damaged goods to me." Just what is the mark of molestation—and why, pray tell, is he so familiar at spotting it? It is a damning, heartless phrase, especially from the mouth of a character we know so little about. But more than that, it reveals a chronic aggression, a persistence on the part of the film to go out of its way to distance us from Dave. While not the monster we think he is, the boy nonetheless will grow up to be a killer. The line betrays the film's phobic baggage. In a better world, one hopes such damaged goods might mend.

A striking revelation: On the morning after the crime, not only is Silent Ray still carrying the hockey stick he used to bludgeon Katie, but he walks it right into her father's store. (After, one assumes, he has sponged off the gore with Hannibal Lecter–like aplomb.) The film is really an indictment of today's miscreant youth.

Today, the overhead shot in which 20-odd cops struggle to restrain a grieving Sean Penn and the excitable Savage brother is hilarious—a comic spectacle of fruitless action (one man goes frantically between the two piles, lightly touching people on the arm). The scene, however, cannot beat the breathing dead.

The woman behind me does not like all the drinking and makes little noises of disapproval. An older man walks out. John's kick to the face gets its biggest reaction yet—squirms, groans, even shouts.

When Tim Robbins slashes the pedophile and when Sean Penn stabs Tim, the sound effects are great. Even a knife hurled into the river flies forth with a *shhhh-ching*!

Later, over burgers, I notice I use a line from the movie in conversation. The pitiful part is that it's not even a big line, just some throwaway filler. I look around the table, but no one has noticed. I have a quiet moment of shame and worry about the saturation of my subconscious.

THE SEVENTH TIME
Tuesday, February 3, 2004
AMC Empire 25
234 West 42nd Street
New York, New York
4:00 p.m.

The snow has turned to rain, and I am skipping out on work—again—to trudge through puddles and slush to the movies. Even the downpour doesn't dim Times Square's Technicolor brilliance and claustrophobic congestion. There are 13 people in the audience today. These are the best seats yet: plush, red, well spaced, and with the proper amount of spring. The screen is huge and at a comfortable height. My mind is on other things, however—namely, the freelance job that I have just learned will no longer exist for me or any of my officemates come Friday. (They're in a bar; I'm in here.) Wet and feeling sorry for myself, I am peeved at the characters and the demands they are trying to make.

I sit close to the front today, so that my eye has to travel across the huge screen. This theater is fantastic.

I notice more Sprite in Sean Penn's office and in his pantry.

I flirt with the idea of reading the book of *Mystic River* then decide it would only cloud my judgment. The movie needs to stand on its own.

I hear a child's voice in the darkness—a woman two rows down has brought her toddler! She best not give him a hockey stick.

There are many, many crosses—around the neck of the molester, on Marcia Gay Harden's wall, across Sean Penn's back. Point made: They're Catholic.

I am no detective, but it seems to me that two boys (first-time killers at that) panicking in the dark might leave some shred of physical evidence—a hair, a fingerprint, a drop of their own blood—but apparently not. More fodder for the cold-blooded psychopath theory.

The first time we hear from The Mouth, Kevin Bacon anticipates the call. He doesn't quite reach for his cell before it rings, but he begins doing something pointless with his arm that then slides over to answer the phone.

I nap through the interrogation of Tim Robbins by the Bacon/Fishburne dynamic duo. I am woken by a man walking out.

My favorite line now belongs to Sean Penn. Right before he kills Tim Robbins, he says, "We bury our sins here, Dave. We wash them clean." Then he shoots him—and goes on to become a crime lord! (Or at least a wanna-be crime lord.) I love it.

The audience reacts at nothing today, though another guy leaves right before Tim gets shot.

It is a strangely conservative movie, despite the presence of political wild card Sean Penn. (There is a funny moment when someone mentions that Just Ray used to carry around enough loose change to make "a phone call to Iraq." I like to think Sean Penn winces a little, but it might just be me.) Despite the fact that we are supposed to deplore what happens, the moral of the film seems to be—judging by tone—that it is okay to kill anyone you think you have to in order to keep the girls safe in their beds. Sean Penn might spill the wrong blood, but we are to admire his tortured resilience, his terse poetry, his leather duster. He makes hard decisions, then shrugs off the consequences—literally, at the parade, as he gives Kevin Bacon a look that says, "What, me?" He is the only one whose children sleep well at night, the only one who finds any faith in his partner, the only one who gets to have any sex (albeit with a homicidally rapacious Laura Linney). Watching the film, I get an uncomfortable feeling that he is supposed to be right. The innocent are acceptable casualties; swift action is preferable to labored justice. These days, some would claim this reminiscent of U.S. foreign policy. I wonder what Sean would say to that?

THE EIGHTH TIME
Thursday, February 5, 2004
Clearview Chelsea
260 West 23rd Street
New York, New York
3:50 p.m.

While those at the office shred, I go to the movies. There are 12 other patrons, all over 65, though I saw a few kids in the lobby suspiciously already out of school. We are floors above the concession stand, and yet the smell of popcorn permeates the theater—no doubt an underhanded psychological gambit. When I enter the theater, the volume is up too high. The ads are booming; some seniors are visibly upset, motioning toward the projection booth while trying to cover their ears with their hands. A lone hipster arrives in shaggy hair and leather, followed by a priest in a collar and frock. I no longer know if this is strange in real life or just because I am taking notes.

The seats are worn blue velvet. Today I know every line in every preview, a new low. Someone at work asked whether my hatred for the movie grew with each viewing. To be honest, it started high, crested around screening number five, dipped slightly once I began taking comfort in the disgrace (the familiar pleasure of going through the paces), and has since plateaued now that the end is within view. That said, the sight of the gray Warner Bros. shield, followed by the emblematic Village Roadshow Pictures *V*, induces a mild fight-or-flight panic.

I notice that what the molester says to get Dave into the car differs slightly in the flashback—whether that is a *Rashomon*-like comment on the vagaries of memory or simply a mistake, I don't know.

I must remember not to fault the actors, some of whom I enjoy in other movies. Film is a director's medium, through and through.

Today I am dead to the movie and it is dead to me. The images, words, and music have no purchase; they slide right off like disjointed patches of color and sound.

Two minor sins: The slow-moving man coming down the street who vanishes while Tim Robbins is telling his son about the storm drain, and Kevin Bacon's odd pause for breath in the climactic line, "This is my daughter…I'm talking about."

One of today's audience members feels he must react—audibly—to every minor plot convulsion. "Yeah." "Nuhhh." "Unnnh."

Laura Linney has become a compelling cipher. Her first line—"She no-shows at work? What if she no-shows at church?"—is awfully harsh, considering she is talking about a stepdaughter we already know is dead. When Sean Penn rebukes her for overcriticizing Katie, she reminds him that he has two other daughters—hers. I become convinced that Laura Linney has orchestrated the whole thing: The wicked stepmother has paid two fresh-faced goons to whack the apple of her husband's eye. We know very little about Laura before her unmasking in the final act as a horny and heartless Lady Macbeth. She spends a lot of time looking sad in a brown leather jacket; the first night she is upstairs, off camera, having needed to take a pill. We know she quit smoking ten years ago but cracks under the strain, sending Tim Robbins out to buy her a pack. Men seem to do her bidding. Her second line in the film is an order to her husband—not to make their daughter laugh in church.

Indeed, despite what Mr. Denby says, that "by the end of the movie, we know this place, for good and for ill—the sour flatness of the accents, the women clinging to the men," and despite the trademark Eastwood machismo that colors both character and style, it is without a doubt the women who rule the roost. (That they rule through manipulation and disloyalty, that they are either dead and pure or alive and treacherous helps reassert the misogyny. Whether that is merely a holdover from noir is up for debate.) Thus Laura Linney proves to be a black-widow bride, and mousy Marcia Gay betrays her husband to the enemy. Faithful Kevin Bacon is slave to the wayward Mouth, who names their only child; when she decides she is coming home, he stammers, "Everything is the way you left it!"

Speaking of Kevin Bacon, his clipped delivery—"Hey. Take it easy. That's the father."—fails to impart the authority he's striving for; instead, he sounds like he's channeling Keanu Reeves in *The Matrix* or *Point Blank*. When Laurence Fishburne sends "his biggest, ugliest troopers" to haul Tim Robbins in for questioning, Kevin shoots him a look like a bemused mother hen ("Oh, *Whitey*...").

I am sick of being shot by Sean Penn; I am tired of the aggression. The next day, I will find myself humming the parade march in the office, not recognizing the tune immediately, then growing very sad.

I am nervous this time when Laura Linney embraces shirtless Sean Penn from behind, her face so near the big mole on his neck, her eyes closed, her nuzzling mouth open—I fear she is going to chomp it off.

In a strange footnote, I go home and find *Groundhog Day* playing on TV. With two viewings still left, I don't appreciate the irony.

I watch it, of course.

THE NINTH TIME
Saturday, February 7, 2004
UA Battery Park City Stadium 11
102 North End Avenue
New York, New York
1:00 p.m.

On a rainy Saturday, armed with tuna in a pita, a bag of chips, a vanilla Coke, and a hefty sack of M&M's (my own product placement), I settle in for a self-imposed double feature. I am going to rip off the Band-Aid, tie the tooth to the doorknob and slam it shut. The execution cannot be worse than the dread. I had hoped to mitigate the pain by going to the historic Ziegfeld Theater, an appropriate blockbuster finale, but I read the schedule incorrectly—the film is no longer playing there. So I end up downtown, where I buy tickets to the one o'clock and the four o'clock shows. The woman in the booth doesn't bat an eye.

When I arrive at the theater, there has been a mistake; the film is already well into the second reel. I walk back out—as I refuse to see one frame more than necessary—and watch someone else alert the management. Once the projector is shut off, about ten patrons follow me in. The seats are new but stiff. We are 15 minutes early, but it seems too quiet for me to tuck into my sandwich. Again, everyone is over 65. At two minutes to the hour, 17 twenty-somethings come in. It seems only the retired and I arrive early.

Another disappearing act, this time in the morgue cafeteria. The man at the adjacent table—now you see him, now you don't.

Why does Laura Linney's father check the water heater? As he's talking to Sean at the wake—about "domestic responsibility"—he licks a finger and thumps the boiler. Does he think Sean, in his grief, might have forgotten to pay the utilities?

I nod off in the usual part, right when Brendan's mom enters in her robe. I wake, refreshed, when Sean and Tim are on the porch.

There is a big laugh and even some clapping when Tim Robbins mouths off to the cops—are there anarchist sympathies in TriBeCa?

I notice that I know the background traffic patterns, as I wait for cars to turn in the distance.

This realization leads me to play a game: I pretend I am the one controlling everything; I pretend I am God. Let the child raise the SpongeBob SquarePants balloon! Let the Savage brother spill whiskey down his chin! The fun lasts for a little while.

Many people sit through the credits, including me. I notice the vampire clip is from a John Carpenter movie. Once all the names have finally rolled off—and we have been assured that this has been a fictional work in which any intersections with real life are purely coincidental (no comment)—the theater is empty save for me and a guy in glasses.

I head to the concession area for my "intermission." Lacking the four quarters necessary to play a video game, I stare out the window.

THE TENTH TIME
Saturday, February 7, 2004
UA Battery Park City Stadium 11
102 North End Avenue
New York, New York
4:00 p.m.

I come back into the theater for the four o'clock showing—and the guy in glasses is still there! He hasn't moved. He is looking at me. What is he doing? Who is he? Why is he watching me? Is he an undercover theater agent? My second ticket, which I applauded myself for honorably purchasing (rather than just sneaking in on the first), has not been torn—making me mildly nervous for no good reason. Has this *Esopus* story been double-assigned? Is this an indication of editorial mistrust? Has he been tailing me all along? The wheels spin faster. Am I a patsy—am I the real story? Is there someone out there writing a piece about me, a piece about someone stupid enough to see the same dull movie ten times?

The theater fills with some 80 people. We get the usual previews with the usual women (Angelina Jolie, Ashley Judd) in the usual roles (cops, investigators) that place them in the usual degrees of bodily peril. Then *Mystic River* begins barreling to its unpalatable denouement, but I can't focus. My thoughts range as to the intentions of my journalistic döppelganger.

Despite the fact that this is the last time I will ever see this movie—rest assured—all is bitter, nothing sweet. I see nothing new, nothing fun; the omniscient agent-of-God game does not work. A woman shouts at the child molester—"No!" The breathing corpse only brings unknowable despair. The plot twists fall like body blows. And I keep thinking about my double out there in the dark.

Mystic River has failed me in ways more pernicious and methodical than almost any other movie could have failed me after ten viewings. Continuity errors I can live with; product placement has become an amusing necessary evil. However with each viewing the film did not grow richer, but more sinister; odd lines, vague motivations, thematic echoes—the amusing hiccups I had hoped to encounter—were never whimsical, were never charming, but instead resolved themselves into troubled designs.

Despite the many claims to the contrary, the film offers only a water cooler catharsis, one in which we earnestly pat ourselves—and those around us—on the back for having endured something so discomforting. Rather than confront tragedy, the film finesses it. *Mystic River* is little more than a passing shell game: Vicious where it should be kind, manipulative where it should be brave, it blames—by dishonest means—those it should forgive and forgives those it should blame. The overweight, passive, and irreversibly "damaged" boy is trampled relentlessly (and in increments so regular, so persistent, they defy the much-touted realism) until he dies—at the hands of an executioner who not only gets away with murder, but does so with the film's only dash of panache. Never mind the plot. In the bare-knuckled, old-world school of *Mystic River*, you are either born a victim or you are born a king, and it's best that never the twain shall meet.

Too much! Buckling under the crushing psychic weight of the *Mystic River* and the steely-rimmed gaze of my sinister twin, I grab my stuff and slip out the door—a coward, painfully aware of my failure of nerve, but instantly, irrevocably happy to see if I can catch the end of *Big Fish*, or something like it, somewhere, anywhere, in the wide-open cineplex.

POSTSCRIPT
March 1, 2004

Mystic River *went on to win two Academy Awards. The Crane Shot of Anguish clip was used to highlight Sean Penn, who won for Best Performance by an Actor in a Leading Role. Tim Robbins was the film's other winner. In his acceptance speech, he made an emotional plea to victims of abuse: "There is no shame or weakness in seeking help or counseling—it is sometimes the strongest thing you can do to stop the cycle of violence."*

Blue

BY CHELLI RIDDIOUGH

As a child, David loved the cartoons where a boxing glove would pop out from a character's chest like a hilarious, haphazard game of Pop Goes the Weasel; years later, when he punched his girlfriend for the first time, he was amazed by how it felt just as he'd imagined it. In the darkest corner where body and mind share horrible truths, he knew this punch was a long time coming. The moment his arm drew back, he acknowledged it as a release he'd been resisting for years. It shared the spasmodic building-up of an orgasm and the pleasant self-indulgence of a yawn. He was rubbing his knuckles, *fuck, that hurt*, before he realized what he'd done, and by then Amy had already crawled across the floor to the telephone and was punching in numbers that he recognized with a sick twist in his stomach were surely 9-1-1.

He shot out of his apartment and into the winter night, forgetting to pull on shoes and colliding with the door frame. The rum echoed on his tongue, Amy's words still ringing in his ears. These two sensations took on the quality of a metallic sheen, glazing his face against the cold. He could still feel it but his brain was putting it into a separate box. He noticed a strange pain in his toes and looked down to see that his legs were walking; his feet, bare. Amy would have scolded him for that. But she would never scold him again. He had failed her at long last. If he had been a better man, he would have found the guy she was fucking and punched him instead.

"Wake up," she had said to him. Those two words seemed to be the shared refrain of every woman in his life—not like there had been many. He didn't count all the girls he'd met at bars, chubby girls with sad, smudgy eyes and bulging tube tops, lost girls with red lips and perfume that wounded his nostrils as he breathed. His mother, of course, was always telling him to wake up. Lucy was too. God, Lucy. He hadn't seen his sister in years. Before Amy there'd been Carmen, his only other true love. "David, wake up," she would whisper to him in the morning, then hide under the covers. "Where in the world is Carmen Sandiego?" he would ask, then dive beneath the sheets and grab her. But that, too, went sour. "Wake up," she said to him the night they broke up. "Some men your age are married. Some even have children." She met someone who looked good with facial hair and moved back to Spain. David wondered if she was happy, but she didn't have a Facebook page so he couldn't tell.

His hand was still aching from the punch. Was she bleeding when he saw her at the telephone? He could only remember her eyes, which were wild and green and had scared him. He was glad they didn't keep a gun in the house.

He cradled his hand in his sweatshirt pocket and told himself that he never would have ended up in that situation if he weren't cursed by his dad. It was so clichéd it burned: an alcoholic father who passed down his legacy of abuse. Father-son tales. It was the reason David had gotten a vasectomy at 22. He wasn't going to continue the cycle.

Though he couldn't remember a time before his dad became mean, things had gotten worse when Lucy turned 14. David was 10, a veteran of the tense silence inside his house. Lucy had been about to blow out the candles on the cake their mother had just baked. She and David were wearing party hats. She was smiling, her mouth huge with braces. Their mother lifted a disposable camera. "Don't smile so big," she was saying. It was taking her forever to get the perfect shot. He wriggled in his seat, wanting cake. He was the one who saw the candle first. It drooped sidelong, stuck briefly in the frosting, then toppled off the edge to spill wax onto the tablecloth. He was still watching it when he heard the slap. He looked up. His sister's cheek was smarting, its freckles lost in the red splotch that was developing into an imprint of their father's hand. He'd seen that mark on his mother before, but this was new. His father had never hit one of them, and David's world teetered with the queasy realization that the rules had been changed.

"Lucy," he choked, the word webbed into a sob. Wed to the violence that came before it, her name sounded like a dirty word.

"Shut up," his father said. "Or you're next."

So he shut up, and things went on as normal. Only Lucy wouldn't smile at him anymore, or sing to him before he went to sleep. He barely noticed, too busy waiting for the day his dad would turn to him with a fist. But he never once got hit. And he was glad. He wished he were the kind of brother and son who would stand up for others, who would say "take me." But, he told himself as he drifted off at night, that's just not who he was.

Most of his father's abuse came in small splinters: a backhand here, a "fucking fatso" there. His mother got the worst of it, but the older Lucy grew and the more womanly responsibilities she had to adopt, the more of his father's hatred permeated her life, too. One afternoon when David was 14, he went into his basement to grab a Sprite from the fridge. Lucy was at the ironing board, singing to herself and running the iron across one of his father's dress shirts. Over the collar, down the sleeves. He didn't like the song she was singing. It sounded familiar and funereal all at once.

He heard his father before he saw him, as usual. Angry thumps down the stairs. He'd learned, like a meteorologist, to read the vibrations of the floor as a barometer for his father's moods.

Lucy, too, must have heard, for she froze at the ironing board. Her head tilted down. The shag rug beneath David's bare feet curled between his toes. It occurred to him that she'd never learned to hide behind her hair. When it was pulled back in a bun, he could see the terror on her face.

"Do you know what you're doing?" their father asked her.

She raised her eyes to his neck.

"I'm ironing," she said in a child's voice.

"No you're not," he said. "You're not ironing. You're burning my fucking shirt."

She looked down: Smoke was rising from the iron's place on the breast pocket. "I'm sorry," she said. Everything about her seemed to be shrinking. The girl who had stood six feet tall on her 13th birthday, laughing as she touched the ceiling with her hands, at 17 had the posture of an old maid, slinking around corners and disappearing into chairs. His father was a giant standing over her, stabbing his finger in the air before her face.

And David stood watching, the glass bottle sweating onto his palm, one hand still on the refrigerator door. His bangs fell into his eyes, a tendency that bothered his mother to no end. "David, show your eyes," she would say, tucking a loose strand behind his ear. "You were such a beautiful child." He hated it when she did this, and would return the hair with a righteous shake of his head. One time he swatted her hand away, and she held it to her chest and looked at him. She hadn't touched him much after that.

As David raised the Sprite to take a sip, his father hit his sister across the face with the iron.

For years to come, he would pause at this point in the story to take a swig of beer and gaze at the bar in front of him. Then he'd turn to whichever Kristy or Laurel was on the stool next to him and say, "That sip tasted like death." In truth, it had tasted only like Sprite, and he'd enjoyed it countless times since, both with and without vodka.

Lucy fell to the floor in a flourish of skirt and skinny legs. Her jaw was broken, and she was out of school for six weeks with her mouth wired shut. David heard a rumor that she had gotten braces and was too embarrassed to show her face. "Something like that," he had said. Her jaw never healed right, even once the bruises had faded. Each time she closed her mouth it angled slightly right, which would have given her smile a possibly charming crookedness, had she ever smiled. He never saw it, at least, when she passed him in the halls.

He saw his feet were turning blue and laughed. So that actually happened: blue feet. He wondered if his lips were blue too. What Amy's eye looked like.

He was in front of a door. He knocked. Though he'd never visited, apparently he knew the way to his sister's house after all. She only lived a mile away, but he hadn't so much as dropped by to say hello since she'd moved there three years earlier. Lucy had tried, in their twenties, to eliminate some of the distance between them. She'd invited him for dinner and holidays. But he couldn't face her. He knew he had helped ruin her life.

The woman at the door was not his sister. Yet she seemed to know him.

"David?" she said. She was so tall. She was tall and beautiful and appeared to be wearing makeup. In addition, there was a man next to her. He was tall, too, and had a hairy chest. David was shocked. Where were the knitting needles? Where were the cats? Why was his sister suddenly so tall?

"This is my brother, David," Lucy said, pulling him inside. "Jack, get a blanket. David, what happened to your shoes? Are you drunk?"

Jack wraps a blanket around his shoulders, steers him to the couch. David realizes he's shaking, and Jack brusquely rubs a hand across his back. This male touch feels so comforting that for a moment David worries he might be gay.

"David, what happened?" asks Lucy. She's holding one of his ice-block hands. Shouldn't she be hitting him and hating him for what he did?

"I hit Amy," David says.

Lucy and Jack exchange a glance.

"I hit my girlfriend," he says, in case they don't know who Amy is. He's expecting a punch from Jack at any moment. The words "get out" to fall from Lucy's lips. Instead, she is looking at him, then leading him upstairs, tucking him into a bed that seems far too small. His feet are hanging off the edge. She covers him with a blanket and says, "We'll deal with all that tomorrow. For now, you need to get some sleep."

She turns off the light and leaves the room, cracking the door. He can hear her voice and Jack's in low murmurs, from downstairs. Their voices sound nice.

They wrap around him like the blanket and settle everything into a haze. Just before he falls asleep, though, he's seized with a sudden fear for his body, that fragile vessel of animal flesh that hurtles through time like a sped arrow. He's helpless to stop its course, and cannot predict the pain he may encounter at any time. This theoretical pain, mental or physical, sits waiting in the dark hallway of his future, unseen and silent as wolves. He imagines them smiling and licking their chops as he floats beneath the surface, into sleep.

When he sifts into consciousness the next morning, he has a feeling of wanting to return to his dream, because in his dream the room is an arc over the sky, and his feet, blue and barely comprehensible, feel no pain. He shuffles to the edge of the arc and looks down; below, he can see all the people he's ever loved, his first kiss, his childhood dog, his mother as a young woman holding a baby to her breast. He thinks they can't see him, but every now and then one of them will look up and say, in words that do not form on their lips but rise up from them like evaporating rain, "David, go back to sleep."

"But I already am asleep," he says once, and they smile, knowing.

Obituary Birthday

BY PAMELA A. IVINSKI

No one had to wait for April 2004—the 10th anniversary of Kurt Cobain's suicide—to begin the inevitable reassessment of his life (death) and art. With the publication of his *Journals* late in 2002, critics and fans had reason to begin weighing in on Cobain's legacy. The first example I came across was a review in the online journal *Salon*, in which Bomani Jones restated what I had always believed: "Simple and plain, Kurt Cobain was a fuckin' genius." But Jones failed to make a case for his claim, merely locating Cobain's brilliance in the "confusion" of his journals and in Nirvana's lyrics: the way he hesitated between opposing states, in the same manner that "the lack of clarity in Monet's work allowed the connoisseur to decide what he was really trying to paint." Jones then cited one of the most-quoted passages from the Nirvana catalogue, from "Smells Like Teen Spirit" (recently named "Greatest Song from the Past 25 Years" by VH1, and ranked third on a *Rolling Stone*/MTV list of "The 100 Greatest Pop Songs Since 1963"). According to Jones, Cobain's infamous line—"a mulatto, an albino, a mosquito, my libido"—made "absolutely no sense, and that was cool."

The next day I eagerly scanned *Salon*'s letters column, thinking someone would surely refute this dim-witted idea that the "mulatto" line is meaningless. Should have done it myself, I guess, because most of the letter writers not only agreed with Jones's (non)interpretation of the lyrics but also violently challenged the contention that Cobain remains worthy of admiration for any facet of his life or music. "Comparing Cobain's work to Monet's is simply shameless. 'Simple and plain, Kurt Cobain was a fuckin' dangerous loony' might be more accurate," wrote one reader. Another, more sympathetic to Cobain's anguish, remarked, "'A mulatto, an albino, a mosquito, my libido' is silly and random and arbitrary and obscure—but if you believe in an omniscience, or in an omniscient deity, then Kurt Cobain's silliness is another [fruit] of nirvana, a facet of eternity, where everything and nothing are on the dance floor all at once." But most of the respondents took a tone similar to the reader who declared, "Cobain was a whining crybaby, not an artist; a loser, not a role model....Nobody wants to hear this crap about [his] 'pain.' Life is hard. You either deal with it or you quit and die. Cobain quit. Not much of a hero."

I was shocked and hurt. *Salon*'s articles usually have a liberal-lefty, bleeding-heart bent, but these readers were killing Cobain all over again, failing to find artistic value in his work, and denying him a place of honor in the pop pantheon because he "quit."

But they're wrong, so very wrong. Of course, musical taste is highly subjective, but you don't need a Ph.D. in literature to find great poetic flair and even "meaning" in Cobain's lyrics—and taste is actually beside the point. A mulatto, an albino: two kinds of people who have been shunned for their skin color, one for being "too" white, the other for being neither black nor white enough. A mosquito: an insect penetrating the skin with a needlelike proboscis, sucking blood, possibly transmitting disease or infection, bringing to mind drug use and HIV. My libido: the hunger for skin on skin, to penetrate or be penetrated; to exchange bodily fluids and, with them, perhaps disease or infection. This is not the classic narration of an emotional state, like, let's say, "Yesterday, all my troubles seemed so far away." But Cobain's words suggest a vivid emotional landscape nonetheless, chasing a chain of seemingly unrelated signifiers to evoke ostracization and intimacy, fear and desire, in an extraordinarily visual as well as rhythmic manner, underscored by the song's remaining lyrics ("I feel stupid, and contagious," etc.). It's not T. S. Eliot exactly, but it's far more compelling than, say, "I can't get no satisfaction." Silly and random, my ass.

As angry as I feel about this denial ("a denial, a denial...") of Cobain's admittedly uneven literary gift, as well as the general failure to consider and contextualize Nirvana's musical contributions in tandem with his lyrics, the idea that as a suicide he is no longer worthy of our respect and affection makes me truly despair. Not simply for his memory, but for anyone with a personal experience of mental illness. That so many people find it impossible to empathize with his pain (many dismissing him as a mere "junkie," as if that, too, were somehow unrelated to his mental illness) makes me fear for what happens when they encounter anyone with similar symptoms in their own lives. Readers and reviewers have complained that the *Journals* and lyrics are painfully adolescent. This doesn't strike me as terribly strange, given that he was really still a boy when doing most of the writing, and that all he ever wanted to be was a rock star. But his childishness went beyond the limits of ordinary celebrity petulance, to the point that it becomes evident he was tormented by, yet unsuccessful at repairing, childhood damage that left deep scars.

At the same time, Cobain's obsessive interest in matters of birth/infancy and death furnished him with one of his richest veins of imagery, thick with the primal experiences that we've all shared to some degree. Nirvana's third and final studio album, *In Utero*, was originally titled *I Hate Myself and I Want to Die* (after a song of the same name), suggesting the force of this womb/tomb duality in his life and art. Simon Reynolds and Joy Press note in their discussion of Nirvana in *The Sex Revolts*, "Cobain's desire to retreat from the world into numbed-out sanctuary passed through heroin addiction, then blossomed into a full-blown death-wish (a surrender to what Freud called the nirvana principle, a tendency in all organic life to revert to the lowest possible level of irritation, to become inanimate)." If Cobain didn't consciously know about the nirvana principle, he certainly intuited the concept: "Paper Cuts," a harrowing first-person song from his band's debut album, based loosely on an actual episode of child abuse that took place in his hometown, ends as he chants the word "nirvana" seven times. In his *Journals* Cobain complained bitterly, "Why in the hell do journalists insist on coming up with a second rate freudian evaluation on my lyrics when 90% of the time they've transcribed the lyrics incorrectly?" But his life as well as his music begs for a psychologically oriented consideration, and for our own benefit—because so many of us have identified ourselves with him, and because so many of us refuse to find any points of identification with him—and not merely because we're voyeurs. I'm no psychologist, and in any case I doubt the most highly qualified doctor could make a reliable diagnosis, considering the patchy documentation regarding Cobain's mental health. But it's worth trying to hold his pain in our minds for a while, to try to imagine something of what he might have been feeling, in order to gain some insight into why he continues to captivate and to repel us.

Cobain began life on February 20, 1967, in Aberdeen, Washington, the first child of high school sweethearts who had eloped after discovering the pregnancy. Given his fixation with birth symbolism, it seems plausible that this event played into his later feelings of guilt, as if the fact of his possibly unwanted conception made him somehow responsible for creating the family that eventually collapsed and abandoned him. That both parents went on to form new families after their 1976 divorce—families with no place for him, a disobedient, sometimes violent child—would have confirmed this unconscious but powerful belief. (According to to biographer Charles R. Cross, during his high school years Cobain lived with 10 different families and at one point spent about four months living more or less on the streets.) The *Journals* include lyrics for an unrecorded song in which he confessed some unnamed sin: "I was the originator, I'll take the blame, me, it was me, I was the instigator, the grandfather, the first and foremost," as if he had sired the entire troubled family that preceded him.

In fact, as a child Cobain liked to tell friends that he had "suicide genes." Suicide was likely the most impressive example of adult behavior in his family—on both sides. We learn to be adults by observing adults, preferably the well-balanced kind. Cobain never truly matured, having lacked the opportunity after the divorce to internalize the constant parental model needed for healthy emotional development. Of course, you can't believe everything you read, but if just a fraction of the stories in the Cobain biographies are true, his pathologies become easier to understand. For instance, in one famous incident, his mother discovered her new husband was unfaithful. Feeling a murderous rage, she collected his guns and dumped them into a river to prevent herself from doing anything more rash. Cobain dredged them up and pawned them for an amp. How's that for symbolism?

Those who lack "good enough" parents or a stable home life, or who have suffered abuse at the hands of someone outside the family (which seems entirely possible in Cobain's case), at times have the luck to find a substitute, a teacher or coach or even a boss, to provide psychological support or at least a few hints as to how mature adults behave. Cobain appears to have had little of that. Instead, he was exposed to spectacular scenes of threatened and actual violence, including a number involving male relatives who savagely destroyed themselves. Long before Cobain was born, his maternal great-grandfather stabbed himself in the abdomen. After surviving the initial trauma, he ripped open the wounds in the hospital (the same one that administered shock treatment to one of Cobain's heroes, Frances Farmer) and succumbed within two months. In 1978, his paternal grandfather's brother, an alcoholic, died from an aneurysm caused by a drunken tumble down the stairs. In 1980, another of his grandfather's brothers killed himself with bullets to the head and gut, and in 1982, the third of these great-uncles repeated the gunshot scenario. No wonder the artistically inclined youngster made a Super-8 movie in that same year titled *Kurt Commits Bloody Suicide*. Self-murder was the story of his family life.

Suicide even played a prominent role in Cobain's journal account of an early sexual experience, occurring when he was around 16. He relates a story about his first month as a regular pot smoker, noting that it coincided with "the Epitomy of my mental abuse from my mother." When pot failed to dull his pain, he decided to kill himself, but not, he announced dramatically, "without actually knowing what it is like to get laid." However, disgusted with the intimate odors of the "half-retarded girl" he'd chosen as the object of his desire, he failed to consummate the act. The girl's family sought to have him punished, and he became known as the "retard fucker" at school (that is, when he bothered to attend). At this point, he wrote, he did attempt suicide: "I got high & drunk & walked down to the train tracks & layed down & waited for the 11:00 train & I put 2 big pieces of cement on my chest & legs & the train came closer & closer. And it went on the next track beside me instead of over me." The experience "scared me enough to try to rehabilitate myself & my guitar playing seemed to be improving so I became less manically depressed." Eventually he met Krist Novoselic, who became his closest friend and the cofounder of Nirvana, and music evolved into his main reason to live. Yet he kept thoughts of suicide nearby at all times for their guilty comfort, and he increasingly self-medicated as a means of dealing with depression and the excruciating stomach pain he'd suffered since childhood.

From this moment, Cobain devoted his energies to achieving his dream of rock stardom, never imagining any other career path, never even holding a regular job for long. He predicted, with the wry humor that frequently lightens his otherwise agonized and often perverse journal rants: "Nirvana. 3 time Granny award winners, No. 1 on billbored top 100 for 36 consecutive weaks in a row. 2 times on the cover of Bowling Stoned, Hailed as the most original, thought provoking and important band of our decade by Thyme & Newsweak." In a mock-up for a publicity flyer, he joked, "Nirvana Can't Decide whether they want to be Punk or R.E.M. Indecision can often at times kill a band, and NIRVANA are suicidal." The journals are less the confessions of a tortured soul than Cobain's workbook for becoming an icon, a safe place to scrawl material for lyrics, brainstorm PR campaigns that would appear suitably unscripted, draft loopy business letters, and practice surreal ripostes to befuddle prying interviewers.

And if he could be funny, Cobain could also rise above his disordered childhood to create music of tender and brutal joy. *Bleach* (named after a health-department campaign urging drug users to sterilize their works) sounds like what it is: a first album, recorded for $600 borrowed from a friend who never got his money back. But it's also a remarkably sophisticated piece of work, given its origins in the disturbed imagination of a young man who'd experienced little of the world outside his chaotic existence in small-town Aberdeen. "Blew," the first track, introduces the band as practitioners of the rumbling Northwest "grunge" sound without being especially memorable except as proof that Cobain already knew how to sing. (Listen to the first U2 album to hear a vocalist who doesn't yet have a clue.) On most of *Bleach*, Cobain howls in a rough voice, an instrument of torture that drills its way into your brain and stays there. But after a while, you start to appreciate the company, even if it hurts sometimes.

The second tune on *Bleach* twists a beloved relic of American pop culture, *The Andy Griffith Show*, into a scene of rape and murder committed by "Floyd the Barber," plus Barney, Opie, and Aunt Bee, with Cobain as their victim. The chorus, repeating "I was shaved" and "I was shamed," brings out another key Cobain theme: his overwhelming sense of humiliation and worthlessness. He sarcastically celebrates these aspects of himself in "Negative Creep," then protests when others offer the same opinion in "Scoff" before launching into a pleading yet strangely rapturous chorus of "Gimme back my alcohol." "About a Girl," written for his girlfriend at the time, ironically contrasts gently loping chords and his growing penchant for Beatlesque melody with a cynical lyric that withholds rather than promises affection. "Swap Meet," about a man and a woman who love each other more than they'll admit, utilizes fierce, spiky riffs to emphasize another of Cobain's strongly visual choruses: "Keeps his cigarettes close to his heart, keeps her photographs close to her heart, keeps the bitterness close to the heart."

Soaked in feedback and distortion, *Bleach* rolls along with all the fervor and aggression of three musically ambitious young men pumped full of hormones, recreational drugs, and cheap beer, but with no better place to go than the parking lot behind the local convenience store. "Smells Like Teen Spirit," the opening track of Nirvana's second album, *Nevermind*, picks up where *Bleach* left off, but ventures into more expansive emotional terrain. The alternating soft verses and hard chorus perfectly embody the simultaneous hopelessness and exuberance that characterize our extended American adolescence: Cobain's coinciding self-hatred and self-confidence writ large for a generation. To understand the song and album as the quintessential "slacker" statement is to ignore the frustration and longing for change inside the anguish and rage of the music, lyrics, and vocals. The blistering chorus and final screaming refrain—"a denial" (repeated nine times)—invert the passivity of the song's last verse, "I found it hard, it's hard to find, oh well whatever nevermind." The ultimate message is not only "whatever" used in the manner of the stoner who can't get himself worked up enough to care. It's also meant as a warning, as if to say, "You're not listening and I act like I don't care, but someday you'll pay with your guilt and your tears."

Nevermind lets us have it both ways: The songs acknowledge fear and despair but make the experience bouncy and even uplifting—thanks also, of course, to Novoselic's steadfast yet playful bass lines and Dave Grohl's extraordinary, in-your-face drumming. "In Bloom" employs a simple singsong melody to present a harsh view of the audience that Cobain would come to despise: macho, gun-loving cretins who bellowed his words so loudly they couldn't hear his pain. The song's two short verses characterize adults as instinctual animals who procreate indiscriminately and then feel justified in pimping out or abandoning their offspring to serve their own needs ("sell the kids for food"); after all, these already damaged children ("bruises on the fruit") can always be replaced ("We can have some more, nature is a whore") when the parents move on to form new families. In "Come As You Are"—the third *Nevermind* song in a row to reference firearms—Cobain sings of welcoming enemies as well as friends while reiterating (guiltily?), "And I swear that I don't have a gun." "Drain You" cheerily explores how love often returns us to an all-consuming state of infantile narcissism and dependency. Lovers are equated with newborns, and love itself with the hunger for a partner who is also a substitute mother ("Chew your meat for you, pass it back and forth, in a passionate kiss"). Other phrases conjure up birth, physical and emotional sustenance, and drug addiction all at once ("It is now my duty to completely drain you, I travel through a tube and end up in your infection"), their juxtaposition insinuating Cobain's extreme and unfulfilled needs.

"Lithium" likewise functions on a number of levels, offering a story of bipolar disorder or schizophrenia ("I'm so happy, 'cause today I found my friends, they're in my head"), as well as a sarcastic tale of religious conversion ("Light my candles in a daze, 'cause I found God"). At the same time, a number of lines suggest something of Cobain's profound concern with sexual fidelity ("I'm so horny, that's okay my will is good"), a notion generally foreign in practice to rock stars. Themes of sexual jealousy also arise in "Lounge Act," in which desire is likened to a punishable offense ("And I wanted more than I can steal, I'll arrest myself and wear a shield"). Scent, too, is again invoked, here more specifically as a marker of sexual conquest ("I'll go out of my way to prove that I still, smell her on you"), in keeping with the origins of the title "Smells Like Teen Spirit," which was taken from a graffito scrawled by a friend that proclaimed "Kurt smells like Teen Spirit"—in other words, he was imprinted with (and emasculated by?) the scent of his strongly feminist girlfriend's "Teen Spirit" antiperspirant. (Reportedly, Cobain was unaware of the full connotation of this phrase until after the album was released, but in my opinion the "Smell her on you" line throws this claim into doubt.)

Two of the most musically gentle songs on *Nevermind* are out-and-out bleak. "Polly" weds a hauntingly beautiful melody counterpointed by delicate harmonies to a cruel narrative of abduction and rape told from the perpetrator's point of view, as he considers his victim's requests: to untie her, put out the blowtorch, feed her, and so forth. Like the earlier "Paper Cuts," the song was based on a true story, this time of a girl kidnapped from a punk rock show in Tacoma. On the other hand, the album's last cut, "Something in the Way," portrays the singer as the antithesis of Polly's abuser or the child-selling parents of "In Bloom." The narrator (presumably Cobain himself, who liked to claim that he'd lived for a time under a bridge in Aberdeen) would rather try to live off grass and "drippings from the ceiling" than eat the animals he's trapped, which he now keeps as pets. (Fish are literally fair game, however, because they "don't have any feelings.") At the same time, the almost catatonic melody and nearly whispered vocals imply that he's too weak and sensitive to survive, and the chorus, which merely repeats, "Something in the way, yeah," reads both as the self-definition of an unwanted child and as a half-completed thought, perhaps the memory of a Beatles song with its loving message of faithfulness long forgotten. Yet despite the muted melancholy of this final tune, the cumulative effect of the album is upbeat; *Nevermind* is a collage of agony and affliction that feels life-affirming, like the cheerleaders wearing the "Anarchy" emblem in the "Teen Spirit" video.

The final Nirvana studio album, *In Utero*, is another matter entirely. With *Nevermind* Cobain achieved all he'd ever thought he'd wanted—and none of it changed anything that really mattered. It sounds sappy and self-helpy to say this, I know, but all the world's adulation (and he came closer than most to becoming a figure of universal adoration) doesn't amount to shit if you can't love yourself. Cobain never quite managed to do that. In many ways, his roots in the "alternative" or "independent" music scene to which he remained devoted despite having signed to a major-label record company intensified his double bind. Defined by his self-contempt, he was able to salvage a shred of good feeling for himself by transferring some of the loathing to all those who weren't initiated into the mysteries and rituals of his particular scene. But when millions who didn't know or respect the secret Seattle/Sub Pop handshake embraced his music, it only served to confirm in his mind that he was no better than the people he claimed to hate.

In an underappreciated *In Utero* song titled "Milk It," Cobain crafted a phrase to match fellow-suicide Sylvia Plath's famous passage, "Dying, Is an art, like everything else. I do it exceptionally well." Cobain's line, "Obituary birthday" (found in a chorus that opens with "Look on the bright side is suicide") encapsulates the degree to which the dark side of the birth/death dyad had come to dominate his life, becoming the primary theme of his art. The legacy of pain and the suicidal tendencies that occasionally seeped to the surface in previous albums now become the substance of the recording. "Serve the Servants," the opening track, impotently refutes the idea that his parents' "legendary divorce" merited the press attention it had received while also admitting, "I tried hard to have a father, but instead I had a dad." "Scentless Apprentice" incorporates aspects of a favorite novel, Patrick Süskind's *Perfume*, which ends when the protagonist entices a frenzied mob to murder. While "Rape Me" ostensibly presents a metaphor for Cobain's horrific experiences with the press (among them, the *Vanity Fair* exposé of drug use that led him and his wife, Courtney Love, to lose custody of their child for a time), it echoes many passages from his pre-fame journals in which he graphically imagined himself as the victim of sexual assault. "Frances Farmer Will Have Her Revenge on Seattle" treats similar issues, expressing the hope that the entire city would someday pay for the abuses visited upon the actress by those in the psychiatric profession who claimed to be helping her. "Radio Friendly Unit Shifter" again takes on the press and ignorant fans, sourly declaring, "I love you for what I am not, I did not want what I have got." The chorus despondently growls, "What is wrong with me, what is what I need."

Cobain was never comfortable with the high-gloss production on *Nevermind* and sought something raw and more *Bleach*-like for *In Utero*, in keeping with the album's generally despairing lyrics, hoarse vocals, and frequently dissonant, sometimes unlistenable music. "Dumb" and "All Apologies" feature gentle melodies but still express suffering and guilt. These feelings seem associated with his now full-blown heroin habit, revealed in sweetly amusing but quietly disturbing lines like "My heart is broke, but I have some glue, help me inhale, and mend it with you." Another such passage, "I'll take all the blame, aqua seafoam shame," brings to mind Love's description of Cobain's pallor when she discovered him moments from death due to his first, possibly intentional, overdose, as well as his claim to have remembered seeing the hospital's aqua floor tiles at the moment of his birth, after which he attempted to clamber back into the womb. The two strongest songs on the album, "Heart-Shaped Box" and "Pennyroyal Tea" (the two songs said to exhibit the positive influence of Love) effectively exploit his signature bipolar soft verse/hard chorus structure to mediate, but not reconcile, beauty and brutality.

While working on *In Utero*, Cobain became fascinated with the idea that the male seahorse "carries the children and gives them Birth," a phrase which he proposed to inscribe on the front of Nirvana T-shirts that would list "mandatory breeding laws" and socialized medicine, among other demands, on the back. By this time he had become a father to Frances Bean Cobain, but the birth imagery of the album appears to relate more closely to his own conception and to the lure of Freud's nirvana principle. In the poignant "Pennyroyal Tea," Cobain sang of this supposed herbal tonic for inducing abortion: "Sit and drink pennyroyal tea, distill the life that's inside of me." The lyric speaks not simply to a Buddhist quest for spiritual purification but also to his strong desire to abort himself. In the recorded performance, the first syllable of "distill" is barely vocalized, so that the line sounds more like "Still the life that's inside of me," emphasizing the notion of pennyroyal tea as an agent of self-abortion and suicide.

A similar fantasy of erasing himself at birth is repeated in "Heart-Shaped Box" when he sings, "Broken hymen of your highness I'm left black, throw down your umbilical noose so I can climb right back." Though said to have been inspired by a token of affection given to Cobain by Love, the heart-shaped box of the title just as readily symbolizes the womb he was once "locked inside." That the song was originally called "Heart-Shaped Coffin" underscores his hatred of the fact of his own birth. Like many of his best tunes, this piece is characterized by vivid imagery, contrasting feathery "angel's hair and baby's breath" (on which he still manages to cut himself) to the dark malevolence of "magnet tar pit trap." Certain phrases betoken greater ambivalence. In context, "I wish I could eat your cancer when you turn black" could be construed as a Jesus-like attempt to cure and save—or as his unmerciful wish that the addressee be stricken with disease so that he could be avenged for some wrong and then share in the torment. Cobain's vocal is in turns heartbreaking and irascible, from the way he cradles the word "heart" roundly in his mouth to his tone in the refrain "Hey, wait," in which he, a man adored by millions, still sounds abjectly desperate for attention, and then, with "I've got a new complaint," merely churlish.

The confusion or undecidability that Bomani Jones describes as the salient characteristic of Kurt Cobain's art might be understood with regard to various currents of postmodernism, such as the idea that meaning is never fixed, that nothing is truly coherent or whole, and that art functions better as a field of free play than as a force for social change or emotional catharsis. Cobain was anointed the voice of a generation, a role he both relished and rejected, because we recognize ourselves in his ambivalence. But to hear him shriek "Obituary birthday, your scent is still here in my place of recovery"—to hear him with the heart as well as the ears—is to acknowledge that many of us are still frantic to fix meaning, feel whole, and experience emotional catharsis or effect social change, and that music, more than any other art form, seduces us into imagining that all these things remain possible. Cobain brilliantly married his misery to insistent, hummable melodies, validating our pain while providing the hope that we, too, could rise above it.

Cobain never succeeded at the recovery he sang about in "Milk It." *In Utero* had been out only for about six months when he overdosed on tranquilizers and champagne in March 1994 (Love revived him, again), and in April, he shot himself right and proper—in the family way.

Was Kurt Cobain a genius? He never produced an oeuvre as consistent or broad as Monet's, but then again, I've never known anyone to look to an Impressionist painting for company, for sexual stimulation, for consolation, for encouragement, in the same way that I've turned—and millions of others have turned—to Nirvana songs for all these things, and more. At their best, Nirvana's songs hold the listener like a baby, soothing and exciting us with their savage lullabies. They never promise that everything will be okay, but they agree that looking on the bright side too often feels like risking blindness, and they assure us that we're not alone in that ("Lost eyesight, I'm on your side"). Though Cobain never aspired to be a writer in the ivory-tower sense of the word, he did conceive of his lyrics as shreds of poetry, and at times they match the allusive richness and primal force of, say, Anne Sexton (yet another fellow suicide). And god, how those melodies make you want to sing along.

Was Kurt Cobain a "whining crybaby," "a loser, not a role model"? Role model, maybe not. But I don't buy the argument, expressed by one *Salon* letter writer, that "What always seems to be forgotten in the 'tortured genius' myth of Cobain is that he had choices." To the contrary, the more famous he became, the more he was "loved" by millions, the more his choices were drastically limited. Whatever trauma he suffered as a child—and from the vividness of the abuse stories in his writings I suspect it was far greater than we will ever know—left him emotionally ill-prepared to enter into adult life. At the moment when most of us were struggling with midterm exams and dorm-room dramas, he was shoved under an unforgiving international spotlight. After his *Vanity Fair* experience in particular, how could he have trusted that anything he told a doctor or fellow 12-step participant wouldn't find its way straight to the tabloids? Cobain epitomizes how we are most drawn to those artists whose need for approbation and attention is even greater than their enormous talent. And then when they fuck up, we pretend not to understand why. Cobain showed he understood this when he remade Süskind's *Perfume* into his own self-portrait in "Scentless Apprentice." The book's antihero, lacking any kind of human scent, formulates a special fragrance to sprinkle on himself for the purpose of compelling a crowd of undesirables to slice him to shreds and consume his flesh. This act represents the only thing they'd ever done "out of love," as Süskind explains. "Teen Spirit" had the very same effect. Though Cobain derived little pleasure from the devotion of his fans, he nonetheless apologized repeatedly in his suicide note for having lost enthusiasm for the music they venerated. At that point, he wrote, it was better to burn out than fade away.

Those who reject Cobain as a loser or quitter probably cannot understand what it feels like to live an existence where "I Hate Myself and I Want to Die" is not just a mordantly amusing song title but also an interior monologue playing on an endless loop: *I hate myself I hate myself I hate myself I hate myself I hate myself I hate myself I hate myself I want to die*. If you've never heard that in your head all day long, or have never had to try to reason, to coax, to trick it out of the brain of a friend or parent or sibling, then you ought to thank your god, if that's your thing, or thank your lucky stars that mental illness has not touched your life, and knock on wood for good measure to keep it that way.

That Kurt Cobain found a way to quiet his self-contempt long enough to write a line as fiercely beautiful and true as "a mulatto, an albino, a mosquito, my libido" makes him my hero and still fuels me, even if it still hurts. I loved him—I still love him—as much as a person can love someone they never had a chance of meeting, and I'm not the only one. No, I'm not the only one.

The Cameraman

BY MAUREEN O'LEARY WANKET

Late in May, Ephraim wanted me for a job, so he sent Walter. Sometimes Ephraim called my cell phone, but usually he sent Walter. I wasn't that hard to find. It was a big school, but I spent most of the time in the back room of the computer lab downloading images onto the yearbook's program, and when I was done with that, looking at MySpaces of people I saw around. This one freshman girl named Felicia kept talking about putting on a strip show in the cafeteria to get back at the principal for expelling her boyfriend.

I wasn't surprised to see Walter at the door. Business with Ephraim picked up when the weather turned hot.

Walter had an old man's name, but nobody made fun of him for it. I wanted to, but he was big. You could just imagine the hurt if he slammed you into a wall or got you in a headlock. I myself saw him in action a bunch of times, so I didn't mess with Walter.

"Hey, Jordan. Ephraim wants you," he said.

Ephraim was waiting in the hall. He liked having excuses to tell bigger guys what to do. Walter stood behind him with his arms crossed like he was a rock star's bodyguard.

Ephraim's hair was buzzed to the scalp except for a thin strip of long, silky black hair that went down the middle of his head in a ponytail that hung all the way past his shoulder blades.

Nobody ever laughed at Ephraim, either.

"Bay Point by three?" he wanted to know. His forehead knotted in a squat dash between his eyes, his mouth tight as an asshole.

We'd done Bay Point once before, a high school in a nearby town. I could make it if I ran to my car right after seventh period.

"I'll give you extra if it's on the website by tonight."

"Fine," I said, and we sealed our deal with a handshake like we were in a movie. I concentrated on keeping my hand as firm as his. Ephraim and I had the same build. It's a myth that skinny guys are weak. It was one of the secrets we knew about each other.

I had Modern Civilizations sixth period. It was a guest speaker day. A Buddhist monk wearing an orange toga and Birkenstocks sat on the teacher's desk, waiting for us. He was a big black dude with the shiniest bald head I ever saw in my life. He must have spent hours waxing it.

"We're all connected," he said, weaving his fingers together in front of his belly. "What we do to one, we do to all. Even to ourselves."

Somebody asked him what he'd come back as in the next life.

"A rich white man with tons of power," he said. I expected him to say a leaf on a tree, or a butterfly. Then he started laughing like crazy at his own joke. It was very entertaining.

My seventh-period English teacher showed a movie about what would happen in regular neighborhoods after a nuclear war. A nuclear winter buried everything in poisonous snow, and this lady's kid shit in the sink. I kept my mind on the Bay Point job. It wasn't a good idea for me to get all bummed out over a movie kid who wasn't even real. I sat back in my seat with my arms crossed and watched the second hand on my watch. I practiced holding my breath for a whole minute.

The school's handheld video camera would work best for this one. I could hide it in my pants pocket, and it would take a steady picture.

Bay Point High School's security depended on defense of the doors. You could only get in through the front. They locked every other entrance. Four guards with wands stood at either side of the metal detector ramps. We needed to get in, do it, and get out in 15 minutes. There wasn't time to dick around with security.

Ephraim stood on the Bay Point front steps, but I pretended not to see him. He wore a trucker's hat and tucked in his ponytail. I put on my fake reading glasses.

I got in behind a bunch of girls. They smelled really good, like peppermint gum. The detectors beeped as they walked through. The girls took their cell phones out and waved them at the guards. At my turn, the detector went off, and I did the same thing. I always got nervous during this part, but nothing ever happened. Their eyes never really saw me.

I got to the boys' bathroom first. One of the toilets overflowed like a fountain, and the water ran over the rim and into a pool on the floor.

The door slammed open, and Ephraim and another guy I didn't know came in with this Indian-from-India-looking kid. Ephraim's friend held him around the neck under his arm. The kid was short, eye-level with Ephraim himself. He looked scared as hell, and I didn't blame him. I switched on the camera.

Ephraim socked him in the stomach. The Indian kid retched and bent over. Ephraim's buddy pushed him away, then kicked him in the butt. The boy splashed onto the floor. Ephraim pulled him up and slammed him in the face and there was kind of a wet crack. Ephraim kicked him so he rolled over like a log, face-down in the water. Ephraim went in to start kicking some more, but the other guy dragged him back and they ran out.

With the camera still going, I reached down and pulled the boy's shoulder to flip him. His eyes rolled back, and he sputtered and choked. I did a close-up on his face right quick. Blood ran in watered-down streams from cuts on his face. His cheeks had already swelled up, and there was something wrong with his jaw.

Later, I passed a few teachers working with students in classrooms, tutoring people who hung around for extra help. The halls were quiet except for the murmur of the students and teachers and my footsteps squishing on the floor. Schools were always nicer after the regular school day was over.

The Bay Point beating was on the website by 5:30. I left in the part where I turned the kid over and he was all gagging in the toilet water. It was a nice effect. The beatings were starting to blend one into the other, and that detail set it apart.

The crack of his jaw stuck with me, especially after watching the video. It was pretty loud. But there was nothing I could have done. It would all go on with or without me. I was just the cameraman.

Mom wasn't home when I got there. I ate dinner that night in front of the television, watching Animal Planet. It was *Animal Cops New York*, my favorite show. There was this one animal-control officer with blond hair. She had a good body and a really pretty mouth. She looked sweet, but she acted tough when she found people being mean to their dogs. If I could find a girl in college like her, I would learn how to talk to girls. Rather than just trying to get into their MySpaces set to private profile.

I ate dinner with a glass of milk and my vitamins.

I watched Animal Planet until I felt sleepy enough to go to bed.

That night I dreamed I was underwater. I couldn't get to the surface. I couldn't breathe. But it didn't matter because I was already dead.

The next morning, the local newspaper headline read "Taped Beating Posted on Internet." I guess the police discovered Ephraim's website. It also said that Ephraim broke the kid's jaw and that the kid's name was Rusty Nandkeshwar.

Rusty would have his jaw wired shut for two months. He had to be in intensive care with a lung infection from aspirating dirty water. Turned out, he nearly drowned.

Rusty didn't tell who hit him. He said he might have remembered five or six black guys, but he never saw them before. He had no idea who would target him or why. But the police found my video online and saw two Hispanic guys, not the five or six black guys that Rusty said. The cops searched for two Hispanic boys, medium build, who may or may not attend Bay Point. They also wanted to speak to the cameraman, also probably Hispanic.

I felt pretty safe that the cops would never catch me. What would they arrest me for, anyway? I didn't hit anybody. And people got in fights in school every day. People gathered around like crazy, taking pictures on their phones. Nobody ever arrested them for watching.

At school, Ephraim charged me in the computer lab. He was on me before I could stand up. I saw a white flash, and then purple dots.

Now I understood why Ephraim's victims didn't fight back. There was no time.

"What the fuck?" I said. My cheekbone felt hot and greasy when I touched it.

"You should have let the motherfucker die, man." Ephraim said. He came up close to me, his chin right in my nose.

We probably looked like we were about to kiss. It was stupid. I wanted to stop it, but I didn't know how.

Ephraim smiled. Scariest thing I ever saw in my life. Then he sat down and kicked a chair out so I would do the same.

As soon as I graduated, I'd never have to see Ephraim again. Sometimes it helped to remind myself of that.

"They think it's someone from Bay Point," I said, forcing my voice to stay even. "And so far Rusty's not talking."

"Who?"

"Rusty. The dude you jumped in the bathroom."

Ephraim waved a hand. "He ain't saying nothing. Not if he wants to live."

"Then what?"

"You should have let him die," Ephraim said. "Quit interfering in my shit."

"Fine."

"Just let it alone, man. And if I leave somebody facedown, leave him facedown."

He got up and rolled the chair hard across the room so that it slammed into a row of shelves.

A thin line of blood oozed along the bone under my eye. I grabbed my backpack and got out of there.

At lunch, that girl Felicia climbed on top of a table in the middle of the cafeteria. She kicked away people's food and started stripping, unbuttoning her shirt first.

It was my first time in the cafeteria since freshman year. I got there early with my video camera and staked a spot near the door.

She opened her shirt and everyone started hooting and hollering, even a bunch of the girls. She ran her hands all over. I held my breath to keep from shaking the camera.

She just got her shirt off and unhooked her bra when two of the deans body-slammed her to the ground. She screamed and spit and bit down on Mr. Miller's forearm.

I stepped back out of the doorway while people rushed forward, jumping on the tables, whipping out cells and taking pictures, howling like dogs.

I watched the whole thing with two sets of eyes, the ones in my head, and through the video camera. I caught everything.

I liked the effect of teachers running out, students running in.

Later on, I had to watch *The Breakfast Club* in English class. Ms. Garrett sat at her desk and stared at the TV, mouthing the words along with the actors. She liked to show us movies from the '80s. She gave me an A on my essay, and she seemed like a nice person, with her black stockings and clunky shoes. She looked like she may have been cool once, a punk or whatever. Now she sighed a lot and seemed kind of disappointed. She did like *The Breakfast Club*, though. I think she loved that dirty guy who catches his own spit.

The thing that bugged me was that even though a girl stripped that day in the cafeteria, and then bit the dean, nothing changed. The school just closed up over her like she was a rock thrown into a pond. It rippled for a second, and then went straight back to routine.

It was like when Mom made me go to school the day after my sister Rebekah's funeral. I remember thinking that somebody would have had to come through and start shooting people to make anybody care.

I got up from my desk and walked out like I was late for something. I don't think Ms. Garrett noticed.

I walked around the halls really fast and just looked down at my feet. I made myself just think about walking. Then I went in to the computer lab and checked out the local news online. They had arrested Ephraim's friend for the beating.

Police were still looking for the other guys.

Rusty refused to talk more, not that he could say much with his jaw wired shut. They caught Ephraim's friend because a teacher recognized him from my video. The police who found Ephraim's website watched the footage frame by frame, and in one, Ephraim's friend turned his face to the side, and you could see him. His name was Dante, which I didn't even know before. The police showed the picture to the teachers at Bay Point, and somebody recognized Dante as a guy they expelled.

I fished for the video camera in my backpack. The bell was about to ring. I scrolled through all the footage of the Bay Point beating, and then of Felicia lifting her shirt. I fast-forwarded past her white stomach, her sad face, and the deans, two old guys twice her size, pulling her down.

With my thumb, I pressed delete, delete, delete.

Ephraim waited by my car in the parking lot. "Come on," he said. "We're going somewhere."

I felt like getting in and driving off by myself, leaving Ephraim alone in the parking lot, his hand reaching for the door handle. But that would be suicide. If I did that, I'd better just keep driving. Don't even stop to piss. Just keep going until I run out of gas and then fill up and drive more. I didn't know where I'd have to drive to in order to get away from an angry Ephraim. Iceland, maybe.

I unlocked the doors, and Ephraim got in. While I started up, he twisted around in the bucket seat.

"Damn," he said. "This car is fucking neat."

"It's just my mom's old Accord..."

"No, I mean neat. There's not even a can on the floor or nothing. Do you vacuum every day or what?"

I didn't know what to say. I turned on the air conditioner.

"Drive," Ephraim said. "You are so fucking weird."

He wanted me to go out into the hills. I followed his directions, trying to hide how slippery my palms were against the steering wheel.

This close, I could smell him. He smelled like soap and fine cologne. I could also really see how close-cropped the underside of his hair was, and how his shirt seemed like it was starched. His jeans were baggy and loose, but they looked ironed too. I wanted to ask him about it. If he was taking me out into a field to beat me to death, at least I'd die knowing that this wired-up, gang-banging punk had gotten up that morning early so he could iron his pants.

"What are you smiling at?" Ephraim asked. "I'll knock your mouth right off your face."

He didn't even make sense.

We headed down a road past orchards where the trees were all lined up in even rows. When I was a kid, I liked looking at those rows from the road. I always wanted to know how they got the trees that straight. Then we passed them and got to the reservoir. Ephraim wanted me to go in to where you could see the water. There was a park there, and picnic tables.

"My parents took us swimming here a couple times," I said.

"So did mine," Ephraim said.

I parked and cut the engine. Ephraim got out, and I followed him. For a split second, I considered letting him get out, and leaving. But I didn't. To be honest, it was like I had to follow that guy. It was like he hypnotized me.

We went over a hill and down onto the sandy beach. A big oak tree with branches like old-man arms grew out of a patch of stubby grass. We stopped under its shade. Ephraim reached down, brushed the grass with his hand.

"Sit down, man," he said.

At four o'clock in the afternoon, the shade barely helped. The air weighed a million pounds. I wished I was back in my car by myself with the air conditioner blasting, just driving.

"Relax," he said, eyes out at the water. "I ain't trippin'."

"Right." Ephraim telling me to relax did not make me want to relax. I got more nervous when he was in a good mood.

"I used to come here all the time," he said. "I used to cannonball off that raft."

An old wooden plank raft floated about twenty yards offshore. A long time ago, they found bacteria in the water and they stopped using it as a public beach. It was E. coli from baby shit or whatever. Now you could visit, and have picnics, but you couldn't get in the water. My family never went there after the ban on swimming, and seeing how deserted it was, I guess nobody else did either.

Ephraim went off toward a dock with two rowboats lashed to it with coiled wire ropes.

"Check it out," Ephraim called. "This one ain't locked."

He stepped in the boat. "Come on, Jordan! Fucking slowpoke."

I did what he said, and the boat rocked under us.

"Sit down, fool. We're about to tip over."

He grabbed the oars from the sides and started rowing. His forearms flexed and we got going pretty fast. It reminded me of this show I saw on the Discovery channel about crew teams at colleges in places like Massachusetts. They had teams of guys who rowed long, skinny boats and raced other teams. They were synchronized like they could read each others' minds, and their oars barely made a splash in the water.

Once Ephraim got going, he made barely any splash. He'd have been awesome on one of those crew teams. I wondered why he hadn't gone out for any sports. Too bad they didn't have boxing at school. Kickboxing.

"What are you looking at?" he asked. We flew past the raft, past the buoy line.

"Why aren't you in sports? You're strong, and I know you're fast."

A strange smile played on his lips. "How do you know I'm fast?"

"I've seen you run from the scene of the crime."

He let out a dry chuckle. It sounded like a dead person laughing. "The coaches hate me."

"Why?"

"How the fuck should I know? They're all prejudiced." Ephraim stopped the rowing and tilted the oars in. He stroked the sides of his face with one hand. "Besides, sports ain't me. I've got other obligations."

"Right."

"You going to college?" he asked. A breeze blew up, and little waves lapped against the sides.

"Yeah."

"Where at?"

"I don't know yet." A lie. He didn't need to know where I went after graduation.

"Nobody wanted you?"

"I didn't say that."

"You too ugly." He covered his mouth and pointed at me like I was the funniest thing he ever saw.

My fist clenched. "I got into college," I said.

His smile widened, and he lifted up his shirt to reveal six-pack abs behind a black handgun as shiny as the back of a cockroach.

He pretended to be retarded. "Duuuh..." he said. He pulled the gun out of his waistband and drew it up his body like he loved himself. Then he grabbed the back of my neck and wedged the barrel under my jaw. I ducked and pushed him away. The boat rocked.

"Duuuh..." Ephraim said, and he wagged the gun around like his arm was made out of rubber. Then he leveled it at me and sat still as a swami on the narrow rowboat bench, his elbows on his knees.

The boat settled.

"You know I could kill you, right?" He cocked the lever.

I thought of all the suckers under bleachers and in bathrooms, trying to get away, trying to reason with him. I thought of what he did to all of those boys.

It seemed like a long time passed when I was just looking into the ugly hole at the end of Ephraim's piece. So what if he shot me and dumped me in the water. I'd be nothing but bones on the bottom of the reservoir before Mom even noticed I wasn't in my room. I grabbed the oars.

"I don't give a fuck," I said, and started to row back to shore.

Ephraim watched me for a second, like he didn't know what to do, then he spit in the water like I wasn't worth the trouble. He slid the gun back into his pants. He put his hands behind his head, lay back. and closed his eyes.

Close to the dock, I stopped so we could glide in.

The sandy bottom of the reservoir glittered with fool's gold. The surface was cold and smooth under my fingers. It would be awesome to jump into it that minute. There was no one around to stop me. Ephraim still had his eyes closed. He was only pretending to be asleep, but he looked almost innocent, like just a kid in a rowboat. I couldn't imagine Ephraim as anything other than the freak show he was, but at some point he must have been young. He couldn't have always been this hard and crazy. Or maybe he was. Maybe he was a kicking, scratching, pissed-off baby.

I dipped my hands in to the wrists. My head was about to crack open in the heat. All the things I usually didn't let myself think about flooded my brain and my chest hurt really bad, like I was drowning. We had been camping at this lake in the mountains with my mom's new boyfriend, and he took Rebekah out on his boat. When he came back, she wasn't on it anymore. He said she'd fallen into the water when he wasn't looking. He kept saying he tried to save her but she sank, and it was too deep. He was a liar because when they found her body, she was all beaten up and worse.

If I'd gone on the boat with her, she'd be 13 now, just like Felicia. I closed my eyes for a second, and for the first time, I stopped fighting.

When I opened my eyes, I took a deep breath, and pulled us into the dock.

I had the key in the ignition when Ephraim jogged up and got in like nothing happened.

"I need to meet somebody at six," he said, falling into the seat. It was too hot for human life in the car. I drove out of the parking lot. I wanted to go home and watch TV.

"We're shooting up some 10th Street bitches tonight," he said. I acted like I didn't hear.

I dropped him off at a gas mart. "I'm not taking any more pictures for you," I said. "No more websites, nothing. After today, I don't even know you."

"You know me," he said. "You will always know me."

Then he got out without looking back, without closing the door behind him.

The next day, the news said that four guys got shot on 10th Street in the middle of the night. The police called it a gang-related incident. They didn't have any suspects at that time. But they were working on it.

Maybe he would get caught. Maybe I would get caught too. Maybe in the end, we would both go under.

Soft Serve

BY DANIEL T. NEELY

In the spring of 1999, I was an ethnomusicology student living in Brooklyn's Boerum Hill neighborhood. That semester, in addition to my regular coursework, I had been working hard to prepare for our program's ritual exam called "The Comps," which would earn me my master's degree and qualify me for doctoral study. Its preparation was an all-encompassing experience, and the emotional release caused by taking it left me exhausted. I spent the following two weeks eating, watching as much television as I could stand, and wondering what those jingle-bearing ice cream trucks passing by outside were doing disturbing my loafing. They were annoying, these trucks, simultaneously compelling and repelling me with their relentless signature tune played over and over...and over again...straight through their routes, day in and day out.

When I found out I'd passed the exam, I was flush with a new sense of academic achievement. So why not, I thought, use my freshly credentialed research abilities to learn something about the truck's music? After a little exploration, I discovered that virtually all writing about this music takes one of two predictable approaches: Either the ice cream man and his music are warmly symbolic of "Main Street U.S.A.," an idealized, mythic space resistant to objective curiosity, or ice cream truck music is a scourge on the urban soundscape, produced by tin-eared engineers whose saccharine and invasive noiseboxes drive neighborhoods to distraction and necessitate more restrictive anti-noise legislation. Neither approach seemed particularly informative, and I had other questions: Where did ice cream truck music come from? When was it first used? Who came up with the idea?

I started by simply striking up conversations with vendors and patrons. The first driver I approached was an Eastern European gentleman in a Mister Soft truck. Though initially confounded that someone would want to talk to him seriously about the subject, he eventually (and graciously) explained that his song was on a cassette that played through a deck wired to a loudspeaker. But most other trucks, he said, used "a little black box with two knobs," because cassettes could melt in hot weather. He didn't know much about these boxes (he hadn't owned one), and soon his truck was surrounded by kids who had been drawn from a nearby apartment building by the incessant chiming that could be heard for blocks.

As my inquiries became more and more detailed, vendors began referring me to their employers' garages, where people might know more. When these people were stumped, they would direct me to chime-box manufacturers who, in turn, put me in contact with old-time ice cream vendors who had long since retired. With all of this information under my belt, I started digging around library archives for relevant material.

Oral histories and written records show that during the 19th and early 20th centuries, ice cream vending—usually from pushcarts or goat-drawn carts—had been accompanied by shouting, bell ringing, harmonica playing, and even barrel-organ music. The earliest reference I could find to an American ice cream street vendor's cry was in the *National Advertiser* in 1828, in which "I Scream, Ice Cream!" is reported to be one of New York City's common street cries. Some 50 years later, M.H. Thornton composed "I Scream; or, Ice Cream," a "serio-comic song and chorus":

VERSE

'Twas on a hot and sultry day
When passed my door a team
The driver cried with monstrous voice
I scream! I scream! I scream!

CHORUS

(SOPRANO) I scream! I scream! I scream!
(ALTO) Ice cream! Ice cream! Ice cream!

While street vending was fairly common in the early to mid-19th century, it increased dramatically in the period after the Civil War, as ice cream gained in popularity as an American comfort food. Its fame also resulted in a proliferation of ice cream parlors and soda fountains, where the refreshment took several new, idiosyncratic forms, including the ice cream soda, the ice cream sundae, and, a bit later, the ice cream cone. In many of these retail outlets, owners installed coin-operated music boxes, which were both novel amusements for patrons and important generators of revenue. Their sophisticated appearance and pleasing tones created an idyllic space in which to enjoy ice cream, and with their ubiquity, the association between the two strengthened.

At that time, music boxes were to parlor entertainment what phonographs were to the early 20th century, and what televisions are to today. The best were elaborate contraptions, as sophisticated musically as they were mechanically and decoratively. Although limited in timbre (they generally produced a chiming sound), some were capable of playing full movements of major orchestral works, including Wagner's *Tannhäuser*, Weber's *Der Freischütz*, Mozart's *Don Giovanni*, Bellini's *Norma*, and various arias from Verdi's operas, without interruption. Their mechanics featured a cylinder with small, pointed "teeth" interspersed over its surface. Set into motion by a spring-loaded motor, these teeth dragged against a musical comb whose tiny tines produced melody and, sometimes, harmony. Unfortunately, they had one major limitation: In order to change a box's song, one had to replace the cylinder, a time-consuming procedure.

Music box technology took an important step forward in 1882 when Miguel Boom, an inventor in Haiti, received a patent for the first "disc-type" music box. The advantage of these boxes was that songs were recorded on easily interchangeable flat discs with impressions that dragged along a musical comb to produce sound. In 1890, they appeared on the market and were used to attract business in the shops that sold ice cream. This was fortunate, for not only could a shop retain the "sound" of the music box, it could maintain a repertory of songs the shop's proprietor felt were popular with and/or appropriate for his or her clientele.

Although the disc box's popularity sent the cylinder boxes into decline, the emergence of the phonograph and, later, the gramophone, did them both in. Music box authority Arthur Ord-Hume remarked that it "went through the musical instrument industry like a virulent blight. Everyone wanted talking machines and the outcome was immediate." By the early 1900s, music boxes were more often seen as toys than as musical instruments with artistic value. With the age of more realistic sound reproduction nigh, chime music fell out of popular fashion and faded into obscurity.

Just as technological advances ushered in a new era in the music industry, innovations in the automobile industry were changing the way companies sold ice cream. Vendors who delivered ice cream from horse-drawn carriages or pushcarts in the 19th century turned to trucks in the 20th. Change was slow at first, but when they finally started modernizing in large numbers, the sounds they used to attract business began changing as well: On a truck, shouting would not only have been perceived as old-fashioned, but was impractical over the roar of an engine.

The Good Humor Company of Youngstown, Ohio, appears to have been the first company to introduce substantive change in its announcement method. Good Humor was established in 1920 by Harry Burt, a confectioner and ice cream parlor owner who found inspiration in the success of Christian Nelson's 1919 invention of the chocolate-covered ice cream bar. Burt went to work on his own frozen novelty, creating the first ice cream bar on a stick. He dubbed it the "Good Humor" because he believed that the humors of the mind are regulated by the good humor of the palate. Burt decided to sell the bar from a white truck fitted with a rack of bells similar to those on his family's bobsled. The bells were a pleasing way of announcing the truck's presence in a neighborhood, their sound doubtlessly evocative of the nostalgic and positive ambience of Burt's own childhood.

The change this method introduced was significant, and consistent with a trend of the day: the comfortable predictability of mass production. An array of bells on a motorcar, chiming in a fixed way—as opposed to ringing a single handbell, for instance—was fresh, and carried a commercial authority different from that created by shouting or using other assisted announcement methods (often dependent on the mood and talents of the vendor). By making a rack of four bells a standard feature on his fleet of Good Humor trucks, Harry Burt's intention was to create a kind of aural promise guaranteeing the best ice cream.

While the rack of bells was rather unambitious mechanically—one needed only to pull a string to make the bells chime—it was the immediate forerunner of a more decisive technological advancement. After Burt died in 1926, a group of businessmen from Cleveland bought the rights to the Good Humor name and established the Good Humor Corporation of America, distributing franchise rights throughout the country. Good Humor's branch in Los Angeles (Good Humor of California), founded by Paul Hawkins in 1927, replaced Burt's bells with mechanical music on its trucks shortly thereafter. Using a custom-made music box based on a carillon design (the device had a cylinder with nails hammered into it that struck bells as it rotated), Hawkins's trucks played a song proprietary to his branch of the Good Humor franchise, a Polish folk tune titled "Stodola Poompa," or "Farm Pump."

This appears to have been the first time mechanical music was used in the sale of ice cream from trucks. More relevant, however, was the fact that "Stodola Poompa" linked Good Humor of California to a specific, proprietary melody. Hawkins, a savvy businessman, was known for his innovative approaches to publicity (he made sure his ice cream trucks were often parked outside of movie studios and radio stations), and his decision to use a music box–like device suggests that he was looking to re-create a nostalgic ambience similar to the one Harry Burt intended when he chose bells. That Hawkins's device actually sounded like a music box and was associated with ice cream must have invoked an association between the coin-operated automata of the Victorian era and their use in ice cream parlors.

According to Paul Dickson, author of *The Great American Ice Cream Book*, U.S. ice cream sales increased dramatically after World War II. (During the war, ice cream's availability was limited both by the scarcity of ingredients and truck-tire rationing.) With the country brimming with happy feelings from a hard-fought war won, 1946 turned out to be an especially good year for the industry, and sales continued to grow until they reached a plateau in 1948 that remained more or less constant for 30 years. These booming postwar years were good and bad for vendors: There was much more business, but subsequently more competition, and drivers had to be constantly on the lookout for a competitive advantage.

Chime music provided this advantage, and as drivers experimented with different methods of playing music, innovation followed. In 1947, John Ralston, a driver for the Swelltime Ice Cream Company in Los Angeles, created a more practical system for making chime music by taping to his steering wheel a toy cylinder-type music box, an army-surplus carbon microphone, and a toy car motor, connecting the entire apparatus to a tube amplifier. ("It worked," he said, quite simply, when I spoke with him in 1999.) That next year, Ralston brought his ideas to the Nelson Company; shortly thereafter, chime-music boxes began to be manufactured expressly for ice cream trucks.

The Nelson Company made one crucial change to Ralston's system: It removed the toy cylinder movement and replaced it with one made by the Thorens Company, called the AD-30. Similar to the disc boxes of the late Victorian era, the main advantage of the AD-30 was that it played small, interchangeable discs, enabling a driver to choose the music that would identify him or her to customers. Once it began to be manufactured, it quickly became customary for all vendors to play music. A 1949 article in *The Saturday Evening Post*, for example, provides a short list of song titles associated with ice cream vending—"Strawberry Blonde," "Little Brown Jug," and "Sidewalks of New York" among them—and suggests that many vendors were adopting songs to remain competitive and unique in the field.

Although music proved a boon for business, the amplification method was impractical: The tube-based amplifiers required a lot of electricity, and their continual use quickly drained a truck's battery. In 1957, Ralston approached

Bob Nichols, an engineer with experience in the era's emergent transistor technology. At Ralston's behest, Nichols built the first transistorized amplification system for ice cream trucks. He also improved the music box's amplification by winding the comb of the music works with wire, like a guitar pickup, so that the entire apparatus put less stress on the battery and improved the device's projection and timbre when amplified. Nichols's change revolutionized the industry.

He went into the chime-music business under the name Nichols Electronics, building both chime boxes and amplifiers. Although his earliest units used the Thorens AD-30 movement and he continued to service these models well into the 1970s, Nichols began manufacturing chime-music systems in 1962 that returned to the cylinder movement. This move might have seemed strange, since cylinder boxes restricted drivers to one tune, but these models proved more reliable than those using the AD-30 movement, and a driver could simply (and cheaply) order the box with the one song appropriate to his or her identity. Thorens originally manufactured the movements for these boxes, and Nichols used them until 1975, when Thorens halted production and Nichols Electronics switched to cylinder works made by the Sankyo Company of Japan.

The problem with all of these mechanical movements, however, was that they were prone to breaking. The AD-30, for example, had dozens of moving parts and required constant upkeep to remain in good working order. Although much more reliable, the more commonly used cylinder boxes presented problems as well. Most of the ice cream truck garages I visited had a music box "graveyard"—usually, a set of shelves containing cylinders with broken teeth or tines.

In 1985, Nichols began to manufacture electronic boxes that used a chip with a single tune programmed on it. Nichols's best-selling early digital box was simply called "the Digital." Without moving parts, it proved far more durable, and therefore more economical, than its predecessors. But Nichols tells me that this first version had a sound that was more like an organ than a traditional music box, and he remembers receiving complaints from drivers about the timbre not being "the same." He worked to perfect it on subsequent versions and has since produced three models: the Mark II (with eight tunes to choose from), the Mark IV (capable of 70 seconds of custom-programmed music), and the Omni (with 32 songs programmed onto two separate channels). Indeed, these are the "little black box[es] with two knobs" mentioned to me by the Mister Soft driver. They are the standard against which all other boxes are compared—and not only for vendors in the United States, but around the world as well. I have seen Nichols's boxes on ice cream trucks in Jamaica and have heard reports that they can be found all around the Americas and even in parts of Asia.

Though the technology of music production has changed dramatically over the years, one thing in ice cream vending has remained remarkably stable: the way the music sounds. For years, a brief snatch of the twinkling sound—the chime, almost totally detached from melody—has been highly evocative of ice cream and, increasingly, the trucks that sell it. What is it about the timbre of this music—and the music itself—that has resisted change for so long?

Someone like Good Humor's Harry Burt might have reasoned that the continuing association is natural, that only chime music evokes the appropriate synesthetic moment in which the hearer's various senses—primarily taste—are stimulated by the music's reception. This viewpoint is rooted in 19th-century musical thought, where the affinity between chimey sounds and the naïveté and pastoral tranquility of childhood were commonly exploited. Of the Romantic composers, Hector Berlioz wrote most poignantly about the aesthetics of chimey timbres in his 1844 *Treatise on Instrumentation*, in which he states that the glockenspiel's sound is "soft, mysterious and of extreme delicacy" while that of the high bells is "more serene in character; it has something rustic and naïve about it." While the object of nostalgia may originally have been music boxes, today this reasoning goes hand in hand with the nostalgia associated with ice cream truck music.

Others, like the author Jacques Attali, might argue that timbral variation was unnecessary because the chimey sound established its place early on, when ice cream vending was relatively new. Once it found its niche, it never needed to change, because its sound became symbolic of the kind of repetitive consumption and ersatz sociability to which we have become predisposed over time.

Although aesthetics and consumption theory mean little to most drivers, all acknowledge that the timbre of the "kiddie tunes" they play is an important part of ice cream vending: As long as the music sounds the same, it is good for ice cream trucks. Because the chime sound was well suited to the task, the technology developed around it.

But as crucial as timbre is to its appeal, I wonder if perhaps the effectiveness of ice cream truck music's melodic simplicity hasn't been underestimated. Although it would sound novel, a chime version of *Tannhäuser* would likely not be appropriate or effective in practice, especially as a truck drives through spaces as architecturally and culturally diverse as New York City neighborhoods are. In contrast, the simplicity of a jingle like "The Entertainer" is not only effective for nostalgia's sake, but for the easily recognizable sonic message it carries in a variety of urban environments.

Probably the most recognizable ice cream jingle in the New York City area is that of the Mister Softee company: "Mister Softee [Jingle and Chimes]." Nichols Electronics has provided the little black boxes for the company since 1975, shepherding the simple tune and its distinctive timbre through various technological breakthroughs. Although it has been the target of much critical and public hostility—witness its starring role in the recent furor surrounding anti-noise legislation in the city—the jingle's power is undeniable, which may explain why Mister Softee is known for bringing legal action against those who play it without authorization. And why wouldn't they? Whatever else it may sound like—a music box, a 19th-century ice cream parlor automaton, or a nostalgic "kiddie tune"—it is, first and foremost, "ice cream truck music."

Early Works

INTERVIEW WITH KENNETH LONERGAN

"Early Works" was a series in *Esopus* whose purpose was to make periodic incursions into the purest source of creativity: the unbridled sensibilities of a child. The goal was to feature examples of youthful work that represented the first glimmers of creativity from well-known artists and writers. We inaugurated the series in 2013 with a contribution from acclaimed playwright and filmmaker Kenneth Lonergan, who shared with our readers a collection of science-fiction books he began writing and illustrating as a young boy. Coming from the creator of such keenly observed plays as *This is Our Youth* and *Lobby Hero* and the nuanced, character-driven films *You Can Count on Me*, *Margaret*, and *Manchester by the Sea*, their subject matter comes as something of a surprise.

***Tod Lippy:** When did you write these books?*

Kenneth Lonergan: I think I started writing them when I was in fifth grade, so I guess I was about 9 or 10 years old.

What attracted you to science fiction?

I just liked it. It was my favorite thing. I liked *Star Trek*, which I remember watching on Channel 4 in prime time. I liked *Planet of the Apes*. And I liked comic books—*Superboy*, the *Legion of Super-Heroes*. I was brought up in the space age: astronauts, space guns—all of that stuff was very, very popular in toys. My brother Peter and I loved to play with the Outer Space Men action figures—I used some of them for the characters in *The Wonderful World of Pluto*. I still like science fiction. I don't think there's enough of it—or enough of it that's any good.

Have you thought about writing it now?

I have, but I've never been able to come up with a story I thought I could pull off. I wrote a play in college called *A Space Play*, which was kind of a good idea but it was basically juvenilia. I've thought of revisiting it from time to time, but I haven't, at least not yet. I've never seen a play that took place in outer space, and I think it could be a good theatrical setting. At this point, I think I like watching science fiction more than I like writing it. I spent so much time on it when I was a kid: I really didn't write anything else from the moment I knew I wanted to be a writer in fifth grade until ninth or tenth grade.

Where did you get the ideas? Was each of these stories inspired by a specific source?

A lot of them were. *Rulers of the Earth* was stolen—or let's just say it derived very heavily from—the Tripods Trilogy, a series of books by John Christopher. It's about these very large, unpleasant space creatures living in tripods that have taken over the earth. *The Planet of the Furs* is obviously from *Planet of the Apes*. It was based on our Irish setter, Mandy, whom we called Fur Dog. It is a very grim story, as was *Planet of the Apes*—nothing good ever happened in that series. I just sort of copied the narrative directly, except I replaced the apes with Irish setters. *Wild Space* is an outer-space version of *Butch Cassidy and the Sundance Kid*, interspersed with different sci-fi stuff. It's partly a novel, but then every other chapter features a different science-fiction story that I had written elsewhere and decided to stick in between the narrative. There's also some *Planet of the Apes* influence in *The Wonderful World of Pluto*, but that one is fairly original to me.

Pluto *seems like the most ambitious story you worked on: It features not only typewritten text but a number of elaborate illustrations. How many pages is it in total?*

I think it's nearly 200 pages. I remember I was so happy when I got to 100 pages that I wrote *100* in red letters. My mother said that I was "writing by the pound."

How long did Pluto *take you to write?*

I want to say two years. I remember that by the time I got to the end of it, my writing had improved enough that I felt like the whole thing needed to be rewritten from the beginning, which was too much work. That happened all the time. I would write only the first volumes of three- or four-volume books. I wrote the first chapter of a book about Lucifer after I'd seen the Frank Langella play about Dracula and then read the Bram Stoker novel. I would usually write about 100 pages of the introductory section and then when I finally got to the main plot I would dry up and move on. I used to show these to a great teacher I had in seventh grade named Jo Anne Kraus. She actually wrote me a very nice letter recently, and told me she remembered me turning in "page after page" of these science-fiction stories.

It almost sounds like she was your first editor, or dramaturge...

Well, no, but I remember I kept in touch with her for a few years after she left—she was only at my school for one year. I finally told her I was writing something other than science fiction and she said, "Oh, thank God." *[laughs]* I really like science fiction, but the truth is, at least two-thirds of it is explanation.

It's funny you mention that: All of these stories include extremely detailed descriptions. In Pluto*, at one point you even interrupt the narrative with the declaration, "I think that an explanation is due." This runs for several paragraphs—and an illustration—and then you write, "Explanations are now at an end, and the story continues."*

Well, if you read real science fiction it does contain a lot of description—you know, all of the talk about the spaceship, the guns, the planet's atmosphere. I read a lot of Isaac Asimov at the time, and Robert A. Heinlein, and well, I was 10 or 11 years old—so I think was very self-aware about all of this.

Your treatment of typos in Pluto *is fascinating. For instance, in the first chapter you mention that there are 3,000,000 people on earth—*

Right, I was going down the list of how many inhabitants there are in all of the planets and I accidentally typed 3,000,000—I missed the last three zeros, because at the time there were 3,000,000,000 people on earth. So then I "fixed" the typo by explaining later on in the book that the entire rest of the population had been wiped out by Martians.

You actually say, "By the way, earlier in the book, I said that there were 3,000,000 Earthlings. I made no mistake."

Well, there was no Liquid Paper, and this was all done on my mother's Olivetti manual typewriter. I think I rubbed some things out with an eraser in *Pluto*. But I was very concerned about the appearance of the page. In *Wild Space*, I became very obsessive about the margins...

You're saying you actually manually *justified the right margins of every one of these pages?*

Yes.

That's incredible.

It's a little bit reminiscent of the writing Jack Nicholson does in *The Shining. [laughs]* I don't know what to say. I wanted it to look like a real book, so I would twist the sentences around, and put in parentheses or dashes—do anything—to get it to have a right-side justification. Later I switched to an electric typewriter—the kind where you put in the different cartridges. I got it for one of my birthdays in high school, and I used that for the next 10 or 15 years, until computers and word processing really came into being.

In Pluto, *there is a marked concern on your part with grammar, which often manifests in dialogue. For instance, Electroyed-E mentions to a visiting Jovian whom he's just met that he has a friend who might be able to share "their apartment," and the Jovian responds with "Their apartment. You said a friend of yours."*

All of the editing in that book was done in the text. It's just corrected on the go.

But what's particularly fascinating is that you're not editing yourself; it's one of your characters editing the other.

Right, it's like that typo about the earth's population: I incorporated it into the story, because if I made a mistake I didn't want to go back and have to retype or rewrite it. I would just either explain the mistake as something deliberate or I would correct it in the narration. *[flipping through* Pluto*]* Look at this one, on page 14. I typed "Yes it does" with two d's by mistake. I now recall deliberately adding two s's at the end of it so that it was spelled ddoess. And then somehow I justified this in the following line, where it says "Plutonians always pronounce does as doaz." Here's another one: I mistyped general and then immediately followed it up with "Plutonians spell it, 'genarle,' not 'general.'" I don't what this says about me, but it's certainly odd.

Your "colleagues" in Rulers of the Earth *are parenthetically referred to as your best friends; were these stand-ins for your actual friends?*

No, no. Not at all, they were all made-up. Anything autobiographical in these is certainly unintentional—or psychological. I think the book that it was based on had three main characters that were all friends.

Your illustrations play a major part in all of these books. You mentioned to me that at this point in your life you were trying to decide whether to become an artist or a writer.

Well, I was primarily interested in drawing until I was in fifth grade, and then I wrote this short story called "A Voyage to Titan" in a composition notebook that was four pages long. I was so excited that I'd managed to write a story that was four pages long that I decided then that I wanted to be a writer. I also had this vague awareness that there was no career in being an artist. I mean, I didn't exactly want to be a great painter or anything, but I liked drawing so much.

Were there any particular artists you were inspired by?

Not really. As I said, I read a lot of comic books: *Thor*, *Captain America*, *Ironman*—all the superheroes. They were my main influence; in fact, they may have been my only influence. I don't think I had yet started looking at paintings at that point. The first drawings I ever did are these poster-size images of all of the superheroes. I drew them with Magic Marker on a big roll of shiny paper my parents gave me. They didn't have arms or legs; their appendages were just rounded off. I still have four or five boxes of comic books, and I tend to reread them in those periods when I'm having trouble focusing on anything else.

You're known as such a humanist in both your plays and your films, yet you were, and it seems still are, drawn to these genres that are traditionally more schematic.

Yeah, I don't know that's about. I guess what you like and what you end up doing aren't always the same thing. I really like action movies—if they aren't insultingly stupid—but I don't think I could ever write one; I don't think I have a gift for that. I mean, I have occasionally worked on these types of scripts, but I always tend to think in terms of people talking to each other, which is sort of a limitation in filmmaking.

In Rulers of the Earth, *you write, "Jimmy had a hard life. He had somehow gotten stuck with a racist for a roommate." Where did that come from?*

I probably didn't even know what a racist was. There were no black kids in my class. I'd obviously heard a lot about racism without realizing that I was growing up among classic liberal racists—and I was one of them. There's my social consciousness at age 9. But that's okay, it has to start somewhere.

You know, there's a sort of theme running through these books that the earth is bad. I think this is actually a reflection of the Upper West Side liberal household I grew up in this period: There was the Vietnam War, and the opposition to the civil rights movement, which my parents—and everyone I knew—were horrified by. They really considered America to be a "bad country." So I didn't grow up thinking the country was such a great place, and that somehow translated into always making earth the villain in the stories.

Speaking of your parents, they are prominently listed in the acknowledgments page of every book; can you talk a bit about their influence on your writing in this period?

They were very supportive. My mother read everything I wrote, but she always complained that there were too many explosions. I gave her chapters of *The Wonderful World of Pluto* as I was writing it, and at some point she said, "Someone gets blown up on every page!" So my conscience pricked me and I wrote a chapter at the end of the book—which was somewhat insincere—in which the main character wanders around, feeling glad that there's "no more violence." *[laughs]*

And my father praised my dialogue, which actually helped point me toward the theater and playwriting. He said something I'll never forget: James Joyce was the master of masters when it came to dialogue—no one made their characters sound as distinct and different from each other as he did. When I later read James Joyce I came to agree with him. Whenever anyone compliments me on my dialogue, I immediately take it to heart. When it's something that I think I'm actually good at, I'm more motivated to do it.

The Pepsi

BY RICK STINSON

Pulling a rake through the detritus Eddie's upstairs neighbors had thrown out their window, I turned up empty packages of beef jerky, condom wrappers, diapers, mealworms, earwigs, centipedes, dead leaves. Everything went into a garbage bag that I tossed in the dumpster behind the pizza place. It was the only restaurant in town. The pizza was terrible.

I made sure to take off my shoes before entering the apartment. Eddie stood just inside the door, holding out some hand sanitizer for me to use before I touched any of his bathroom fixtures.

"Andrea is in the parking lot, in the blue Honda," he said. "I don't know what she's doing here, but I want her to leave."

I washed my hands, arms, neck, and face, and then went to the window. Eddie's sister, heavyset, sat in her car, glaring at the house. Of course Eddie's family wouldn't leave him alone. Of course his new neighbors were piling up trash outside his apartment.

"Thank you for dealing with all that garbage," Eddie said. "I just don't have the stomach."

"It's a housewarming present," I told him. Eddie's recently deceased uncle had left him $28,000. No one knew why—they weren't close. Personally, I thought it was because Eddie looked exactly like his dead father. His hair was even thinning the same way, starting in the back. Eddie had chosen to use this modest inheritance to rent an apartment in a building dozens of miles from the house in which he grew up—the first time in his life that he'd ever lived away from his mother.

I had taken off my jacket while dealing with the trash, and I was acutely aware of how cold it was when I stepped outside to talk to Eddie's sister. She rolled down the window as I approached her car.

"Hi, he's in bed. Not feeling well," I said.

"Do you think I want to see Eddie? After how ungrateful he's been to Mom?

Are you kidding?" she said. She was wearing a gray sweatshirt with the logo of a minor-league hockey team from Albany.

I waited for her to continue, and she did.

"I have some Pepsi for him, in case he gets thirsty." There was a case of Pepsi sitting next to her on the passenger seat.

"Do you want me to bring it in?"

"No, because it's a *gift*. From his *mother*. I'll give it to him. And I'm going to sit right here until he lets me in."

I went back inside and told Eddie what was going on. He'd replaced all of the fixtures in the apartment, sanded and refinished the floors, and was now using a fine-pointed brush to repaint the walls and ceiling with a degree of meticulous detail not normally attempted with white interior house paint. I could make out minuscule vertical brushstrokes on the door frame.

"Are you just going to let your sister sit out there?"

"Yes."

"She has a case of Pepsi for you from your mother."

"I can get my own Pepsi," he said.

"I'll bet if you take it, she'll go away. And besides, free Pepsi."

"Nothing from my mother's house will enter this apartment."

"I'll take it."

"Neither of us is going to take it, all right?"

Eddie couldn't touch unfamiliar surfaces or hold a conversation with a stranger, couldn't endure changes to his daily schedule, and had an unpredictable temper. He was not well liked and couldn't work on a farm, so in a town of fewer than one thousand people, he did not work at all. I was trying to steer him towards filing for SSI, but first he needed a diagnosis of some sort, and a teenage stint in a psychiatric hospital had left him terrified of shrinks. I was Eddie's only friend and had been since kindergarten, when I asked him to teach me how to draw—at that age, he'd already mastered two-point perspective. I was the only non–family member to be invited to his father's funeral, when we were both 11 years old, but only at Eddie's insistence. His mother and sister refused to talk to me after the service. I hadn't set foot in their house in over a decade.

Showing Eddie how to make eye contact with well-meaning strangers, open a bank account, purchase clothing: that's how I spent my formative years. As a teenager, a typical Saturday night would be spent trying to get a completely disengaged, borderline-catatonic Eddie to call up and order a pizza. My world bifurcated the moment he and I met—there was my life where I pursued romance and edited video and attended parties with people I call friends; and then there was my life with Eddie. Decades of effort had done nothing to bring these two worlds closer together, and the gulf between them was becoming each year more difficult to traverse. Every few weeks I rented a car and drove upstate to hang out with him. It occurred to me that I would probably still be doing this as an old man. I missed the simplicity of our childhood friendship, where keeping him safe was as easy as inviting him for a sleepover or taking a beating for him.

We were supposed to go grocery shopping, but Eddie didn't want to leave until he'd finished painting the door frame, and he could not be convinced to use a normal-sized paintbrush. While Eddie painted, I grabbed one of his sketchbooks out of a box. It was filled with exquisite photo-realistic drawings (mostly of horses) rendered in blue ballpoint pen, and then, offset slightly, the same image repeated in red ballpoint pen. Ballpoint pen had long been his medium of choice.

"You'll need 3D glasses for those. There's a pair around here somewhere," he said.

In the afternoon we left Andrea to stew in her car and headed to the grocery store. The morning's snow was melting quickly, and sodden, flattened cardboard boxes covered the floor by the entrance. As we entered, Eddie pulled on the brown cotton gloves that he always wore when outside his home. He purchased a lot of frozen food, several bags of potato chips, and a case of Pepsi, which I carried for him. We waited in line while a hulking farmer bought a case of Miller Genuine Draft and an Entenmann's coffee cake with a personal check.

"Do you want me to show you how to cook pancakes when we get back?" I said.

"No, no, no . . ." Eddie said. "Thank you, though."

"You don't have any cooking utensils yet?"

"Not yet," he said happily.

"You should really get some. This microwavable food isn't so great, you know, healthwise."

"There's enough stuff in my apartment as it is."

"That's what your kitchen cabinets are for," I said, and Eddie didn't reply.

"I'm going to get you a spatula," I said, but Eddie grabbed my arm.

"No. No, no, no," he said, squinting his eyes shut.

We returned to find Andrea's case of Pepsi sitting on the doorstep. Eddie burst into the apartment to call his sister. I unloaded the groceries, placed them in front of the door, and decided to wait outside. He screamed at her that she should stay out of his apartment, that he didn't want any Pepsi from their mother and it wasn't his job to make her happy, that he'd never wanted to live in his mother's house for such a long time and he wasn't going to spend his inheritance renovating it, and that buying a new television for the house wasn't really a repair per se, and he wasn't wasting his money by renting his own apartment, and it wasn't his fault that she'd chosen to sit out in the cold for so long. Et cetera.

When the yelling stopped I came in and put the food Eddie had purchased into his refrigerator, which was otherwise completely empty. When I finished, I turned around to see him staring at two identical cases of Pepsi on the kitchen floor.

"Which is the one we bought, and which is the one my mother tried to give me?" he asked.

"I don't know," I said, before I could think better of it. I should have just lied. He stared at the soda with a look of mounting horror.

"We have to give them both back," he said. "I won't have anything of hers in my apartment."

"What, give them to Andrea?"

"To my mother. She doesn't have to know we put them back."

"You're kidding."

"No, we'll just take this Pepsi back, get a new case from the store, and then come back here," Eddie said.

"We could just throw this in the dumpster and then get you a Pepsi from the gas station. How about that?" I said. Eddie's face reddened ominously.

"Why don't you want to do this?"

"I don't know, because it doesn't make any sense. At all."

"The Pepsi doesn't go here. It goes back in her house."

"That doesn't really explain anything."

"If it doesn't go back to her, it's still mine, and I have to take care of it."

"Can't you just 'take care of it' by throwing it out?" I asked. Eddie looked at me, stricken, his hands twisting.

"Fine," I said. I was drained.

In a few months, when the snow really began to fall, Eddie's mother's house would be nearly inaccessible. Clad in white vinyl siding, the house gleamed in the headlights as we drove past, shining through the dark foliage of the trees crowded around it. I parked the car on the side of the road, out of sight. Eddie unfastened his seat belt and struck out for the house, moving quickly and silently. The school bus that Eddie's mother drove for the district was parked on the lawn near the basketball hoop, sans net. I remembered practicing left-hand layups while Eddie sat on a rock near the stream, sketching.

"We should try not to wake her up," he whispered as we approached. His mother had been stalled in the second step of a 12-step program for the last few years.

We entered through the garage, which was piled to the ceiling with boxes—there was barely room to move. Five dogs were tied up in the far corner. They didn't bark or acknowledge us; they didn't wag their tails or even stir. They weren't acting like dogs at all. Three push lawn-mowers, two of which were brand-new with tags, were lined up against the wall. I struggled with the weight of both cases of Pepsi.

The accumulation began after Eddie's father died. I first noticed that Eddie's mother had a lot of bird feeders, but kept buying new ones that she would leave in their boxes in the garage. As a kid I didn't have a reference for what was or wasn't normal behavior, so I never thought to tell my mother what was going on. By the end of the year, when she drove me to pick Eddie up on the weekend, he would meet us outside the house, even when it was raining.

Now I was looking at a mountain of boxes where an electric-blue Dodge Charger had once been, balanced on jack stands. It was entirely possible that the car was still there, buried. We took our shoes off and walked through the front door.

It took a moment for my eyes to adjust to the darkness. Dozens of coats hung from the wall, three or more on each coat hook, some with their tags still attached. They were down-filled and dull-colored, gray and forest green mostly, except for several bright-orange hunting jackets. A number of these were on the floor in clear plastic garbage bags, which did nothing to contain their rancid smell. Estrus, probably. A row of shotguns stood upright in a homemade rack, boxes of shells next to them. The couch was piled high with birdhouses, packages of white tube socks, and shrink-wrapped boxes of Christmas ornaments.

I was trying to figure out how to navigate through everything when Eddie pushed past, nimbly making his way across the floor to the staircase at the other end of the room. He climbed the steps, his narrow legs swiftly picking through the clutter on the stairs, his pale hands visible in the dim light as he held his arms out for balance.

The cases of Pepsi were getting heavy. Not being particularly agile, I advanced through the house slowly. I thought I'd put them in the kitchen, which was off to the right. To gain access to it, I had to step over two 50-pound sacks of bird feed. The room was filled with dozens of bags of dog food and teetering stacks of magazines and catalogs. The kitchen table and chairs were nearly covered, as was the counter. I made my way to the refrigerator, which was humming, and carefully shifted some boxes so I could open it.

The temperature had been turned down as low as possible, and I flinched at the plume of cold air that escaped. The refrigerator was filled with blue jays sealed in ziplock bags, dull and frozen solid, stacked in neat rows. I closed the door quickly. Eddie appeared in the stairwell and stared at me, exasperated.

"We're going to put it upstairs, so come on," he said.

I hefted the Pepsi onto my shoulder and gingerly ascended the stairs, which were cluttered with vases and appliances. The second floor was worse than the first. At first I didn't understand what I was looking at—the spacious living room I remembered from years before was completely obscured. Boxes blocked the windows. Eddie leaned in and whispered as quietly and furiously as he possibly could: "What were you doing in there?"

"I was trying to put away the Pepsi."

"We don't use that kitchen anymore. The new kitchen is up here. Besides, we're not going to put it in the kitchen."

"There's a bunch of dead birds down there, in the refrigerator."

"I know. They're in the second-floor fridge too, and in the freezers in the basement." He cocked his head at the kitchen window. There was a pellet gun sitting on the sill, next to a few cardboard cartons of Copperhead pellets. "She says the blue jays are mean to the other birds at the feeders."

Eddie didn't make any sound as he moved down the hallway; although I was trying to be silent, I kept stumbling over things. We were close to his mother's room. I could hear her snoring. Eddie reached up and pulled on a short length of nylon cord hanging down from the ceiling, but very slowly. The attic door came down, and Eddie gingerly unfolded the stairs, which were painted a bright orange. We pulled them up after us.

I squinted when he turned on the lights. Eddie sifted through the piles of newspapers that cluttered the floor.

A pile of Christmas presents, wrapped in brittle paper, sat in the corner of the attic. I picked one up to read the tag: *Merry Xmas, Eddie! Love, Dad.*

"Put it here," he said.

"These presents are all from your father?"

"No, they're from other people in the family too. My mother withholds Christmas presents from me if I haven't been good enough."

"You never told me that," I said. Eddie looked at me like I was an idiot.

"Why would I?"

"Do you still want this stuff?"

"No. Put the Pepsi here. This is where it belongs."

From downstairs I heard coughing, and then the sound of a door opening. Someone was grunting. Eddie reached past my head and turned off the light.

"Someone in my house?" his mother muttered. "Better not be. I know my goddamn self-defense rights." The sound of her going downstairs, and then, for a minute, nothing, and then a nearly inaudible litany of curses. She belched loudly as she staggered through the mess.

I was trying to remain as silent as possible when I suddently heard a soft wet sound and smelled alcohol; Eddie, silhouetted against a window, was rubbing his hands down with hand sanitizer. His mother pounded up the stairs, panting. She was right below us. There was another sound but I couldn't understand what it was. When I tapped Eddie on the shoulder and raised an eyebrow, he mimed drinking, and then cocking a shotgun.

I was nauseated, galvanized with panic—I had no idea how to get us out of the house. Her heavy, faltering tread pounded the floor downstairs, and I could hear her ramping herself up to take care of things. The look on my face must have been priceless, because for the first time that day Eddie was smiling; he was struggling to hold back laughter. Composing himself, he leaned forward and whispered very quietly in my ear: "Don't worry. I know exactly what to do." I wanted to throw my arms around him. I was sure that he was right; I knew that he would save me if he could. He sat there in the dark, his hands sanitized, perfectly calm.

Oddments

BY JESSICA RAE ELSAESSER

Dousing Rods

Our bodies
are more honest
than us, when it
comes to finding
what is needed:
water, home,
the wayward soul,
our fingers forge
onward, signing out
our message to
the intended.
This is what
we want, and
it is decent,
modest,
deserving of
divining.

Whale Watching

Beings of a certain greatness
impress us with their
gravity, how much
they displace,
the density
of their communions,
sounds like the
immutable lament
our marrow is made of,
as though if we
were made larger
our sorrows would
grow likewise,
expanding
– it could hardly be withstood –
that unfulfilled need
to believe that
mountains could
move.

Weathering

How a passing
leaves you
bleached by it,
a white tree
among the others
as though this
were not the
taking of something
from you,
but a mark,
one that spreads
abating what you were
before replacing you,
your memories like
petrified wood that
has been stone
so very long.

Absurd Regrets

There was all this light –
stuff floating around you
like pollen. It came out
of me in tufts, you brushed
my coat and I fell apart.
There were others nearby
who gathered it up, made it
into something usable
like love. The sun is on
your shoulders and
it is a sight to behold.

Force

Inside the knife-
sharpener's truck
is an array of blades,
dull and sharp, and if
you ask him which
is more dangerous,
he will tell you blunt
and sternly warn
above the belts still whirring
of all the force
we may place unwittingly
upon an old edge.

A Far Sight

A common memory
for those with poor vision
is the leaves on trees
separating, still green
but traced, through
the newly fitted
lenses and
surroundings
which at once
are full of edges,
wanting always
to come apart,
until the pleasure
is so specific
it is something like
a stitch and then
the only relief
is in semblances,
letting the leaves
and such loosen
and diffuse
until even
the meagrest lights
have halos.

Boxing the Compass

Everything proceeds
from a point, all our
lives' undertakings
divided by the most minute
of angles. Begin listing
the winds and all their names
will sound familiar
in the end
the peril is not
in unknown shores or
courses outflown
but in spinning and
spinning and
spinning.

Tallying

Tally marks
are useful
for counting
over time,
when though
a finite number
may exist,
we've no right
to expect it.
Each anticipates
another, none
thinks it is the last,
but fashions stars
of totals and sums,
answers, wholes and
worths, amounts,
ends, reckonings,
and spends its days
gazing.

The Outer Problems

INTERVIEW WITH JOHN CONWAY

In Donald E. Knuth's 1974 novella *Surreal Numbers*, an Adam and Eve–ish couple come upon a tablet that reads, in Hebrew, "In the beginning, everything was void, and J. H. W. H. Conway began to create numbers." The Conway in question is late mathematician John Conway (1937–2020)—whose discovery of surreal numbers in 1970 rocked the world of mathematics—and the godlike status conferred upon him is hardly hyperbolic. Over the course of his career, he did groundbreaking work in group theory, knot theory, coding theory, and the theory of finite groups. He was particularly revered among amateur mathematicians for his invention of the so-called Game of Life (which inspired the field of cellular automata), as well as the Doomsday Algorithm, a formula that calculates the day of the week for any date in history.

When *Esopus* invited Conway to contribute something related to his working process, he came up with an extremely generous offer: An inveterate model-builder, he proposed creating a template for a three-dimensional geometric polyhedron that our readers could then assemble on their own, effectively allowing them direct insight into his working methods. In the Fall of 2006, we paid a visit to Conway at Princeton University's math department, where we photographed him building a prototype of the model while he mused on aesthetics, symmetry, and the therapeutic benefits of drawing knots.

Tod Lippy: *Is it common for mathematicians to build models?*

John Conway: Actually, I'm not so sure it is, at least with professionals. But certainly it is when they're young—I first started building them when I was in high school. I've just never outgrown the habit. You know, I don't really like the process of doing it. I do like having the final things. It's like when people say, "Do you enjoy traveling?" Well, who enjoys sitting on a plane for hours? But you like getting there. That's the thing.

How many of these have you made?

Well, there might be a hundred or so in my office, and you know, double or treble it, maybe. These things, you see, are some of my friends. Like the guys on the wall, the famous mathematicians. Most of the models you see there were made between attacks of laziness.

Can you tell me a little bit about this particular polyhedron you've chosen for our readers to build?

This is the small stellated dodecahedron, which was named in the early 1600s by Johannes Kepler, the great astronomer. Kepler spent a good part of his life trying to understand the planets and how they are arranged. When he was trying to work out the ratios and distances between the planets, he thought they might have something to do with irregular polyhedra, and so he started studying these irregular solids—Platonic solids, they're called.

Along the way he discovered that if you prolong the edges of an ordinary dodecahedron, they meet again, and you get this thing with star-shaped faces. The faces of this particular one are called pentagrams. So he came up with this beautiful object, a star-shaped polyhedron. He also found another one, the great stellated polyhedron, and then a few hundred years went by. In the early 1800s, Louis Poinsot found the other two: the great icosahedron, which has an ordinary pentagon for its intersecting faces, and the great dodecahedron, which has triangles. These make up what are called the Kepler-Poinsot solids.

There are just four of them?

Yes. Augustin-Louis Cauchy, a really great mathematician of the 1800s, proved in the end that there are only four of these star polyhedra.

Were models of them made when they were discovered?

Actually, there were some models of polyhedra that were believed to have been made by Leonardo. You can see pictures of those in various places. The edges were made of wood, sort of hinged together in various ways.

How does model building relate to your theoretical work?

It's sort of funny, really. As I said, this is a rather childish pursuit for a grown-up mathematician. I tell people that I make them for teaching purposes. That's not really true. I make them because I think they are sort of inspiring. You know, the subject that I studied for a long time and made some progress in is called group theory, which is the study of symmetry. And the progress I made was all in high dimensions. I studied the symmetry of this wonderful object in 24-dimensional space, which was actually the first big discovery I made. Things like this stellated dodecahedron, they're in three-dimensional space, because, unfortunately, we don't live in 24-dimensional space. But, you know, they have the same sort of ring about them. So they're a sort of substitute. Really not so interesting, but still quite beautiful.

So even if they only barely approximate these much more complicated objects, they can still prove useful?

Well, I should say that what I do is neither simple nor complicated; it's sort of big—or maybe *subtle* is a better word. But yes, often they're nice, easy examples. And people aren't very familiar with these things nowadays. I really can't rely anymore on a student knowing what I'm talking about when I mention a dodecahedron. So it's nice to have a model around. But the theory of these three-dimensional things was really all finished off by the 19th century. So it's old. But you know, what's the difference if it's old? It's still beautiful. One could argue that the same thing is true with modern art. You sort of arty types frown upon the older, straight representational stuff. It's no longer so much in vogue. So there's a parallel in a way.

Well, that raises a question: Would you call these models abstract or representational?

No, these things are real things. You know, how can I say it? Some people like the human—or the earthly, let's put it like that. And I must say I do, in a way. But ever since I was a teenager, I've been more interested in what I would call the outer problems. Things that concern our species, or our planet, I regard as parochial. Somebody might write a history of their own little town, but then who's going to be interested in it? Well, I don't know, but probably most of the people interested in it will be the town's inhabitants. You know, *Fifty Interesting Walks in New Jersey* sells to people who live in New Jersey. Fine. I'm also a member of the human species, and live on earth, so I have a slight amount of interest in geography and the humanities. But I'm more interested in things that have a certain universality. I'm very intrigued by what would interest some creature I haven't met yet. Like a Martian, or some other intelligent being from a long way away, who won't be especially interested in human concerns. The fact that someone is human doesn't especially turn me on.

Do you think most mathematicians share that perspective?

No, not necessarily. And I don't totally have it myself. For instance, I'm very interested in etymology, and particularly the etymology of the English language. That's not a mathematical pursuit. But professionally, so to speak, the things that interest me are the ones that I can imagine interesting somebody from some other place.

This model is an instance where rationality intersects with aesthetics. I mean, there is a beauty about this. It's not everybody's cup of tea, I'd imagine, but it's undeniably aesthetic. I should say that mathematics is an aesthetic subject. A phrase you will constantly hear my colleagues applying to something is "It's elegant." That's what we do. We study beautiful things. And there's a subtlety to the beauty. And there are rules to the beauty, specifically. You can't just sort of invent something and say, "I find this interesting." Well, you can, but then you're not doing mathematics. It's a wonderful fact that there are only four of these Kepler-Poinsot solids. I can't invent another star-regular polyhedron.

Can the process of building a model like this help people who know little about math to better understand it?

Well, you know, a former Princeton colleague, Bill Thurston, used to say that geometry is the user interface of mathematics. It's "user-friendly." The fact is that much of mathematics is really hard to learn or understand—and by the way, there's no reason why everyone should do it. But people might like to know why we strange people are so interested in it. And the answer is, often, because of its beauty. Additionally, with geometry—unlike, say, algebra—the layperson can get some clue about it, because geometry is about shapes. You look at the shape and you don't have to do any calculations to create the shape. You can just appreciate it. "Oh, that's nice." So you know, that gives you a little bit of a clue about mathematics without any pain.

I think geometry is pain-free to its practitioners. Well, there may be some pain when you're doing calculations. I did a little calculation when I was drawing this thing, to work out exactly how to draw the pentagon. So there was a little bit of pain there.

Do you find the assembly part to be therapeutic?

It can be. I remember when my first marriage was sort of breaking down, and it was a real mess, you know. At the time, I was planning on publishing a dictionary of knots, which would include about 1,000 different types, and every now and then I'd take out my drawing instruments, which included my special pen and india ink, and French curves to trace around with, and sort of draw knots for a half hour or hour at a time. There's a certain sensuality to knots that polyhedra lack. This kind of geometry has straight lines. Knots have sinuous curves. So there was a certain pleasure and comfort in drawing those curves, arranging them.

When one finds templates for these various polyhedra in books or on the Internet, they tend to be one large form that you then fold together and glue down. Your assembly method is somewhat different—why?

You see, that's what they call a "net" for polyhedra. It doesn't actually save time. Well, it saves time if you don't actually have to draw the thing in the first place. But the problem is, if you make a net, some of the edges are folded, and some of them have tabs and glue. So there are two different kinds of edges on your model. What that means is that it won't be symmetrical. You will see round edges in certain places, and sharp edges in others. Basically, it doesn't look nice.

As far as I know, I'm the only person who's ever assembled them in this interlocking way. It's a bit tricky to do, but it has this great advantage in that the faces stay plane. Also, sticking the faces through each other—this intersecting jazz—is fun in a way because, at least to a certain perverse type of mind, it's all about solving a puzzle. And it's not at all obvious you can do it. There's a sense of achievement in forcing the things through.

How much of your time is spent on process as opposed to, say, the completion of a theorem?

Well, the way I work is a bit peculiar, really. I sort of do the same thing over and over again. I'm not a systematic person; I don't keep notes. And in fact, the only way I ever keep notes of anything is when I've published a paper. That's my note. But you know, I'll work out a piece of mathematics one year and then forget about it. And next year I sort of vaguely remember how I did it, but I don't remember the answer, so I do it again. And then I forget about it again, and five years later I get back to it and do it again, and every now and then, I discover a sort of slight improvement. So by the 10th time I've done it, it's actually getting pretty good. It's just a perennial polishing. That's not actually answering the question as you posed it, but that's what I spend a fantastic amount of my time doing. Only every now and then do I actually sort of really discover anything that's entirely new. Those are the great times. During those, I do not sleep. I'm awake for sixty hours in a row. When I discovered the surreal numbers, I was in a permanent daydream for six weeks, thinking how beautiful this thing was, and thinking, "How clever you are, John, to have discovered it." I was lost in admiration of the discovery—the abstract things—and lost in admiration of my own accomplishment.

I haven't met anyone else who works quite in this way. It's sort of like contemplating your navel, in a sense, except it's not your navel, it's whatever it is. I spend such an enormous amount of time just looking at this one thing from every conceivable point of view. I'll count its vertices a thousand times. And you might go away and come back the next day and I'll still be there, looking at it from a different angle.

Plate Tectonics

BY LESLEY CLAYTON

"Because India is plowing into Eurasia," she said, propping a pillow up on the window to block the sun coming in.

"But India is so much smaller. Won't Eurasia win?" He pulled a handful of blankets up from their twists at the foot of the bed.

"Eurasia won't win."

"Why not?"

"Because Eurasia isn't fighting."

"It's just sitting there? Being plowed into?"

"Basically."

"So the Himalayas are growing?"

"The Himalayas are growing."

He made a light clicking noise with his tongue on the back of his teeth while he thought it over. "When do you get off tonight?" he asked, scratching the beginnings of a beard, a different noise altogether.

"I don't know. Maybe ten?"

"But India is attached to Eurasia. Why aren't they moving together?"

"India is headstrong. It's on a plate by itself."

"And it's plowing into Eurasia?"

"And it's plowing into Eurasia."

"And the Himalayas are growing?"

"And the Himalayas are growing."

"And they'll just grow and grow until they plow through the atmosphere and we can climb them to outer space?"

"No."

"Then they'll grow so tall that they'll knock the moon all the way across the universe like a pinball flipper?"

"No."

"And the nights will be pitch-black and the waves will stop waving and the ocean will stand stock-still for all eternity?"

"No."

"And our children will hear about the moon like they hear about Santa Claus and Christopher Columbus and never see it in the sky?"

"Who said we're having children?"

He blushed, and laughed at himself for it. "Well, maybe not our children, but, you know, 'Our Children.'" He said the words like a news anchor, with one hand in a loose fist on his chest.

She laughed too, not because it was funny but to put him at ease. "Well, no. 'Our Children' will see the moon."

"What, then?"

She raised her head from its post on his shoulder and propped herself up on one elbow, to look him in the face. "It will plow all the way through and snap Russia in half, then move into the Arctic." He was quiet for a moment and she lay her head back down.

"So unsuspecting Russian families will wake up to find that India has come through and split their homes in half?"

"No. They'll see it coming."

"How so?"

"It will take one hundred thousand years."

"So they will have to choose the east or the west while they helplessly watch India split their nation?"

"No."

"Will political parties run to their respective corners and cheer India on—*C'mon India! Break the bastards off!*—then never need to debate again?"

"God, you're frustrating."

He was quiet again. She watched dust float in the lines of sunlight projecting onto the far wall and thought about coffee, about how long she had to lie there with him before going to the kitchen.

"Why isn't India more ambitious?"

"Breaking Russia in half isn't ambitious?"

"Why Russia? Couldn't it be more constructive?"

"How so?"

"Couldn't it separate the Koreas?"

"Oh, God."

"Or Israel and Palestine? That would be helpful."

"Do you want coffee?" she asked him.

"Sure."

She started to get up, but couldn't pass his body without knocking him off the narrow bed and onto the cold hardwood floor. "Then you'll have to move," she told him.

"You'll have to get past me," he said playfully and rolled toward her, anchoring his weight.

"Don't mess with me, kid. I am tough."

"Uh-huh."

"I will headbutt you."

"India style?"

"Yes. India style." She pushed against his chest with her hands and shoulder. He laughed, and she felt the muscles in his stomach and chest tensing up to combat her. Her hair fell down over her eyes, and for a second, she liked the way her dark fingernail polish looked against the bright white of his T-shirt. She gave up, backed off, and brushed her hair out of her face.

"Eurasia's totally gonna win," he laughed.

"No, it's not," she shook her head. "Just give me one hundred thousand years."

"You can have it," he said, and it made her uncomfortable. She was sitting upright with her legs crossed in front of her. He lay on his side and traced a scar on her knee with his forefinger. "You could break me in half, you know."

She nodded slowly, her eyes fixed on the tips of her toes.

"I know I could," she said, and climbed over his body to the cold shock of the bare winter floor on the soles of her feet.

From *Esopus 22* (2015)

Critical Conversations: A 360° Clinical Portrait

BY DANIELLE SPENCER AND STEPHANIE ADLER YUAN

Annie Baker is a sixty-something retired English teacher in treatment for colon cancer that has metastasized to her liver. She receives medical care at a large suburban oncology practice in the northeastern United States. The office is a busy one, part of a cancer center adjacent to a regional hospital.

On a cold, foggy day in December 2014, we accompanied Annie to a routine appointment with her oncologist at this office, and we visited her a week later in her hospital room when she was admitted for inpatient chemotherapy. Over the course of those two visits we interviewed Annie and staff members involved directly and indirectly with her care in various capacities: receptionist, nurse, physician, phlebotomist, administrative assistant, and many others. We spoke to them about their lives, their work, and their experiences of illness and caregiving, in an effort to portray the delicate and complex constellation of care surrounding a single, and singular, cancer patient.

While recent years have brought an increasing number of memoirs about illness, along with accounts by clinicians, few writings have bridged the two and offered a depiction of a health-care experience from multiple perspectives. The portrait that emerges here prompts many questions, such as: Which accounts of illness and caregiving are culturally accepted? How do certain narratives serve us in difficult times? How might we address the erosion of agency one experiences in the face of illness and medical treatment? How do we understand experiences of care, of grace, and of facing mortality itself?

All names have been changed to preserve participants' anonymity, and interviews have been edited for brevity and clarity.

VIRGINIA (RECEPTIONIST, ONCOLOGY PRACTICE)

Virginia: I'm breaking out in a sweat here...I'm just like—God, you're making me nervous. I'm really not good at this stuff. Okay, all right.

I'm a receptionist. I greet the patients as they come in, new patients. Sign them in and take co-pays, and just hope that they have a comfortable, relaxing visit. It's scary, and they're nervous when they come in. I connect with a lot of them. It's kind of sad a lot of days, when we lose people and stuff, because we do tend to connect. When they don't come anymore, you're like, "Hmmm..." You wonder. I don't know anything [about their clinical status]—it depends on how much they tell me. Some will stand there and talk to me for 10 minutes. You just see what they're going through.

I've been here six and a half years. I was actually in OB/GYN before, and there you see babies, from the beginning. So, from one extreme to the other. Of course, lots of bad things happen there also. But they're both rewarding.

I really didn't know anything before working here. I'd had family members go through cancer, but I never really knew how it affects everybody. And visit-wise, if you see people come in by themselves, you wish they had somebody with them. I don't know, it's sad. Then again, like I said, it's rewarding also, because I do enjoy the patients and stuff.

I'm sure they enjoy you.

Virginia: So they say. *[laughs]*

Has it gotten easier over time?

Virginia: Yeah. Some days are harder than others. We have that dreaded list in the kitchen where when people pass, it's...sometimes the minute you walk in, in the morning, and it's just...that can make a day bad.

There's a list in the office kitchen of patients who have passed away?

Virginia: Yeah. It's just 8.5 by 11, so it goes down, and as the page fills up, the top goes off. It's actually right on the refrigerator.

How many names are there per week?

Virginia: It depends. On there now, I think the latest one has probably like 12 or 13 names. That could be over a two- or three-week span. Some times it's larger than others.

I see. That is a lot. Two or three weeks?

Virginia: Yeah, it's sad. *[quiet pause]*

Do you talk to your colleagues about it?

Virginia: We do, because we get close to the patients. Unfortunately we've lost a lot of good ones...I'm sorry... *[starts crying]* That's one thing I don't like about it.

You have to carry around that sadness and grief but also, being the first person who people see when they come in, do you feel like you have to be upbeat and cheery for patients?

Virginia: I don't feel like I have to be; it's just me. I wouldn't want to be sitting there like this when you walk in, that's for sure. So you just put on the face, if nothing else. We do it, but also the three of us working at the front desk, we're pretty close, we talk. Like, "Hey, we haven't seen this one in a while, I wonder what's going on..."

So you don't necessarily know?

Virginia: Yeah, we don't always know. We're not really told a lot.

Do you feel comfortable asking, if you're concerned about someone?

Virginia: Yeah. But then sometimes we don't really want to know. You know? If they're in a hospice or something like that...I don't know...

That first encounter in a medical office matters so much. It's an important part of patient care.

Virginia: Yeah. I don't even like going to my own doctor's office, they're just so nasty. I've told my doctor, "If I ever acted like that, first of all I wouldn't be able to go home and sleep, and it would bother me. *And* I would lose my job in a heartbeat, and so I should." I've gone into my doctor's office and I'm like, "Oh no, it's *her*!" I say to myself, "God, I hope people don't say that about *me*." *[laughs]*

Everybody has a bad day, and not everybody is going to like everybody, unfortunately. There's people who come in, they are upset, and sometimes they take it out on us, like it's our fault that they're sick, and you have to try to understand that sometimes you just don't click with somebody, no matter how hard you try.

But Annie's just so pleasant all the time. She usually comes at busy times, so it's usually, "Hi, how are you?" She'll come out with something funny. I was actually checking in a new patient when Annie came in, and she said to the patient, "Is this your first time here? You are going to have such a wonderful experience." And I was like, "Thank you." Then she goes, "And especially starting with *Virginia*!" I'm like, "Oh my God." You know what? You don't hear it a lot. When somebody does say it, then thank you, I appreciate that.

Is there anything that surprises you about your job?

Virginia: That I enjoy it. My friends say, "I don't know how you do that." They don't know how I go here every day and deal with everything, but I just like the interaction with the people. I talk to the ladies about their wigs. They tell me, "I like it," "I don't like it," or they might say, "Okay, you didn't say anything, that means you didn't like this one." I'm like, "Oh, no, I just didn't notice, I'm sorry!" *[laughter]* Yeah, it's kind of weird. They name them. They name their wigs. One lady came in the other day and said, "This is Barbara here. This is our first time out together." I enjoy that. It's just little things like that.

You must see the whole spectrum of how people respond. Some with humor, and some not, right?

Virginia: Right. Some are mad. You can understand that side too. They're just mad. Why them? So that's a bad part of it.

Do you ever end up on the receiving end of that anger?

Virginia: Oh, yeah, all the time. You just try to defuse it. It happens mostly when they first come in, because they're scared. Then we just try to guide them through and tell them, "Listen, you're in a good place." They'll look around and see the waiting room, how packed it is, and I'm like, "But that's a good thing, because people keep coming back."

Some people come back a year later and they're like, "I stood outside shaking for five minutes, and I didn't want to walk in here." I'm like, "I don't blame you. But look, we're still here!" *[laughs]* Everybody reacts differently. I try to keep in mind, how would I want to be treated if I were walking into some place for the first time, or any time?

[Indicating Virginia's crucifix necklace] *Do you mind my asking if you ever pray for patients?*

Virginia: We do, a lot. I pray for them. Most of them, actually. Just everybody that walks in. Sometimes you see them leaving, you know you're never going to see them again, and the family and everything.

You mean if they're being discharged to hospice?

Virginia: Yeah.

It must be hard.

Virginia: Yeah, it is. Don't make me cry again.

DR. SHANTI ROY (ONCOLOGIST)

What's on your mind going into this visit with Annie?

Dr. Roy: I'm excited for Annie because I just saw the report from her surgeon and the CAT scan report. It showed that there was a response, further response, in the cancer in her liver, the liver metastasis. All along [since I met her nine months ago] I've been hoping for her to have an adequate response so that she can have surgery.

She has metastatic colon cancer, and we've been doing chemotherapy up front to try to shrink this liver lesion. If it's shrunk to a certain degree, she may be a candidate for surgery. And that is really her only chance for a cure. Without that, we would just be giving her more chemo and it would be more palliative. And this sort of gives us more hope that there could be a cure for her. If she can have that liver lesion taken out—and she'll have to have colon surgery as well—that would put her in a different category, like a potentially curable situation.

I literally just got the report from her surgeon yesterday, and I spoke to him today and he also was optimistic about it. It's going to be challenging surgically and anatomically, but he is eager to do the surgery now. Whereas previously, at every step when we had been doing CAT scans, he was like, "Well, there's some shrinkage, but not enough. She needs more chemo." So we've been going through this now for months, so this is sort of a big step. Now, she's probably heard it from her surgeon, but I'll be able to talk to her more about it.

Do you generally think about your patients between visits?

Dr. Roy: I do, especially if there's a scan or something going on, and then I have to talk to them about the results. Sometimes I'll call them before the visit because I don't want them to wait. I always look at my schedule for the week before it starts, so I know what's coming and who's coming and what issues there might be and stuff. So, yeah, I do think about them in advance.

Do you ever share your thoughts and concerns and fears with the patients as you consider them privately?

Dr. Roy: Hmmm. That's a tough one. I think, no—I don't. Because I think, as an oncologist, you kind of have to be the strong person. You have to really be the authority figure. You have to give them direction and hope. So fears, no. It's not really about fear. It could be about making different decisions, like maybe not continuing chemotherapy but rather going on palliative care or hospice.

But it's part of our job to be the leader, the person who gives guidance and advice. I don't think it would do the patient any good if I were afraid or if I conveyed that to them. At times, I think it's natural to feel that way, but I don't think it's part of our job description.

Do you ever dream about your patients?

Dr. Roy: Mm-hmm *[affirmative]*. Yeah, yeah, it happens once in a while, yes, yes. I think it probably happened earlier in my career more than now.

Why do you think that is?

Dr. Roy: It's a very emotionally taxing field. Learning how to cope with that is a process. It's part of the training, really, as much as it is learning about the drugs and the side effects and everything. There's a whole emotional learning curve that goes on with it. I think you just sort of get a little bit better at that part of it, about dealing with everything and absorbing it and communicating, and all those things.

How do you manage that aspect of your work?

Dr. Roy: It really helps to talk to people who have been doing it for longer, because they're like the Yodas. They've done it. They get it. They understand. They just know what it feels like to be in a situation where you're trying to guide somebody, you're trying to help somebody, and it's really hard, because you know there's not much more you can do, medically. There are no more drugs to offer. There are no more treatment options. So—they've been there. I think just talking about it helps.

I guess it sort of helps to be somewhat spiritual. Also, on a personal level, just to know that things could be worse—and I'm dealing with adults, not with children. So I think it helps to put everything in perspective.

How do you typically go about establishing a connection with a new patient?

Dr. Roy: I think a lot of it is the first visit. It's really important to get to know who they are the first time you see them, because that's when you have more time. I try to spend time getting to know them and getting to know who their family members are, and what kind of support they have at home. Just to know what they did for work, and if they're retired, what they do now and how they spend their days. I try to write it down, because I can't remember everything, so the next time I see, I remember: This is the guy who likes to play golf or likes to fish or whatever. It helps. Just little things that you can kind of connect with them over that are outside of their disease, that make them real people.

What do you hope to discuss with Annie during this visit?

Dr. Roy: I think we're just going to talk about these CAT scan results, her conversation with her surgeon, and then what the plan is going to be—which is that she's probably going to have surgery. But we might need to do some chemotherapy just to tide things over because otherwise it's a long gap between now and when the surgery is, and the surgeon didn't want her to have any progression of the cancer in the interim, so we might do one more hospital admission. She may or may not be excited about that. Probably not, but I'll have to talk to her about it and try to explain why that's important, and we'll see how that goes.

She always has something interesting to talk about, like what book she's reading or something. She's just an interesting person, really well read, very dynamic. We have a lot of trust and respect mutually. I really feel for what she's going through. She's had a hard life and this sort of hit her like a ton of bricks when it happened. She was really shocked, surprised, but she's come a long way in terms of coping with it. She's expressed this before, that "Anything that happens, it happens, and I feel like I'm in the best hands." She's very grateful. Many patients aren't. They're angry, and it's understandable, but she's not like that. She's just very grounded. She's an amazing person.

Do you feel like her attitude or your relationship with her impacts the care relationship?

Dr. Roy: That's a good question, and I think it does. It has to, because as physicians, we're human beings first. I think that people go an extra mile for somebody that they really know well and that they care about. As a physician, you try to have that with every patient. And I think you do, but then there are some people that make you want to do more.

Is there anything that you feel can go unsaid, not necessarily between you and Annie, but between a physician and a patient in a clinical relationship?

Dr. Roy: Yeah, I think so, because it's all about timing. For example, we deal a lot with patients who are at the end of life, and the conversation about stopping chemotherapy and moving on to palliative care and hospice has to happen at the right time—and they have to be ready to hear it. Although we may be thinking about it for a long time, the actual presentation of that discussion might not happen immediately. So that can be a little bit hard because you know you're on different planes—you're thinking different things—but you have to allow the patient some time to get closer to where you are before you can have that kind of conversation, because otherwise it might not go well.

I think the patient experience is so—what's the word—it's just a very difficult one. Having been on the other side, whether it's myself or a family member, being a patient—I always go back to that and think about what the experience was like for any of us in dealing with physicians and nurses and the whole team.

As physicians, I think we often forget what the patient experience is like. And probably for many of the staff here, everyone kind of gets stuck in their routines and forgets that the patient is the one who has the disease and they're the ones who are experiencing something that can be very difficult. There are so many things that you internalize or that you perceive as a patient that you're never really given a forum to express.

Do you also feel like you don't have a forum to express aspects of your experience as a physician?

Dr. Roy: Definitely. There's just not enough time in the day. There is just not enough time. I'd say 90 percent of what we experience gets internalized and there's no place to let it out, you know?

And I love what I do. I love my job. So I don't feel ever that it's not the right place for me. I feel lucky that I ended up doing what I'm doing. I feel that I can help people at a very critical time in their lives. And it's unlike many other fields. Cancer—still, it's just so hard to hear that word. I think that coming into people's lives at that moment is unique. No other medical field has that kind of impact. That's what I was drawn to.

I do talk to my husband. I think I used to talk to him much more, again, earlier in my career, when it was really heavy on my mind. But with time I think I've been able to process things a little bit better myself and kind of realize, "All right, well, this is how it's going to go, and this is what happens," and just, again, put it all into perspective. I think with time, with experience, it just naturally happens.

As you become a Yoda yourself, gradually.

Dr. Roy: Eventually, yes.

ANNIE BAKER (PATIENT)

So what brings you here today?

Annie: I am here to see Dr. R. after having had 14 chemo treatments and having seen the surgeon. The tumor on my liver, which is in a very bad place—as he says, it's in the crotch of the liver—it has shrunk and he is going to do the surgery. About which I am *ecstatic*.

Everyone is very, very, *very* optimistic about my outcome. When I first met Dr. R., we clicked immediately. She's just this amazing woman—and she looks like she's 12 years old. I told her I didn't know how she had done all this schooling, being 12—*and* she had children! *[laughs]* Golly. I felt like asking her, "Does your mother know you're here and wearing a white outfit?"

Anyway, my first question to her was, "Do I have reason to be cautiously optimistic?" She looked at me and said, "You have every reason to be *completely* optimistic." Dr. S. is going to be doing the surgery. I'm going to be having a procedure next Tuesday in which a catheter is going to be inserted into the lobe of the liver to block off the blood supply so that the other side will enlarge. The idea being, keep as much healthy liver as possible and also reverse the colostomy, which has been... *[blows raspberry]*

The brochure that one is given when one gets a colostomy is an absolutely flaming pack of lies: "You Can Live with a Colostomy." The problem with mine is that it was an emergency surgery with a blockage. I was very fortunate, because nothing ruptured. Dr. S. didn't have really an option or time to choose where to put it and to really do all of the closing up. There's a huge hernia underneath it, which makes it stick out so much more. That's why I look...I keep covering it up.

Going into this particular visit, what's on your mind?

Annie: What's on my mind now is that I'm in transition from the chemo stage to the operative stage. One thing that brings me here is that I knit a little scarf for Dr. R., and I want to give it to her. Then, just to find out when the next chemo will be, since Dr. S. wants another one before the surgery. Just to check in.

DR. SHANTI ROY (ONCOLOGIST)
ANNIE BAKER (PATIENT)

[Walking down the hall, Annie and Dr. Roy talk.]

Dr. Roy: How are you?

Annie: I'm good. I'm going to have surgery...I'm gonna go, baby! And I know he wants one more chemo.

Dr. Roy: You know about it? He told you?

Annie: Yes.

Dr. Roy: Okay, good, now I don't have to tell you.

Annie: It's fine. At this point—please, please. It's, whatever. Tell me where I need to be and at what time. No, but it was such good news! You should be thrilled!

Dr. Roy: *[laughs]* I *was*!

[They enter Dr. Roy's office.]

Annie: Okay! *[gives Dr. Roy a wrapped gift]* You have to open it now.

[Dr. Roy starts to open the present.]

Annie: Just look at the reindeer as seasonal...

Dr. Roy: It's very nice. *[still opening paper]*

Annie: Oh, just rip it! Are you one of those savers? *[laughs]*

Dr. Roy: Beautiful.

Annie: All right. Now, I made it small.

Dr. Roy: You made this?

Annie: Yes, I did.

Dr. Roy: Are you kidding me?

Annie: Yes. Now, I made it small because you're so petite.

Dr. Roy: That is beautiful. I love it.

Annie:: I thought...get your hair out of the way. I thought it would just fold.

Dr. Roy: It's perfect.

Annie: Like that.

Dr. Roy: It folds perfectly. Thank you. Thank you so much.

Annie: Wear it with a T-shirt or a dressy dress or whatever.

Dr. Roy: Or a white coat.

Annie: Or a white coat. You're too petite to wear the big scarves that I like.

Dr. Roy: This is awesome. This is really beautiful and sweet, and I will always think of you, wearing it.

Annie: Good. Enjoy it.

Dr. Roy: Thank you so much.

Annie: Think of it is a hug around your neck whenever you put it on. Okay.

Dr. Roy: How are you?

Annie: I really am okay. I had to up the prednisone this morning because I am going into a little bit of a flare.

Dr. Roy: What are you on now?

Annie: I was down to 5 milligrams for a few days, and today I took a 10. I had seen my rheumatologist and she said that if I felt the flare coming, to pop a 10 and not even think about it. I'll just call her and let her know.

Dr. Roy: All right. She gave you a little bit of freedom with that, what to do with the prednisone?

Annie: Yeah. When I call, she'll tell me how many days for 10. Then I'm scheduled for the outpatient occlusion on Tuesday.

Dr. Roy: What's that?

Annie: I'm going to have a catheter inserted into my liver to block off the blood supply. It has a long name. I called it *occlusion* because I couldn't remember it. So that the other side will grow over the next few weeks. Are you familiar with this procedure? What is it, putting a bubble in there or something...

Dr. Roy: "Embolize left portal vein."

Annie: It's probably an $850,000 piece of sponge that's going to be wedged into the blood vessel. *[laughs]* So, another chemo, and when do we need to do this? Can it be after Christmas?

Dr. Roy: My preference is to do it next week, because if we do it after the holiday, then there are two things: One is that it's going to be a longer interval between chemo sessions, and then a shorter one between that chemo and the surgery, and you don't want it to be too close.

Annie: Okay, *not* after Christmas. I knew that was going to happen. Good thing I had my hair cut again. I knew it. I knew it. I was just talking about the difficulty with the rheumatoid arthritis in terms of the chemo and all of that kind of stuff. So, pick a problem: Rheumatoid? Cancer? Colostomy? Pick one.

Dr. Roy: Okay. We'll have to coordinate a little bit. All right, and your medicines otherwise: Can I run down the list that I have here?

Annie: Mm-hmm.

Dr. Roy: Ativan, as needed. The Biofreeze roll-on gel, Centrum, vitamin D, Neurontin, Plaquenil. Prednisone—10, you told me. Sandostatin, we're going to do today. Synthroid, Tylenol, and B12. Is that everything?

Annie: Yeah. And D? Did you have vitamin D?

Dr. Roy: Got it. Two 2,000's a day.

Annie: Yeah. My rheumatologist really pushes that. Something with the arthritis.

Dr. Roy: How's your energy?

Annie: Fine.

Dr. Roy: Any new issues? Shortness of breath, chest pain, cough, palpitations?

Annie: No.

Dr. Roy: Nausea?

Annie: Sometimes I get a little queasy. I find myself taking a couple of Ativan a day. I take one in the morning just by habit, I think. I find that around 4 or 4:30, something like that, sometimes I take one.

Dr. Roy: That's fine. Then, constipation, diarrhea, anything like that?

Annie: No. Well, it's hard, no, I don't have...

Dr. Roy: Not like excessive output [into the colostomy bag]?

Annie: No.

Dr. Roy: Okay. Then you told me about the pain from your rheumatoid. Rashes, headaches, confusion, depression, anxiety, any of that?

Annie: No.

Dr. Roy: Okay. All right. You look fantastic. You look pretty.

Annie: Thank you, dear.

Dr. Roy: You look really good. I'm so glad I was not the one to tell you that you had to get another dose of chemo.

Annie: No, it really...if my years to be, whatever they are, involved having to go in for chemo every week and a half—you and I talked about this—I would have a very serious decision to make, because it's not any way really to live your life. But it's just adding one more. I've had 14, so it's 15.

Dr. Roy: I know, but who's counting?

Annie: No. I know, and it means I can have the surgery.

Dr. Roy: It's something to look forward to. I think this is wonderful.

Annie: Yeah. I'm in the glow of the surgeon saying how happy he was about the shrinkage and that he was thinking he was going to do it. I was saying, too, as we started down the hall, that now the enormity of the surgery and the recuperation from it is starting to...but I tend to be pragmatic. It's just, you have to do it, so that's fine.

Dr. Roy: Maybe it's like the next phase and the unknown.

Annie: Right.

Dr. Roy: You have had surgery before and you recovered from it. This is good. This is where we wanted to get to. This is what we wanted.

Annie: Yes, because then, my maintenance after...it shouldn't be chemo, chemo, chemo, chemo, chemo.

Dr. Roy: We'll have to see. I think, you know, nothing is set in stone. It all depends on what he finds, how much he can take out, what he can do. Sometimes, they just don't know until they're in there—

Annie: I know.

Dr. Roy: —what they can do. As much as there is uncertainty about it, we have to sort of accept that.

Annie: I understand. He's going to reverse the colostomy at the same time.

Dr. Roy: If he could only do that, right? I know that that's been such a burden for you.

Annie: When I went for a checkup, Dr. S. said, "Well, if it's a problem, we can always just *move* the colostomy." No, no, no, no, no. No.

Dr. Roy: That's not what you're signing up for.

Annie: No, no, no. If I had to, I could live with it, because the hernia would be corrected and I wouldn't stick out so much. It wouldn't be so grotesque. No, no, no, no, we want the colostomy reversed, not just moved. No.

Dr. Roy: Let's be very clear about that.

Annie: Yeah.

VINITA (PHLEBOTOMIST, ONCOLOGY PRACTICE)

Vinita: I've been working here for two and a half years. I'm a phlebotomist here. I do blood draws.

You have to cause patients a little bit of pain and discomfort, even though it's necessary. Is it hard to do that?

Vinita: Yeah, sometimes. Like, sometimes the patient didn't drink, so they get dehydrated. One patient was hostile because she didn't drink any water, so I had to stick her again. I stuck her one time, and then I stuck her again, and I couldn't get the blood, because she didn't drink the water. She got mad and she was in pain, so I can understand her feelings, too. It was bad: She was in pain, and I didn't get the blood, so she was angry. I told my manager, so she had somebody else try, and then we just put some warm water over there so the circulation could get better. We got a little bit of blood from the other arm, but it was still a little bit sore. I knew it was difficult for the patient and for me, too, to stick them again. I feel bad that I couldn't get anything when I stuck a second time.

Do you find that most patients want to chat?

Vinita: Yeah, most of the patients. When I came, I didn't talk too much, but once I got used to it, with all the people, I just talk. Some of the patients always ask for me, because I talk a lot. *[laughs]* They're so nice. They feel the home environment here.

I've known Annie for a long time. She's always nice. She always talks about the grandkids. I always talk about my daughter. We stick her finger, but she never complains about the pain and stuff. She's good. She's always a laughing person.

What's the most difficult part of your job?

Vinita: When we pack the tubes with the patients' requisitions we have to be very careful that we don't mess up the labels. We have to make sure two or three times that we packed the right tubes. Otherwise the results will come out different, and they will end up giving the chemo to the patients wrongly. It's a big responsibility when we do all the blood work.

We always ask date of birth first, then look at the patients. Sometimes we have patients with the same name but with a different date of birth. When we call patients with their last name, two people come. So we have to make sure who's the right patient. You have to be very careful.

Do you know about what's happening with patients' treatment, or do they just show up for the blood?

Vinita: Yeah, we only do the blood work, so after that we don't know. Sometimes we can see the patients' face having pain or they're not feeling well from the treatments and things like that. Sometimes they come fresh, energetic. Sometimes they look so tired.

Anything else that you want to tell us about your job?

Vinita: I love my job! *[laughs]* That was my dream, to take care of the patients. When I was in school, I was thinking to do patient care. I wanted to be an RN, but then I just changed my mind, then I went to the phlebotomy subject. So I like my job, yeah.

ABBY (LABORATORY MANAGER, ONCOLOGY PRACTICE)

Abby: I'm the laboratory manager and I've been here for 13 years. We run a few tests here. We run CBCs [complete blood count]; we run urinalysis occasionally. We run PT and INRs [prothrombin time and international normalized ratio blood tests]. We do occult blood occasionally. That's about it, but basically everybody who comes into the office gets a CBC run and that needs to be collected and processed in the computer before either the nurse or the physician sees the patient.

So we're dealing with the patients, the physicians, and the nurses. The nurses can't do their job until we have the CBC; only then they can make sure that the patient can have their chemo, or, if they are here for a nadir check, that they may need to have a Neupogen shot or a Procrit or something along those lines.

We try to make it seem like it's running as smoothly as possible and not have any issues. Sometimes it's a little hard to do when we have a staffing issue or something, but usually it works pretty well. I pretty much do whatever is needed to make sure that everything runs as smoothly as possible. One of us, a med tech, has to be running an instrument and verifying the results.

What is the instrument?

Abby: It's on the counter. It's really an amazing machine. [We call them] Pentra 1 or Pentra 2. One or two.

What do you see as the lab's role in contributing to a patient's experience here?

Abby: We try to do it as quickly and efficiently as possible, but also with the patient's personality in mind, too. I think we're a lot luckier than secretarial staff or somebody who's on the other end of a nasty phone call. People are a little apprehensive about having their blood drawn, so they are not going to complain to the person or be nasty to the person who's on the other end of the needle until after they do the needle. Most times my staff does really well, so people are very complimentary...

Even though they are actually the ones possibly causing some pain.

Abby: Yeah, but it shouldn't be painful.

When results come out when you're running something in-house, would you necessarily understand their clinical significance?

Abby: Yeah. Most times I do. Yeah. If somebody's got leukemia or something like that, we can see that maybe they're in a crisis again or that they're going to need blood. We're obviously the first people to know because we get the counts, but then we're not the ones who tell the patient. We just put it up for somebody.

Do you ever have anyone ask you for their results?

Abby: Yeah. Some of them we can give. Some of them that we know. [One patient] comes in all the time for his PT and his hemoglobin is up really high sometimes, so he'll sit and wait for the doctor, but meanwhile, I'll just give him a copy, so that makes him happy.

I've had several family members come through here and a few of them haven't survived, just because of the cancer that they've had. It's just interesting. It's like being on both sides.

CAROL (ADMINISTRATIVE ASSISTANT, ONCOLOGY PRACTICE)

Carol: I'm an administrative assistant for the nurses in the treatment room. I've been here 15 years.

It's very hard to put what I do into words. I schedule patients. We do planned admits. We do...and this is not the right word to use, but I often feel like we're doing a little social work with patients. We're comforting them and their families, for lack of a better word. I might refer people to social work if I think they could benefit. We order lab work. We do all the chemotherapy scheduling, which is new. We hadn't done that before. That's a whole other learning process for us.

I don't know, I do a little of everything. What everybody asks us to do. I mail out schedules. I talk to patients. We triage many phone calls all day long, give out all the symptom calls to the nurses. Figure out if the calls need to go to the nurse practitioner, if they need to go to a treating nurse. It's a little hard to put everything into words. I tried to do a résumé once and it came out blank, because I couldn't really put everything down that I do in any given day. It's basically a customer-service job, if you want to look at it that way; you're making sure that everything runs smoothly for the nurses.

Do you have a pretty good view of what a patient is going through at any given moment?

Carol: You do get to know what the patients are going through, what their families are going through. Annie, I've always dealt with her, so I know her. But she doesn't get her treatment in our office. She was getting it in the office, but then she got really ill. So that's when Dr. R. decided that they should admit her to the hospital when she gets her treatments. She was having reactions. She was, I guess, very, very nauseous and everything following treatments, and she would call and we'd bring her in for a hydration, and it was too much for her. So Dr. R. discussed it, I guess, with the nurses and the other docs, and they decided to admit her. Every time she gets admitted, Annie is so on top of everything. She knows exactly when she needs to be admitted. So she'll call me and say, "Arrange for my admission," and I'll say, "Let me check with Dr. R. and then we'll take care of everything for you."

You have to be aware of everything that's around you. Like, if you see a nurse running with the vital-signs machine, we stand up right away because it might be a code. The nurses will yell out, "Call a code!"—purple, blue, whatever. Yes, you have to be aware. And you see where I sit [at the hub]. I mean, my God,

I hear everything. That's not a bad thing, because that helps me know what's going on. I can interject if somebody has a question without it seeming like I was eavesdropping.

How do you balance the paperwork when there's all this human stuff happening? Is it like an improvisation?

Carol: It can be. It can be. There will be times like, especially if the others are at lunch and I'm by myself, and this one is coming at you from here and the doc is coming down this way and there's another one coming at you this way. I don't even sit. I just stand and go.

I don't know if you saw what happened today. There was a transport that came to take a patient to radiology, went into the waiting room, asked for Donna. So *Dana* gets in the chair. He starts to wheel her out and she finally realizes she's not supposed to be going in a chair. So she's like, "Help me! Where am I going?! Aren't I just getting Procrit?" I had to make sure she was okay, calm her down. I say, "You're not going to radiology. It was a mistake." She had spent two months in ICU. She does not want to go anywhere, just get her shot and go home. While that was happening, someone else is asking a question, the phone is ringing.

It's a little of everything. It's very frustrating, but I love it. I feel I make a difference. I'm not patting myself on the back or anything. I just feel that at the end of the day, you can go home really frustrated, but this place humbles you. If you can make a little bit of a difference—I mean, I know I get paid, but you still feel good when you can help somebody or just give them a hug or whatever.

Do you talk a lot with your colleagues about the humbling aspects of the work?

Carol: Not so much. I talk—not by patient name or anything—more to my son because he is a hospital-security chief, so he understands the concept of working in a medical environment. The rest of my family doesn't. They tell me I have no sympathy for anything they're dealing with. I don't, really. I'm like, "Come work with me for a day and see." But I don't think I've really told anybody, except for my family, that it humbles me to work here, because that's a personal thing.

What about the hard parts of losing patients and the sadness? What do you do with it?

Carol: Pray. I pray a lot. My brother-in-law died at 38 of pancreatic cancer—that was twenty-something years ago. I've been through a lot of things in my own life, so I can deal with things here. Patients that we've all been really close to—even if they're older, you've gotten really close to them and it's just really sad. You have your coworkers to talk to about that, and that's good, you know, that you can say, "He was a funny guy, he was a great guy, he was always happy when he was here." You need to talk that out. You can't keep it in.

Do you think your patients understand how deeply they affect you?

Carol: I hope so. I still have it pinned to my desk from when I first started working here—somebody sent me, anonymously, a note with an angel pin that said something to the effect of, "It's not important who I am. It's important that I realize how much you do and how much you mean to me." I still have it. Because when you're having a really bad day, sometimes you need to pull that out and look at that, and remind yourself that you are making a difference. I'm not a nurse. I'm not a doctor. But I feel I'm part of the team.

This is not an end-of-your-day-you-go-home job. This is tomorrow you have to finish this up and follow through on this and make sure this was done. I've actually started keeping a pad in the well of my car because I'll be halfway home and think, "Did I call that patient?" I scribble it down so I remember in the morning. A lot of times, I'll just text my colleague in the morning and say, "Could you just check on this when you get in?" I know they're coming in before I get there.

Do your friends and family understand what you do?

Carol: Here's the thing: A lot of my family and friends think that I know many things that I don't. My sister's had heart problems most of her life and she'll ask me questions, and I'll say, "I don't know anything about cardiology." Or she has a friend who has breast cancer, who unfortunately just passed, and she would ask me if the medication she was getting was a drug they use here. I'd be like, "Yes, they use it, but every case is different. I don't know." I always say, "I'm just a secretary."

You probably know more than you realize you know.

Carol: It will surprise you sometimes. Somebody will ask you a question and something will come out and you'll realize, "Oh! I really did know!"

On the whole, I think this is a very good job. I work hard, and I get paid well. But it makes me feel good that I'm doing this. The doctors yell at you sometimes. The nurses yell sometimes. Everybody gets frustrated, but you have to take that in stride.

ANNIE BAKER (PATIENT)
KATHLEEN (NURSE, ONCOLOGY PRACTICE)

Annie: Hey, motorcycle lady.

Kathleen: Hi! How are you?

Annie: I'm good. I'm here for a Sandostatin shot.

Kathleen: Okay, I'll go start getting it prepped and ready. Have a seat.

Annie: Kathleen took care of my chemo once here before I started going in the hospital. She's a motorcycle mama.

Kathleen: It's true.

Annie: Just bought a bigger one.

Kathleen: That's true.

Annie: And she's so wonderful.

Kathleen: I just took your Sandostatin out of the refrigerator, so it's got to come to room temperature first. I've set a timer for 15 minutes. After 15 minutes, I have to mix it. So you've got a good half hour to sit and wait.

Annie, when you got the diagnosis, did you have any sense of what was ahead?

Annie: I had no idea it was going to be so isolating. I really didn't have an idea of the total impact it would have. That's gotten me down a few times. And I have an amazing, amazing support system. Still, it's your disease and it's this quiet little thing doing whatever it's doing inside of you.

But I don't want to talk about how I'm feeling with people all the time or whatever. And so in some ways—and my friends and family understand it—I need space. Also, I am consciously protective of others involved in this process with me. Like my son in Chicago. They're going through some stuff of their own right now. He will be here for the surgery and so on, but I said at one point, "Put me at the bottom of the concern list. If I need to, I'll call you." Were there times that I would have liked him to have been able to visit more? Sure. But he doesn't have to know that.

And again, the pragmatism, what's the choice? What's the choice? For me it's similar to my divorce, what I like to call my "domestic realignment." What am I going to do, spend all my time being angry? I think I'm the only person who is not angry at my ex for all of the years of the stress and all of that, because

I understand now the pathology in his personality that led to it all. So what's the point of bad-mouthing? Please. It's such a waste of energy, and I need my energy for this. I don't need it for that.

In the beginning it must be an adjustment, applying that "I am a cancer patient" notion to oneself.

Annie: Yeah, it takes a while for that really to sink in. I think one's personal philosophy has something to do with it, whether it's "readiness is all" [from *Hamlet*] or whatever. I am not a religious person at all. Watch me get hit by lightning as I sit in my metal...my plastic chair. *[laughs]* I'm not religious. But I have no fear of dying. I really don't. I never have. I'd like to live as long as I can, but there will be a time when I will stop.

Sometimes it kind of feels as if I'm watching myself going through this process. And I think that's a coping skill. And see, I've been fortunate, too: I've kept my hair, and I don't have the look of someone who's been going through... *[whispers so that other patients can't hear]* do you know what I mean? And that's been fortunate for me, selfishly. It's been important for me. So it's not, "Aww, look at Annie." Because I hate that crap. I hate that crap.

Have you written about your experience at all?

Annie: No. One of my girlfriends asked me, "How is your journal going?" It was at a moment when this was all fresh and new, and I said to her, "Why the *fuck* would I keep a journal of this?" On a cozy, snowy day, I'm going to say, "Oh, Annie, why don't you go get your journal and read all about this again?" My God! I don't think so.

Have you read any other accounts by people who had cancer that interested you at all?

Annie: Oh, maybe if I'm thumbing through a magazine and there's something about someone who is a survivor and it's wonderful and all of that. Some tend to be a little too God driven and a little too religious for me. I got a card from a dear friend that said, "God only gives you what you can handle," and I thought, "If anybody ever says this to me face-to-face, I will not be able to control myself."

I think the hardest for me is when it's religious. It's wonderful that people are praying for me. I mean that sincerely. It is wonderful that they are applying their faith to my outcome. There's a wonderful, wonderful nun who comes to visit the hospital, Sister Martha. Right from the get-go I said, "I'm sorry, I'm not religious at all." She said, "It doesn't make any difference." And we just chat.

And again, this is not to toot, but as far as being strong, I go, girl. I can handle a hell of a lot. Which is why, when I went in with this flare and I started crying in front of the rheumatologist, she said, "This is bad, then." I have a very high threshold for pain, but I couldn't take it. And I can take a lot.

You're in treatment for cancer and you have rheumatoid arthritis...

Annie: Don't forget my colostomy.

I'm not forgetting. Well, I guess I did. [laughs]

Annie: My melon. My melon.

But it sounds like the RA is very difficult to deal with and incredibly painful at times...

Annie: I have a disease that is ultimately crippling and I have another one that ultimately could be fatal. So I guess it's pretty helpful that I don't have a fear of dying. Because if the RA gets too bad, give me a car and I'll find a tree. I tell you. God. *[laughs]* Anyway.

KATHLEEN (NURSE, ONCOLOGY PRACTICE)

Kathleen: My name is Kathleen. I have worked here for a little over a year. I am a registered oncology nurse, so I get to work mostly in the treatment room administering chemo, but once in a while I float into this room, which is our nadir room. Here we field patients who are coming in to have lab work done. We also administer injections when people need them for their blood counts. We review labs if people need blood transfusions, things of that sort.

I feel that being an oncology nurse is the absolute epitome of what a nurse is, because we really get to see people at a critical time in their lives. When somebody is diagnosed with cancer, it's like no other disease. It is a scary, scary time: They don't know what they're going to encounter on their journey. Whether they come through it and they go into remission or whether their journey doesn't end, we really have the opportunity to participate in their care like no other nurse does in any other field.

Did you always know you wanted to work in oncology? How did you come to it?

Kathleen: I didn't want to be a nurse. When I was a little girl growing up my father was a police officer and I always thought I wanted to be a cop like Daddy. Right out of high school, I went to school for forensic psychology. I was a double major in criminal justice and psychology, and when I got out of school I started working for a criminal attorney and I hated it. I lasted for three months.

I got a job just on a whim working as a medical receptionist and immediately knew that I had found something that I really, really enjoyed. I worked for 11 years doing basically administrative work and I transitioned into an EMT and medical assistant and eventually I went to nursing school and I found something that I truly, truly loved. It was a second career choice for me. I have no doubt that it was the right one. I don't ever leave work at work. It's with me all the time. It's part of who I am.

How do you manage the emotional aspects of the job?

Kathleen: A lot of it is acceptance. We're all going to die someday. Everybody's going to go, one way or another, and cancer is some people's fate. It's helped me to learn a lot about the dying process. It's absolutely sad and overwhelming, but it's given me a greater appreciation for a lot of things in life and it teaches me a lot about perspective. It reminds me to be present every day.

Does your work ever enter your dreams?

Kathleen: Not really dreams, but the funny thing is, there have been a few times where I've woken up to my alarm clock and I've been convinced that it was an IV pump beeping. I'm like, "Wait a minute. I'm at work already? No, that's the alarm!"

Have you come to know Annie over time?

Kathleen: I have. I really enjoyed taking care of her when she was being treated here and I love when she comes in here because she is one of those people who is a fighter no matter what her situation is. She always has a smile on her face and a positive view of things and nothing seems to get her down. She shares my view of positivity. I enjoy her sense of humor and she and I get along great. She's a lot of fun.

How do you usually go about establishing a connection with patients when you're getting to know someone?

Kathleen: I tend to be the resident goofball. I jokingly say a lot of times that I encourage the patients to channel their inner child and part of that is because I never grew up myself. I like to have a lot of fun and I use my sense of humor a lot. Life is too short.

I think if you take all of this too seriously—even though it is a *very* serious thing—it can be overwhelming. I'm just myself. A big part of this job has nothing to do with clinical work. It's just about being a human being and knowing that the people sitting in these chairs for the most part are completely terrified. Some of them are spiritual, some of them are not. A lot of it is about the holistic aspect. We're not treating a disease; we're treating people. If we as nurses can't recognize that, then what do we have to give?

I wear my heart on my sleeve. I share a little bit of myself with all the patients here because I feel in order to make them comfortable, I have to let them into my world, too. It makes them a little more comfortable.

Is there anything you feel patients need to know that they don't, regarding what you do here?

Kathleen: I think they need to know how much they matter to us. A lot of times they come in here and then, after their treatment, they come back to thank us. I don't think they know how much that means to us, because we wonder when they walk out the door what happens. We're like, "What happened to so-and-so?" They are such a big part of us.

How many patients do you see in a given day?

Kathleen: In our treatment room there are usually anywhere between 30 and 65, and then we'll have another 20 to 40 here in the nadir room.

What does "nadir room" mean?

Kathleen: The nadir is a low point [the drop in white blood cells and platelets following chemotherapy]. That's the room we're standing in right now, and it's for people who are coming in to get their labs checked when they've had chemo. Or they're coming in here to get injections. It's really a multipurpose room where patients come in for anything other than chemo or for seeing the doctors.

Who named it?

Kathleen: I don't know. The room is [specific to this office] but *nadir* is a common term used in chemotherapy.

I'd like to get to those patients...

JACOB (NURSING AIDE, HOSPITAL)
EDEN (PHARMACIST, HOSPITAL)
ANNIE BAKER (PATIENT)

[One week later, Annie has been admitted to the hospital for another round of chemo; she is in a gown, seated in a chair, an IV pole beside her.]

Jacob: I started as a nursing aide, and I started oncology because my mother was diagnosed with cancer. I was in med-surg [medical-surgical nursing], but when my mother was diagnosed I specifically applied to the oncology unit—so I think I was meant to be part of the oncology team.

I'm a unit representative. I'm the front line: I'm the person you see at the desk when you walk off the elevator. I'm the first person to say [brightly], "Hi, how are you?" I'm also the person who answers the call button. [The calls are] a variety; patients call if they are in pain, they call with just small, little requests that make them happy: "Can you tell me which channel such-and-such is playing on?" We get a lot of calls about different things. Sometimes it's like, "Where is my lunch?"

Annie: I think part of that is because when you're a patient receiving cancer treatment you have absolutely no control over anything. You know, the doctors tell me where I'm supposed to be, and at what time. So little things like getting a TV station or having somebody come and bring you ice water—just to feel like you have a little bit of control—becomes very important to you. And the staff has to be patient because sometimes it can be again and again and again. When I volunteered at the nursing home I saw it too. You know, there wasn't enough pudding at dinner. They wanted more pudding. To have some control over something, that's what it's about. [gesturing at IV pole] They hang whatever they're going to hang on there. I have no clue. I mean, I know that's the saline drip, and all that. But I don't know what's in the cocktail or anything like that. So they hang it and then I just wait to see what happens.

Is there anything comparable to this experience in modern life, where you go into an environment and have to surrender so much of your own personal autonomy?

Annie: I think if you're arrested and put in jail.

Eden: *[laughs]* Wow, okay.

Annie: No, but seriously, that's the only thing I can think of. Or if you have some kind of a very traumatic injury that puts you in a wheelchair or gives you paralysis—anything that takes away your ability to control what you're doing. Being a nun, I guess, would also be...but that, too, they make a choice.

What about the military?

Annie: That's still a choice. It's still a choice.

Eden: Ultimately doctors try to explain as much as they can, tell you what's being treated and explain your schedule. But how much can you take in if you don't know the medical field and you're like, "What are you saying? When am I coming in?" A lot of times they have to give a med urgently. So it's not like we don't want to tell [patients] but at the same time, how much can you grasp of what's going on?

Annie: That's a very good point, because it is almost, it's almost too much to absorb. And that's why I often go with my sister or a very dear friend to an appointment. Because I just can't get it all when I'm sitting there. I just eliminate [a lot of the technical information]—I don't get it, so what's the point. It's not going to mean anything to me.

You have to be a special person to work on this floor. I think it was the last chemo—14 or 13?—there was a young man who had children down at the far end of the hall who passed away. And he was a young man. That was hard on the nurses and on everyone. He did pass away, didn't he, yes?

Eden: *[nods]* We had a few that week.

Annie: It's hard to be on this floor. I know this is a floor that I have to be on, because I have cancer. But it's hard to be on this floor because there are some very, very sick people here. But that's just the reality of what the floor is about. And thank heavens we have this floor. But if I—*when* I am released, shall I say—and on maintenance or whatever it's going to be, I want to volunteer on this floor. There was a wonderful woman the first time I came here, gray-haired, very attractive. She pulled up a chair and she sat right close to me—I think I was crying—and she said, "Doesn't this *suck*?" And she was a cancer survivor too. And I think you have to be a cancer survivor in order to understand where people are coming from.

JACKIE (NURSING ASSISTANT, HOSPITAL)
ANNIE BAKER (PATIENT)

Jackie: Normally, my shift is 3 to 11 a.m., and it's patient care. We have to do a.m. care, which is cleaning them up. If they need anything to drink, making sure they're okay. You do their vital signs. Like every four hours. Everything.

What's it like when you have to wake patients up in the middle of the night to get their vitals?

Jackie: *[sighs] Not* good. You sometimes don't even want to do it because they're sleeping, so we'll ask the nurse. It's sad because you know that they didn't sleep like the whole day or the whole night. If the nurse says let it go, then we'll go back and do them later. But if they're sleeping and we have to, we gently just put their arm up, and sometimes they don't even wake up. Not even to, like, get a sugar check.

Annie: Jackie and I connected during my first chemo here, I think. We bonded over the colostomy bag.

Jackie: Yes, the first time I learned how to empty it out was with you. I was brand-new, and I learned with her. *[laughs]* She goes, "I'll show you," and we just did it, and that was it.

Do patients get embarrassed at people seeing their body, or do they get used to it?

Annie: At this point, I could walk across that courtyard naked—it would be a horrible sight to see, and anybody who saw me would probably go into a monastery or a convent—and I wouldn't care.

Jackie: Yeah, they don't get embarrassed. You see them, clean them, naked. They're used to it. And you give them the confidence so they can feel okay. You keep them covered always, while you're cleaning them or something. So they can feel comfortable.

Annie: Oh, this morning it was awful, because it was just, all let go. *[gestures toward colostomy bag]* I was covered in...um...fecal matter. It was absolutely disgusting. I want this reversed. *[pats abdomen]*

Jackie: I love working here. I love caring for patients. It's just, you have to have it in your heart to do it. Not just anybody can do it. You can't even say it's for the money, because...you have to feel it and you have to really like it. You carry it with you day in and day out, that's it. You go home with them, and you think about them. It's like your second family.

TATYANA (NURSE, HOSPITAL)
ANNIE BAKER (PATIENT)

Tatyana: I'm involved with direct patient care. I do injections, I give them medications, we administer chemotherapy...

Annie: She sits and talks with me if I need to.

Tatyana: We do a lot of the education for the patients and their families. The families are a big, big, big piece of who we take care of. So we don't only get five patients per day, you know, to take care of—that's our typical ratio—but we get a whole bag of family members who are worried, who are scared just like their loved ones, who are sharing the diagnosis of cancer with them. They're holding it in their head and changing their lives, you know, rearranging it. They have to, because no one can or should be fighting the battle alone. It's really difficult.

Is there something about working here that you think most people wouldn't know, or something that would surprise them?

Tatyana: Oh, yeah. It's my opinion—and I've heard other nurses share it with me—that a cancer patient is absolutely very different from patients who have other conditions, chronic ones like diabetes, heart failure. A friend of mine says, "I will take a patient with a tumor"—direct quote—"in a heartbeat over anybody else." They have a different insight on life, you know. A totally different approach to people, how they accept help, how they ask for it. They are a little more appreciative, I want to say. They are more pleasant to deal with, and they're warm. They listen to what we tell them and actually follow it. There are a lot of people who have chronic conditions, and they have them because they don't really follow advice.

So you think it has to do with getting a diagnosis that nobody is ever expecting?

Tatyana: I think it's also the uncertainty of what the outcome is going to be, and what the future is like. When it's going to be the end of your life becomes so uncertain from the moment of diagnosis. Even people who get cured, you know—that fear that it's coming back remains in their mind every day for the rest of their lives. And the uncertainty puts a totally different perspective on their lives and how they see the world, and how they see themselves in that world. How they approach other people, and how they relate to other people.

Everybody is different. A lot of people get very depressed, very withdrawn. I think they're angry and fearful of the diagnosis and what's coming with the treatment. I think fear of the unknown is the biggest.

Annie: Every once in a while I'll get a little—have a little pity party, but it doesn't last long. Because that's not who I want to be. *[pauses]* But I've seen people at the cancer center, you can tell they're very frightened, especially if they're just starting out the treatment. Because they don't really know what is going to happen. And it can be a bitch, it can really be a bitch.

DR. RAJIV PATEL (HOSPITALIST)
ANNIE BAKER (PATIENT)

Dr. Patel: Annie is very popular. The nurses fight over her—

Annie: Stop, stop, stop.

Dr. Patel: No, it's really like that!

Annie: Stop, stop, stop.

Dr. Patel: When have you seen, when you've gone to a room, that the nurses have written on the whiteboard, "Welcome back"? You don't see that on any other door—

Annie: This man is amazing, anyway.

Dr. Patel: It's a pleasure to take care of her, I mean, you know, the first time we met, she was in Room 6 or, no, 8—

Annie: Well, I've been in 14 of them.

Dr. Patel: Room 8 was the first time I saw you; that was the first bad episode of the chemo that she had. She came in there, there were accidents with the ostomy. It was getting filled up so fast and we had to put her on a short TPN [total parenteral nutrition]—remember when we put in the TPN for the first time? It got better and then she went home and then that's how we got to know each other. Then the second time she came in she was all—

Annie: Loopy, I had no—

Dr. Patel: She...those 24 hours, she still doesn't have any recollection of what happened.

Annie: No, I forget. I have no clue about the 24 hours, when I'm out of it.

Dr. Patel: After which we decided that it is not safe for her to take the pump and do chemotherapy at home. After that she comes over here, and gets her chemotherapy here, and it's like every two weeks. I mean she was dehydrated, electrolyte-wise she was depleted, and there was a lot going on at that point. We gave her a very fancy diagnosis, remember? Transient global...

Annie: ...Amnesia, which the nurse said means that the neurologist had no clue what happened. *[laughs]*

That sounds very impressive, you know.

Dr. Patel: *[laughs]* "I had *transient global amnesia*," yeah.

Annie: And Dr. Patel takes care of all of us on the floor.

So you're a hospitalist?

Dr. Patel: I'm a hospitalist, yes. I just stay here on the oncology floor. We have a big group, 13, 14 docs, and we used to rotate. I did a few stints over there and I sort of liked it. Then they came to me and they said, "Do you want to just stay here forever?" And I said, "Yeah, I don't mind."

And in that time, and even now, none of the other hospitalists want to come here. One of them was here just two days and she still has nightmares about it. She just can't see the pain and suffering over here. She's like, "Oncology is too much for me, I can't handle it. I'd rather deal with my cardiac patients." On the cardiac wards it's huffing and puffing, but it's the same huffing and puffing every day, you know. My group members will only do weekend stints when I'm not here.

I've had a couple of patients say, "Where were you over the weekend? I was here! There was some other person who didn't know anything—he kept on asking questions and questions, and I kept on saying, 'But why are *you* here? Why isn't Dr. *Patel* here?'" *[laughs]* Like, yeah, you know, I have a family also!

Do you ever take a vacation?

Annie: He took one to Canada.

Dr. Patel: I took one, yeah, that was the day I discharged you.

Annie: Yes.

Dr. Patel: I discharged you and we ran.

You were saying that your colleagues can't or won't work here—why do you think you can?

Dr. Patel: I don't know; I don't think that there is anything special with me. I sort of developed a soft corner toward some of the cancer patients. It's not like sympathy or pity or anything like that, it's just that I feel for them. I mean I...it's just that I want to, you know—it's a difficult journey. I just want to take the trip together, that's it. *[pauses]*

Nobody can understand their pain. It's wrong to say, "I understand what you're going through." *No, you can't.* None of us here can understand what Annie is going through. None of us can. We can try, but we can't. It's very individual, and every person has different issues. Emotional issues, physical issues, pain issues. It's a systemic diagnosis. It's not, let's say, Annie's colon [cancer]—it's not just the colon. It's everywhere. I mean it alters their lifestyle. It alters how they do things, how they travel—you know you have to take into consideration so many factors now.

People all shout about heart attacks and hypertension and everything. How many people became depressed after having a heart attack? There are statistics of depression in people post-MI [myocardial infarction], but you know, cardiology is so advanced now. You put a stent in, you put them on this drug, that drug, you function. People are going about their usual lives. My dad had a bypass seven years ago, and he is very active now. He's feeling younger after the bypass, which is normal.

Annie: Yeah, my father-in-law said, "I feel 25 years younger," because he had new plumbing put in.

So is cardiology more like plumbing?

Dr. Patel: Technically, all of the human body is wiring and plumbing—but it's all alive. At home you are in control of the plumbing and the wiring: You can turn the switch on and off and the tap on and off. Here, it's all automatic inside.

You were talking about how everybody's experience is individual and also holistic, and I wonder if your training in internal medicine contributes to that perspective?

Dr. Patel: It does. I mean, the oncologist usually tells me the same thing, he's like, "Okay, we'll just give the chemo, so you will take care of the rest, right?" In that way it feels okay. I mean, I shouldn't be bothering them about the patient's blood pressure going high or the blood sugar going here and there. They should be focused just on trying to get the patient better with *their* magic. And I can take care of the rest.

Annie, do you ever talk about your rheumatoid arthritis when you're here?

Annie: Well, yeah. *[to Dr. Patel]* What did you say, my hand was—swan something?

Dr. Patel: Swan-neck deformity.

Annie: Yes.

Dr. Patel: It's not there yet.

Annie: I know.

Dr. Patel: It won't be.

Annie: *[holds out her wrist, turns it to the side to demonstrate]* "Oh, look, you're going to have a swan-neck deformity." "And good morning to *you*, Dr. Patel!" *[laughs]*

Dr. Patel: I was just telling her, it's so weird that, you know, they describe these deformities in such beautiful language. You know when you look at a swan, you look at how elegant it is, and then they describe the rheumatoid-arthritic changes as a swan's neck. *[laughs]*

Is there anything about working here that you think people on the outside would be surprised to hear or that would be important for them to know?

Dr. Patel: Yes. Cancer is not a terminal diagnosis, you know. If this person wants to live, it's not what *you* think that matters. It's what *they* think that matters at this point. You can't make a decision for a patient. You can give them information. You can guide them, but you can't make the decisions for them. And plus, you cannot make a prognosis based on a diagnosis. In the ER the patient may just be acutely ill for some reason and you just treat the patient and carry on, you know, and that's it.

I have arguments like this with medical residents, and with some of the ER attendings. They are like, "But she has cancer." It's like, "And? How does it differ? How does it differ in how you're treating the patient?" I just feel when you say that, you're saying, "surrender," you know, white flag.

Annie: "Go get your affairs in order."

Dr. Patel: You didn't even *do* anything. You have to *do* something before you say, okay, you know what, we tried everything.

Annie: And there is so much that can be tried now.

Dr. Patel: Yeah, there are so many options nowadays. It's not 10 or 15 years ago. I mean, we have Dr. X. over here who has exclusive pancreatic-cancer patients who are surviving for two years and three years. I mean he has something going on over here—you go anywhere else in the world, and in six months you're *done*, with pancreatic. If you're *lucky* you have six months.

Annie: Overall, there is not a gloom-and-doom feeling on this floor at all. You felt it when you got off the elevator.

Absolutely.

Annie: It's not, "Give up all hope, ye who enter here."

What is it, then? What is the motto that crystallizes the experience here?

Annie: Hope, I think.

Dr. Patel: Yeah, exactly. It's hope.

Annie: Hope and cooperation. Hope, cooperation, and commitment on the part of the staff.

Dr. Patel: And I give 100 percent to these people that are here. I don't know how they do it. They've been working more than me, I've been here just three years with the staff. One of the nurses has been here for more like 25 years, and some people for 12 or 13 years working on the same floor.

Annie: They do a lot of taking care of cancer patients. I don't get down because certain people won't let me. I feel very optimistic about the outcome, if I can get through all the surgeries and stuff like that.

And you were thinking you were done with the chemo, right? When we saw you with Dr. Roy last Tuesday—

Annie: *[sighs]* Yes, I thought I was done at 14 cycles, and then little petite Dr. R., in her very mild-mannered way, says, "The surgeon feels that you should have one more chemo," and I said, "How about after Christmas?" Then she pulls out that invisible cudgel from behind her that no one sees and says, "Ohh, I don't think after Christmas would be good," and the cudgel goes *whack*. Okay. *[laughs]* And she's only 12 years old. I said that to her the first time I met her: "Does your mother know that you're out pretending in a white jacket?"

Dr. Patel: Did you really say that? She has two kids! *[laughs]* It's not just you. I hear nurses over here say, “Oh, Dr. R. could drive a car over me and I wouldn’t even say anything.”

Annie: She’s wonderful. She’s a sweetheart, and she’s smart as anything.

Dr. Patel: She is very smart, yes.

Annie: Well you’re no slouch either. You’re smart. He’s also a reader. I mean, honestly, and don’t be modest. Don’t you think that your attitude is in part responsible for mine?

Dr. Patel: No, I—

Annie: I’m a positive person anyway, but don’t you think that you reinforced—

Dr. Patel: No, it’s human nature, Annie. I try to do the same thing for everybody. Okay? I try to encourage even the most negative people. I have a very difficult patient on the floor; she even tried to fire me twice, and I said, “No, that’s not happening, I’m not going to abandon you.” She said, “I have my rights,” and I was like, “Yeah, even I have my rights. I’m still going to come here and see you. I’m not abandoning you.” But you know, she can’t bring that out of me, what you bring out of me. So, part and parcel I think some of the patients are also responsible for how I react. When they say, “Oh, you’re so good,” it is because *they* are so good, you know?

Annie: Yeah, but you *are* good. *[gets up and gestures toward IV pole]* This is my buddy—I’m going to start making faces for these.

Dr. Patel: Yeah, I call it Tommy. [n.b. “Tommy” is a common pet name in India.] I used to cover the cardiac floors, and I used to tell the patients, “You know, Tommy over here has a bladder problem, so take him for a walk.”

Is it always Tommy, or do they have different names?

Dr. Patel: It’s always Tommy. *[laughs]*

[Annie and Dr. Patel exit together.]

We thank everyone who agreed to be interviewed and are particularly grateful to Annie for her generosity and kindness.

Reading

BY KATHERINE J. LEE

We were reading in bed. It was something we liked to do—talking with our brains is what she called it, instead of talking out loud. Which was okay before we found out about the cancer and she started looking at every book like it was a Bible. It made me sad just watching her.

"What's wrong?" she said, putting her book down and looking at me. After a minute she picked it back up.

I rolled over and thought about turning off my bedside light, but didn't. Sometimes the best part of my week is waking up as she's balanced over me on both knees and one arm stretched across, breasts or belly over my face as she goes to turn out my light. Other nights I must sleep through it.

The light's still on when she wakes me and we make the trip to the emergency room. They spend thirty minutes just getting her information down. It makes me regret rushing her when she couldn't find matching shoes. It's even worse when she goes to hold my hand, because I know she's trying to make me feel better. Twenty-seven years and it feels like the first three were the only ones I ever had a grip on.

Back then I had a job selling paper products four hundred miles from where she lived in Minneapolis with her parents. Some weekends I drove all night to see her. I'd crawl into her twin bed and feel like we were kids again. "Maybe we should get our own place," she said, one of those weekends.

"We'll be together," she said. "How bad could it be?"

"How can we live like that?" I started quoting expenses at her and she cut me off.

She said, "It's how much it's worth to you." She made me sleep on the floor that night to prove her point.

After that, we moved to the suburbs. Somehow she knew everything. I felt a million miles behind. Don't give honey to the baby, she'd say. Or, The couple next door is getting a divorce. Before I knew the neighborhood, I'd get lost delivering paper, and I'd take forever, finding the way home.

In the waiting room, I point out the big aquarium. "Isn't that the kind you wanted?" I ask.

She looks up. "Yeah," she says. "Though ideally ours wouldn't be empty."

"What kind of hospital can't even keep their fish alive?" I say.

I must look pretty bad, because she's doing this thing she does to let me know she's taking care of me. She touches the pulse in my throat until it slows. Checks my teeth, moving my lips with her fingers. Drops her head and puts her ear to my chest. I can feel how hot her face is through two layers. But we stay like that until someone calls her name.

The nurse asks how she'd rate the pain, one to ten.

She says, "Oh, I don't like to complain." She has this look on her face like she had just enough energy to get through everything until they asked her this.

The nurse says, "Ten is intolerable pain—"

"Eight," she snaps. "Maybe eight and a half."

Before the surgery they give her something that makes her hallucinate, and I can't stay in the room.

When I come back from the cafeteria, she's lying down but lucid. It's like getting her back from the dead.

"You look nice," she prompts.

"You look nice," I tell her. I tuck the sheet in around her like a cocoon.

I say, "My jaw hurts."

"That's because you grind your teeth at night," she says.

"I don't," I say. "I do?"

"Going on a year now," she says.

"Why didn't you say anything?"

She shrugs. "I didn't think I needed to."

"Well, you did need to," I say, which makes her look at me. "If I was keeping you up at night."

She scratches her hand where they've put in the IV. She says, "I meant, I thought you knew."

We have to stay overnight at the hospital. While she's sleeping, I try to stay awake. Generally I'm the kind of guy who's in pajamas by dinner, but I'm worried I'll miss something.

Around three in the morning, I'm working so hard to stay conscious, my stomach hurts from the effort. Whenever I close my eyes, the room starts rocking.

I call the boys to let them know their mother's all right. The two older ones don't pick up. I get the wife of the youngest, and she passes the phone to him as soon as she hears it's me. He says, "Dad, save the late-night calls for when Mom's not all right, okay?"

"Sure," I tell him.

There's a pause. "You're taking good care of her."

I can't figure out whether he's making fun of me. After a minute, I ask, "Is that what it looks like from over there?" though I know he'll take it the wrong way.

When the cancer progressed from her colon to her liver, they stopped the chemo and let her leave. As it turned out, it was either my staying home or finding someone else to stay with her all day. So we found a place outside Whitefish, Montana, and threw out every calendar in the house to make time crawl. After a cool night, when the sun rose, you could watch the fog roll away from the front porch.

I thought I'd be a new person. But mornings, when I'd finally convince myself to get up, everything would be where we'd left it the night before—dishes to the ceiling, shoes kicked off in the hallways, hair clogging our drains.

"Why don't you say anything anymore?" she'd ask, on her bad days. On better days, we'd lie in the dark, not touching. One night it thundered so violently, the ceiling fan swung above our heads, working loose from its base. The sound of it in the quiet made me resolve to leave.

"This is killing us both," I said.

"I'll give you one take back," she said. It was dark but I could practically hear her smiling. After a while, she said, "Do you ever find that you have any regrets?"

Two days after we're released, she has an infection in her arm. It's three times the size it should be. The flesh is red and blue overlaid by a mottled yellow.

"Sometimes there are complications during surgery," our doctor says.

"My arm is nowhere near my colon," she says.

"We'll know within an hour," he says. "We'll try to save it."

"What do you mean, try," she says. Don't get scared, get loud: something she learned from three sons.

He says, "If the antibiotics don't work, we'll have to take the arm off."

She says, "Forget it."

They both look at me. The doctor says, "It'll spread to the vital organs."

She pats my arm with her good hand and looks at our doctor. She says, "I'm really attached to this arm."

I'm blank. I'm thinking, Take mine instead. Instead, I say, "Your arm isn't as important as your life," as if that were guaranteed.

She says, "Can we all please stop acting like I'm the one making decisions here?"

We listen to the guy across the hall in the body cast play with the volume on his TV until she finally says okay. Then she cries for the first time all night and the doctor watches me while I try to make her feel better. Sometimes I wonder how I can get through it, standing here watching my wife become a stranger. It makes me nervous to think she can see it, that same strangeness in me.

When she stops crying, the doctor holds the clipboard while she signs with her left hand. Her signature is strange and wide, like her left hand's scheming against the right. She passes it to me and I have a hard time keeping it steady. I make sure my name touches hers.

The doctor swings the clipboard back up to his chest and says, "Thank you," like he has better places to be.

The day after I told her I was leaving Whitefish, I watched her chucking little twigs and things from her pockets into a fire she'd built in the yard. It was drizzling, but the woman could light a fire during a flood. She'd felt too sick for dinner again, and I was taking my time in the kitchen even though I was only washing one plate. I wanted her to come back in and see me.

Eventually I went upstairs and fell asleep waiting. When she walked into the room, the smell of smoke followed her and made her seem alive again.

I told her I wasn't leaving.

"Okay," she said. She fell asleep before finishing the word.

I wanted her to know I was taking her back. I was going to drag her across the finish line, promises intact. I said, "If I let you ruin my life, I'll never forgive myself."

She said, "If you put your mind to it, you can forgive anybody."

After the arm comes off, she has phantom pain and won't believe us when we say it's no longer there.

"It hurts," she says. "Make them fix it."

Then she says, "Do you have to stand there?" and recoils from me, scratching at the operated shoulder until the staff asks me to leave.

"She doesn't know it's you," a nurse says to me, softly.

I disagree, but leave anyway.

One thing we never got around to was that fishing trip. She'd been at me for a while about it, the whole deal, with the Styrofoam tub of nightcrawlers and fluorescent lures. We'd take the boat out at dusk and anchor near the shoreline, where it was deep enough and murky.

"It would've been nice," she said, during our final hospital trip. "To be in a boat with you."

At this point, I'm not crying into my beer. Since I remarried, Sandy has consumed my energies. She may look like the workhorse she is, but I'm grateful for her strength and company. She makes our meals for the week on Sundays and freezes them. We choose what to heat up and when.

We're moving to Vermont to die near her kids, as she puts it. She has a mentally unwell daughter and two normal ones in Montreal. She flew ahead to Albany, and I'm taking the train from Montana, which is okay by me. I stayed in Whitefish two years after the end, and each year the winter got worse. I felt like everything beautiful was behind me. I was cold all the time.

When we pull away from the platform, the college kid sitting next to me lets me borrow his cell phone so I can let Sandy know I'm on my way. He has to show me how to use it, which is why I'm flustered when she picks up.

"I'll be there soon," I say.

"Honey?" she says. "Is that you?"

I hang up and hand back the phone. The kid, Lou, wants to know if I'm okay. I nod toward the window so he'll stop staring, though everything outside for miles is so flat we can practically see the end of the line. Back in 1904, Whitefish used to be called Stumptown, because they cut down all the trees in the area to build the railway.

He gives me a funny look. My wife used to say, Don't make sounds, make sense.

So I ask him where he's going. He shrugs and says, "Where do I start?"

I wake up half an hour before Chicago, when a woman goes into labor. We make an emergency stop in Irving Park, near where I used to work, and where an ambulance is waiting at the station. The whole car listens to the baby cry for twenty minutes before the mother's stretchered off. The woman across the aisle whispers, “That tiny person stopped a train.”

Some of us step out for fresh air, so we're all standing on the platform when the father pulls up in a taxi. The EMTs have his wife mostly packed up, but the guy's so busy beaming and slapping everyone on the back he doesn't notice when they try and steer him toward the seat next to the driver. He comes over to the line of us and pretends to xylophone our shoes.

“Hey, man,” Lou says, “your family's waiting for you.”

But he just climbs up on the platform in his suit and wipes his face with his tie.

I know how he must be feeling—how I felt all those years I was away from home, selling printer paper and TP and rolls of paper towels. I want to tell him how lucky I felt, being away from her and still knowing she was there. How I'll never forget the time I half woke with her hand in my hair, and how I could live in that overlap forever, being pulled from my isolated world into hers.

“I used to live here,” I tell him, but the train whistle blows and he passes by me.

The conductor calls everyone back onto the train. Not one of us moves an inch. Which goes to show—it's got a grip on us all. Whatever it is you want to leave, you can't leave. It put her in a box. It buried me.

She's gone, I tell myself. She's not coming back. But even now I don't believe it.

The man moves toward the ambulance where his wife is waiting. “Roll her out,” he shouts. “Let me see her face.”

Then he turns to wave at our train, and all the passengers cheer.

From *Esopus 16* (2011)

New Colors

BY ANTHONY CHEUNG

Early Musical Experiences

The first time I remember seeing a composer alive and in the flesh was when the great Polish modernist Witold Lutoslawski conducted the San Francisco Symphony in a program of his music, about a year before his death. It was a revelatory experience; heady stuff for a kid of 10, and unlike anything I had ever heard. But I was absolutely enthralled by the palette of sounds that Lutoslawski drew from a traditional orchestra and soon went out and bought a recording of his riveting string quartet. The idea that a composer could be living and thriving among us was absolutely foreign to me, as my concept of a musical creator was of a half-mythical creature endowed with indescribable genius, who frequently went deaf or mad or otherwise met his demise under mysterious circumstances. A few summers earlier, on a family vacation, my parents had taken me to the Zentralfriedhof (Central Cemetery) in Vienna—the final resting place for such venerable figures as Beethoven, Brahms, and Schubert—so I knew these men (always men) were once mortal, historical beings. But to be faced with the freshly penned music of someone known for his "controlled chance procedures" was both a major shock and immense liberation. It opened the door to a kind of personal expression that was unfathomable, and shattered my preconceptions of what a musical experience could actually be.

I had dabbled in writing music from about the same time I had taken up the piano, so trying to imitate the long-deceased composers whose music I was practicing didn't seem too out of the ordinary. I never thought that such activities would eventually lead to a life in writing music. If anything, preparing to be a serious pianist seemed a much more tangible reality. But after the initial Lutoslawski encounter, there were a series of aftershocks. I heard much more contemporary music mixed in with the standard repertoire at the symphony, which I attended nearly every week. I grew as a composer, having important experiences working with local chamber ensembles and orchestras. Before I left for college I had been to hundreds of orchestral, chamber, and solo concerts and amassed a huge collection of CDs and scores. There were frequent treks to secondhand record stores like Amoeba in Berkeley and weekly trips to the San Francisco Public Library. The famously autodidactic Frank Zappa once remarked that all one needed in order to learn how to write for the orchestra was to spend time at a public library. This was to an extent true for me, though I also took lessons with wonderfully supportive teachers. For my geeky self, being rebellious meant attempting to scandalize my audience of grade-school peers during an assembly by playing Schoenberg's third piano piece from his Opus 11 set, the wild and no-holds-barred conclusion to the first piece of freely nontonal music. Early modernism and the radical works of Mahler, Stravinsky, Schoenberg, Webern, Debussy, and Bartók were constant sources of inspiration. In these very different composers, I admired the formal innovations, the harmonic risk-taking, and the refined use of color, which made earlier music sound positively eight-bit.

The other formative experience was with improvised music. My uncle played jazz guitar as a hobby, and he gave me copies of his fake-book lead sheets. We would fumble through tunes together as I attempted to improvise over the chord changes. I bought a book of Bill Evans transcriptions, matching what was written with the recordings, and eventually just tried to play things by ear. Miles Davis's autobiography, fraught with expletives and colorful anecdotes, opened my world to an attitude about music and a list of collaborators that was an entire education in itself. When I got to high school, my jazz teacher Tim Price turned me on to great modern big-band arranger-composers like Thad Jones, Clare Fischer, and Bob Brookmeyer, whose advanced approaches to harmony and ensemble sound excited me.

Rather than see the differences between the improvisational tradition of jazz and my training in classical composition, I embraced what were obvious links. Charlie Parker's harmonic extensions, which he called the "pretty notes," had much in common with the sensual chords of Debussy and Ravel. The harmonic language of post-bop pianists like McCoy Tyner and Chick Corea had parallels to Bartók, Hindemith, and Stravinsky. I heard a lot of Messiaen in Brookmeyer's charts. And these links, if often left to the imagination, were sometimes right out in the open. In Gil Evans's arrangement of "The Meaning of the Blues" on the album *Miles Ahead*, he quotes at the outset the opening of the second movement of Berg's hyperromantic, expressionistic, and dodecaphonic (yes, those three things can coexist) Violin Concerto. The idea that "third-stream music"—as so labeled by musical polymath Gunther Schuller—could be a natural confluence of elements from jazz and modern-classical music greatly inspired me, not so much as an era-specific aesthetic, but as a creative ideal.

These early discoveries formed a large basis of my musical personality at the time, and their direct impact on my own music is much less obvious now than it was initially, now that I have been exposed to many other strands of influence in subsequent years. Yet I think a lot about how we as composers grow exponentially when we are least experienced, since we respond to things instinctively and without prejudice, and how many of our initial encounters stamp us with bits of euphoria that never leave us, even if we spend a lot of time away from them.

On Finding Inspiration, and the Creative Process

A composer's creative process is subject to so many variables that one can often speak only of incomplete traces. Historically, it has been a subject always shrouded in mystery and hyperbole. Stravinsky got scenarios for pieces like *The Soldier's Tale* and *The Rite of Spring* in dreams, claiming that he was "the vessel through which *The Rite* flowed," all but captive to its inner workings. Mozart could summon forth entire works in his head and copy them out effortlessly, whereas Beethoven's genius was hard-earned and masochistic. Examining composers' sketchbooks reveals the immense trials and tribulations of a work's birthing. One sees angry and obsessive corrections in Beethoven's drafts, elegance and refinement in the penmanship of Chopin and Ravel (both nevertheless labored obsessively over each phrase), musical and psychological/autobiographical angst in Mahler. And then there is the enigma of Brahms, who destroyed all his sketches so as to leave no trace of the process itself, only the unblemished outcome. Though improvisers create in the moment, they access the complex circuitry of muscle memory (fingerings, runs, patterns) and a thousand previous attempts at a similar thing, if working within a given vocabulary. A true improvisation is never entirely free, still bending to rules, techniques, and parameters set up by the performer or aesthetic. Thus attempts have been made to simulate these creative activities on a computer, with mixed results. If you're ever willing to be pleasantly surprised, however, try listening to Band-in-a-Box improvise on Coltrane's "Giant Steps," or a computer-generated Beethoven's Tenth Symphony that uses the artificially intelligent software of David Cope.

My creative process tends to change according to the nature of each of project, and my methodology of finding a way into a new work really depends on what the piece is trying to convey. Very rarely does the message of the piece actually reveal itself at the outset. There might be, for instance, a metaphor or allusion that forms the poetic basis of the work. The instrumentation itself is often a starting point that leads to that elusive image. My piece *Windswept Cypresses*, for instance, arose out of thinking about the sonic possibilities of a combination of flute, viola, harp, and various percussion instruments parallel to the image of the sinewy branches of Monterey cypress trees along the California coast at Point Lobos. I jotted down verbal notes such as "continuously sculpted by wind" and "frozen in time," thinking of analogues in sound that could approach such a representation, given the instrumentation. That led to the dramaturgical direction I wanted to pursue, followed by a skeleton of the structure.

While in the mode of precomposition, the actual materials of a new work begin to reveal themselves: a consistent harmonic language (which is often the most audible stamp of a composer's identity), rhythmic and melodic considerations, etc. If the piece does not depict external sources, its internal structure can still be influenced by existing forms. In my orchestral work *Pantoumime*, I used the structure of a pantoum poem—a kind of spiraling, regenerative form based on recontexualized repetitions of lines across stanzas—to create a dialogue between musical phrases. In my work *Enjamb, Infuse, Implode*, I started with the metaphor of the line break as the connective thread between the melodic phrases of the piece. The piece ends with the musical equivalent of an envoi, tying together the previous stanzas' material with entirely new commentary.

Many musical forms are so tied to poetic structures that it is easy to forget why they are so effective. Stretching back throughout music history, examples include strophic verse and the early rondeau (related to its baroque counterpart, the ritornello, and in the classical period, the rondo), with constantly recurring refrains. Then there are those musical forms that, in turn, have inspired the literary arts: Thomas Bernhard's *The Loser* (variations on a theme, in this case Bach's *Goldberg Variations*), Milan Kundera's *The Book of Laughter and Forgetting* (again variations, especially those of late Beethoven), James Joyce's *Ulysses* (fugue and polyphony in general in the "Wandering Rocks" and "Sirens" episodes). And more recently, musical forms have taken on parallels to the sciences, such as the stochastic processes of Iannis Xenakis and the equivalent of fractals in the music of Per Nørgård. Sequences of data gleaned from biology and astronomy can make for fascinating and unpredictable rhythmic patterns, as the recent Japanese experimental sound artist Ryoji Ikeda has proven. György Ligeti used as one of his titles a phrase from philosopher Karl Popper, "Clocks and Clouds," to describe both regular and irregular patterns found in nature.

Once certain ingredients are assembled in the precomposition stage, my actual writing process resembles a synthesis of both the extemporized and strategically planned. Every gesture that I conceive is first felt, then "transcribed." This may explain my very odd habit of walking—usually in circles—while generating new material, trying to feel out the rhythm of a phrase in real time. Each sonic event depends on what has come before and what is anticipated next, and though there may be a general road map of a section already in mind, the moment-to-moment details are to a large extent improvised during the compositional process. Organizationally, I may choose to have a harmonic progression in place, over which new material is generated, or vice versa. This ambiguity of cause and effect is quite attractive to me, and the constant shifting of roles (background versus foreground, solo versus accompaniment) entices a listener's senses, so I try to keep these events perceptually (and perpetually) multidimensional.

I also find links and analogies to language very interesting, and not just in terms of overall structure. Rules of grammar and rhetoric fascinate me, as they create expectations that can be fulfilled or deliberately thwarted. Repetitions can be emphasized to drive home a point, materials reordered or redirected, the appearance of themes and cadences delayed, etc.—all in the service of the sensory experience. My large-ensemble piece *Hyperbaton* plays on the rhetorical effects of abnormal word order, and the final section of my piece *Centripedalocity* takes Thelonious Monk's tune "Epistrophy"—itself a play on the epistrophe, or repetition of phrase endings—and moves it through a series of looping, metrically disjunct figures.

Sometimes, though increasingly less often, I work at the piano trying out rhythmic or harmonic figures for sketches. Many composers write a short score first, consisting of a reduction that can be fleshed out, and these are often done at the piano. Some of the greatest orchestral composers of all time, master colorists such as Stravinsky and Ravel, worked somewhat paradoxically in this manner, although one finds it difficult to hear in their final orchestrated renditions the humble short-score or even pianistic origins of a work. Others prefer to orchestrate directly onto the full score, hearing each sonic detail as it comes into play, with every decision being fully formed as it is written. My use of the piano as a compositional tool comes from the need for a physical connection to an instrument as I write, though my materials do not fit its confines. Harmonically, my language has reached outside the standard equal-tempered tuning system of which the piano is the exemplar, and into the domain of microtonality. When using such a language, one must tread carefully to avoid sounding simply out of tune or unfamiliar. My musical aims have not been compromised or changed in any way, but rather have been enhanced by this new palette of tonal relationships. One can, it is hoped, hear traces of improvisational influences in the use of fluid, flexible rhythms and phrases as well as a satisfying formal logic and consistent approach to harmony. I try to take no sound for granted and am constantly searching for new colors, not just for cosmetic purposes, but to make deep structural connections.

The Work of a Composer

The contemporary composer is perhaps the oddest duck of all. For one, composers themselves don't even know what to call the music they write. *New music, art music, concert music, serious music, contemporary classical music, notated music*: the nomenclature is as varied as the public personae of its creators. I can't think of a more esoteric or misunderstood profession. Whenever a creative artist in another discipline attempts a portrayal of a contemporary composer, it only adds to the mystique and confusion. Our most famous example in literature is Thomas Mann's Adrian Leverkühn, the Schoenberg/Adorno–inspired modern Faust who bargains away his soul for unbridled, yet calculated, creativity. Recently, there has been another Adrian, that of Jonathan Parker's 2009 film *(Untitled)*, a sort of caricature of the brooding, highly irritable avant-gardist who spews forth the most unbearable sound-art clichés, the kind that give contemporary music a bad name. These days it is difficult and rather useless to take the human-interest or biographical angle in introducing a composer's work. All that is left for the public to decode is the music itself, which is never as attractive as how its maker happens to be a good pastry chef. For the most part, composers of the last few decades have led rather uneventful day-to-day existences, chiseling away at their scores in preferred isolation.

One problem is simply that talking about aesthetic aims often involves being technically precise. And the abundance of programmatic scenarios and narratives that defined much earlier music, particularly that of the 19th century, simply doesn't apply to much new music, which needn't reference other forms of expression or experience to define itself. Contemporary music can be *about* almost anything: For classic minimalists, a simple process of overlapping, gradually desynchronizing rhythms is enough, and in more recent spectral music, a transformation of a bell sound into human voice can be the entire raison d'être of a piece. Of course, pieces using such techniques can be more than purely conceptual, but the worlds they inhabit are more often than not similarly unfamiliar and nonreferential. Gérard Grisey, one of the pioneers behind the spectral-music aesthetic, famously wrote, "We are musicians and our model is sound not literature, sound not mathematics, sound not theater, visual arts, quantum physics, geology, astrology or acupuncture." Such a matter-of-factness toward one's art could be a turnoff to the uninitiated listener, except for the fact that Grisey's music is some of the most sensuous, humanistic, and visionary of any recent composer.

The fixation on the purely sonic model arose slowly through the early decades of the 20th century and accelerated rapidly following the end of the Second World War. Earlier ideas of representation and mimesis underwent the same revolution in music as they did in other forms of art. Gradual abstraction away from fixed forms of affect, formulas for structures, and traditional handling of tension and release led to an era where received common-practice traditions were questioned critically. But certain ingredients found to be persuasive developed into movements, and out of the vast plethora of initially unclassifiable techniques arose consistencies that morphed into styles. These new modes of expression could be complementary or wildly contradictory and often played out together or against one another in dialectic fashion, or so their respective critics and chroniclers liked to attest.

Some of the most inventive composers bypassed trends and alliances altogether, producing outputs so entirely unique and unlike those of their contemporaries as to have defied any claims of obvious influence. The American tradition of maverick composers that began with Charles Ives extended to such lonely figures as the expatriate Conlon Nancarrow—writing mechanical music for the player piano based on impossibly difficult rhythmic canons—and microtonal pioneer Harry Partch, who was so unsatisfied with the system of equal-tempered tuning that had dominated Western music for two centuries that he invented his own instruments capable of being tuned to the strictest overtone ratios. These composers, working outside the cloistered caste system of the classical-music world, espoused ideas of rugged individualism and were largely unknown during their lives. Yet their innovations had far-reaching consequences on subsequent generations of creators throughout the world. The fiercely original Hungarian composer György Ligeti, himself a great critic of stylistic dogma and fashionable trends in contemporary music, found in the music of Nancarrow, Partch, and other American mavericks such as minimalists Terry Riley and Steve Reich a great deal of inspiration and freedom that he eventually adopted as part of his own language.

Throughout the 20th century, electronics and the recorded medium were two great liberating forces, freeing music from restrictive conventions of musical parameters such as register, harmony, timbre (tone color), dynamics, and rhythm. This paradigm shift made listening and considering sound on a more microscopic level possible. Not just discrete rhythms, but granular ones, teetering on chaos; not just rhythmic units based on ever-smaller divisions of note-values, but the possibility of any fraction of a second as a measure of time. John Cage, writing in 1937, anticipated how composers working with the electronic-tape medium a few decades later would approach time: "The composer (organizer of sound) will be faced not only with the entire field of sound but also with the entire field of time. The 'frame' or fraction of a second, following established film technique, will probably be the basic unit in the measurement of time. No rhythm will be beyond the composer's reach." Even as tape technology has become obsolete, Cage's words now ring truer than ever in the age of digital software sequencers.

Synthesizers proved that producing sounds from anywhere on the frequency spectrum was possible, and at any desired volume. And even in the purely instrumental works that followed such developments, composers could not ignore the impact of these new technologies. The orchestral works that Ligeti wrote following his stint in the electronic studios of Cologne reflected his new attitude toward sound. In light of such discoveries, the idea that "notes" as autonomous entities could be abstracted and reordered suddenly seemed rather archaic. For when a composer considers a note, he or she is really hearing a timbre of a particular instrument played in a particular way, and with it, an entire overtone structure comprising individual frequencies, which is responsible for the outcome of timbre. The same note played by two different instruments separately, and then by a combination of both, will reveal completely different colors and overtone configurations.

If you're a musician, try this experiment. Take the first chord of "A Hard Day's Night," probably the most famous and recognizable chord in rock history. Transcribe it by ear. Playing it back on the piano, it doesn't seem too out of the ordinary. Jazz musicians might hear in it a great similarity to the vamp chord from Herbie Hancock's classic jazz tune "Maiden Voyage." No matter what theory jargon you use to call it—a D7sus4, a predominant in the key of C, a diatonic pitch collection—something is lacking from this reductionist approach to analysis. It disregards what makes the sound of that moment so special, which is not the chord itself, but its timbre. For decades, listeners wondered just how it was obtained. A few years ago, mathematician Jason Brown used fast Fourier transform (FFT) analysis to deconstruct the frequencies of the chord. From this he could identify the exact pitches being played along with their frequencies, as well as the instruments, separating them by timbre. It was known that George Harrison played a 12-string electric guitar and John Lennon a 6-string acoustic guitar, with Paul McCartney's low bass note, and even a small percussion hit from Ringo Starr. But the secret ingredient—not necessarily audible on its own, but part of the blended sound of the chord—was producer George Martin playing a few notes on the piano. The combined overtones of all these instruments played together in that particular register is what creates the unforgettable and ambiguous quality of the chord.

Contemporary composers have long been aware of this microscopic approach to analyzing sound. In 1975, Gérard Grisey wrote "Partiels," a work that opens with a low E on the trombone and bass followed by what sounds like an electronic halo emanating from it. The chord is in fact an entirely acoustic orchestration of the partials, or overtones, of the single trombone note; the information came from an electric sonogram of the sound that Grisey then applied to his ensemble. This process, known as instrumental synthesis, is one of the cornerstone techniques of the composers belonging to spectral music. In the opening four minutes of the work, Grisey takes the listener on a journey from a pure, consonant overtone spectrum to an increasingly unstable one, as the low fundamental that triggers the spectrum becomes dirtier and noisier. In doing this, Grisey demonstrates that a continuum between a pure overtone series and white noise can be mapped onto the traditional model of absolute consonance and extreme dissonance. At the vague intersection where timbre and harmony meet, the slight shifting of overtone configurations that make up individual sounds can dramatically alter both the material itself and one's perception of it.

These days we can see a graphical representation of any sound in the world and alter its inner components into something entirely different. To a composer, it presents a source of immeasurable sonic inspiration. We are now in an era where musical material demands that we not only discuss notes and rhythms, but also *sounds*, with their constantly shifting timbres evolving from attacks, resonances, and decays. If Cage's model for musical time consists of divisions of seconds and not beats, then notes too have their counterpart in the overtone series and the components thereof. And if music has an area of indefinite possibilities, a final frontier, it is in the domain of timbre. It remains the challenge of the imaginative composer to take these discoveries and tools and shape them into a personal language, and to elevate pure techniques into poetry.

From *Esopus 2* (2004)

Painting

BY LEV AC ROSEN

Lisa's hands are dirty. Not just unwashed, but gritty from lifting boxes all day. They feel raw, as though the skin itself is the dirt, shaken loose by the stress, hanging off her open nerves. She tries to wash them in the sink, uses soap heavily, but nothing seems to help much. The line between her hands and the grime is indistinguishable. Everything would have been easier with John around, but her hands still would have been dirty.

The apartment is white, except for one wall, which is, for some reason, purple. A bright, somewhat offensive purple. It had been the one thing she and John had hated about the apartment when they first saw it, but it seemed so petty at the time. The rest of it was wonderful, with a large living room, a big kitchen, no walls except to divide the bedroom and bathroom, and the window. The window was Lisa's favorite part: a huge, smooth glass wall looking out on midtown Manhattan. She liked the feeling that there was nothing there at all, just a hole into the apartment, no privacy left. The fact that the opposite wall was purple was unfortunate, but it, they had reasoned, could easily be painted over. A can of white paint and brushes sit over by the purple wall all ready, dry, but glossy with anticipation. She can almost feel the soft hairs of the brushes rippling over her hands, but fears acting upon the desire to touch them. She doesn't want to get them oily before she uses them. When the wall is white, she will hang her photography on it. Her project.

The boxes are all in now, and she is very tired. The bed isn't built yet, though, and her mattress lies on the floor in the middle of the room, still covered in plastic. She tears the plastic off ferociously. Plastic wrappings have always terrified her with their easy suffocation, their eerie power to cut everything off. She sometimes has nightmares of being mummified in it, staring out as it binds her arms to her body and seals her open, screaming mouth like a vacuum. When the plastic is off, she throws it aside, falls onto the mattress, and is soon asleep, surrounded by towers of brown boxes.

Lisa's parents are both artists. They had adopted her in their 40s, after being married for two years. Lisa was a half-Japanese, half-Italian orphan, then being raised by the government, all of her blood family having been recently deceased. They took her from social services and raised her as their own, with great artistic prowess expected from her from that point on. After all, they had chosen her. They had even given her a beautiful, artistic name: Mona Lisa Genji Wells. The Mona Lisa, they told her as she grew up, was for her Italian blood, and the Genji was for *The Tale of Genji*, reflecting her Asian background. They had proudly shown her the adoption papers they had signed which identified her blood family. She remembers her mother displaying them on her 12th birthday, over dinner. She had been working on a project for school, a family tree, and had asked about her family's background. Her mother had jumped up from the table, a blur of colors and strange beads, and quickly come back with The Papers, placing them over Lisa's food, pointing to her father's name, where it said "murdered" and to her mother's name, where it said "suicide."

"Your parents were brave and extraordinary people. We can only hope to raise you to be as wonderful as they were." She had then put the papers down and eaten in silence.

During college, Lisa had investigated her parents' deaths on her own. They had been married two months before her birth, and one month after it her father had been killed, apparently by the man whose wife he had been sleeping with. Her mother, an immigrant, had few skills of her own and had hanged herself in her one-bedroom apartment when she couldn't come up with the rent. The landlord broke down the door to find the body swinging over Lisa's cradle, wearing nothing but a white nightgown, which had started to slip. Apparently, Lisa had been batting at the edge of the robe, pulling it further down off the corpse and into her cradle.

When Lisa wakes up, it is storming outside. The huge wall-to-wall window is navy and occasionally flashes white, highlighting the tops of buildings with lightning. Rain hits the pane hard and smears it, distorting the image further, turning the whole wall into a nightmarish video mural. Lisa gazes up at it and lets the picture, cold and raging, fill her for a few minutes. Then she gets up and presses herself against the glass, pushing it, daring it to break, but of course, it doesn't. The glass feels cool, and when she puts her ear to it, the beat of the rain sounds like a thousand dropping marbles. She stays against the window for a few moments longer, her ear to the glass, her arms spread out, suctioning her to the image of rain. She takes a deep breath and turns on the overhead light, creating a reflection on the skyline but not dampening the steady noise. She glances at her watch—3:53 a.m.—and decides to begin painting the wall. She pushes the cardboard boxes and bags of her things into the bedroom. Then she opens the large can of white paint. She and John hadn't bothered to check if it was an exact match with the white of the other two walls. John figured one was as good as another, but Lisa, knowing how many shades of white exist in the world, made sure to buy enough paint to cover all the walls.

John had suggested buying a roller, of course, as it was the practical thing to do, but she craved the feeling of the clean brush, running over her fingers, and then the weight of it, dripping thick paint, and afterwards, washing it in the sink, slowly rubbing the paint out of the plastic hairs under the running water of the sink. John hadn't protested, but maybe, Lisa thinks, he had already known that he wouldn't be living with her, wouldn't be repainting the wall.

He had already helped enough with her project, anyway. She had posted an ad online, looking for a model—male, attractive, white, blond, preferably with blue eyes. She had wanted the All-American Man to pose in the photos with her, her dark, foreign looks contrasting even more against the archetype. This would show how most people saw her, she thought: compared to someone else.

Photography had been Lisa's choice of art form, though she had never had a choice about being an artist. As a child, she didn't draw much or tell stories, but instead liked to play on the swings, or with small yellow toy trucks. Soon, her parents' friends began to talk: "Where is her genius?" Some had blamed it on her adoption, but others insisted that her parents' natures could not help but instill artistic talent into the child.

It wasn't until college that she even began experimenting with a camera. By then, her parents were pushing her: Why didn't she pursue something artistic? So she started taking pictures. It seemed easy at first, a point-and-click art form that required little work. Something to make her parents happy, or to prove to them that she wasn't really an artist. But after a while, the ruse became a fascination. She loved how the camera could slow down moments or imprison them. She loved how a single breath could be divided into 20 neat photos. This was when she decided to begin work on her project.

The project was almost an excuse. It kept her parents and their friends at bay. Whenever they asked why they hadn't seen any pieces, her parents could say she was "working on the project." It had such weight. And Lisa didn't have to worry about being too much of a disappointment. But while it was an excuse, it was also becoming a mild obsession. Especially since the photos with John. Which is why she needs the wall to be white.

For the first coat of paint she doesn't follow any particular pattern. She takes the brush, heavy with white paint, and runs the length of the wall, creating figure eights, stripes, sometimes painting smiley faces or lightning bolts. Soon, one layer of paint has covered the wall, running over itself, dripping, and just barely covering the purple. She sits down and waits for the paint to dry before beginning the next layer. It withers slowly, clinging to the wall under it, becoming more transparent in its desperation to join completely with the purple. It reminds her of plastic wrap, slowly shriveling tighter, and so she turns away and tries to think of how she will begin to place things on the wall. The photos of her and John are important, of course, but she wants to spread them around, like a blanket underneath her. Something behind her.

The photo shoot had been surprising. John had come over, and after talking for a while they had decided to go out for coffee. He had studied art but never felt a need to create. He was in graduate school but taking a semester off. He was attractive and blond, tall and well dressed and well spoken, but single. His appearance was perfect, but under it all, so many sidebars. In the soft light of the café, he looked like a model, she some odd creature he had tamed. She wore her dark hair short and parted to the side, and had on a sports jacket, a man's button-down shirt and tight pants. With her olive skin and narrow shoulders, she knew she looked androgynous to the people around her. Dark, mysterious, and sitting next to the captain of the football team. The contrast felt weird in public—it unnerved her. That is what made her decide John was the one for the job. They had arranged a date for the photos and exchanged phone numbers, and Lisa had left feeling she had made a new friend.

The first layer of paint is dry, and she enjoys the swirls and texture of it. But the purple still peeks out behind the white, as though it's being viewed through a veil, or thick rolling fog. Lisa gets up and begins painting again, this time in straight lines, up and down, up and down, the wavelike motion relaxing her mind.

When she was little, her parents had found her an inspiration. Her mother, the sculptor, had taken casts of her six-year-old hand in a variety of poses, then used them to create a poured concrete sculpture which looked like a garden of small hands, grabbing, clawing, waving, pushing out. It had been painted gold and green and titled "Cabbage Patch." Her father, the poet, sat her on a stool in his study, writing metaphors for her eyes. He had shown these to her after every "session." She saw in his writing as her eyes went from "innocent inkwells" to "black pebbles on an exotic shore" to "black pearls peeking out from between the dark-colored lids of a clam's mouth." Later, he had published a book of poems entirely composed about or inspired by her. He had dedicated it to her birth parents.

Once, a boy in college, upon learning her full name, had said that her parents must have really wanted her to be an artist.

"The *Mona Lisa* and *The Tale of Genji* aren't artists," she had responded. He didn't reply then but two weeks later had asked her out for coffee. She had accepted, and over the warm caffeine, she had asked him why he wanted to go out with her. He was handsome, with dark hair and blue eyes, and wore a black turtleneck and thick glasses.

"You seem so fascinating," he said.

The second layer dries fast, but seems to have less effect. The wall is still purple with splotches of varying depth of color, some places dark like a bunch of grapes, some light like a sprig of lavender. One spot resembles a dark purple- blue rose. She starts painting over these specific images, trying to whitewash them from her mind. Then she paints over the rest of the wall, haphazardly, just throwing the paint on. As it dries she goes to the window. It is still raining and dark. The storm seems to have nestled itself above the city, possibly right above the building. The thunder is now booming and seems to make the window shake slightly, and Lisa wonders if it will fall out and the wind will come in to grab her as well. She likes the idea of the rush of air and the static of the storm fizzling through her as she plummets downward. She doesn't want to die, despite her recent losses, but she would like her lungs to fill with so much air that she might explode.

The first shoot with John had been the naked one. She felt comfortable with it, and he said he did as well, so they had stripped down. She had explained what she wanted, positioned the camera, and they had begun posing as lovers on her bed. She wanted everything to be clearly posed and fake, the overdramatized love of opposites. She had assumed John was gay, and so had he. She thinks perhaps it was how her small breasts looked like a man's chest when she lay on her back, or the short hair. Or the Asian blood, which she knew took away gender when she was viewed through others' eyes.

On her 16th birthday, her mother had given her a kimono. It was custom-made by a friend of hers, white on the outside with a cherry blossom pattern, and soft pink silk lining the inside. The friend had shown her how to properly tie and wear it, all the time with her mother murmuring approvingly in the background. When the kimono was fully in place, she said to Lisa, "Now let me take a picture."

She still had the kimono but wore it around the house over her pajamas, like a bathrobe. She liked the fabric, the smooth feel of it, but couldn't think of it as a cultural marker. She still has the photo, though, which she had framed in silk and bamboo. This will go in the lower right-hand corner of the wall when it is ready.

She also has many photos of herself before she had chopped her hair off, in the kimono, with heavy makeup on, her hair up with beads and chopsticks, and a fan, behind which she demurely hid her painted lips, as if trying not to giggle. She developed them so that they were black on brown, like old parchment. These photos also will go on the wall, overlapping the single moment of her bowing her head behind the fan, creating a background in the lower left part of the project. That is, if the paint ever covers the purple.

The third layer is dry now, though Lisa doesn't see any improvement. The white is like some great, thick wall of ice, but behind it she can still see the purple lounging against the wall, smoking a cigarette, regarding Lisa with wicked eyes. Teasing her, she thinks, slipping out of the way of her paintbrush, running into the far corners where she has difficulty painting, and then sliding down the white streaks back into the middle, or the side, or wherever it chooses to be.

The photo shoot with John had slid from a self-aware mockery of lovemaking into actual lovemaking without either of them being completely aware of what was going on. It was smooth, like the lining of her kimono, and almost natural, despite all the things that should have been keeping them apart. The fake kisses became moist, and harder, the poses became less romantic and more real, rough, and the noises were soon the real unpleasant noises of body on body, sweat mingling, not the carefully choreographed noises of a love scene. The heat of the lamps had made them both drowsy, and John had fallen asleep in Lisa's arms. When they woke up two hours later, they had talked briefly, wondering if things would be odd or different now, trying to incorporate this puzzle piece into their lives. John had said that while he was indeed gay, he had no regrets about the sex; he had in fact enjoyed it. Lisa had liked it, too, but had trouble distinguishing whatever physical pleasure she had experienced from the pseudo-intellectual pleasure of the unlikeliness of the match. Her physical deviance of appearance matching with his hidden deviances—deviances that were so well hidden by his physical ideal form. Could people see how perfectly they worked together, or would they just see difference, instead of their dirty similarities? Would his WASP mother be happy he was with a woman, or upset that he was with her, adopted, mixed race, and so dark to look at? They had decided, without saying it out loud, that the experience would not stop them from being friends, but neither would it stop it from happening again. It wasn't a romantic relationship, it was sex with a friend, then living with a close friend as he moved his stuff into her apartment, then buying a new place with a best friend. A one-bedroom new place. They didn't think they were together, but they didn't act as though they were single anymore, either. Lisa was never completely sure where they were, but as her time became almost exclusively spent, and enjoyed, with him, she knew they were a couple to the outside world, if not to themselves.

He was part of her routine, sleeping over most nights, going out to buy groceries. She would wake up in the morning to find him lying on his side, looking at her.

"What do you want to do today?" he would ask.

"I should work."

"I should go see this new exhibit at the Met."

"Okay, well why don't you go and see the exhibit, and while you're doing that, I'll work on the project. Then we can meet up for dinner."

"Good plan, but I really hate going to museums alone." He would say this with a mock tremble of fear in his voice.

"Oh," she would respond, with the appropriate level of mock concern, "then I'd better go with you." And then they'd go to the museum, and hold hands while looking at art.

In the textured bands of the white paint, dry again now, she can see the fleeting shape of the purple, always sliding, just out of view. She picks up the brush, this time so heavy with white paint that it drizzles a line on the wooden floor as she moves it to the wall, and once there, she begins to beat it with the brush, paint exploding like fireworks overhead, splatters raining down on her and painting her white. She is going to erase any trace of the purple now. She needs the blank wall for her project.

Three weeks ago, she was at her parents' house, sitting around the table, with the two of them in the cozy rose-colored apartment she had grown up in. Her father, who finally had come to resemble the old poet he had always wanted to be with his tiny spectacles and white beard, had picked at the bright orange sweet potatoes on his plate.

"How is the project going?" he had asked.

"It's all right," she had said, trying not to look him in the eye, not wanting him to know that it had been less and less a priority as John had become more and more of one. "It's hard to really work on it right now, 'cause I'm packing everything up for the move."

"Of course," he had said.

Her mother was in a long shapeless purple dress that accented her breasts and the mass of orange-gray curls around her head. They bobbed suddenly as she jerked her arm towards Lisa, pointing at her with the fork, then quickly retracted it.

"You know, Mone, we're a little worried that maybe you're not taking this project as seriously as you should. You said it was about you, after all, and you should be taking you very seriously." Her parents called her Mone, a nickname she had shed as early as possible in the outside world.

"Don't worry, Mom, I'm taking it seriously. I've been trying to figure out why my mother killed herself. That's pretty serious, I think." She had hoped that would end the conversation. Her mother sighed, almost relaxed.

"If I could have children, and had to give one up because I couldn't provide for her, I would probably kill myself, too." This hung in the air a little while among the scrapings of metal on ceramic.

"Maybe," Lisa said, trying to sound as if she weren't instigating a fight, "she was just upset that my father was cheating on her."

"Oh," said her father quickly, "I don't think a woman like her would be bothered by that. From what I read in her file, she seemed very traditional."

"Traditional?"

"Your mother was a real Japanese lady. She was probably raised to act that way from birth."

"She moved to America. She had a child with an Italian. None of that is very traditional." Lisa had held her fork tightly and could see the red marks on her fingers.

"Well," he said, leaning back in his chair, "when she got herself into a crisis, she did turn back to her racial customs."

"I don't think you knew anything about her."

"No, but I can guess, from you. Sometimes I think you've absorbed some of your birth mother's character. Like her soul dripped into you as she hung over your cradle."

"That's a lovely image," her mother had said, in complete sincerity. "You should write it down." He had nodded and quickly gotten up to go to his study. "You know, Mone, you shouldn't be so hard on your father. He tries, but sometimes stereotypes don't leave the head easily. They're part of everyone's culture."

"But I'm his daughter." Lisa hated this conversation, it always went on, like a circle, renewing itself every time they spoke for long periods of time.

"Even so." Then silence. "Even so" always killed the argument, or at least stalled it until next time. Her father came back, happily patting his stomach after digesting his poetic phrasing.

"So," her mother had said then, clearly trying to pretend nothing had happened, "how is John these days?"

John was fine in those days. Better than fine. After dinner with her parents,

Lisa had met him, waiting outside her apartment, even though he had a key.

"Don't change," he had said, "we're going somewhere." He had taken her by the hand and led her down the street. She lived downtown then and the walk to Little Italy wasn't very far. She considered telling John about the events at her parents' house, her frustrations, but she didn't. She didn't want to bother him with her own issues, issues that didn't exist now. What was a bother with her parents became beautiful with John. Lisa didn't know the name of the fair going on, or even that there was a fair going on. The street had the sort of darkness New York has late at night—blue and yellow and murmurs of mint green. But all along the street were booths selling things—fried dough, handcrafted purses, even cotton candy. Lisa half expected to see a Ferris wheel in the place of a brownstone around any corner. The light was stained with pink, and John led her through the booths one by one, gently pulling her along by the hand when she stopped to look at something. Finally he stopped her in front of a small booth, draped with red cloth. "Pick one," he said. The booth was filled with flowers. An old woman, her head covered by some sort of shawl, stood amidst the red fabric and the flowers, which crept up the walls, the beams, the desk in front of her.

"Silk," the woman said, "I make them myself." Lisa tentatively approached the stand then, and looked all around its interior. The flowers looked real, but when she touched them, they felt softer than real and had a musty sweetness she had smelled only once before and couldn't place. She spent what felt like hours going over each of the flowers, the red orchids, or the green lilies, but eventually she picked out a rose, dark midnight blue, with a long red stem and soft ivy green edging the petals.

"This one," she said to John, who was still holding her hand.

"Perfect," he had said, and bought it for her.

"If white roses are for friendship, and red ones are for love, what are the blue ones for?" she had asked him, feeling playful.

"Well, now they're for us."

The window is bending in and out with the wind outside, being pushed like a sheet of transparent cloth. And the wall is still purple. Lisa stands back, taking a breath, and looks again, and smiles. Not entirely purple. Improvement has been made. To anyone else, the wall would look white. Textured, white, with a faint hint at another color hiding in the shadows. If you didn't know that there had originally been purple, you would just think it was an interesting white wall. So no one would know except her. Well, except her and John.

He had left two days ago. She supposes she should have seen it coming. This friendship, this wonderful knowing of him—his mind, his personality, and his body—had to end eventually. He was gay, after all. She wasn't so much sad that it was over, but more disappointed with herself for thinking that such a pleasant part of her life could last forever. He had packed his bags—only two suitcases, really—without saying anything, and had stood in front of her as she lay on the bed in her old apartment.

"I've met someone," he had said, looking stiff, "A man. I'm moving back to my place. I'm sorry. I don't know why we thought this would work. We don't even know what it is."

"I know," she had said, not feeling much of anything at the time, just gazing at his pretty blue eyes and pale hair, his sad, perfectly painted expression.

"I should never have let you, or me, think that we could somehow be a couple. We were never a couple."

"We never were. We were just close. Close friends."

"We're still close friends. Right?"

"Yes. Of course." And somehow, she had found it in herself to stand up, and to smile, and to hug him. What a pair they had made, light and dark, his seeming perfection, her obvious differences. And how wonderful he was to talk with, to drink with, to hold or lie next to in bed. How wonderful it was to have a best friend and a lover in one body, even if they had never been in love. Her eyes were a little blurry when she pulled out of the hug, and looking up at him, his golden hair seemed like a bright light around him, with only the dark shadows of her hands blocking the glow. She pulled her arms back and wrapped them around herself.

"You should go, I guess. I'll call you once I'm moved into the new place."

"Okay," he had said, genuinely smiling, the fear she hadn't seen slowly being released as the relationship oozed into something more fathomable. "There's an opening at MoMA next Friday. Want to go?"

"Of course," she had said.

Now, hanging up photos and pieces of the project on the barely dry, still sticky white wall, she smiles as she thinks of the exhibit they'll be going to. It's for emerging artists from Southeast Asia. She is looking forward to it, and to seeing John, and maybe meeting his new boyfriend.

The photos she hangs don't make much of an image yet. There are still many empty spaces, and in them, she can see the color lurking in the shadows of the texture. She decides to make peace with the purple, though, the strangely colored shadows on the project over which she tries to post these images of her imaginary past.

The window continues to shake with the cracking of thunder, and the room is still lit with flashes of lightning. The only sound Lisa can hear, though, as she steps back to look at the wall, is the pattern of rain.

Haunted

BY CHRISTOPHER WHEELDON

I have been choreographing professionally for about nine years now, and over that relatively short period of time you could say I have covered many bases. Some assert that I spread myself thin, others that I seem to lack a distinctive voice; both are right in some respects. Thrilled by a challenge and never content to settle too early into a predictable creative pattern, I take on many different projects. My world is the ballet, but I didn't say no to Broadway or the movies. Actually, choreographing a short segment for *Sesame Street* was quite possibly one of my favorite commissions. It may be clichéd to say it, but for me, variety certainly is the spice of life. Of course, it can be comforting to have a favorite designer you can count on, or certain dancers who inspire you—what's wrong with coming home once in a while? In my mind, however, the only way to learn and grow as an artist is by living a little dangerously, and that often means packing your toothbrush and setting off into the unknown. Having said that, over the past three years I have had a musical relationship with one man whose magical and often frightening world seems to have me hooked: the Romanian-born composer György Ligeti.

My interest in Ligeti came about purely by chance. In the fall of 2000, I was on holiday in London with my partner at the time, Jock Soto, for whom I was about to create a new work for New York City Ballet. I had just opened a production of Vivaldi's *The Four Seasons* for the Boston Ballet, and having struggled with it, my confidence was very low. I knew that it was time to steer away from what had been until then rather conservative musical choices. Never having been a conformist, Jock urged me to make a departure and to find music that not only interested me, but more important, frightened me. It was time to be daring and unconventional. The City Ballet was calling me daily to ask what the rehearsal pianists should be preparing for the approaching rehearsal dates. So off I headed for Tower Records in Piccadilly Circus.

I randomly went to the L section, and there, I came upon a CD by György Ligeti. "Why does that name ring a bell?" I thought, and then recalled that as a 12-year-old piano student I had been given a simple piece by Ligeti to learn. I had scoffed at the atonality and secretly dreamed of playing Chopin. Now seemed as good a time as any to reaquaint myself with Ligeti—and atonal was certainly daring. So I bought a collection of piano works and took them back to the hotel for that all-important first impression.

The first piece that struck the right chord with me was "No. 2: Mesto, Rigido e Cerimonale" from a collection of pieces called *Musica Ricercata*. I had heard it recently in Stanley Kubrick's *Eyes Wide Shut*—it was a four-minute piano work that had been stretched out over a two-and-a-half-hour movie. At its intended length, it was startlingly hypnotic. I knew this was where I would begin, but beyond that, it was anyone's guess; the other pieces seemed like a complicated web of rhythm and atonality—grotesquely poetic to an extent that I found interesting, yet deeply intimidating.

It's worth noting that for me, physical preparation and preproduction for a new ballet is nonexistent: There are no long sessions in the studio creating sequences of movement for the dancers to learn the following day. I make up for this with a detailed knowledge of the music. Though my technical skills as a musician are basic, I can, through saturation and a certain amount of natural understanding, get to know a score so that I can sing the phrases in my head and follow by translating them into movement. This, combined with a healthy dash of self-confidence and a trust in my instincts, is my approach to creating a new ballet.

Back in New York, rehearsals began on what would become the signature pas de deux of the ballet that I decided to call *Polyphonia*. I was still undecided, however, on the choices of music for the other dances, and with about 25 piano works to choose from, I embarked on a very different selection process.

Daily, I would spend one hour in the studio with my rehearsal pianist, Cameron Grant, and we would decide on a piece for the rehearsal that followed. What had previously been a precarious gamble, in which I relied purely on my instincts, backed up by many weeks of listening to the music, was now a random selection of music minutes before the dancers arrived. The challenge presented by this was compounded by the attitudes of the dancers, who can at times be a grumpy species—having been one, I can attest to that. Daily self-scrutiny can affect one's willingness to participate in the creative process! Luckily, the group of dancers I had chosen were more than cooperative and seemed to relish the randomness of the process.

We choreographed each dance phrase by phrase, after first listening to the entire piece a couple of times. The results were spontaneous and exciting. As we progressed, the complexities of the music unlocked themselves, and I found myself delving deeper into the material than I ever had before. The ballet was completed in two weeks, and the experience of working with Ligeti's music had profoundly affected my choreographic approach. The ten piano pieces in *Polyphonia* sparked something in my imagination, giving me the courage to explore a darker, more angular world of muscular, sculptured dances that were both erotic and tender, yet strangely untouchable and distant.

I went to Ligeti for inspiration a second time after I was commissioned by the San Francisco Ballet in 2001 to create a new work for its impending season. Rehearsals for the ballet *Continuum* began on September 18th, exactly one week after the dreadful events of September 11th. America, still reeling from the tragedy, felt like an open wound. Many artists chose to create work very specific to the attacks. I responded through creativity because I had no choice, but I remember feeling very resistant to jumping on the "9/11 bandwagon" and tried to avoid addressing the events directly in the choreography for the piece.

It wasn't until seeing *Continuum* again this summer at a presentation of my work at the Edinburgh Festival that I realized how reflective, at least obliquely, some of the imagery of the ballet ended up being. The centerpiece of the ballet is danced to Ligeti's "Continuum for Harpsichord." Here, the composer creates a monotone by rapidly playing two notes in succession. (The harpsichord has no pedal to sustain notes, so this virtuoso trilling is the only way to create continuous sound.) The droning siren quality of this piece inspired an ominous slow-motion pas de deux, in which dancers Yuan Yuan Tan and Damian Smith gaze up at the sky and then shield their eyes as if to block out a bright light. Their movement continues at a snail's place as each dancer sinks sideways into the ground.

In the final pas de deux, dancers Muriel Maffre and Benjamin Pierce press palms together and open their fingers as if carrying something precious. At first, they look away, as if disgusted by what they hold, but later they stare longingly into their empty palms. I remember telling both of them to imagine themselves as gods protecting a miniature world that soon falls away, disappearing into the movement.

One of the most startling discoveries I made during work on *Morphoses*, my third ballet to the music of Ligeti, was the result of one of those serendipitous moments that I suppose have been a mainstay of my career as a choreographer, since I've always preferred to work on impulse. I decided that as my two previous adventures with Ligeti's wonderful piano pieces had been so fruitful, it was time to get to know the man whose music so inspired me. I bought Richard Toop's biography *György Ligeti* and in the first chapter discovered that a traumatic incident Ligeti suffered as a small child had a formative influence on his life and work. In the book, the composer recalls: "When I was three years old, I stayed with my aunt for three months, as construction work was going on at our house. She was a teacher at an elementary school and had the idea that children had to overcome their aversions. When she realized that I was afraid of spiders she made me collect cobwebs with my bare hands. It terrified and disgusted me."

Toop goes on to say that "Ligeti remains an arachnophobe to this day, and one essential aspect of his early work—the weblike 'micro-polyphony' that enters his work from the late 1950s onwards—arises, arguably, from the need to exorcize this persisting horror, or else to transmute it into artistic gold."

This brief passage caused me great excitement. The previous day I had completed a pas de deux for Jock and his fellow NYCB principal, Wendy Whelan. We had had some problems finding an ending for the dance, and Wendy, sensing my discomfort at being blocked, had instinctively gotten down on all fours and crept offstage sideways, like a sexy half woman/half spider—a perfect ending to the pas de deux, and a serendipitous moment.

This is not the only insect reference in my Ligeti-inspired ballets. In *Polyphonia* Wendy climbs on Jock like a praying mantis preparing to devour its prey. These and many other descriptive images are stumbled upon randomly, sometimes by me, sometimes by the artists I am working with. Often, one striking image can act as a catalyst for the movement that is built up around them, later forming the entire ballet. I'm convinced, though, that these images are unlocked by the poetic, nightmarish world of Ligeti and the instinctive responses of the artists working with his music.

Although *Polyphonia* marked the beginning of a more personal choreographic style, it was clearly aesthetically influenced by my long-term exposure to the works of George Balanchine; my seven years dancing in the house of Balanchine remain invaluable in my development as a choreographer.

The most successful way to study Balanchine is to dance Balanchine. I remember being a dancer and looking out from the back of the stage, toward the end of *Symphony in Three Movements*. From this vantage point, the brightly lit bodies of the dancers stand out in relief against the dark stillness of the auditorium, and the multilayering of music and thematic movement is distinctly clear. My role as one of six couples in the corps de ballet involved gently marking time with a simple pulsing step. A certain amount of concentration is necessary, but having danced the ballet many times, I found myself watching the dancers in front of me as they took on another musical theme, and then in front of them, the principal dancers yet another. By identifying isolated rhythms and then layering them, the effect is rich and complex, yet never so complicated that an audience member's eyes have to fight to know what to focus on. Up there on the stage you are involved as perhaps an instrument is involved in an orchestra: in building a world in which music and movement are a seamless symphony.

These were all important lessons that gave me the confidence to explore the often intimidating rhythms of Ligeti's music. On first hearing, most would say that this was not dance music. However, by grasping on (sometimes for dear life) to a rhythm from within the polyphonic structure, it is possible to ride through even the trickiest of Ligeti's studies. *Desordre*, the first piano étude in *Polyphonia*, lives up to its name as the pianist maniacally crashes through a series of fiendishly difficult passages in which the two hands are frequently playing different rhythms. To the ear, the sound is complete cacophony; yet by arranging a highly structured, almost academic dance to work over the music, the movement serves to punctuate it, helping us to see order within the disorder.

The ballet audience is an intelligent, discerning group, yet in this country, outside of New York City Ballet, where Balanchine so deftly educated his audience by exposing them to Stravinsky and even to the electronic music of Pierre Henry, atonal music is usually considered inappropriate or too difficult for ballet. Of course, there are those who have a taste for more contemporary sounds, but I am afraid that the majority will always prefer the *oom-pah-pahs* that are typically associated with ballet music. Combining this more challenging music with movement, however, can help to solve some of the problems contemporary music has for a traditional ballet audience.

Ligeti is a man I have much to thank for. He has contributed a great deal to my maturation as an artist. I now listen to music differently, searching for the less likely way to hear it—the hidden rhythmic patterns, the impact of the stillness between the phrases. I always admire how Balanchine so effortlessly seemed to be able to choreograph in a way that allowed us, as an audience, to appreciate the music and listen with so much more care and attention. I think that working with Ligeti's music has shown me how I, too, can play a part in helping an audience discover and come to love a piece of music that they might switch stations from if they heard it on the radio. Ligeti is not instantly accessible for most, but if you really take the time to listen and absorb his work, he will transport you to a fascinating, dark, poetic place that will haunt and transform you.

Yesterday's Mail

INTERVIEW WITH ROBERT WARNER

In the late '80s, Robert Warner first came across a piece of mail art sent by the artist Ray Johnson to a mutual friend. Intrigued, he contacted Johnson, who called him a few days later. That phone call initiated an intense, fascinating exchange between Johnson and Warner that lasted until Johnson's death in 1995. Over the course of their relationship, Warner received hundreds of pieces of mail art from Johnson, ranging from collages to a piece of driftwood hand-delivered to the eyewear store where Warner, an optician, worked at the time. The conversation below, conducted with Warner in early 2011, was accompanied in *Esopus 16* by 18 painstakingly reproduced facsimiles of items sent to Warner by Johnson. *Ray and Bob Box,* a related exhibition and series of performances by Warner, was featured at Esopus Space in June 2011.

Tod Lippy: *When did you first become aware of Ray Johnson?*

Robert Warner: In 1988, I noticed a postcard on the bulletin board of Laura Bohn, a friend of mine. It had a hand-drawn heart with *Laura* written on the inside of it, and while the ink was still wet it had been tipped up: a bleeding heart. I said, "Laura, what's up with the postcard?" and she said, "Oh, that's from Ray Johnson." She took it down and turned it over and said, "This is Ray's return address. I'm not sure if he's still there, or if he's still up to it, but he used to like collaging and corresponding."

At the time I thought, Well, an artist I could correspond with would be good. So I wrote down his return address—actually, I think I probably Xeroxed it—and I sent him what I thought would be an appropriate thing to send to an artist: a paper palette that had an oval hole in it.

What was his response?

He liked it. He actually called me; I guess I was listed in the phone book. The first thing he said was, "Where do I get more of those paper palettes?" Apparently he wanted to use them for another project. I told him I got them at an art-supply store in Sausalito, California. I didn't know the name of it, and you know, there was no Google at the time, so there were back-and-forth conversations—"Was the store called Orange Art?" "I don't know." "Was it Siciliano?" "I don't remember." Finally I said, "Listen, I have another dozen of them and I'll just send them to you." On the outside of the package I rubber-stamped the image of a cow. A few days later he called me, and the first thing he said was, "You know, I was friends with Andy Warhol." And I was kind of confused about why he had brought this up until he said, "You know, the cow wallpaper." It soon became clear to me that this was how many conversations with Ray began. He would make an oblique reference to something I'd sent, or something he was working on, and I'd sort of have to figure out what he was talking about. It was never very easy, but it was always intriguing; it was like being led into a dark chamber with all sorts of questions.

Chance, of course, played an enormous role in his work; it sounds like it played a similarly important part in his social interactions.

Yeah, it was like ping-pong. And he really liked having a gaming partner; he really liked the back-and-forth. One time while I was talking to him on the phone I said, "*Blondie and Dagwood* just came on television," and he responded, "You know, Dagwood Bumstead has no nipples. Next time you look in a comic book, you'll see; when he's in a bathing suit or a towel, he has no nipples. Trust me." And then of course he would insist that I track down the comic book, and then I would cut up parts of it, you know, like the bathtub scene, and send that to him, which would lead to a phone call where he'd say, "Have you ever seen Walt Whitman's bathtub? I'm sure it exists. It's probably in Camden." And then the conversation would go on and on about bathtubs for a week.

What were you doing at the time the correspondence started?

I was an optician at a store called Morgenthal Frederics Opticians at 62nd and Madison, which was a great place to be in New York in the '80s, because you got all of the old New Yorkers coming in. Anyone from Adolfo to Jackie Onassis to Tom Wolfe. Because I came into contact with all of these socialites, artists, and performers, they would become a part of this ongoing conversation with Ray. For example, one day I brought up Gypsy Rose Lee, and Ray said, "You know, Jasper Johns's house was once owned by Gypsy Rose Lee. I'll send you something and I want you to hand-deliver it there."

Did you?

I did. I found the address of his townhouse and just slipped the envelope under the door. I have no idea what Ray sent to him.

It seems that assigning tasks like these to respondents was a fairly important part of his mail-art practice.

Definitely. Once, for example, he Xeroxed the Declaration of Independence and asked me to take it to John Cage to have him sign it. And one day—it was the Fourth of July—he called me and told me that John Cage was expecting me to bring it over. He told me where he lived, and I delivered it.

Did Cage sign it?

There was another person going into his loft on Sixth Avenue at the same time, so he just took it. I don't know if Cage ever followed through or not. Ray would also make appointments for me. One time he called and said, "David Bourdon has one of the *Marilyns*. A chorine." And I said to him, "I have no idea what a *chorine* is." He said, "A chorus girl. Marilyn Monroe was a chorus girl." So I arrived at Bourdon's house—he was an art critic for *Life* magazine at the time—and he said, "Hi, I was expecting you. Ray wanted me to show you some things." He had some stuff laid out on the table, which he took me over to. I remember he had a yappy dog that nipped at my heels the whole time.

Another time Ray asked me if I knew where he could get a photograph of Carmen Miranda, and I went to Jerry Ohlinger's movie-stills store on 14th Street. I sent the photos to him and he sent me back a Carmen Miranda portrait in multiples. I said it reminded me of Warhol's portraits of Elizabeth Taylor, and he told me that early on in his work, Warhol and he would go and get movie stills together. He told me that toward the end of Andy's life he went to an exhibition that had one of Andy's *Triple Elvis*es on the wall, and Andy asked if he'd like the triptych, and Ray said, "No, I have no room for it." He said to me, "Oh, Bob, if only I had a *Triple Elvis* now..." I asked him where he'd put it, and he said, "Well, I guess under my bed." *[laughs]* A *Triple Elvis* under your bed.

How old were you at the time this began?

I was 32.

It sounds almost like a teacher-student relationship, although more intimate in some ways.

It was definitely an education. I really enjoyed it. Other people in my life were more equivocal about it. My partner, Joseph Lembo, was really annoyed by all of the phone conversations.

How often did you speak on the phone with him?

Every day. Sometimes twice a day. He would call me at work, and finally my boss, Mr. Morgenthal, said, "This has got to stop, Robert. This is just excessive." And I said, "Well, everybody else gets phone calls from their family." And he replied, "Ray Johnson is not your family." So I told Ray, "Mr. Morgenthal thinks we shouldn't talk on the phone so much." And he responded with this very clipped "*Oh*." So I kind of knew that he would do something. About a week later he sent Mr. Morgenthal a Xeroxed image of a pair of Mickey Mouse glasses that he'd found out on the beach collaged over one of his rabbit heads with the message: "Mr. Morgenthal, please give this to Robert Warner." I believe it was his way of saying that he felt the response to the phone calls had been a "Mickey Mouse" thing to do, you know, kind of a cheap, disposable thing. When he got it, Mr. Morgenthal handed it to me and said, "What do you think he's trying to say to me?" I said, "Gee, I don't know. He's curious that way."

The next day, I think, Ray called and identified himself as "Mr. Sassoon." That went on for a while, so everybody assumed I was fitting eyeglasses for Vidal Sassoon.

Did the two of you ever actually meet in person?

We met seven times. The first was when he came to the optical shop on a Saturday with his friend Toby Spiselman. She came in and said to me, "Ray is outside; could you come out to meet him?" I went out and said hello, and he was gone in like two minutes. This was about eight months into the conversation.

At some point, I asked if I could visit him, and he said, "No, do *not* come to Locust Valley. Do not come visit." He seemed to be very private and very much in control of his appearances—and disappearances—and I respected that.

One time I told him I was going to be at a garage sale in Great Neck at the house of my friend Judy's mother-in-law, who was moving to Florida. He called and asked me if I was going to have transportation back to the city, and I told him I would. So he said he would drop by. He pulled up in front of the house in his Volkswagen. You know, he's bald, he's got on his leather jacket and jeans and a white T-shirt—he looked kind of rough—and I introduced him to everybody. He was very cordial and shook hands with everyone, and then he said to Julie's husband, Steve, who was driving me back, "Can I put these things I brought Bob in your trunk?" And I said, "What things?" He proceeded to take out of the car 15 cardboard boxes tied with twine, labeled "Bob Box 1," "Bob Box 2," "Bob Box 3..." The smallest one was the size of a shoe box and the largest was maybe 12" by 15". And then he said, "I'll take you to lunch." He took me to a diner, and we had conversations about his visits with Joseph Cornell on Long Island. There were always stories about other artists. At one point he looked over at the next booth and said, "I think that's Robert Mapplethorpe's brother Edward." It was all very curious.

What was in the boxes?

Mostly found objects. They are a window onto the world of Ray Johnson in the '70s and '80s: everything from signed-and-dated empty toilet-paper tubes to a box that contained nothing but hundreds of envelopes that were addressed but never mailed.

Did you ever make it out to Locust Valley?

Only after he died.

You mentioned there was some awkwardness with your partner. Did you get a sense that he might have had some romantic interest in you?

No. It was always very playful, but I don't believe it ever stemmed from any serious affection on his part. I think it was more from a desire to have a correspondent. Although he did put me on the top of his "Locust Valley Biennale" list one year—I think it was 1989. He would always create these lists with the names of a wide range of people on them. This one had Shelley Duvall, Mary Hart from *Entertainment Tonight*, and a bunch of others. I was number one on the list that year, and Joseph, my partner, was number four.

This correspondence went from 1988 to 1995, right?

That's right, but the true heart of the correspondence was from 1988 to 1992. In 1992, I had a new partner, Joel Conarroe, who was the president of the John Simon Guggenheim Memorial Foundation, and Ray started keeping a bit of a distance then. Our correspondence wasn't as fluid and there weren't as many phone conversations. He would still call me at work, but he wouldn't call my home. Ray called Joel "Dr. Canary." One time, Ray telephoned Joel at the Guggenheim Foundation and asked him to photograph Bill de Kooning's mailbox. Joel had a house in the Hamptons, and so did de Kooning, and Ray gave de Kooning's address to Joel. Joel took the photo, and in return, Ray sent Joel a collage that was a combination of an author's photo of Joel from one of his collections of poetry and an old photo of Judy Garland. And when he got it, Joel said, "This is beautiful, but I don't know what it means." I said, "I'm sorry, I don't know what it means either." It was always a little mysterious, and often I think Ray was doing things as a sort of offhanded put-down.

My understanding is that by this period, Johnson had pretty well divorced himself from the art world—I remember reading somewhere that in these later years he refused to have any gallery representation, for instance.

Well, he would tell me about when collectors came from Europe and he would arrange to meet them in the supermarket parking lot in Locust Valley—he would just open his trunk and take out a box of things and sell work that way. Or he would rent a room at a hotel and let collectors buy things there.

Your question reminds me of something: I had a rubber stamp that said NO GALLERY AFFILIATION, and one time I stamped it on the outside of an envelope I sent to him. He called me and said, "That's not a good idea, because one day you might have a gallery affiliation. I don't think you should be doing that." So it was okay for *him* to have no gallery affiliation, but not okay for me to say anything about such a thing. He was very much a disciplinarian at times, and very direct about communicating when he didn't think things should be done in certain ways.

Toward the end of his life—this was probably early in 1995—somebody had left a dozen hand-blown eggs on his doorstep. And I asked him if he knew who it was, and he said "I think it's the teenage boys in the neighborhood that did it as a practical joke." So I sent a postcard to him saying "hand-blown by teenage boys," and he called, furious with me. "You shouldn't do that. My postman is going to read my mail and assume the worst about me." And I said, "Ray, it was meant to be lighthearted." "Then put it in an envelope!" He was so angry.

And yet a lot of the work he sent to you was fairly explicit and filled with sexual innuendo.

Yes, but it was usually stuffed into a business envelope. So sometimes I crossed the line. He was doing send-ups one year of the artist Sherrie Levine, so I thought I would send him a bottle of sherry, which I thought he would find funny. He called and said, "Do not send this. I won't open it. I don't appreciate it. I don't think it's funny. You've gone too far."

I have a specific question: What exactly is Nipple Beach? It is referred to a number of times in these letters.

That's a good question. The nipple comes up in a lot of Ray's work, not to mention his conversations. He told me he was out walking on a beach on the North Shore of Long Island near his house and he found a piece of wood that had the words *Nipple Beach* written on it in Magic Marker. He asked me, "Did you do that? Did you come to my beach?" And I said, "Ray, I don't even know where your beach is." "But how strange is that, that someone would reference nipples at my beach..." So he started calling it that. And he would often send me objects he found on the beach during his walks. He also peed my name in the sand at the beach. That stemmed from a story I told him about when I was a little boy and I was with my father and sister driving in a snowstorm, and I had to relieve myself. My father pulled over the car, and I got out and wrote *Sue* in the snow. And I got back in the car and told them that I only had enough pee to write *Sue* and not *Suzanne*, and that somehow struck a chord with Ray, perhaps because of Warhol's "Piss paintings." Fluids played a big role in his correspondence: urine, blood, semen, you name it.

Like I said, what he sent was always funny, kind of dark, and always engaging. Some people really felt it was too much. One time I was fitting the women who owned the store Tender Buttons with eyeglasses, and they said, "We were friends with Ray, but at one point it was just too much. We finally said to him, Please stop." And they never received anything else from him.

At the time you were having all of these mailed exchanges with him, were there other people doing the same thing?

I wasn't aware of too many others, except for Rick Yamasaki in Nyack. Rick, who was sending out mail art on his own, learned that Ray was the founder of mail art, and the dean, as it were, of the New York Correspondence School (NYCS), so he asked him if he could use the name "NYCS Nyack" for his correspondence, and Ray gave him permission. Ray would send letters to Rick to send to me. Not just letters, actually: objects, too. Like pieces of driftwood from the beach. He'd give them to Rick and then Rick would come into the city and drop them off to me at work. This is from Ray, he'd say, and he would hand me a piece of wood with *Please Give to Bob Warner* written on it. So it was all very ephemeral in a certain sense, but the objects had a weight to them, you know?

What about everything you sent to him? Does it still exist?

Well, that's an interesting question. Frances Beatty, who worked at Feigen Gallery and ended up being in charge of the Ray Johnson archives, called after Ray died and told me that his house, which was up for sale and needed to be cleaned out, was full of stuff, and they needed my set of eyes to help figure out what should be kept and what should go. So I went to the house, and in the basement, which had already been cleared out, I found a few little scraps from things I'd sent to him. I asked what happened to all of the things in the basement and one of the archivists said that everything had been packed up and was in a storage unit in Brooklyn somewhere. So I assume they're out there somewhere. It might be nice at some point to put all of the correspondence together, since we always dated everything we sent. Although Ray never liked chronology. He would take the *no* from the center of the word and elevate it above the *Chro logy*. I think he liked to work with a more back-and-forth sense of time than a linear sense of it.

You said things started to slow down in the early '90s; how much contact did you have with him before he died?

I talked to him three days before he died. At this point I was managing a shop across from the Whitney Museum, and I called him and said, "I haven't heard from you in a while. Is everything okay?" And he said, "Yeah, everything's fine." And that was the last I heard from him.

Did it ever occur to you that he might commit suicide?

No. I did receive something from another NYCS correspondent, Richard Craven, which was postmarked on January 13, 1995, the date of Ray's death. And I assumed that it was something Ray had sent to him to send to me. It was a "dead letter" notice from the post office, and there was a skull and crossbones drawn on it, so I figured that Ray had meant it to be his last mailing to me. But Richard insists that it was pure happenstance—that he just happened to post it on that particular day.

So there was no sense from him that he might be planning this final "performance" of sorts?

No. He loved doing performances, and he would always talk about them, like his rooftop events, or the helicopter flight over Manhattan with hot dogs, or the silhouette drawings. But I never assumed he would choose one of them for his passing. I didn't see it coming.

How many letters do you think you got from him all together?

I don't know. Hundreds. I was getting something once or twice a week, maybe three times a week in the beginning.

How would you define the relationship you had with him?

It was a conversation, I guess. But also a friendship, because there was the back-and-forth. I remember one time I asked him if he was friends with Bob Rauschenberg, and he said no, because "Bob doesn't really send much." I guess toward the end of our friendship there was less of that—I wasn't paddling back in the ping-pong match. Joel and I invited him to visit us in Amagansett, and he kept saying, Of course I'll come visit, but he never did.

Whatever it was, it was amazing. The whole thing seems like a puzzle that hasn't been completely finished. Like I'm halfway down Chutes and Ladders and thinking, What the hell...? And I think that's the beauty of it, in a way: There will always be a few pieces missing.

Good Friends

BY VICTORY MATSUI

Well, I'm pregnant. My breasts tender and my stomach in turmoil: I should have known. I call my boyfriend, my underwear still hooked around my ankles; I trip, pacing. I give him the facts. I'm sorry, he says, and then goes quiet. I'm impatient; I say something like, So, do you know where we can get a good crib? I listen to him gasp for breath and then remember that's just how he laughs. Not funny, he says in a tone I don't recognize. We don't know each other very well. We hang up, a relief.

I call my best friend next. What's up? she says. I'm getting an abortion, I say. You called me first? she asks, excited, and then: Sorry. A few seconds later, there's a knock on the window and there she is, standing on the fire escape; I open the window and let her in. I wasn't in the neighborhood, but I ran, she says. Let me do things for you, what can I do? I let her make my bed and brush my hair before I realize I should tell my other friends the news so that no one feels left out.

I make a few calls and the word just spreads; soon my doorbell is buzzing, insistent, like it's got something urgent to tell me. I open the door for some friends from elementary school. They have really changed since then. My boss arrives and shakes my hand. The guy from the corner deli shows up with a package of cookies. Each person tells me how sorry they are as they shoulder their way inside.

In the house, people start milling around, looking at the walls, picking up my things and dully inspecting them. They start meager little conversations. I try to play host; I put out every glass I own and open up the liquor cabinet. People seem disappointed, eyeing the cheap stuff, asking if I have any ice or juice or sour mix or even a small amount of tonic water. No, I say, I wasn't really prepared.

Some of the guests ask if they can invite friends over. I say sure, why not. Soon the house is humming with small talk, glasses clinking, friendly party sounds. I introduce myself to the people I don't know. They seem nice. I introduce my single friends to each other. Two of them go upstairs to make out. Use a condom! someone calls after them, and we all really laugh. I'm feeling pretty okay now. I hand out cigarettes and tell people to feel free to smoke inside, what the hell, and soon we're all swimming in a cloud of nicotine. We order in pizza with artichokes on top. We don't care about the extra money; we tip big, we enjoy ourselves.

It gets late and the collective energy drops right off, everyone lying around with their eyes half closed, holding their stomachs. I start preparing to put everyone to bed. I almost fall down the stairs carrying a tower of pillows. I squeeze a bit of toothpaste onto each person's finger and direct them toward the sink, a line of zombies. I go to my room to put on pajamas and come back to a living room full of bodies slouched on every chair, the sink full of dirty dishes, a sweat and sock smell in the air. Good night, I call; they mumble it back.

The next day we all wake up contorted and crusty-eyed. It's a beautiful day: The sun is glaring at us from the sky and the birds are practically trilling themselves to death outside. I have an early morning appointment at the clinic. I find my shoes in an empty pizza box. You don't have to come with me, I say to the crowd as I put on my coat. To be honest, I'm getting a little tired of these people. I don't offer them breakfast, but someone finds the cereal on top of the fridge and passes the box around. They plunge handfuls of cornflakes into their mouths. Of course we're coming! they shriek. We're your friends!

I walk to the clinic surrounded by the crowd. They push people out of our way on the sidewalk. Be careful, I say. At the clinic, they stand hawkishly around me as I sign in. There aren't enough chairs for everyone in the waiting room, so a lot of them just sit on the floor. Are you okay? they roar in unison. They clutch my hands. I'm fine, I tell them. We settle in; we wait.

Then the nurse calls my name and I have to let go and get up. Blood rushes to my head as I turn to look at the crowd. Now I feel very sad to leave them behind; they misunderstand this as sadness for where I'm going. We wave goodbye to one another.

The nurse takes me to a room and lays me down on a table lined with noisy paper. I put my hand on my stomach and try to feel what I know is there. I close my eyes. I feel a cup around my mouth and I breathe and breathe. I can do that, at least. I know I am breathing in; I know I am breathing out. Then a hand shakes me awake and I blink my way back into the world.

In an anesthetic haze, I make my way back to the waiting room. Half hidden behind the chairs are my friends—faces red, balloons lolling at their feet. Confetti flutters down on us: a surprise.

They swarm around me. Do you like this? they ask breathlessly. We didn't know what you would want because we're human, and we have limited predictive powers, and how does one person really know another person anyway?

I see what they mean. Whatever I say next, they'll just have to believe.

Improvisations

BY LONNIE HOLLEY

I Left You Alone (Definition of Why)

So lonely
So lonely, all alone
Missing you, missing you
All of your wonder
Missing you, missing you

I'm sorry
I'm sorry I left you alone
Went away in exploration
Just to show, show, show
How much I wanted to see
Oh, the stars, the stars, all the stars
Of wonder
I left you in search of
In search of
Fulfilling the need to have love
To have loved you

I'm sorry
You were the best I ever had
All of my wishes
Were all granted
Oh, you were my dreams of wonder
And I saw the making of life
Oh, I'm lonely

Even though I fell into wonder
Of education
I know you will be going around
And I know that the light of the universe will shine on you

And even though
The further I get away
I find myself in wonder
Wondering
After your turning
Something about being there
To hear the earthly bells ringing
From a baby, until I got grown enough to lose control
Can I come back?
Oh, wonder please
Can I come back
To where I was born to wonder?
To wonder
To keep on wondering
To the wonder degree

I Bet You Don't Know

I bet you don't know
I bet you don't know where I'm at
I bet you don't know where I'm coming from
Sometimes
I bet you don't know where I'm at
Or where I'm coming from

I bet you don't know where I
Where I'm coming from
But one thing we can learn to know
That we are all on Mother Earth together
And I ain't going nowhere
I ain't going nowhere

I bet you don't know
That we use the same old air
And water
Oh, and water
It makes its way down

In a sense of precipitation
It just rises to come back down
I bet you don't know
Where I'm coming from
'Cause some mistaken and say I'm gone
Gone for so long

When I sing
When I play
I bet
I bet you don't know
Where we are going
And I bet you can't calculate how much time you will spend
Wondering
Wonder when
Wonder when in the wind
Am I going to appear?

I bet you don't know
How much sun it takes for precipitation
To water a nation
And I'm betting you all haven't climbed all of you all's
mountains high
Snowcapped, covered to a humanly degree
I bet you don't know
What it's going to take
For us to see
Beyond the satellites
Beyond the making of technology

I bet you don't know

How many calculations
That it's going to take to add up all us data
Just to matter
For another baby
For another babe
For another baby
To be born

I bet you don't know
Where I'm coming from
Or how long it's going to take me
To get from here to there
Hey
I bet you don't know
My friends, how long it took for Juno to get to Jupiter
How much money did we spend?
To clear-ify reality
Or did I, somehow or another, leave it up to theory
Theorializing
Theorializing
Playing like this
Playing like that
Playing like I was a kid again
While I watch you all spin

I bet you don't know
Where I'm coming from
But I'm on the same Mother Earth going around
I'm sharing the same
The same ground
And I said, it may be our fault
But we don't want to act like we are a part of humanity
When it comes down to ugly
Tricky-ation
Or plans for future generations

I bet you don't know
And it is all right

If sweat got me blind and I can't see
If working, working, working, working
Till I sweat like this, just for thee
I bet you don't know
I bet you don't know
Where I am
Or where
Or where I'm playing from

Looking for All

Looking for all to be rendered
Looking for all to come about from my soul
Looking for all somewhere within

One day it all began
I was needing oh, so bad
All my goodness to show
And one day
One day
At my lowest
At most lowest, I know
That day I needed all
I needed all to show

Looking for all
Looking for all to show
I called upon myself
Called upon myself to do my best
Called upon myself
I was looking for all
All to be rendered
To be the truth
From deep inside
Of my internal self

And I told everybody
I say art is, to me
The A is for all
The R is for rendered
The T is for truth
The I is for internal
And the S is for self

Looking for all
All to be rendered
For the truth of humankind
From an internal place in me
From an internal place
That I called "myself"

Coming Back, Part 1

Coming back
Through the years
Light-years away
Coming back

Oh, from thousands of years, out into space
Humans, how deep it is

How deep the light-year
Just researching to tell
Looking through these windows of my brain's ability to see

Coming back
From the light-year

Machinery
Technically designed
Now, now, now

To digitally define
The distance between the spaces of time

Coming back
Humans
From the distance of spaces
If I can say anything that can help the human brain expectation
See, I know it's going to take; it's going to take to get there
Participation from every generation
Continuation of working forward, together

And nobody, nobody can tell
What it's going to take to make the struggle

Coming back
From the distance of time
To share and try to explain
Why humans, we need to look together
From the small, small space in the spaces
Of what we know as time

Coming back
I wondered what to play

Coming back, yes
From a human's journey out in space
From way, way long deep within

Coming back

Getting to the Mountaintop

See, I had sung about
How high do we need to go up a mountain
Before we can understand a sliding rock?
You know, I had been up and over so many mountains
You see, I know what this city been built off of
By way of the rail

But I want to say
That those mountains
That were struggled over
Had another side
See a lot of my friends don't understand
Getting to the mountaintop
I thought about Dr. King telling all humans
In this struggle
Y'all will get to the mountaintop
Getting, yeah, to the mountaintop
Had been a hard struggle

You know, me and my friends
Have been to the mountaintops
It's scary to look down the other side
We didn't know it would be so many years
Between
Yeah
This rock and that rock
And hey
And those stones
Hey
But I believe
If we work hard and we work on
Getting to the mountaintop
And when we get there
When we get there
Every one of our human brains
Has something to share

We can put it on a bird's wing
And let it fly
Way down low

See, I remember telling my friend
They said, Lonnie Bradley Holley
What do you think about getting to the mountaintop?
I said, some of them took an elevator
And then some of us used an escalator
And some of them caught a flight of lies along the way
But hey
Down and along
Down and along the way
Up the mountain
You'll find evidence
Evidence
Evidence of human struggle
Along the way

See, they say
Humans, y'all will get there
You'll surely get there
You'll get to the mountaintop
But will you be willing?
The Bible say
Will you be willing
To give all you've got
And come, go with me
Some lose so much along the way
Some get burned out
Tornadoes
Earthquakes
Tsunamis
And dying, dying, dying
By many diseases
Hospitals
Old folks' homes
And cemeteries

Is running over
My, my, my, my

And homeless
Homeless
Homeless
Homeless
Hey
Is laying close to the ground
Come on, please, say something for me
I need to be quiet for a minute and just listen
Say something for me, please

I Hear Birds

I hear birds
Outside my window

I hear birds whistling
Every day
Whistling together

Humans, I ask:
Oh, why can't we
Be like the birds?
In a kind of togetherness

I hear birds, humans, all the time
As we say take your hand together
They right outside my window

Do you know I saw them?
Flocking together
Gathering together
Listening together
Humans, why can't we learn from the birds?

All together, what they need
And season after season
I hear birds
I hear them
We are all students of Mother Universe
If we be like the birds
Keep all the water we need
Supply all the food we need
Circulate in season
My, my
Why? Why?
Please, please
Why can't we be like the birds outside my window?

All I'm trying to say, humans,
Is this earth needs us so badly
Needs us so badly
Together
Think about how birds build their nests
Birds work their nests over and over
Making them
When the baby bird comes along

I hear birds
Humans, please prefer to work together
No matter what the aftermath of every occasion be

Searching for Nostradamus

BY STÉPHANE GERSON

Nostradamus. The name reverberates, but the man occupies an elusive place in our collective imagination. He is not Lincoln, the heroic leader whom every generation fashions in its own image. He is not Billy the Kid, the historical figure who spawned a legend while remaining tethered to a particular era. And he is not Robin Hood, the fictional character whose story suffuses mass culture. Unmoored from history, legend, and mythic narratives, Nostradamus is everywhere and nowhere. We have all heard of him. A few among us are even aware that he lived a long time ago. But that is pretty much it.

Take the first episode of *The Sopranos* after 9/11. In one scene, Tony Soprano and his brother-in-law Bobby catch up over steak sandwiches. "You know, Quasimodo predicted all of this," says Bobby, referring to the worldwide turmoil. Tony points out that it was Nostradamus, not the fictional hunchback of Notre Dame, who made these predictions. "Oh, right, Notre Damus," says Bobby—to which Tony replies impatiently that Notre Dame and Nostradamus are different things altogether. Bobby is puzzled and Tony knows little more.

Bobby had heard the rumors that began circulating hours after the planes hit the World Trade Center. Nostradamus, they said, had predicted the attack: "Two brothers torn apart by chaos while the fortress endures. The third big war will begin when the big city is burning." The prediction was a fake, but it went around the Internet. Nostradamus became the leading search on Yahoo and one of the top three on Google. His *Prophecies* jumped to number one on Amazon.

My wife and I lived a few blocks from the towers, and we evacuated our apartment while they burned. Holed up in a hotel room with our sons and our dog, we dealt with this trauma as best we could. Like others, we participated in candlelight vigils and read the memorials posted in Union Square. Nostradamus offered something besides the public outpouring of grief: a mysterious appeal, an emotional pull that seemed to draw in many people. I knew little more about the man than Tony did, but I remembered one evening that Nostradamus had entered my life once before—in Brussels (where I grew up) during the early 1980s. *Paris Match* and other magazines were claiming that he had predicted the Soviet missiles about to flatten our homes. "Maximum Danger: Summer 1984!" Scary stuff. I wanted to quit *Paris Match* cold turkey. Instead, I read on, petrified, mesmerized, and slightly ashamed.

After 9/11, I approached the phenomenon with greater distance but no less wonder. Now a historian, I began digging—in dusty archives, obscure auction houses, databases, image banks, and too many libraries to mention. Nostradamus has inflamed the Western imagination for centuries, generating a staggering output of books, tracts, pamphlets, almanacs, novels, plays, paintings, engravings, songs, movies, and more. The phenomenon is based on ominous predictions and their interpretations across time. It speaks of the lure and mystery that dark, seemingly impregnable sentences hold for us. And it involves the shifting, elusive afterlife of a man who has escaped attempts to pin him down. Posterity has seldom worked in stranger ways.

We might say that the Nostradamus phenomenon has taken the form of a three-act play. During the Renaissance and ensuing decades, Europeans thought of Nostradamus as a doctor, a reputable astrologer, or a prophet, possessing recognizable skills and familiar features. Biography and respectability prevailed. The second act represented a change of inflection rather than a radical shift, but it was a significant one. While legends surrounded Nostradamus from the start, they became much more prevalent from the late 1600s on. Though never completely vanishing, the doctor and the astrologer faded behind the downcast soothsayer, the ghost, the sorcerer, the necromancer, the alchemist, and the magical wizard. Instability triumphed in this act, which lasted until around 1900. Then another change of inflection took place: Biography and legend survived in some quarters, but in the public imagination, Nostradamus became an ambiguous, free-floating name. Act III is where we are today.

1. The Biographical Moment

Nostradamus was the pen name of Michel de Nostredame, born in French Provence in 1503 and buried there in 1566. Tracing the man's path is easy enough during his lifetime: By the time of his death, he was an international celebrity. "One name alone is on everybody's lips," declared a Hungarian citizen in 1559, "that of Nostradamus, famous among all." Europeans visited him in his home in Salon de Craux, known today as Salon-de-Provence (near Aix), and they wrote him letters asking for personal horoscopes. More commonly, they consulted his predictions.

Contemporaries had not always heard about his childhood in a middling family of Jewish origin or his medical studies in Montpellier. They were not necessarily familiar with his wanderings across southern Europe or the potions he brought to plague-afflicted towns. But they knew about his almanacs and prognostications, which began circulating throughout Europe in the 1550s. They knew about the poetic prophecies (the quatrains) that he bundled in series of 100 (the *centuries*) and collated into a book *(The Prophecies)*. Many, like the Queen Mother Catherine de' Medici, also believed that Nostradamus had foreseen the death of French king Henri II during a jousting tournament.

If pushed to explain his predictive powers, contemporaries would point to his astrological skills, his prophetic inspiration, or his acquaintance with magic. He mentioned all three in his writings. In this respect as in others, Nostradamus was a creature of the in-between: a presence at the court who opted for the small Provencal town of Salon, a grandson of Jewish converts who was a devout Catholic, a man of reason who penned exuberant poetry, a recluse who became a celebrity. He moved between worlds in ways others did not, or at least not as visibly.

Still, Nostradamus came across as a learned astrologer, a student of the heavens and human affairs who inspired respect and trust. He was credible. Nostradamus marketed all of this on the covers of his publications, hoping to seduce readers while reassuring the authorities. Together with his publishers, he was one of the first to fashion his own image. People knew who the man was, what he looked like, and from where he drew his knowledge.

The earliest depiction of Nostradamus may well be a woodcut found on the cover of several of his almanacs and prognostications from the late 1550s. These cheap and flimsy chapbooks provided weather forecasts, calendars, fair schedules, predictions, and more. Nostradamus wears the sober robe and hat that were mandatory for doctors and astrologers. Austerity of dress suited hardworking, learned men who devoted themselves to healing bodies and souls. A picture of penetration and inspiration, the humanist is working in his book-lined study rather than preaching to excited crowds.

This image of the scholar in his study surfaced in all kinds of publications for decades after Nostradamus's death. This does not mean that it remained static. The sky and stars, for one, sometimes disappeared from publications geared toward a learned readership that might question the premises of astrology. Indeed, those who believed Nostradamus, or simply chose to publish him, had to address key questions. Could he really predict the future? If so, where did he find his inspiration? Was he a true prophet or an imposter? A good Christian or a satanic envoy? The stakes transcended the person of Nostradamus. They encompassed the cosmology of the world, the foundations of religious authority, and the political organization of society. Debates and justifications thus surrounded Nostradamus, and they revolved around a flesh-and-blood man. At this time, biography ruled.

Along with the image of the studious astrologer, another depiction of Nostradamus has resurfaced again and again: a formal three-quarter bust of a sober savant looking into the distance. The dress, the clipped beard, and the warm, resolute gaze are those of a Renaissance humanist. Inscriptions accompanying these representations make it even clearer that Nostradamus was a doctor, a mathematician, and a reputable soothsayer.

From the start, Nostradamus straddled high and low cultures. The unparalleled success of his almanacs led generations of publishers to use his name in order to sell their wares. They needed an authoritative name, a "doctor in physyck and astronomie" who would brand their publications as ancient and reputable in a competitive market. Commercial forces, too, can shape biography.

2. The Legendary Moment

While images from the biographical moment have survived to the present day, this era began to wane in the late 1600s. Nostradamus the man became obscured behind a plethora of legendary figures.

Various factors came into play. With the expansion of the print market, it became less common for publishers to include the occupation and place of residence of their authors in book titles. Likewise, astrologers and prophets lost some of their allure when reason and logic became normative values in the Western world. As the religious stakes surrounding *The Prophecies* decreased, determining Nostradamus's status and his relationship to Christian creed became less urgent. Critics of Nostradamus were now less concerned about this harmless loony than about his deluded (and no doubt ill-intentioned) interpreters, the superstitious spirit of the Renaissance, or the credulous populace that still believed such nonsense in later centuries. Consequently, supporters had less of a reason to defend Nostradamus by returning to his biography. In fact, these supporters could not agree whether he had drawn his powers from divine illumination, astrology, a sixth sense, or an understanding of human psychology.

Nor could people turn Nostradamus into a popular or national hero. He had become far too menacing, far too incandescent and successful, and far too removed from the public good to play that role. Intrigue, mystery, and fame—yes. Admiration, legitimacy, and glory—no.

An essayist once identified 22 components of any hero's life story. Nostradamus's included only three: He was chosen by God (according to some people), his demise was mysterious, and his children did not succeed him. This prevented his life story from generating a mythic narrative about humanity or the natural universe that would have kept his biography stable. Similarly, the man who circulated between realms belonged to everyone and to no one. As a result, no social group took it upon itself to preserve the contours of his biography. No class identified with Nostradamus or linked its self-worth with the man. No regime or political formation, no organized religion or intellectual school, made him its own.

Nostradamus has remained outside canons, academies, curricula, national commemorations, and pantheons. Memory distorts, but it can also preserve when a social group feels it has something to defend. This was not the case here. As Nostradamus the legend gravitated more and more toward politics, apocalyptic prophecy, and the market, the historical figure gave way to a strange cast of fictional characters.

Threat and consolation have always danced together in Nostradamus's universe, but his menacing quatrains eventually took on a life of their own. In the late 17th century, Nostradamus began his transformation into a prophet of doom, the first of many guises that shared little with the Renaissance humanist of the biographical era. This aspect of the legendary Nostradamus has survived to the present day—just visit your local supermarket checkout stand.

The same mix of fear and warning, of politics and commerce lies behind Nostradamus's transformation into a spirit or a ghost. Tradition has long held that the souls of the dead return to denounce injustice and our errant ways. Nostradamus, the creature of the in-between, easily morphed into a spirit that fraternized with the living and the departed. By the 17th century, some people believed in ghosts while others used them as satire or comedy. Regardless, the man was once again escaping history.

The culture industry ate Nostradamus up but had little appetite for biography. Legend took off in various directions as artists, writers, composers, and publishers refashioned him to suit their own dramatic needs. Readers and spectators could not tell what was true and what was not as they delved into worlds of fantasy and of comedy.

Consider Hippolyte Bonnelier's *Nostradamus: A Novel* (1834), which told a tale of dark predictions, unrequited love, rancor, and vengeance. In it, the Renaissance savant was also an alchemist, a somnambulist, and a spurned lover. Bonnelier's novel ends in Nostradamus's tomb, where the soothsayer had buried himself alive with his paramour—and the ashes of his former wives. He is discovered three decades later by visitors, who come upon his skeleton seated on a chair, quill in hand.

This tomb scene became a set piece in dramas and novels. It worked on many levels: as an entertaining subplot, a source of speculation, a way of exploring the relationship between life and the afterworld, and a means of mocking the phenomenon.

Writers drew from a legend that had surfaced by 1600 and then, like a voracious climbing plant, sprouted off in multiple directions. First came the (false) claim that Nostradamus's coffin had been buried half inside, half outside the church—a fine metaphor for a man who crossed boundaries. People then pored over a quatrain that had seemingly predicted the day of his death. From this, they inferred that he had prepared his tomb, written his own funeral service, or even buried himself alive in a vault with a table, paper, and ink. Some versions of the story claimed that he had cast a spell on those who dared to disturb his quietude. Others recounted the ghastly fate of the reckless souls who had disregarded the warning. Still others held that some visitors had miraculously survived and returned with new predictions.

While the initial story revolved around a real individual, new subplots plunged Nostradamus into the realm of necromancers, necrophiliacs, and the living dead.

Despite the ascendance of reason in 19th-century Europe, supernatural forces held their own through traditional avenues (horoscopes, prophecy, and fortune-tellers) and newfangled ones (magnetic somnambulists, mediums, and Spiritualist séances). All made up what was now called the occult. Contemporaries needed a way of talking about this—a shortcut, an emblematic figure whom they could praise, sell, or disparage.

By this time, Nostradamus was perceived as an old, bearded occultist who had probably existed at some time or another. He could be anything from a sorcerer to a necromancer to an interpreter of dreams. Nostradamus, said one English periodical, was a "prophet, or magician, for he might be called either, or rather both." Whatever.

Visually, Nostradamus now anticipated a Disney wizard, with his pointy hat and multicolored robe covered with hieroglyphs or esoteric symbols. One New Zealand newspaper dubbed him "the Merlin of France." This wizard surfaced in the early 18th century and became a stereotype in the 19th.

3. A Floating Name

Over the centuries, Nostradamus became that rare figure who lends himself to both literal and ironic readings, who elicits wonder, fear, belief, curiosity, and laughter—sometimes all at once. Yet his legacy has remained precarious and marginal, an intermittent phenomenon without legitimacy or consistency. Biography faded due to a dearth of committed advocates. Legend faced the opposite problem: There was a lack of natural limitations to contain the phenomenon as it grew ever more visible. Ubiquity and indeterminacy went hand in hand. Images of a prophet and a magician, of a prognosticator and a wizard, bounced off each other like bumper cars in an amusement park. Eventually, they obliterated one another.

This left only the name, articulated more loudly and freely than ever. "Little is generally known of Nostradamus but his name," intoned Baltimore's *Southern Magazine* in 1875. This change in inflection has played out over the past century. The name outpowered man and legend, ingesting and processing them both and then emerging as a brand, an alter ego, and a metonym for prediction, mystery, horror, and superstition.

One of the ironies of this story is that Nostradamus, with deeper anchors in history than most prophets, has become a floating signifier, summoning new meanings while pointing beyond itself. This does not make him pure abstraction. The name remains laden with the dust of distant origins, the scent of the unknown, and the shadow of a human being who must have existed. The man who circulated between worlds without belonging to any one of them in particular hangs between history and imagination, doubt and certainty, anxiety and mirth, past and future.

This works—at least for some people and at some points in time. In his classic takedown of modern astrology, the philosopher Theodor Adorno wrote that we have come to accept horoscopes simply because they appear in our morning paper. Results alone matter, not their origin. People "don't even see the sorcerers at work any more," explains Adorno. "They simply 'get the dope.'" Adorno was on to something. Our era is not only one of charismatic leaders and celebrities. Anonymous, impenetrable, media-fueled forces exert a strong pull as well. When a phenomenon combines the two, anything is possible.

This is why I did not blink when *Paris Match* tapped the name and the predictions while leaving the Renaissance astrologer in the background. This is why the name flashed across our screens atop forged quatrains after 9/11. And this is why Tony and Bobby did not need to settle their argument about Nostradamus and Quasimodo. They were both right.

Carter and the Kid

BY STUART NADLER

Carter Rawlings wasn't sure when he began to love the Kid.

He suspected it was somewhere near Omaha, where they'd fought for 5,000 men in an abandoned slaughterhouse that reeked of dung and lime. Carter had knocked the Kid cold with two right jabs in the third. He'd got him good on the chin, and just as they'd practiced, the Kid went down. Or perhaps it had happened in Portland, where they'd fought for 250 whooping shellfishermen in winter coats and wool hats. The Kid had put up a good fight then, just as they'd drawn it up, throwing three terrific crosses that clocked the champ on his right temple. Carter could take a punch, but for show, he knew how to bite the inside of his cheek, draw blood, and with the right amount of drama and grit, spit out a wet crimson stream onto the judge's table. It helped sell the crowd if they thought the fight was real.

Two years earlier, at Gleason's in Brooklyn, Carter had picked the Kid straight off the speed bag, tapping him with the edge of his weathered Everlast. "You interested in seeing the country?" Carter had asked that day.

The Kid's real name was Chuck McCally. He was a burly Irish 18-year-old from Bay Ridge with a fading homemade shillalah tattooed onto his left biceps. Together, they orchestrated six fights. Every seventh fight was the same as the first: McCally went down in the third. The only thing that changed was Chuck's name. In German towns, where the men loved to root against an Irishman, he fought as Connor "Shammy" Malloy, a Dublin street fighter. In the dark, rainy towns north of Boston, where the men hated to root for a German, McCally called himself Peter "Der Rock" Krauss, a hardheaded former Waffen soldier. They were foolish nicknames, Carter thought, but they helped sell tickets.

Tonight, outside of Chicago, where the Poles loved to hate a Russian, especially a big, mean one, McCally was going as Ivan Shamarov, a former KGBer. As the advertisement placards read, Shamarov was responsible for training young

Soviets to kill with their hands.

In every town, Carter went as the Champ, even though it had been 20 years since he'd knocked Sugar Sweets cold in Cleveland with a Hail Mary of a roundhouse. That punch, frozen in time by a photograph published in the New York *Daily Sun*, had made him famous. The Champ still remembered how the inside of his eyelids lit up as he stood up on the ropes in Cleveland, the magnesium flashbulbs popping one after the other like firecrackers on a holiday.

As their train pulled into Joliet, he couldn't take his eyes off the boy's face. They'd been on trains together for two years. He was sure that when they left New York for the first time, he hadn't felt the way he felt now. Under the yellow of the train lamplight, Carter saw what two years of fighting had done to the Kid's cheeks. When he'd met the Kid, his skin was smooth, wrapping around a pair of fantastically high cheekbones that had once prompted Carter to ask if he was part Navajo.

"What's the matter, Carter," the Kid said as the train passed through an Illinois grain elevator station. He spoke with the heaviest of Brooklyn accents.

"Nothing, Chuck," Carter said. "Just something caught my eye."

"Sure is snowing," the Kid said, parting the train curtains to see the sky over Joliet filled with snow. "It's gonna be hell getting to the hotel."

"We're staying with the Elks," Carter said, looking down at an itinerary. "In their dormers."

"We getting our own rooms? Getting mighty tired of bunking with you," the Kid said, a half smile on his lips.

Carter sucked down the rest of his Teacher's. Whiskey made his stomach burn. He lit a Viceroy. This was 1949. An older black porter, with skin like caramel, chalk-white teeth, and the salted gray stubble of a two-day beard on his chin, came around to their compartment, knocked on the glass window, lowered his face into view.

"Pie?" the porter said. "Got cherry, got apple."

Carter shook the old man away, looked back at the Kid. He'd busted his lips the night before. They'd fought someplace in Iowa where the wind had smelled like shit the entire time they were there. Someone said something about fields being fertilized. Carter didn't care: Shit on the wind was unpleasant no matter the cause. The Kid wore a cologne that he'd picked up in Tennessee, a scent called Old Smokey that smelled richly of whiskey and cloves and cinnamon. Iowa had smelled like shit for two days, and it angered Carter that he hadn't been able to breathe the smell of the Kid's neck. He thought that maybe he'd been too angry, and looking at the Kid's lip, opened in two places below the nose, he felt sorry.

"Got you good last night," Carter said, drinking more.

"It's nothing," the Kid said. He could take a punch. If they were really fighting, and not dancing, Carter wasn't sure the Kid would be able to walk now.

"Iowa sure was shit, huh?" Carter said.

"I kind of liked looking at it out the window," the Kid said.

"Well, it sure smelled like shit."

"You get with that hussy last night," the Kid asked. "What was her name? That redhead who came up on you outside?"

The Kid raised his eyebrows salaciously at the Champ. The girl called herself Lorraine. Carter paid her 10 dollars, let her kiss his face for 20 minutes, kicked her out, felt like hell, cried on the hopper while the Kid slept. "Sure did," Carter said.

"Good ride?"

"Best kind."

"Redheads," the Kid said, shaking his head wistfully.

"You know the drill for tonight, right, Kid?" Carter asked.

"Down in the second."

"Left uppercut, right jab, left cross," Carter said, giving the cue that signaled when it was time for the Kid to hit the mat.

"Carter," McCally breathed through a smoke. The Kid never smoked, just let the sticks sit on his lips. "I've been doing this for two years. I know the cues."

"You stepped out of line last night," Carter said.

He wasn't going to mention it, the slight deviation from their script that had confused him midway through the second round. Where the Kid was just supposed to stand and grapple with the Champ, he'd danced around, even turned to the crowd, tried to summon support from the Czechs in Cedar Rapids.

Carter let the Kid do his thing, then broke his lip.

"I was just having some fun," the Kid said.

"Don't."

"How about we have a go tonight?" the Kid asked, and for a moment Carter thought that he was saying something that he wasn't.

"How about we stick to the script."

They stepped off the train into the station yard in Joliet. Snowdrifts were piled high against the tiny signal house. Carter and the Kid were the only people who'd gotten off in Joliet, and they were alone in the snow. The Kid shivered in the cold. He'd lost his jacket in a poker game a week earlier in St. Louis. Carter took the fur off his back. His furrier, a crazed Jew in Brooklyn, had worked for weeks on the dyed-black mink that he wore. Carter slung the fur across the Kid's back.

"What's the big idea?" the Kid said.

"You're cold."

"I'm fine."

"It's snowing."

"It gets warmer when it gets to snowing," the Kid said.

"Where'd you learn that garbage," Carter said, beginning to shiver now himself.

"I went to school, you know. We's got school in Brooklyn."

The Kid looked funny with the fur draped around his back, like he was a child king somewhere, the fur his cape, the snow collected around the ring of his scalp his crown. They stood beneath the dim orange flood of a station light. As the train moved on to Chicago, the wheels screeched on the tracks. Carter lit another Viceroy, dragged on it hard, blew perfect rings into the winter. Joliet smelled like cow.

"What is it with the Midwest?" Carter said. "Every state smells like another animal."

"I kind of like this," the Kid said, breathing in. "Makes me hungry."

A week earlier, Carter had hurt the Kid's nose, and now as the young guy sucked air in through what had once been a perfect button of an organ, Carter saw that only one nostril worked. He reached out, put his cold hand on the Kid's face, stroked the soft skin there. The Kid stepped back, startled, and threw both hands in the air, ready to fight.

"Why you always touching me?"

"I'm sorry about your nose, Kid."

"We're boxers," the Kid said. "Noses get busted."

"I hurt you," Carter said, pulling on the Viceroy. He didn't put up his hands. If the Kid wanted to fight, he'd fight. A sportswriter once, 20 years earlier, had written a piece for the *Chicago Tribune* that said that Carter Rawlings could get hit by a truck, get up, and still win a fight.

"Take your fur," the Kid said, pulling the coat off his back, holding the heavy jacket between two pinched fingers as if the animals that had perished for its hide were still alive and squirming.

"You can have it if you want," Carter turned, feeling lousy, looking in his travel bag for his Teacher's.

They were interrupted by the twin, bright eye-lights of a Ford Tudor that pulled into the station lot. The car's engine hummed warmly. A thin man stepped out into the snow.

"Sure snowing like a motherfucker," the man said in a flat Chicago accent.

Carter always thought that the Chicago accent sounded too *nice*, and when people from Chicago cussed, he always felt that it sounded strange. Now that the Tudor's headlights were trained on the station lot, Carter saw that the driver had one arm.

"What happened to your arm?" Carter called out.

"Lost it," the man said.

They stood around for a while, watching the snow falling and listening to the warm whirring from the Tudor's choppy engine. Carter measured the short breaths that shot out of the Kid's mouth, tiny white storm clouds.

"Are we getting in, Champ?" the Kid asked, looking at the car.

The inside of the Tudor stank like rubber and car cleaner. Carter lit another Viceroy, blew smoke at the back of the driver's head. People in Chicago were always losing their arms, he thought. That's what all that beef cutting did to people, it cut up their arms and their hands and made them into hot dogs. He looked to his right, saw how pretty the Kid looked in the Joliet darkness. He wanted to just tell him, to just say to the young guy how pretty he thought he was, but the driver started to talk.

"Saw you 10 years ago fighting against that kraut, whatever his name was," the driver said.

"Jergens," the Champ said.

He'd fought Vic Jergens in Chicago twice. The first time he'd broke the German's face into three pieces. The second time, he'd been paid $2,000 to throw the fight. He went down in the second, lost his belt, went home to Brooklyn a hero. The punch hadn't even got him clean. That still burned him.

"How'd you end up losing to that bastard," the driver said.

"How'd you end up losing your arm?" Carter replied.

Beside him, the Kid shook his head and hissed through his teeth. Travel with anyone long enough and sooner or later anything will sound annoying. Carter had the fur in his hand, and he stroked the jacket with his fingers. He'd heard once that it took 30 little critters to make a coat like his. A shame, he thought.

"I had tickets for when you went up against Johnson," the driver said. "I missed it, though. My girl was in labor."

"That was a good one," Carter said.

"I listened to the radio. It was like I could feel when you downed him in the first."

"I bet," Carter said.

"How long did it take, that fight?"

"Ninety-two seconds."

"Is it true? Was he out cold even before he went down, Champ?"

"Don't call me Champ," Carter said.

Out the window, Carter saw the buildings of Joliet cut out against the sky, the entire place like a tombstone city. The Kid closed his eyes, tried to get some rest. He couldn't sleep on trains; he was always fidgeting and complaining. The driver drove like he had one arm, the Tudor all over the road. Carter rolled down the window, let the snow into the car.

"Look, it's like a snow globe," he said, trying to rouse the Kid.

"Close the goddamned window, Champ."

"Why's he can call you Champ?" the driver asked.

"How do you drive with one arm?" Carter asked.

"Got perfectly good knees," the driver said.

The Tudor took the turns hard, and the Kid slid across the bench seat into Carter's chest. He wanted to hug the Kid, smell his neck, put his hand in his hair. When they got back to Brooklyn, he wanted to pay a real artist to fix the shit tattoo the Kid had on his arm.

"Are we gonna get our own rooms?" the Kid asked.

"You'll like it here. The Elks got nice bunking," the driver said.

"Yeah?" the Kid said.

"Got a pack of good girls, too." The driver said, laughing. He tapped the steering wheel with his one hand.

An hour later they were at the bar, and every man in the place was around the Champ, patting him on the back, asking him how it felt when he knocked Sugar Sweets cold in Cleveland. He'd been 19 then, and now, at 39, he couldn't remember much of the fight. In 20 years, he'd been hit in the head so many times that he didn't know what was a memory and what was a story that he'd read somewhere, in some newspaper, in some rat hotel in the middle of nowhere. All he did remember about the fight against Sugar Sweets was how scared he was as he walked into the ring. Sugar Sweets was a giant, and covered in sweat, the man looked like a piece of wet granite. The punch that downed Sweets, the hook that made Carter Rawlings the champ, was a gift, he always told people.

"It just came up from somewhere," he said to the Elks, so drunk that to light his Viceroy he had to steady one elbow on the bar so that he didn't light his nose on fire.

"From heaven," a man said.

"Or from hell," a fat Elk said. "That was a devil's punch."

"That buck just fell," another Elk said.

"Don't talk like that," Carter said, finally lighting his smoke, turning around to see the short Elk who'd just spoken. Carter had nothing against blacks and didn't like people who did. He stood up off his stool, swayed from left to right. "Don't ever talk like that around me."

"Sorry, Champ," the Elk said.

"You're squirmy," Carter said, grabbing the small Elk by the shirt collar.

The small man was scared, his hands shaking and spilling beer onto the floor.

"I guess," the small Elk said.

"You got something against coloreds?" Carter asked.

The small guy didn't know what to say, shook his head, looked for his friends.

"Say that you don't got no problem with no coloreds," the Champ said.

"I don't got no problem," the guy said.

At the bar, McCally had a derby hat pulled down over his face. In every city they traveled to, it went like this. The Kid had to sit away from Carter, his face hidden so that no one caught on to the act. Now, the Kid stood up and walked to break up the fight. Tomorrow he'd be the Russian again, but now, he spoke with his thick Brooklyn tongue.

"Put him down, you dumb guinea," McCally said, slugging the Champ in the arm.

Carter felt the punch in his stiff arm. He didn't know why he could take a punch and why others couldn't. A good punch stung him like a dog's bite, but it never hurt. Even Sugar Sweets, whose punches had wrecked better fighters than Carter, wasn't able to hurt him. When Carter's dad was alive, he'd said that some men were just built for fighting, while others were made out of glass.

Carter and the Kid sat at the bar. The bartender was a Pole and had pretty blue eyes that Carter noticed. He'd never been with a man before. Once or twice he'd been with a girl, but they were paid women, loose and vulgar. When he had enough to drink he'd find something nice to look at in a man, like the Pole's great blue eyes, like wet spots on a frozen lake.

"I miss Janie," the Kid said.

"Yeah?" Carter said, looking at the Kid and his split lip.

"It's been two years," he said.

"Yeah," Carter said.

"You're drunk," the Kid said.

"How do you know?"

"Cause you don't say shit when you're drunk. You just mutter."

"You got your own room in this shithole," Carter said, spitting onto the bar. "You happy, Chappy?"

The Pole stared at Carter, and for a moment, the Champ was set to tell him how pretty he thought his eyes were. At the back of the room, two Elks were singing a song in another language. One had an accordion. Accordions made Carter think of the circus.

A year ago, a man from the circus had asked him to come around the country with his elephants and his freaks. They wanted some fighters to entertain the men before the animals came out and jumped through flaming hoops. The man wore a black hat and a good suit. He was the only person who ever knew that what he and the Kid were up to was a scam. The man from the circus was full of compliments, said that he was impressed by their stories. Carter still had his business card in his wallet.

"I want to go up and call Janie."

"It's late in New York," Carter said.

"I'll see you in the morning," the Kid said. "Get some rest. You're drunk."

The Kid got up to leave, putting a dollar bill down on the bar. He always left good tips, and the Pole thanked him. Carter sat for a while, dragged on his smoke. The Pole looked at him, and Carter felt his cheeks turn hot. He thought he ought to be tough, so he blew smoke in the Pole's face.

"What are you looking at?" Carter barked.

The hallway of the Elk's lodge was dark and smelled like dirty linen. Carter bumped into the wall when he walked. It felt to him like the floor was moving beneath his feet. He found the Kid on the hallway phone. When he came into the hallway, the Kid turned around, slammed down the earpiece of the phone.

"She's not in?" Carter said.

"No," the Kid said.

"It's late in New York," Carter said.

"I know."

"What's your woman up to this late in New York?"

The Kid slumped against the wall. Carter thought that the Kid was going to cry. He walked over, put his hand on the Kid's shoulder. They stood beneath a lit sconce. Joliet was a cold place. Janie, the Kid's woman, was a right slut, he thought. She'd tried to come on to him the first time he'd gone to the Kid's tiny apartment in Bay Ridge.

Under the light, the Kid's face was smooth. The dark stubble of the Kid's beard made him look good. The Champ leaned in, put his lips against the Kid's lips, felt the sandpaper of his unshaven face. He'd never kissed a man. It felt right to him. The Kid struggled, his hands beating back Carter's face, hitting him first with an open hand, and then, his hands clenched, with bare-knuckled punches.

"Just let me," Carter said, feeling like crying.

"No," the Kid said.

"You look scared."

"You're a queer, Champ?" the Kid asked.

"Don't be scared," Carter said, wanting to kiss him again.

With one hand, the Kid opened the door to his room. Carter took a step into the room, but the Kid stopped him with a right jab to the face, his fist landing square against the Champ's nose. Carter didn't feel the punch. One of the singing Poles came up the stairs, startling Carter. The Kid slammed the door to his room.

The ring in Joliet was brand-new, the ropes freshly pulled, the springs in the corners tight, the mat hard and chalky. As the announcer called out his name, Carter slipped under the ropes. Under his robe, he was sweating. He never smoked on fight night, and he wanted a Viceroy. Carter was announced as the Heavyweight Champion of the World, even though he'd fought never as a heavyweight, but as a middleweight, and even though he hadn't been champ for 10 years. He looked out at the crowd. Over the years, he developed an ability to estimate how many people were in a crowd, and looking over the ropes, he judged that there were 10,000 screaming men waiting for him to batter the Kid. They were fighting in an old meat processing plant. There'd been huge, garish bloodstains on the floor of the locker room. A cow's blood was darker than a man's.

He looked at the Kid. When they'd announced the Kid as Ivan Shamarov, the crowd had thrown bottles into the ring. Usually, before a fight, the Kid would look over at him, nod his head, give a sly grin. Tonight though, the Kid looked out at the crowd, hitting his gloves together.

The way that the fight was supposed to go down was simple, and for two years, they'd never had a problem with the design. As their fights went, it was one of their easiest. When the first round started, they were supposed to rush from their corners and grapple in the center of the ring, wrapping their arms around one another the way a pair of wrestlers might. After a minute, Carter would let the Kid take whatever punches he wanted to throw. At the end of the round, he would level the Kid with a right hook. The fight would end in the second round. There was a three-punch cue: left uppercut, right jab, left cross.

When the judge rang the bell, the Kid darted from his corner, his right hand leading his left. The Kid was a southpaw. Carter had never had any real luck against southpaws. He always ended up taking a lot of damage, and as the Kid came out running, Carter had to duck from the barrage.

The crowd went silent as he got backed up into the corner. He tried to meet the Kid's eyes, but the punches came too quickly. The Kid grunted through his jabs; he hit good. Carter wanted to tell him that he hadn't meant to upset him. He stepped out of the corner. The Kid grunted, ran at him again. Carter was old but could still move, and as he stepped aside again, this time like a matador, he threw a hook that clocked the Kid on the back of the skull. The Kid toppled on the mat. Carter was almost 40, but he could still throw.

The Kid shot up on a four count, looked at the Champ, cussed at him.

"I'm done with you, queer."

"Fine," Carter said.

"I thought we were friends," the Kid said. "I didn't know you was sick."

As he said this, the Kid spit blood onto the mat. Carter saw that he'd made him bleed. He felt ill at the sight.

"I'm not sick," Carter said.

"I don't ever want to see you," the Kid said.

"You've ruined everything," Carter said.

When the fight started again, he backed the Kid into his corner. As a young fighter, he'd always tried to corner his opponent, the corner being a snare that a weak fighter could never extricate himself from, like a small mink in a trap. Carter thought of his fur coat.

"Why didn't you just take the fucking mink," he yelled.

Boxing him against the ropes, he saw the Kid's eyes open in fright. No fighter, however strong, wanted to be caught in a corner against Carter Rawlings.

"I didn't want your lady coat," the Kid said.

Carter had grown up a fighter, the son of a boxer, the grandson of a bare-knuckler. The past two years, circling the country, had been a charade born from boredom. They'd gone from Brooklyn to Seattle to El Paso and up now to Joliet. He didn't need the money, or the blood, or the thousands of drunk men cheering his name. At night, after he was done drinking, he always knew the truth: that he had nothing to go home to, no wife, no kids. For a while with the Kid, he'd been happy, the two of them traveling on trains like Lefty and Leadbelly, a strange marriage made up of blood and boxing and whiskey.

In the corner, he hit the Kid the way he'd first learned to hit a speed bag, his hands quick and strong and lethal. Every punch came down on the Kid's head like an eight-pound hammer against a tenpenny nail. The Kid's face opened, blood moving in a slow current from his crushed eye socket down into his mouth.

Seeing the Kid's face busted open, Carter wanted to cry. He spoke through his punches, told the Kid that he had a pretty face. "You were so pretty," he said, wrecking the Kid's teeth, his chin, the two cheekbones that sat beside his nose like twin china teacups. "You shouldn't have made me ruin it." Carter's right hook broke the Kid's nose. The ref stepped in, and Carter took the old guy down with an uppercut. The crowd loved blood. All crowds love blood.

Outside the hospital in Joliet, the snow still hadn't stopped. Carter spit blood into a snowbank. He'd bit the inside of his lip, needing to feel real, actual pain. The spatter of his blood in the white snow made him think of the way the Kid had fallen to the mat, blood pooling under his head as if a bullet had entered his skull.

Carter smoked, pulling from the Viceroy as if inside the chalky stick there was a secret to be had, and if by dragging on the smoke hard enough, he'd find it. The Teacher's in his left hand was almost empty, but he wasn't drunk. The wind came against his skin and made him wish that he'd died.

A doctor came out, his stethoscope around his neck like a piece of jewelry.

"Are you his friend," the doctor asked.

"I'm his best friend," Carter said. "Is he dead?'

"Not yet," the doctor said.

"Not yet?" Carter said, gasping, his mouth open, his breath greeting the cold air like a rank cloud of cigarette smoke.

"It's his skull," the doctor said. "I'll come out and let you know if anything changes."

Outside of the hospital, Carter waited and smoked and drank. Joliet smelled like beef, and now that he had the Kid's blood caked on him, splattered from his split head, it smelled like Brooklyn, too.

Every now and then, a small Polack with bright blues came to shake the Champ's hands.

"Good fight," one man said.

"Thanks for lashing that commie bastard," another said.

"Yeah," Carter said. "Thanks."

A newspaperman in the third row would later write that he feared for the challenger's life just before the Champ tired, turned away, and let the Kid fall to the mat. A young father in the audience, gifted with a new Canon camera, took the photograph that ran in the *Chicago Tribune* the next morning, the Kid motionless on the mat, blood under his head, his body splayed like a murder victim. Feathers McGonagall, the *Tribune*'s boxing writer, wrote that the only thing that was missing “was the chalk outline around his body, for this was not sport, but a crime.”

By then, Chicago had learned that the Kid was not, as had been advertised, a Soviet, but a Brooklyn boy, an Irishman named Chuck McCally. When asked for a statement, Carter Rawlings was quoted as saying that he hadn’t known the boy was not a Russian.

“I barely knew the kid,” Carter said.

The Lifer

INTERVIEW WITH LARRY AUERBACH

According to Wikipedia, "It's possible that Larry Auerbach directed more dramatic television than any other American director (approximately 3,000 hours)." Nearly every one of those hours was devoted to soap operas, so it might also be fair to assert that no other person knew daytime drama as well as he did. Auerbach was justly rewarded for his expertise: The director received a Daytime Emmy award in 1985 for his work on the ABC soap *One Life to Live* and was also the recipient of the Directors Guild of America's Robert B. Aldrich Service Award in 1991. In 2004, the DGA named him an honorary life member, a designation he shares with an elite group of filmmakers that includes Charlie Chaplin and Frank Capra. Auerbach, who died in 2014, offered *Esopus* readers his recollections of—and frank opinions about—working in soap operas for nearly a half century when I interviewed him in 2010 for our issue devoted to television, *Esopus 15*.

Tod Lippy: *From what I understand, you pretty much jumped right into broadcasting in Chicago after a stint in the army and a degree from Northwestern University's speech school.*

Larry Auerbach: Well, I graduated in June of 1947, and in January of 1948, I got a job writing copy at a radio station in Burlington, Vermont. That was 40 hours a week for 40 bucks, subsidized by the government because I was a veteran. One of my instructors at Northwestern had been Art Jacobson, a moonlighting executive from NBC Chicago. In the spring of 1948, NBC needed somebody to cover the daylight-saving-time network. I had kept in touch with Jake, and he sent me a telegram asking if I'd be available for a summer job at NBC. In 1948, most of the country was still on standard time; it was only the metropolitan areas that were on daylight-saving time. So everything was recorded on great big discs and played back an hour later to the standard-time network. This was done out of

Chicago, and they needed somebody to be out there and supervise the process, since those big discs gained or lost a second or two every half hour. Because the NBC chimes controlled the network, everything had to be exactly on time. So an announcer—often it was Hugh Downs—and I sat in a control room, and at the proper time I would give Hugh, or whoever was assigned, a cue, and he would push the button to ring the chimes. At the end of that summer there was an opening at NBC, and they kept me on. Eventually, Jake went over to television and brought me with him. It's a classic example of being in the right place at the right time.

This was just as TV was beginning to find its footing, right?

Oh, yeah. This was 1950, what is now considered the golden age of television. Dave Garroway was doing his program in Chicago, with Bob Banner directing. Dan Petrie was directing *Studs' Place*, with Studs Terkel, which I was the stage manager on. And I was the first director of *Mr. Wizard*, which was a science program for kids. It was a wonderful time, and everything was live. What you got on the air was whatever you had on camera in the studio, and that worked very well. If there was an error, then there was an error. You had to cover it the best you could.

Hawkins Falls, *which I'm pretty certain is considered to be the first television soap opera, was being produced in Chicago around that time. Did you work on it at all?*

Ben Park was the producer and director on that, and I was one of several stage managers. As a matter of fact, we actually did some location work for it, which was very unusual at the time because the equipment didn't really facilitate it.

How did you get from Chicago to New York?

My father was very ill, so I took a leave of absence and came home to New York. While I was here I thought I would look for work. I went to see Dan Petrie, just to chat, and he said that Roy Winsor, whom I had worked for in Chicago, was now in New York and had been made head of television and radio at an important ad agency, the Biow Company. He said, "You ought to go see Roy; I hear he's going to do a couple of soap operas." So I went to see him, and he put me in touch with the guy who was going to be producing *Love of Life*, a guy by the name of Green. And I wrote him a letter thanking "Mr. Grey," and he didn't like that much, so I didn't get to do the pilot. *[laughs]* As it turned out, they weren't happy with the pilot, so Roy called me one day and said, "You're starting next week." We went on the air with the first show on September 24, 1951, and our last show was in January of 1980—28 years later.

When Love of Life *started, each episode was 15 minutes, which was the same length as the radio soap operas that had been around for some time.*

That's right. And they were in black-and-white.

There is one of these from 1953 available online, and I had a chance to watch it the other day. In it, the show's protagonist, Vanessa Dale, is told by Beanie, her "bad" sister Meg's son, that the man she is interested in is being pursued by Meg.

[laughs] Oh, you really watched.

I found the economy of means to be really compelling: three short scenes, two characters, each taking place on a different, but very basic-looking, set.

Actually, we often had more than two people in a scene, but the budget allowed for only a certain number of performances per week. Therefore, if, say, Vanessa's contract guaranteed the performer three performances a week, that had to affect how many other people we could cast during the week. I don't think the writers actually had to count, but someone would keep track to make sure the budget didn't get out of whack.

We shot the show at the Liederkranz Hall, which had originally been the headquarters for a German singing society, so it had good acoustics. CBS took it over in the '40s and made radio, or perhaps recording, studios out of it. Later on, they put four small television studios in there. It was on 56th Street between Park and Lexington, next to the Library for the Blind, but it has since been torn down.

There were two studios on the first floor up the stairs from the street, and two studios on the floor above it. Every piece of scenery and furniture had to be hand carried in by the stagehands. And there was only one studio in which you could fit a car, and it had to be winched in up a ramp. So if I wanted to use a car, I had to do it at a time when that studio wasn't being used for *Search for Tomorrow*, which was another soap Roy Winsor had started for Procter & Gamble. Later on, he came up with *Secret Storm*.

My understanding is that American Home Products basically created these two shows—much like Procter & Gamble had created Guiding Light*—as a vehicle for selling its products.*

That's essentially right. American Home sponsored them, but hired Roy to create them.

The episode I watched opened with a Chef Boyardee ad, and then, at the end, there was an aspirin ad, I believe for Bayer—

No, it would have been Anacin.

That's right. So these types of ads for American Home Products always bookended every episode?

There were two 30-second and two one-minute commercials in every 15-minute program.

At this point, who actually owned the show? CBS, or American Home Products?

Basically, American Home owned it and just bought the time from CBS to air the show. Eventually, CBS licensed it from American Home—as I recall, American Home didn't want to carry the full weight anymore, and I believe CBS eventually owned it all and sold off commercial spots.

Can you describe a typical day's worth of production?

Well, first I would get the script. I would go over it, and then we would have a lot of rehearsal, which doesn't happen anymore. We would start rehearsal in the afternoon of the day before. It would take three hours, as I remember, and we would schedule the performers to come in as needed—if someone was in every scene, they'd be there all afternoon; otherwise, they'd be there just part of the time. After we had that rehearsal and had done the physical blocking, I would go away and work out all of my camera positions.

How many cameras were you using?

Three cameras. And no zooms in those days. Each camera had four lenses. So I would notate all of my camera stuff in the script, and then we'd come in the next morning and have another hour of dry rehearsal in the morning. After that, we'd go into the studio and have a camera blocking, a run-through, and a dress rehearsal, and then we'd air the episode. That was the preparation when we had a 15-minute, black-and-white, live show. And when it went to a half hour in the '60s, we kept pretty much the same schedule, but if I remember correctly, by then we had gone to videotape, so we were no longer shooting live. And then the next step was color, in the late '60s.

How many writers were working on the early episodes?

The first writer for the show was John Hess, and he did it all himself. My relationship with him was somewhat removed, because the producer, who worked in the office and worried about the budget, was the one who always worked with the writer. I would see John at a meeting or something—I might have some suggestions here and there, but my contact was limited. I'm sure you know about Irna Phillips. She was considered the doyenne of soap operas, and she had originally come out of radio. Basically, every word that flowed from her pen was gold, and you didn't dare touch it, because you'd turn it into lead. Fortunately, I never had to work with her. As I'm told, Irna would sit and watch each show, and as soon as it was off the air, the phone in the control room would ring and she would present her notes, comments, and criticisms to the director. I wouldn't have been able to put up with that, and I didn't have to, fortunately. There was some talk at one point that Roy was going to bring her in to do *Love of Life*, and I said to him, "You'll have to stand between her and me."

I felt there was a difference between the written word and the spoken word, and sometimes it came out of the actor's mouth better if we changed a word or two or four. I felt that as long as we kept the writer's intention—kept the story going per the outline—if it came out more realistically or believably, it was worth doing. So to that extent, I've had some input into the writing. I've often felt that writers should sit there and read out loud what they wrote. I mean, this is a verbal medium, after all.

But the writer was never on the set?

No. It was just the actors and the stage manager.

How about you?

I directed from the control room, with monitors for every camera. During rehearsal I might very well go out onto the floor and talk to one of the actors. Between takes, which is something we had the luxury of only when tape became available, if there was anything that wasn't working, or you wanted to adjust a movement or something, I could either ask the stage manager to convey it to the performer or go out on the floor myself. But generally speaking, communication between the performer and the director would be through the stage manager, who was always on the set. And there were usually two stage managers on every show after the shows went to an hour. The first stage manager was more or less in control of the floor, and the second would help out with the extras or the heavy action scenes, or wherever needed. On *Love of Life*, we had only one stage manager.

Can you describe the control room for me?

There were monitors for every camera, and a technical director who was doing the switching, an audio man responsible for monitoring the sound, and a video guy handling the video signal from the cameras. There was also an associate director who would sit to my right and make notes, since he or she was doing most of the editing. And then there was a production associate sitting in the back, doing timings and taking down my notes to performers, particularly during a rehearsal. I would spew out note after note after note, which the poor PA would have to write down, and then between rehearsal and taping, I'd go out to the floor and the PA would have the notes, which we would then pass along to each actor. You know, "You turned just a little bit too soon." And of course, in the early days, when you had to get on the air and off the air, or even when you were trying to make the taped material meet time constraints, it was very important for the PA to keep you apprised of time. You had to be very aware of scenes speeding up, which meant the show would be short, or stretching, which meant you'd end up with too much material. Today they don't care about that; they just cut it. When it was live, obviously, timing was essential. If you didn't finish, you were finished!

It sounds like you really thrived on these limitations, which sound pretty formidable.

Yeah. Because the pressure to get it done was stimulating. You had to deal with what you had to deal with. If I had a camera go out, I'd have to work around it. That's number one. Also, when you got done, you were done. Once we started taping shows, and the shows became more expensive to produce, supervision increased. It was no longer about getting it done. It was a slog, because there were people looking over your shoulder constantly. The material became much more complicated, and there was a lot more of it. Today, it's just awful—the days can get very long, and in some ways, you're basically just a traffic manager. So, yes, I would like to have kept it to the "shoot live, do it, walk out of here and start again tomorrow" model.

You know, when I first started out, I thought, "I'd like to go to Hollywood and make a movie." After I'd directed soaps for a number of years, though, all I could think to myself was, "I could never work that slowly." I just couldn't do it. Spend four hours on one shot, screwing around? Do it, get it in the can, and let's move on. And I was happier when I was the only director.

From what I understand, that's pretty unusual for soap operas.

That's right. I was the only director for a long time on *Love of Life*. In my case, it changed pretty much when we went to color. And the reason it changed was that Roy Winsor used it as an excuse to get me a raise. He went to the sponsor and said, "This is much too complicated now with color; we can't ask Larry to do this five days a week. We're going to give him the same money and he'll do only four days a week." So that's how I got a second director—as a raise. *[laughs]*

Eventually, when CBS took over the program and we began to have more supervision, the producers felt that I should do three days a week and somebody else should do two.

How did the CBS takeover manifest itself on the set?

Well, they were present. They were looking over your shoulder; they were making suggestions. As long as you had people who had been in the business, who were competent, that could be helpful—however annoying. But when you began to get people who hadn't been in the business, who came from God-knows-where, and who thought that as long as they were there, they had to do or say something, it was terrible. I had one unpleasant so-called executive producer who had come from Hollywood and film and didn't know the first thing about "live on tape" television—it was awful.

What did they want from you and the show?

They wanted to keep their job. I always felt they wanted to be a director but didn't want to take the risk of sitting in the chair and having to actually do it. It was a lot easier to say, "Oh, that shot's no good. Take it from over there." Sometimes it was just easier to say okay rather than stand there and argue about it. They came in without having done the preparation and with this preconceived idea that they had better say something today.

But didn't American Home have suggestions in the earlier days too, or were you and the writer given pretty much free rein?

I don't think American Home ever got involved. They left it to Roy Winsor and the Biow Company, and later just to Roy when he had his own company. All they were interested in were the numbers. The head writers did do a long story outline. Later on, they did a week's outline, and then when we began to have sub-writers, they would do even daily outlines. But it was basically Roy and the writers—John Hess, Don Ettlinger, or whoever—they all sat down and worked out these story arcs and then would work from that. American Home really was interested in only two things: how much it cost and what the audience was like. They were a huge company. They were a major, major advertiser, just like Procter & Gamble. Not as big, but the same idea. And they owned the program, which doesn't happen today.

That reminds me of something else you don't see anymore: In those days, you couldn't have competing products in the same 15 minutes of advertising. Today, you know, a Chrysler ad is followed immediately by a Ford ad.

Speaking of ads, that early episode I saw seemed to run uninterrupted from start to finish. Were there were no commercial breaks when the shows were only 15 minutes long?

Actually, there were breaks for commercials. You must have seen an edited version. There were the four I mentioned earlier—two 30-second ads and two one-minute ads in each episode, and in the early days, they were done live in the studio. We had a commercial set also. Don Hancock, who was the announcer, would do a commercial for Anacin and a commercial for BiSoDol or whatever the agency scheduled. Don would hold up the product and then give his pitch. I'd have to break one of my three cameras from the drama scene to get to the commercial set, and once that was underway, I'd have to get the product "beauty shot" on a second camera, then reverse the procedure to get back to the story material.

Were any of these products ever "placed" into the actual show?

Interesting you should ask that. Not the products, but we had giveaways. You could send in a box top from Anacin with 25 cents and get, for example, a packet of seeds from Mother Dale's garden. Suddenly American Home would decide they wanted to give a premium, and the writer would have to include that in the story. One time they decided they were going to give away perfumed earrings. They were little tiny cagelike earrings that had small pieces of cotton in them, and you would put perfume on the cotton balls. For a box top and 50 cents, or whatever, viewers could get their own pair. So Meg was in jail, and her boyfriend brought her these wonderful earrings, which of course we would have to get a beautiful close-up of. As a matter of fact, I was told that even at 50 cents, American Home made money on the deal. *[laughs]* That kind of thing happened maybe twice a year.

Three different actresses played the role of Vanessa Dale in Love of Life *over those 28 years it was on the air. I know this is a fairly common phenomenon on soaps, especially long-running ones. Was that difficult to navigate around as a director?*

Like everything else in those days, you just dealt with it. When Bonnie Bartlett was unable to come to a contract agreement with Roy Winsor, we shot her going to bed on Friday, and on Monday, we shot Audrey Peters waking up in the same spot.

Speaking of actors, Love of Life *had a pretty incredible roster of talent on the show over the years, including Warren Beatty, Roy Scheider, Christopher Reeve—*

Well, Christopher, who was at Juilliard at the time, actually played a regular character on the show: Vanessa's son, Ben. Beatty and Scheider were there only for small parts.

Didn't Frances Sternhagen appear on the show also?

Oh, Franny Sternhagen, she played several different characters over the years. She's a wonderful lady, by the way.

Was there a certain collegiality between you, the actors, and the other production people off the set?

There was a certain familial feeling in the earlier days because we were all in the pool together. I think that some of the actors befriended one another, and we would occasionally decide to have a cast-and-crew party somewhere, but we didn't really hang out together. At least I didn't—I had to go home and do my homework: There were always scripts to read, story plans to review, and camera blocking to do.

When did you do the actual camera blocking for the show?

Well, the camera blocking followed the physical blocking of the actors, and that came from working in the rehearsal hall. So the camera work was done after the physical work, when I knew where all of the actors were going to be and could see how they were interacting: "Now, what am I going to do with my cameras…" The lighting was done in the morning because we had a lot of rehearsal time in the studio. Eventually, when I was working in the hour format on a show after *Love of Life* was canceled, everything became much more complicated. The sets were bigger and more complex, and the input of the director into the design of the sets became more and more minimal. We'd walk into the preproduction meeting or the studio and would essentially be given the set, which is a bunch of shit.

So in the earlier days, you had input into the set design?

Oh, yeah. I worked with a wonderful set designer named Lloyd Evans on *Love of Life*. He also designed stuff for the New York City Opera. Lloyd and I would meet all of the time. Set design on a soap opera is important, and when you have one director and one designer, it's a very cooperative kind of venture.

As you've noted, so many things related to technology and the production process changed over the course of your career. How did the dramatic societal changes of the '60s and '70s impact Love of Life*? The series certainly had its share of divorces, extramarital affairs, and the like.*

Well, as society began to be more accepting, we were able to do a little bit more. We no longer had to do what the movies had been required to do with love scenes, for instance—you know, one foot on the floor all the time. Certainly there were things happening in society that a writer could pick up on and use.

Did you ever get a script and find its material to be problematic? Or would that have already been taken care of in the meeting with the producer?

That would have been taken care of before it got to me.

Did you ever get a script to shoot and find it inappropriate, or at least not credible in some way?

I was never particularly concerned about appropriateness. I got plenty of scripts that I didn't like. *[laughs]* I was more concerned about whether I could swallow what the script was about. I mean, these people were writing 260 shows a year! You ask a guy to sit down and knock out 260 of these a year and it's not going to be Shakespeare.

It must be pretty draining, though, to have to work with material you don't like—I would imagine it would be tough for the actors as well.

You know, you signed a piece of paper and you said you were going to do your job, so you just try to do it as best you can. Make it better if you can. I mean, you bitch and complain, but you get up and go in and get it done. It was a lot of material. You know, when the shows went to an hour, you would be shooting

70-, 80-, even 90-page scripts in a single day.

Did actors memorize lines, or were teleprompters used?

We didn't use them at first, and then eventually we got them. The first ones held rolls of paper, and every once in a while, the roll of teleprompter paper tore and you would be able to hear this ripping sound off camera. Then at some point we got video teleprompters. On *One Life to Live*, the producer Paul Rauch eventually dispensed with the teleprompters because you would too often catch the actors looking at them. There was one guy who did this constantly—he also happened to be a rotten son of a bitch. He'd be in a scene with another actor who would be having this intense moment of communication with him, and he wouldn't even be making eye contact—he'd be looking for his line on the teleprompter. So Paul, who was a difficult producer but a very good producer, dispensed with them, and the actors had to learn their lines. I don't know if they're used now or not.

You know, the more I hear, the more it strikes me that the whole soap-opera genre is some kind of test of human endurance. Writing this enormous volume of new material, memorizing and performing it, shooting it, etc., day after day after day. There seems to be nothing else like it in the entertainment industry.

It's very difficult. But I think it's worst for writers. I don't know how they last, to tell you the truth. And as a matter of fact, they don't. Writers migrate from one soap to the other more than directors and performers—except maybe for the day players.

Soap-opera fans can be pretty passionate about their shows; did you ever run into any of this while you were directing?

No, I didn't get any of that. I would get reports back from the actors, who would be accosted on the street—*accosted* being the proper word in a couple of instances. Bonnie Bedelia was on *Love of Life* for a long time, and I'm pretty certain it was she who told me about a fan coming up to her at a bus stop and slapping her in the face because her character had been ugly to Vanessa on the show. So, yeah, fans got really involved—they considered the performer's character to be the real person.

Why do you think Love of Life *was canceled in 1980? You have said before that you suspected CBS's decision to move it to a four p.m. time slot in the late '70s was one important factor.*

I think that had something to do with it. I also think the last writer CBS chose, who had failed on other shows beforehand, had something to do with it. And I got the sense that CBS—I mean, this is only a guess, as I wasn't privy to this stuff—wanted the time slot back.

The final episode closes with a shot of you walking through the sets of the show on an otherwise empty soundstage, turning off the lights as you leave the studio. In the background, we hear Tony Bennett's "We'll Be Together Again." It's a nice moment.

Somebody else may claim authorship for that last scene, but I'm pretty sure it was my idea to walk through and turn the lights out at the door.

It serves as a reminder that soap directors don't normally play a very visible role, making the genre not the best home for the auteur theory. As you mentioned, there are usually several directors working on any given show, and of course it's important to keep a certain sameness to the presentation of the material. That said, do you think there is any way to distinguish your work from that of other directors on the soaps you've worked on?

I don't think so—especially today, when everything is so edited. If you managed to look at the tapes and you knew who directed that day, you might be able to discern something once in a while. You might notice, for instance, that there are a lot more close-ups in one episode than another.

Were close-ups something you were partial to as a director?

I had a theory about close-ups, particularly in the early days. You know, we were working for very small screens. If you go to the theater and sit in the back, and there are three people on a dramatically lit stage with some furniture, your mind is able to somehow create the proper size relationship with the performers. But if you're looking at an actor on a small screen in your living room, your eye is also unconsciously aware of the furniture and other objects in the room, and it diminishes the size and impact of the person on the screen. If I want to grab the attention of the viewer, I need to make sure the characters are large enough to be noticed. So in those earlier days, when we were restricted to those small screens, I wanted the close-up. The wide shot, the two shot, were less important. Today, when the screens are so much larger, it's different.

But I don't think you could look at a show and say, "Oh, that's a Larry Auerbach show, or that's a Gary Donatelli show." Particularly now, when nobody does a complete episode anymore. On any given day, one director will do some scenes for a particular show, and the next day, another director will do another group. It's a mishmash. In order to save money, they'll fill the studio with sets—say, on a Monday—and shoot all the scenes that are supposed to take place in those sets in the next week or so. Then they'll strike those sets, put up others, and shoot all the scenes taking place in those on Tuesday. So there could be four different directors' work in one particular episode.

I don't know how it is today, but I was always careful to read all of the scripts, which in itself took a lot of time. And I would talk to a director from whom I was going to pick up a scene to find out where he was leaving the actors and where I was going to pick them up. And then I would call whoever was going to take over that scene from me to give them the same information, so he or she could continue with minimal interruption.

My guess would be that soap-opera actors are probably great with continuity issues, since they've inhabited their characters for such a long time and at such a consistent pace.

Absolutely. That's a big help. Somebody like Susan Lucci from *All My Children*, she knows the character of Erica Kane better than any writer or any director around. She's been doing it longer than anybody. Although with some actors, that can be a hindrance too. An actor who is stubborn might say, "But my character would never do that!" That's shit—the character does what the writer wants him to do.

After Love of Life *ended, didn't you go almost immediately to* All My Children*?*

That's right. I worked there with a wonderful producer named Jørn Winther—he was a guy who really knew how to produce a soap opera, and he was a good director. After *All My Children* I went to *One Life to Live*, and when I had a chance to renew my contract, I intentionally declined to do so, because I didn't like the way I was being treated. I also worked as a fill-in for *Another World* and *As the World Turns*.

And you never wanted to pursue other kinds of directing?

Sure! *[laughs]* I thought about it. As I said, I eventually decided shooting a movie would just be too goddamn boring. And I don't know too many directors who've made that leap. Peter Levin, who directed soap operas here in New York, went to L.A. and had some success doing episodic television, but it's a rarity. Part of it, of course, is that soap operas always have a stigma.

Why do you think that is?

Well, because the material doesn't reach great heights. There has always been a feeling that soaps aren't worth paying very much attention to. You know, people think if you're grinding something out every day, it can't be worth that much. So soap-opera people have always been looked down upon—not actors so much, but writers and directors. But I defy anybody who has shot a movie to come in and try to do a one-hour soap opera in one day in a studio. To deal with that many pages, to deal with the sets—to get it all done in eight hours.

In the past couple of years, several of the surviving long-running soaps— Guiding Light, As the World Turns*—have gone off the air, and the feeling is that more—and perhaps all—will follow. Why do you think the genre appears to be on its last legs?*

It's several things. Economics. Audience. And, of course, technology. Life has changed. First of all, the number of women at home during the day has decreased precipitously. And instead of being able to get only three networks, now you get 103, so the availability of material for the eyeballs to rest on is so much greater. I used to go to a cleaners in Mamaroneck, and the woman who ran the counter there told me she had two VCRs going all the time at her house during the day. Over the weekend, she would watch all of her soaps. Today, nobody cares that much. People don't need a relatively simple story when they can rent or buy a DVD anytime, or for that matter, just go on the Internet. Also, it's expensive to produce these: It's no longer about simple sets with a little wainscoting and a piece of black velour. There are location shoots, stunts. It's gotten to be like making a movie every day.

In the '50s and '60s, we had something like 16 soap operas shooting in New York; now we've got one left: *One Life to Live*. How long that will be around, I don't know.

Your last gig in soap operas was in 1995. Do you miss it?

Well, I'll sometimes occasionally dream about being in the control room and not being able to get on the air. *[laughs]* But no, I don't miss being in that world, particularly as it is today. I'll tell you what I really miss: I miss being back in radio. I wasn't there very long, but I loved it. You had to get in there and you had to do it. If there was a problem, fix it right now, because there is no tomorrow. Just like live TV: Have a real rehearsal, get in the control room, do it, and move on. That I miss.

From *Esopus 23* (2016)

On the Value of Literature

BY KARL OVE KNAUSGAARD

WE ARE BORN FREE. But the moment we open our eyes and encounter the gaze of another, whether that of our mother or father, or merely of a maternity nurse whose shift it happens to be, the matter is sealed. From then on we belong to the community. By the community we are fed and provided with clothing, security, and warmth, but also language, and access to the wealth of knowledge and information that is accumulated in our culture. What does it ask for in return? Not much. And yet nothing the community has brought about, be it food or clothing, warmth or security, language, knowledge, or information, is self-sustaining. It is the duty and responsibility of each individual member of the community, to the best of his or her ability, to ensure that the community keeps on providing. Some of us must collect the available information on car engines so that they may be constructed and repaired, and so that the construction and repair of car engines does not sink into oblivion. Some must learn what is known about shoe soles, and the rubber caps we afix to the metal legs of chairs that make their feet look like little hooves. Some have to find out about constructing staircases, and then learn that skill. Some must gather knowledge of coffee varieties, flashing lights, bridges, carrots, socks, fencing, plastic bowls, bricks, cables, knives, dresses, elevators, barns, livers, hamburgers, mailboxes, ashtrays, windowpanes, airplanes, brains, hearts, monkeys, windmills, radios, soil, rifles, cell phones, raincoats, suitcases, and asphalt. Some of us must furthermore endeavor to find alternatives to car engines, since car engines, all their advantages nothwithstanding, seem also to have disadvantages that have turned out to rather seriously impact the environment. At the same time, some of us must make provisions for that work to take place, either by financing it or by passing the requisite legislation, allowing the scientists to conduct the research, others to put it into practice, and still others to sweep the floors of the spaces in which all of it takes place. Some of us must look after the children of these people while they are at work, and some must take care of the workers should they become sick, or in the event that some accident should befall them. Such is the way of things throughout our society. A pleated skirt requires its own set of knowledge and skills, likewise the computer mouse, the drinking glass, the toilet bowl, the electric lightbulb. To many of us, our society is the very sum of these elements of work, whose function is to ensure that the wheels continue to turn, trains and trams arrive on time, food appears on tables, and heating is delivered to our houses, whereas everything that has nothing directly to do with such matters, for instance art, literature, film, photography, philosophy, history, or archaeology, is considered secondary, something by which we can distract ourselves to the extent we can afford it, but which is not in any way essential, and therefore not important, at best something nice to have, by which we can pass our time.

To a large degree this assessment is correct. We read books for entertainment, to escape from reality for a few hours, learning little from them, except, say, that human desire is a powerful force that can give rise to a great many problems. We watch films for entertainment, and even if a film has any greater ambition than telling a story in which the main character, having encountered difficulties of a near-insurmountable nature, eventually ends up getting what he or she wants, our experience will still usually be summed up in the form of banal insights we already possessed before we started. Art can be invigorating to look at, but what is art exactly, if not the arbitrary product of human beings who never really learned how to adapt to society, people who believe themselves to be so special they don't need to contribute to the community and instead may spend their time giving form to the encounter between their precious inner being and the community's external manifestation, in the shape of earth piled up on a floor, an erect penis drawn with a marker on a sheet of metal, a motorcycle suspended from the ceiling, or simply an untidy room with an unmade bed, reconstructed in a gallery space? These things might conceivably give the beholder pause, but apart from that they are play, more properly speaking frivolity, at least when seen in relation to the toil of a fisherman off the coast of northern Norway, or the day-to-day travails of a nurse in the emergency room of any large regional hospital.

Most of you reading this might now consider that I, the writer of this essay, do not believe this to be the case. Perhaps you are now waiting for the turning point to come, the juncture at which the piece begins to build up arguments in favor of the opposite viewpoint, that art and literature are what *really* matter in society, and that everything hitherto mentioned is in fact dependent on them, not in any superficial, quotidian kind of way, but quite fundamentally, and existentially so.

You may even be right.

But still you are not clairvoyant. That method of arguing a case, beginning by presenting matters in such a way as to demonstrate understanding of the opposite viewpoint, is a well-known ploy of classical rhetoric, a method exploited by speechwriters and public debaters alike. The trick is to accommodate one's audience. By falling in with its opinion, one is seen to take one's audience seriously; its viewpoint has been deemed valuable, and if an audience senses as much it will take a liking to the speaker or writer and be more inclined to listen to what he or she has to say than if the actual arguments had been put forward first. In the latter case, the audience would have stood aloof and the remoteness thereby established would first have had to be overcome. The pathway to success in such cases goes through the emotions rather than reason.

Few people can teach us more about this than Adolf Hitler. He writes with great skill about what it takes to win over a reluctant audience. This, he contends, is all but impossible to achieve in writing, insofar as the written form privileges rational argument, and minds are generally made up beforehand. So no one ever became a Nazi by reading *Mein Kampf*. Of this Hitler is acutely aware. For its power of persuasion, he found oral communication so superior to the written word that he is able in his writing to describe his methods, to detail his tricks, his entire repertoire of manipulations, without in any way compromising his credibility. What he knew was that everything depends on the physical encounter. As long as he had a stage or a podium on which to stand, and an audience of people gathered together in a space, he would be able to win them over, regardless of how skeptical they might be. If the audience members stood with their arms folded against their chests when the meeting began, it didn't matter, because by the time it ended their arms would be raised in the air. What he had to do was to create an identification, a feeling of togetherness, of sharing the same world. To this end he needed to know who they were, what thoughts they possessed, what feelings. Workers, housewives, soldiers, university professors: As soon as he had established himself as one of them, they began to listen—he describes it in terms of penetrating their defenses, the same as reaching into their feelings—and after that he could lead them wherever he wished.

So much stronger than reason is emotion that such a method, its simplicity and transparency notwithstanding, does not appear manipulative. Rather, it dons the garb, so to speak, of reality, and is thereby the only aspect apparent to us, since emotion draws us closer, and what is required in order to see the method, or the form, is distance.

To what purpose did Adolf Hitler exploit this enormous talent for manipulation? What did he make people believe? What he did was to create a fiction, a deeply romantic one, about a great people and a great nation, and to translate this fiction into reality, to play it out, as it were, like a theater piece relying on a vast collective suspension of disbelief. Primarily in visual terms, since what is visual goes directly to the emotions, but also in the written form, by redefining the words of the language, and by a widespread use of euphemism, whereby words concealed actual events that were occurring in their name—emotion once again being primary. A triad was established comprising form, emotion, and reality: form roused emotion, and emotion suppressed, colored, or re-created reality.

What can we learn from this?

That what moves us to tears, sends shivers down our spines, or enhances our self-esteem is not art, but emotional manipulation?

Where, then, would the difference lie? All of us possess emotions; they belong to being human, and since the theme of art and literature is being human, it naturally embraces our emotions, too.

The difference is that emotions, as they occur in our lives, do so without aim. Grief isn't meant to lead anywhere in particular. Likewise joy or pride. Feelings come over us, they color our moods, and we view the world through their filter. They are a part of us, and since we always feel something, whatever it might be, feelings are central to our very existence in the world. They do not appear at random, but are always awakened by some factor, known or otherwise. As such they are vulnerable to manipulation and may be triggered by others wishing to exploit them to some end. In that way, emotions become useful. Hitler, who lived in an age in which mass communication was a new phenomenon, exploited emotion to political ends. In our day there is little we fear more than this, so when politicians play on our emotions, as we so aptly say, as though our feelings were strings inside us to be plucked or strummed at will, they do so discreetly and with caution: no more the stadium rally or the fervor of religious revival, no longer the fluttering flags and proud uniforms, the flaming torches and gigantic cheers of the crowd. Yet such manipulation is by no means foreign to us; it has merely shifted location, to a quotidian realm we hardly perceive as a realm at all, a place in which it runs without end, in the manner of a successful play, with but one aim in mind, the awakening of our emotions. I am thinking of the mass media. Advertising permeates every aspect of our lives, and its language gives our emotions a purpose beyond merely existing: it persuades us to buy. Its aim is to give pleasure, and thereby to make us purchase. To arouse feelings of pride, desire, shame, envy, all in order to make us consume. The news industry exploits grief to that same end: feeding on accident and disaster, it functions as a communicative apparatus capable of presenting collective events in wide-screen panorama, the great earthquake in which 5,000 perish, and zooming in on the individual fate, the boy bullied at school who eventually hangs himself, and this it does with zest, under the pretense of keeping us informed. But we pay for all of this, and because almost nothing of what we are informed about is of any practical use to us, what we are really paying for is the awakening of our emotions. If this were not the case, the news might just as well come in telegrams, without photographs or moving images, neutral and objective, devoid of embellishment. That would be information, but it would be of little interest to us, because what we crave is fully illustrated disaster, in all its sensational splendor. And the more sensational it is, the more we feel. Our emotions are thus besieged: on the one hand by those who urge us to buy, and who must first manipulate us emotionally so that may happen; on the other hand by those whom we insist should rouse our feelings, and whom we pay for the privilege. The film industry is part of the same complex, inasmuch as nine out of ten films and TV series are made to stimulate our emotions—to stir feelings of excitement, joy, sorrow, and sympathy—this being their purpose, the sole reason they are produced. And again, we pay readily, yearning to feel these great emotions within us. In all this, an almost entirely visual culture has developed; as Hitler demonstrated, the potential to manipulate emotions is greatest in sound and vision.

And what could be wrong with that? Even if the feelings thereby awakened in us are of the same essential nature as those Hitler once awakened in the German people—which indeed they are, because feelings are feelings, and as such do not arise collectively but in each and every person individually—they will nonetheless come to nothing, for the fact is that we do not kill or go to war on their account. They are innocent, harmless, something that makes life easier and brings to it a certain pleasure, small jolts of stimuli received during the course of a day, little presents delivered to the soul.

Rhetoric is the study of the art of communication. It concerns how best to convince others of a matter, and mastering it is the same as possessing power. Such power may be exploited for ideological, idealistic, or religious purposes, or it may be used to make money. That money, one might argue, does not merely disappear, but is spent on maintaining the production of goods and services, greasing the wheels of society, as we say, and thereby benefiting us all: capitalism is the system in which we live, it is us, and we are it, and the business of buying and selling, what we usually think of as commercialism, pervades all aspects of our lives and makes up such a large part of our identity that we are no longer aware of it. Standing in front of the mirror to brush one's teeth before bedtime, who gives a thought to the fact that their toothbrush, toothpaste, mouthwash, dental floss, even the glass they fill with water, are commercial products of a capitalist system? I, for one, certainly do not, and it would not surprise me in the slightest if the nurse in the emergency room and the fisherman off the coast of northern Norway gave as little consideration to the matter as I do. Perhaps every now and then they might even check the news on their smartphones while they are in the process. I know I do. One last little gift for the soul before sleep.

Now, you might think, surely the turning point in this text will come? Society has been described in terms of a community in which everyone has their jobs to do, their responsibilities and duties to fulfill. The relationship of this community to human emotions continuously awakened in unforced yet well-rewarded ways has been laid out. And, while I have not been conscious of it, there is nonetheless something almost dystopian about that description, a state of somnambulation, as it were, in which dreamlike images no longer populate only the night, but also the day, in which everything is about passing, via emotions, into some reality other than the one we actually inhabit.

A turning point would therefore seem appropriate, a glimpse of light in all this darkness, a little hope to which we might cling, in the anticipation that it could grow and spread—for surely I cannot be alone in feeling displeasure at the fact that everything is reduced to images, that everything is for sale, that the world in all its material might is gradually vanishing?

I refuse to believe it.

Is literature then that light, that hope, that alternative?

No, because literature is not the other, outside or beyond. Literature is us, in the same way as capitalism is us. It belongs to the community, in the same way as language, and is something into which we are born, that we must address and then depart in death. Literature exists, so it seems, independently of the individual, even as it is sustained and nourished within the individual. Literature is created by individuals, yet belongs to us all, and what it does, it does collectively: a solitary book is a contradiction, like a language spoken by a solitary human being.

But why literature? We have films, TV series, news, advertising, and music to keep us entertained, allowing us briefly to escape our lives and to experience things otherwise remote to us, in ways quite unparalleled. And, not least, in ways that exclude no one, for such media are made for all.

So why books, sentences, words?

Language is a living entity, in the sense that words we no longer need fall by the wayside, while new ones appear according to what we require. Moreover, language is above all a practical means for us to designate the world around us, identifying the elements of which it is comprised, thereby making it possible for us to comprehend and manage. Go and fill the mug with water, I say to my daughter, and she picks up the mug, takes it into the kitchen, and fills it with water. Or else she says *no, I won't,* and in the exchange that ensues, the simple act of filling a mug with water becomes a representation of a power structure—daddy commands, daughter obeys—against which she protests. Why does she do that? The reasons are many, and concealed within her, but because of what she says, some are revealed to me, and because of my experience in the world, I understand, or at least think I understand, others that remain unspoken. One of the most important things children have to learn when growing up is how to manage their emotions. To come to grips by themselves with their griefs and sorrows, and all their disappointments, but also their joys and pleasures, too. To distinguish between their inner lives and what is external to them, between themselves and others. Naming by means of language is one way of distinguishing. To name is to isolate and identify. It is not the only way, but it is the most important. I am not thinking about the conceptual apparatus of psychology here, which is a metalanguage of analysis. I am thinking about that aspect of language that we do not perceive or consider, because it forms such a natural part of ourselves and our identity; the language we reside in, that in which we are so snugly sheathed that we cannot think of ourselves without it.

This inner, private language is the domain of literature, and only there, in literature, can it manifest outside the self and make itself visible to others. Literature extends across many other domains—social, historical, political—and it assumes many forms, of which the narrative story is perhaps the most predominant, but only this is specific to literature: only literature can offer up our inner, private language and make it visible.

Why should it be made visible?

Language is above all practical: think of a workplace, the way everything in it has a name on which everyone agrees, so that no doubt ever arises as to what's what, and therefore only rarely as to what's to be done. Hammer, nail, plasterboard, paintbrush, bucket, paint. Scalpel, saw, latex gloves, apron, mask, lamp. Steering wheel, gear lever, clutch, hand brake. Dishwasher, chopping board, refrigerator, cucumber, saucepan, whisk, frying pan. Now think of a workplace abandoned by time, a place no longer in use, because what was made or done there is no longer needed. Imagine that the words once used to designate its various tools and instruments have been forgotten. They would then merely be objects, nameless effects left lying around, without purpose, bereft of meaning. One might give them names—a thrinch, a ling, a gridget—though without knowledge of what they were used for, the contexts in which they were employed, such words would be meaningless. Now imagine a space likewise abandoned, though one within our human existence, formerly taken for granted, with its own obvious place in the scheme of things, but now disused, because no one any longer has need of what used to be found there. Religious ecstasy, for instance: reading texts from the Middle Ages or the Renaissance, one may come across descriptions of feelings and moods that to me, at least, are unfamiliar, as if they conceptualize something that is not found within me, but which nonetheless clearly belongs to the inner human experience. And this is where things get complicated. For is this any loss? We seem to get on rather well without such ecstasy and the language that accompanies it. Similarly, we might wonder about the new language that came to replace it, that introduced by Freud and the paradigm of psychology at the turn of the last century, which entered directly into our everyday speech and the way we perceive ourselves in a very fundamental way: the subconscious, the id, ego, and superego, repression, projection. Might such words, too, fall into disuse and become incomprehensible to us? Would it matter if they did? Would it not merely indicate to us that language names the things we need, making available what is useful, abandoning that which is not? Would it not merely suggest that what we are dealing with here is some kind of evolutionary principle taking care of things on our behalf, allowing what must die to die, what must live to live?

I believe that to be the case. But the sphere in which this occurs is not exhaustively that of literature. What belongs to the inner experience and which is invisible to all others but ourselves, is nonetheless common to us all, and this is what makes literature both possible and important. Reading is an intimate matter, something we do on our own, and it is remarkable in that by allowing our gaze to pass along the page we thereby evoke within us the voice of another, a voice to which we submit, in such a way that we ourselves vanish—to a greater or lesser degree, obviously, but with the best books, we vanish entirely. What happens in such instances? For some hours, our ways of thinking and feeling follow new paths, and we see ourselves simultaneously from the outside and from within. Our emotions are awakened, not to fulfill some external purpose, but so they may be acknowledged.

Why is this important?

If, indeed, it is important at all.

The fact is that we can get along quite nicely without reading literature. I know plenty of people who have never read a book in their lives, and they are neither better nor worse humans than I, who have read thousands of books. Nor is it the case that their lives are lacking in any way, or are incomplete because of it—on the contrary, I suspect, it is I who am lacking, and this is the reason I read—so, once again, why literature?

In the community into which we are born there are certain conceptions, certain ways of looking at the world, notions about the nature of reality, and these forms are complete, they await us, as it were, await our entering into them. This we do. Now and then, when the great ideologies arise, we are able to perceive this, that the way we view the world, society, and the community is a form we apply to reality, as it were. We see this because the form never quite fits, because life is something else, always in the making, forever incomplete, forever tentative.

These two things—life and our conception of it—are continually chafing against each other, and have done so for as long as human beings have existed. All plans, systems, and theories belong to our conceptions about life and must constantly be reassessed and altered, insofar as they belong to what has come to an end, whereas the life they seek to describe and govern is always in its beginnings and itself oblivious to any boundary. In nature, boundaries do not exist, all entities and phenomena merge, the earth is round, the universe infinite, time eternal. What this entails, none of us is privileged to understand, for to be human is to categorize, classify, identify, and define, delineate, and frame. This is true of our own lives as we live them inside our homes, separated from the rest of the world by roofs, floors, walls, and, outside those structures, if we live in a house, by the boundaries of our gardens and yards. It is true also of our own selves, which we associate with the body and its boundaries, and with a certain set of thoughts, notions, ideas, opinions, and experiences. And it is likewise true of our reality, what we refer to as the world, which we divide up into entities, groups of entities, phenomena, and groups of phenomena, understood on the basis of the ways they differ from other entities and phenomena. This division is a frame; it establishes an inside and an outside and is not in itself considered to be a part of any perceived or understood reality.

These frames, without which neither we nor the world itself might be considered, are found in all areas of existence. They are valid not only for what is, but also for what ought to be, because there are clear boundaries for the ways in which we behave, too. Since life is fluid, discrepancies will occasionally arise between what we ought to do and what we want to do, made manifest in a desire to overstep the established boundaries. If such desire is fulfilled, a state of flux will occur until new frames are constructed. So it is in the life of the individual, most obviously in adolescence in what we refer to as teenage rebellion, and so it is more widely in culture, too, where we speak of uprising, revolution, war.

Literature is one of the few areas within the great community we are born into and in which we live our lives where the predictable has been dissolved, or is sought to be dissolved. The space of literature is a space between our conception of reality and reality itself. Literature seeks to keep that space open, in order to reach, perhaps even determine, those moments in which our conception of reality and reality itself correspond, and are one and the same. This seldom happens, but when it does, it immediately assumes a form, and thereby once again remoteness is established. So why do we even try, and continue to try? Why publish all these thousands of books, year after year? It is surely a meaningless endeavor, an idiotic exertion leading to nothing, and yet it is exquisite, in its own singular way, and it resembles life—perhaps this is where literature's legitimacy is to be found?

Literature is as tentative as life itself, as meaningless and as diverse, and quite as directionless, and every now and then, like life itself, it condenses into enormous clusters of meaningfulness and nearness to the world. These clusters are like huge floodlights, reaching out to us all, directly and indirectly, elevating us, not to what we should or could have been, but to what we are. There, in that striving toward such clusters, which are good because they are true, and which illuminate the entire community, however seldom it succeeds in reaching that goal, lies literature's legitimacy: its value consists in its endeavor toward the light, not in the light itself. And this is so because we are not human beings, but endeavors to become human beings.

Translated by Martin Aitken

The Sissy Monologues (#3)

BY STEPHEN ADLY GUIRGIS

Dear Sissy—

I'm not supposed to write you anymore because every time I do, you never write back, and then I feel bad. I got this friend now, she's, like, a counselor, and she says; "If you wanna feel bad, write Sissy." She says that after two years, healthy people move on, and that I don't really love you anymore, I just think I do because I have a tendency to want to feel bad in order to punish myself, because I feel guilty that I didn't do better when you were my girl. She says I have to forgive myself; and every time we talk, she keeps using the word Acceptance, like 58 billion times. It's real fuckin annoying. She keeps telling me that nothing in this world happens by mistake, so, if "me and you" aren't "me and you" anymore, it's because it's not a mistake and it's supposed to be like that. She tells me people do what they wanna do, and they don't do what they don't wanna do, and that if you wanted to write me back, you would, but you don't wanna, so you don't. And she also says that if I wanted to be a better boyfriend, I woulda been, but I wasn't. She tells me I'm a good guy and that I did the best I could and that I will learn from the experience in the future. Sometimes I try to argue with her, but she always wins cuz she's smarter than me and all her arguments make sense, and all my arguments don't make sense to anyone but drunks and the mentally ill people that I work with down at this place I started working at. Mostly, I tell this counselor lady; "I don't wanna learn something for the future, I just wanna learn about when Sissy's comin' back." And she tells me; "If you really wanted Sissy back so bad, then how come you never went down there to try and get her?" I told her I did try, but you wouldn't see me, and she tells me that I should have insisted on seeing you, but that I didn't insist because of 2 reasons: either I knew it was really over and seeing you would confirm it and I didn't want it to be confirmed, OR, I didn't insist because I didn't really, in my heart, wanna get back together with you, I just thought I did. She says that since

I hurt you the first time we broke up, and also the second time we broke up, that now I wanna get hurt back because I feel it's what I deserve and also because it's easier to walk away hurt than to walk away being the hurt-er, and also because I think I have to be punished or something cuz I come from a real fucked up mountain family where everyone's nice but real fucked up.... Anyways, that's why I haven't written you for a while, it's not because you aren't in my heart. The truth is, you are never too far from my thoughts or my heart, and I don't think it's because I'm unhealthy, or a stalker, or a pain-junkie, or anything like that. My counselor is real nice—you'd like her—and, it's not like she don't have a point from time to time, cuz she does—but all those theories and explanations, Sissy—they just don't wash clean. I love you, Sissy, and as long as I love you, I'm gonna love you no matter what anyone says. Sissy, I know this girl who had a messed up time with her boyfriend and then they got back together, but then she walked away because even though she still loved him, and even though she still really wanted to be with him, she just couldn't because she said that something had been broken and that it couldn't be fixed even though she wished that it could and it killed her that it couldn't. Maybe I broke something with you, Sissy, and it can't be fixed. I don't know. Maybe that's why I've written all these tons of letters and postcards and stuff and you never write back. Megan Rogers says you read all my letters, and that you always ask her about everything I'm doing. And maybe that's not enough reason for me to have hope, but, Sissy, I'm gonna be who I am and take my Hope where I can find it.... I can still picture us real old sitting on a porch somewhere, Sissy. And we're real old and stuff, but when I look across my rocker over at your rocker, I look into your eyes and it's the exact same you that you've always been—and I smile at you, and you smile at me, and I quietly think to myself how I'm without question the luckiest son of a bitch in the whole entire world. And then you take my hand, and we don't say nuthin, but the feel of your old hand against my old hand is all the confirmation I'll ever need. Because our hands are old and rickety and lined and scarred and gnarled and broken, Sissy, but crease for crease, line for line, and gnarl for gnarl—like some old wooden jigsaw puzzle, Sissy—our old twisted hands—they fit clean. You will always be the oxygen of my heart, Sissy. There's a lot of stuff that people know, but there's also stuff that no one can tell you. And the stuff that no one can tell you is the most important stuff to know. And even if I never get to see you or smell you or feel you or love you again, it'll be okay. I just want you to know that you were and are like that 'ol Barry White said: "First. Last. Everything." Not in a bad way, Sissy, but in the only way that really matters.... So, I'm comin' down there, Sissy, I bought my bus ticket this morning, so, if you don't wanna see me, this'd be a good time to skip town. And tell Johnny Bassner he can bang me around all he wants. Sooner or later his arms will get tired.... I was a dumb, fuckin' ass, Sissy. And prolly,

I'm still a dumb fuckin' ass. But maybe if you look into my eyes, Sissy, you'll see that I've changed. And all I'm saying is that I'm more than willing to take a beating from Johnny Bassner to find that out. And then maybe you'll be willing to, like, have a cup of tea with me or something just for like a minute. And if it's the last tea I ever drink with you, well then, I'll just haveta to sip it like your daddy does—long and slow. And I guess that'll haveta be just fine. I gotta go to work now cuz I'm already late. I grew a Fu Manchu mustache up here, but I'll shave it before I come down. Everyone's got mustaches and stuff up here. But I'd rather just have you. All my love, Sissy. For real. And Always.

PS—I just got accepted to journalism school at this place called City College. They got classes for everything up here. Just in case you wanna know.

Nothing Personal

BY HEATHER McPHERSON

Receiving a marriage proposal is a funny thing, especially when you just met the fellow who's asking you over a plate of deviled eggs in the sweltering kitchen of the first trailer on the right in the lot on the 5th of July. What's funny is that it made the death threat that followed close on its heels seem somehow quaint. Different man, but just as sincere—which, both assured me, was plenty. I could have been married and died in the space of one day. Technically, that's not really true, as the pledge to hunt me down in my home of New York City and shoot me twice between the eyes as I slept (he'd make sure I woke up just in time to see the muzzle bearing down, he promised) was contingent on him not liking this, the article I had gone to West Virginia to write. And since getting this right is pretty important, what with me being too lazy to change my locks and too poor to hire a full-time bodyguard, I'm going to start from the beginning and give it to you straight, as best I can, and hope it's good enough.

I started out for Palestine, West Virginia, in search of a Jessica Lynch story. The ex-P.O.W. whose filmed rescue from a hospital in Nasiriyah, Iraq, captured the attention of the world and the media, or likely the other way around, had been born and raised in the tiny mountain town. Rumors were printed and retracted about the details of her capture on a weekly basis, Diane Sawyer had sent her a locket with a photo of her family home to tempt her into talking, and CBS was being accused of unethical "bundling," having accompanied a request for an interview with promises of other Viacom deals: a book, a movie, an Ashanti concert in Jessica's hometown. Having no illusions of getting *the story*, the idea was to get the story of trying to get *the story*. My hometown is a small one in rural Missouri, so I had a pretty good idea that whatever had gone on in the months since Jessica's rescue on April 1st had thrown the town into a tumult. The trick would be to get people to talk to me—a reporter like all the rest of them—about all the rest of them.

The closest motel to Palestine is in Mineral Wells, which has a choice of four. It's an interstate exit, just a few miles south of Parkersburg, not far from the Ohio Valley, squarely in Appalachia. I arrived the evening before July 4th, and, with not a small measure of trepidation to go where my cell phone could not, I headed in the direction of Elizabeth, the biggest town near Palestine and seat of Wirt County. I was surprised first at the manicured lawns and groomed homes along the highway in Mineral Wells, and then at the road itself. Winding and hilly, it was nonetheless smooth blacktop, and I hummed the inevitable tune, John Denver's "Country Roads," the lyrics of which Dan Rather would recite on the national news just a few weeks later after Jessica's homecoming. I cruised along the hairpin turns as the houses fell away, enjoying the occasional pastoral overlooks of rolling hills dotted with hay bales, and literally laughed out loud when I switched on my radio and heard Lee Greenwood's "I'm Proud to Be an American." The intro of my piece, I thought, had just written itself.

Satisfied with my day's work, I hit the seek button, half expecting every channel to be devoted to America's favorite patriotic tune. Instead, it was an NPR segment about a new biography on Benjamin Franklin, the signal strong. Franklin had likely never flown the kite or followed his own common sense, and his son had been illegitimate, born of a woman of low repute. The announcer mused that popular ideals of the "Founding Fathers" and "family values" were, perhaps, rooted in historical fiction. I sympathized. The most compelling stories are, of course, a witch's brew of fact and fiction—just ask Jayson Blair. The very existence of an NPR broadcast in this region had shot my tidy Lee Greenwood allegory, and I considered how easy it would be to conveniently ignore it. Bookers the world over were salivating at the prospect of getting Jessica on their show to talk about her ordeal, despite the likelihood that she was unconscious for much of it. NBC was in the midst of casting its TV movie of Jessica's capture and rescue, regardless of the fact that the particulars of her capture were nonexistent and those of her rescue disputed. Dan Rather's commentary would be a lyrics recitation. I had the opportunity to write about something true, newsworthy or not, and it was a pain in my ass.

Twenty minutes later, Elizabeth loomed...then was gone. The highway leads to a T-intersection, dead-ending in a bank, with the courthouse to the left and the rest of the town to the right. I chose right, and within a couple of minutes I was on the other side of the city limits. The high school, home of the Tigers, was near the courthouse, which was by the home of the *Wirt County Journal*, just down from the Pizza Den, across a parking lot from the fire station.... After driving around for another few minutes, not only did I feel I'd sufficiently covered the territory, I'd passed two adolescent girls out for a walk three times, and I began to fear being discovered and ejected for suspicious activity. There were people sitting in front of the Pizza Den, so I pulled into a patch of gravel and approached, hoping to get a slice and directions to Palestine before heading back for an evening of cable TV in my motel room.

A salt-and-pepper-haired man in a mesh cap and oversize golf shirt sat on a folding chair, flanked by a skinny redheaded girl and a boy whose baby face belied his impressive height and weight. I was unsure what was required in my passing them, but having gone to school in North Carolina and figuring any state that serves sweet tea in fast-food joints follows the same basic principles, I said hi and smiled. I got a couple of nods, a returned hey, and the girl rose to follow me inside. She worked there, apparently, and they were sitting outside to escape the heat of the ovens. I asked if they had any pizza, not seeing any, and then immediately remembered that New York City is unique in its vast availability of pizza at any moment of the day. She raised her eyebrows. "I can make you a pizza if you want one." In town 10 minutes, I was already exposing myself as the stupid city slicker. I apologized, told her not to bother and, desperate to keep the conversation going, asked where Palestine was.

"R.T!" she shouted. "Hey! Tell her how to get to Palestine!" she ordered, banging the screen door open. "I'm not from around here," she explained. "I'm from Parkersburg." I'd driven through Parkersburg that day—it was about half an hour away.

"Don't you know how the hell to get there?" R.T., the older man in the cap, shook his head in disgust at the redhead, then turned to me. "Take this road right here, follow it off to the right, keep going, and don't blink," he said.

"That's 14. You mean it's on Highway 14?" the redhead questioned.

"Yes, Highway 14, dummy. What the hell other road you think I'm talking about? You might know that if you wasn't so goddamned stupid."

"Then what the hell you talking about going to the right?"

"Well, goddamn. There's a kind of funny place in the road and you got to go right."

"That's another road, and you got to turn left to go the wrong way. Just tell her to keep going." She looked at me. "Don't worry about 'go right.' Just keep going on this road and you'll get there."

This was not good. If they knew I was writing a story, they wouldn't be speaking like this in front of me. "I'm sort of writing a story," I said, hoping to sound innocent while dutifully informing them of the presence of media in their midst. "Like everybody else, I guess."

There was a pause. “You mean you’re writing on that Jessica Lynch?” R.T. said.

“Duh,” said the redhead. “What the hell did you think she was asking about Palestine for? Vacation?”

The boy piped up. “Aren’t there, what, three bridges you got to cross to get out there?”

“Goddamn it, dummy, don’t go talking about bridges,” R.T. said, taking a swipe at the boy. “You just go and then turn when you see the sign for Mayberry Run Road for the Lynch’s place. That’s all they is.”

“Oh, come on, Pappy,” said the boy, cheerfully taunting R.T.

R.T. obliged with another swipe to the head, which was deflected. R.T. pointed at the boy’s face: “Boy, I will kill you.”

The girl turned to me. “Wouldn’t you think R.T. and Levi was father and son if you didn’t know?” she said. I didn’t know, but I saw the look on R.T.’s face and refrained from comment.

“And I can kick your skinny ass, too, while I’m at it,” he growled at her.

“Oh, bring it on,” she said, resuming her slouch in the sidewalk folding chair.

“I’m really just writing about the town and all,” I clarified to no one. “You know, all the media that came through here and everything that’s been going on?”

Nods.

“So was it, uh, crazy? I mean, did reporters talk to you?”

The girl shrugged. “I’m not from around here, so it’s really not my place to talk about it.” I wasn’t sure if this was a brand of etiquette that had kept her from talking to the reporters or kept her from telling me about talking to the reporters. Or why, if Parkersburg was considered so distant, she’d taken an after-school job in Elizabeth.

“You mean they asked you questions but you just wouldn’t talk to them?”

R.T. answered, shaking his head impatiently. “They come in to eat and all, but anybody with a lick of sense heads the other way when they see a TV camera.” It was an inadvertent admission that the redhead had, in fact, some sense. It was also the end of the discussion. I thanked them and headed off to Palestine. I returned in 20 minutes.

“You back?” R.T. said, more a statement than a question. I’d found Palestine just as had been described. The town was signaled only by a city limits sign and a vague proliferation of homes. There was one store, the What-Not Shop, and a post office along the road, then a sharp bend to the right, a few more houses, a couple of homemade banners fashioned from sheets and spray paint praising God for Jessi’s rescue, and then farmland. Three miles later, I assumed

I'd missed the turnoff for the Lynch residence and was slowing to double back when I saw a tattered ribbon hanging from the Mayberry Run sign—it used to be yellow, like many of the bows I'd seen posted to trees and front doors. The road had been paved just days prior, I'd read, but it was still a narrow affair with respectable ditches on either side—this was, I realized with growing excitement, a real, live "holler." Another mile down past a handful of homes here and there, a few ramshackle, a few downright decrepit, and the road veered to the left. On one side, a deep embankment gave way to a trailer and yard complete with trampoline and scattered toys. On the other, a construction site with retaining wall, freshly turned red earth, new flagpole, and, set back down the gravel driveway, an A-frame house with a new addition and incongruously white siding. The home itself was modest, but the effect was impressive. This was legitimate backwoods down an honest-to-God country road, and local volunteers, funded by the donations pouring in from around the country, had effectively ruined what had no doubt been a newscaster's dream background: It was entirely normal.

And so I was back at the Pizza Den, starving, too shamefaced to make the redheaded girl fire up the oven just for me, asking for ice cream, which would, I hoped, allow me a few more questions. "I wanted to see what time you all would be around tomorrow," I said. "Would it be all right if I came by?"

"We'll be closed for the next four days," R.T. said, leaning toward me, eyes wide. "And we're going camping, too—getting the hell out of Dodge. There'll be a parade and the firemen's ice cream social on Saturday, and this place'll be full of people." He walked into the restaurant, the screen door slamming behind him. I pushed it open and followed him in, crestfallen. I was going to have to start all over in the morning.

Another customer had replaced the young boy, Levi, and was telling the redhead about his trip that afternoon into Charleston, the state capital.

"I'm surprised they didn't run your ass right outta there," said R.T.

"Well, my truck ain't running so I was driving my mom's green pimpmobile. They didn't know it was me," said the new guy, chuckling. I was unsure if he was returning R.T.'s teasing or offering an explanation for a legitimate concern. He was wearing skintight jeans, black lace-up boots to his knees, a tight purple T-shirt with the word "cuz" printed over his heart in orange, large yellow wraparound sunglasses, and a floppy hat with a wide brim. A blond ponytail hung halfway down his back. "I was driving there, and they was just whizzing past me—everybody just *vooom...vooom*...right on by. I looked at my *spee*-dometer and I was going 112 miles per hour! And everybody's passing me! I could not figure it out. Well, come to find out that damn thing's in *ki*-lometers." Then, suddenly turning and acknowledging me for the first time, he smiled, "And that word took me 10 minutes to remember earlier."

R.T. had sidled up next to me and muttered, "Randall there is the one you ought to talk to," nodding toward the man. "He's Jessi's cousin." Don't ask how, but I knew that the proclamation on his chest had nothing to do with this. "He's not quite right in the head—fried his brain. But he'll damn near do anything for you if he's your friend."

I ate my ice cream slowly, afraid that finishing my cup would mean I'd have no excuse to stay, waiting for a pause in the conversation. It was a while. "So, I hear you're Jessi's cousin, right?" I blurted out. The sign on the courthouse had referred to her as Jessi, as had several others. He looked at me blankly. "Jessica? Jessica Lynch?" A pause. "She's your cousin?"

"Well, goddamn," said Randall, shaking his head. "Ain't nobody in this goddamned town can keep their goddamned mouth shut." R.T. threw his head back and laughed. "You're the one that's writing that book?" Randall said, fighting the smile curling his lips.

"No! No, definitely not a book. Just an article. About, oh, the town and all the media and everything."

"Well, I live up in the mountains, and I don't know nothing about it," he said. "I stay the hell away from all that stuff. I only come down to town maybe once a week or so. Sorry." Everyone nodded. And that was that.

My ice cream was gone, but I lingered. No one wanted to talk to me about anything having to do with Jessica Lynch, but they really didn't seem to mind my asking, either. In fact, for the most part they didn't seem to betray any awareness that I was there, talking about Randall's broken truck, his "old lady" and his old lady's daughter, who'd recently left to join her latest boyfriend at his army base in Missouri. (Trying to add something to the conversation, I asked Randall a question about his "old woman." In what was perhaps the most gracious example of hospitality I saw all weekend, he held back his laugh as I stammered a correction.) Outside, a vehicle pulled up to the door and Levi and a man walked in. He looked about Randall's age, 30-something, and a little like the strawberry-blond version of Violet Beauregarde's blueberry in *Willy Wonka*. No one looked up.

"Renee, your hubby's here," someone said to the girl, who was just a few feet away. She rolled her eyes and kept wiping the counter. Surely this man was not actually dating this young girl? But if not, if maybe he had an unseemly crush on her, it was grotesquely inappropriate that he be called her "hubby" right in front of both of them. And then I noticed the small gold band on her wedding ring finger.

It was several minutes before someone mentioned to Renee's husband that I was writing a story. He looked at me, possibly for the first time since entering, and Renee asked him who I should talk to. "The *Register* lady," he said to me. "I don't know her name—Renee and I aren't from around here—but the woman who does the *Wirt County Register*. She knows everything and everybody. If you don't mind riding in the rust bucket, I'll drive you over and show you where she lives."

His car was a well-beaten white Suzuki, and he explained how he'd recently put the doors back on. The boy, still mostly silent except for the occasional yelps he'd emit after provoking another swat from R.T., climbed in the back. I thought we were perhaps headed for the hills and wondered how long it would take the news of my death by Suzuki-crushing to reach my family. About two blocks later, the car stopped in front of a cute little brick house, and Renee's husband jumped out and strode up the sidewalk. I looked at Levi. He shrugged. The front door opened, and a cluster of children and a barking dog pressed against the glass of the storm door. A middle-aged woman cracked it, pushing the crowd out of the way with her body. I trotted up the sidewalk for what was to be, it now appeared, my introduction to the *Register* lady. She wrestled to secure the dog and then stepped onto the porch. They greeted each other with the familiarity of small-town neighbors who know more about your husband's infidelities or your financial problems than they do about you, and Renee's husband introduced himself as Rob. He acknowledged he knew her only as "the *Register* lady," and she cackled that most people knew her as that or "Brian's mom." She was sorry but they were just leaving town to go camping for the weekend; but I could always call her at the paper next week. I was getting the sinking feeling that the locals were all going to vacate to make room for people like me that weekend. She didn't have much to tell me, she added, as had everyone I'd spoken to so far.

There were three minutes on the drive back for me to get the scoop on Rob and Renee: She was, I was relieved and amazed to hear, 24, and he was 31. They'd been married for four years and had moved to Elizabeth to work at the pizza place her aunt and uncle opened a year ago. Rob had managed a few pizza parlors in his day and Renee had wanted to be near her family—they'd moved to North Carolina for nearly a year after their wedding and she'd never really gotten over the homesickness.

Back at the restaurant, R.T., Levi, Randall, Renee, and Rob sat in chairs and kicked gravel in the street, hoping aloud that each approaching car was not coming to eat. Often it was someone just coming to idle in the road and say hey, and R.T. and Randall would alternate muttering to me their story—a tale that generally had something to do with, as Randall described one woman with a car full of half-dressed kids, "loving to have unprotected sex." Randall also told me about selling homemade moonshine at a concert in upstate New York. "Them Yankees paid two dollars a shot for the stuff," he laughed, and claimed he'd made a few thousand dollars in a couple of days selling it and bowls of spaghetti. "Around here you have to make your own jobs," he explained. He put up hay in season and, he admitted, had some websites that did a pretty good business.

When patrons arrived at the Pizza Den, R.T. and Renee would begin a game of chicken, each refusing to rise and serve the customer until, usually, Renee would stand up, cursing at R.T. (Rob had the night off and Levi, like Randall, was just a regular), and stalk inside to roll out dough. They closed at 9 p.m. and began discussing what to eat for dinner. Rob turned to me and said, "So what's your name, anyway?" I took it as an offer to stay. They did not consider the restaurant full of food at their disposal, and decided to order from their main competition, an Italian fast-food place in Mineral Wells. Renee and I would go pick it up—a proposition that took close to an hour—and we would reconvene at their home. Randall handed me a pair of black iron horseshoes he'd soldered hooks to. "These are for you," he said simply. "I generally sell them for seven dollars apiece." He was returning to his home up in the hills before his old lady came looking for him, and although I didn't realize it at the time, I would not see him again.

Because I was driving and had been warned to keep watch for deer, the drive to the restaurant adjacent to my hotel took nearly 30 minutes. Renee confessed on the way back that she could make it in about 15, but because the sheriff was a regular customer at the Pizza Den, she didn't have to worry much about speeding tickets. She told me about the distance course she was taking to get her G.E.D., and how she'd begun to realize that almost everything her father had ever told her, including his advice to not drop out of school, had been right. Her real dream was to work with kids—she had two nephews she adored—and maybe someday open her own day care. Right now, though, she just wanted to get her diploma to prove to herself that she could do it. It was hard to do the work, especially the math, after working in the kitchen all day, but she was proud of an essay she'd written about her grandmother. The idea of wanting to write for a living, though—that was pretty crazy. I agreed.

Rob and Renee lived in a trailer, and we sat on the wooden front deck, eating pizza and drinking Tab, until past 2 a.m. Much of the conversation revolved around what R.T. would do to each of them were they to reveal to me the origins of his name, culminating in Renee scampering inside and announcing his name through the locked door. Rob chuckled and smiled at me, R.T. worked his chaw in contemplation of a proper punishment, and Levi exclaimed, "It wasn't me! I didn't say it!" until R.T. tried to push him off the deck backwards. There was a long discussion on how Levi would get home—it was probably a 45-minute bike ride, they reasoned, and wasn't a particularly safe jaunt in the middle of the night. Especially if, as R.T. suggested with a laugh, they gave him a 10-minute lead before R.T. started for home on the same road and they "raced." He was welcome to stay on Rob and Renee's couch, but R.T., they knew, would be happy to give him and his bike a lift in his "Barneymobile," a purple Suzuki. ("The ladies like the color," he'd confided when teased earlier that night.)

At some point in the night it had been decided that their camping trip was postponed indefinitely. After our pizza run, Renee had taken me under her wing and spent some time insisting that everyone concentrate for a moment and think of people who I should interview, and, as they discussed the merits and biases of the townspeople, began murmuring, "We're not really going camping now, right?" With no discussion of the matter that I ever witnessed, Rob announced as I rose to leave that they'd take me to the swimming hole the next day. Because I'd paid for our pizza that night, he said, they'd also take me to dinner in Parkersburg on Saturday. "Let's go Chinese-ing!" offered Levi, but Renee reminded them she didn't like Chinese food. We'd go to Ryan's Steakhouse, Rob said, I as their guest, and when I countered that I was more an intruder than a guest, R.T. looked at me sidelong and said quietly, "If you was an intruder you'da been run off long before now."

I got a late start the next day, having not gone to bed until nearly 4 a.m. I went dutifully to the Food Lion, the swimming pool and Dick's Mart, where a relative of Jessi's, the sheriff's wife, and Jessi's friend from high school worked, respectively, before heading to the trailer as instructed. The relative had told me about a British reporter who, in the melee after Jessi's rescue, had backed into her husband's truck. He and his buddies had given the reporter a hard time, calling the sheriff over and claiming she was going to have to pay for the damages or be shipped back to England, but Jessi's relative had no dealings with the media herself and the truck wasn't really hurt, anyway. I'd missed the sheriff's wife at the pool by the time I arrived there, but Jessi's friend, Miriah Duckworth, made up for it. She'd been interviewed by Jane Clayson ("a sweetheart") and Larry King, among others, and despite her protests that she didn't plan to talk bad about others ("It's just not me," she'd repeated, and meant it) was furious that CBS was being accused of unethical dealings. It was CBS, she said, that was responsible for first getting the story of Jessi's capture out to the world, before any other station had taken notice, "and when that many people are all praying for this one girl, God's got to pay attention," she said. "Well, not that He doesn't pay attention to other prayers, but you know." Since the people at CBS had theoretically led to Jessi's rescue, and since they'd shown, she claimed, genuine concern for Jessi and her family and friends since that first interview, she believed they deserved the story. Besides—lowering her voice in an effort to mitigate the fact that she was close to revealing something bad about somebody—she wasn't saying who, exactly, but practically every other news outlet had done something distasteful, like yell at Jessi's mom. "And around here," she said firmly, "being pushy and rude is not the way to get what you want." Her boss walked by, one of many such passes, and she smiled apologetically and thanked me for stopping in—interview over.

At the trailer, I could hear the TV but couldn't see into the dark living room. "Heather's here," I heard a voice say, and I let myself in. R.T. and Levi were watching a movie on Lifetime starring Julie Andrews and Haley Joel Osment while Renee worked in the kitchen. Rob had the freezer door open with his head inside—his allergies were killing him and this was the house's only air-conditioning. I'd ruined our plans for the swimming hole, and they'd gone fishing while I skulked about deli counters in grocery and convenience stores. We watched the entire movie in relative silence as Renee prepared hot dogs, hamburger patties, deviled eggs and baked beans for a cookout that I was suddenly unsure if I was welcome to join. Jessica Lynch had ruined my day.

Minutes later, Renee asked casually if I was eating, and R.T. and I discovered that it was a good 10 degrees cooler outside. My spirits soared. R.T. had talked a fair amount about shooting people, anyone, really, who might cross him, and I'd questioned the plausibility of this proposition. He now pulled out from his car a .357 Magnum, fully licensed and legal, he assured me, and opened and emptied a full chamber before handing it to me. I'd never seen, let alone held, a real handgun before, and he showed me how to pull back the hammer and laughed when I asked him where the safety was. Apparently they don't come standard.

Renee's brother, sister-in-law, and two nephews arrived with the usual lack of fanfare and introductions. I still had the gun in my hand, fascinated by the weight of it, and was horrified suddenly to be brandishing a real live gun in front of two small children. I considered hiding it behind me but feared that someone might see, and, well, what to think of the strange woman poorly concealing a weapon on the front lawn?

Three hours later, after dinner and several fights about the possibility of setting a neighbor's roof on fire with the boys' bottle rockets, we were shooting fireworks over a lake a couple of miles down the road. Across the water was

Rob and Renee's landlords' house, and they intermittently screamed and honked their horn to see if anyone was home. In the other direction was an expanse of high grass and, beyond, a rise that disappeared in woods. It was in the last minutes before the sun escaped the horizon that Rob said to me, eyebrows raised, "You should take a look at the firecracker R.T. has over there." I figured there was some special Roman candle for the evening's finale, and I chuckled that R.T. was joining in the fun. I swung my head around just in time to see a bluish white bubble wave out of his hands, and then I heard the gun's report. It was, without a doubt, the loudest noise I've ever heard in my life. There was time enough to curse and press my hands to my singing ears before R.T., laughing, of course, was handing the .357 to me. My hearing was irreparably damaged, the kids had now seen me hold a gun and shout obscenities, and I'd interviewed two people since coming to town. I aimed for the trees and squeezed.

The next morning a parade came through Elizabeth. Rob and R.T. (who'd vowed to get the hell out of Dodge in anticipation of this event) nodded to me from a perch on their restaurant's balcony. The building, which also housed a video rental place, sat back from the main road enough that they avoided the specter of Mardi Gras. While I darted about, looking in vain for any sign or reference to Jessica Lynch, I did notice the *Register* lady taking photographs for the paper. She had totally blown me off. I consoled myself by taking my own pictures of the monster truck I'd heard would be featured—just some local guy who'd jacked his Ford up on struts that, with the hydraulics pushed to the max, looked like a chassis on a jungle gym—and local girls in spangled costumes twirling batons.

A few of Rob and R.T.'s friends who had joined them on the balcony congregated in the parking lot below after the parade. I had assumed the town would be crawling with reporters trying to cash in on the holiday with a nice Americana piece, but aside from the *Register* lady and a photographer, the parade seemed populated by locals and residents of nearby towns. This assembly of friends—all men—claimed I wasn't the only one who'd been thinking that. They swore that last year's had lasted 10 minutes instead of 45, and that all the surrounding counties who had sent fire trucks and squad cars to participate had done so only because of the reporters they'd hoped would be attending. They wanted, it seemed, to get in on the Jessi action.

This was not the first time I'd heard rumblings of resentment toward the publicity Jessica Lynch's story was generating. They were quick to say that Jessi herself had little or nothing to do with the phenomenon (some even hoping she'd take all she could get from the frenzy), but most couldn't keep the bitterness from their voices when they spoke of "the Bell boy." Marine Sgt. David Bell had grown up in Elizabeth and had been injured on duty a month and a half prior when a grenade launcher jammed and exploded in his face on his base in San Diego. Nobody was interested in his plight, they said, and he was serving his country as Jessi had been. His picture had finally been hung in the courthouse next to hers, and although a spaghetti dinner was planned to raise money for his family, everyone agreed that he hadn't received his fair share of the attention, and there was one reason only: He was a man.

One, Craig, was quick to point out to me that his opinion was not a reflection of his esteem for women. He loved women, he assured me, although having just watched him call out "look at the shitter on that critter" to one of the comely high school girls working at a car wash fundraiser across the street, I had the notion that our definition of love was a little different. He also, in the course of praising the parade, had announced something so racist that although everyone around him laughed and encouraged him to repeat it, he now asked me not to print it. There were laws against racism, he claimed, and he'd already been to jail once—his sister was pregnant, so he'd taken the rap for her. (Rob told me later that day that if I hadn't noticed, Craig didn't like black people, and R.T. proclaimed him "two bricks short of a load." They both agreed, however, that he'd grown up a lot and was a good friend to have on your side.)

The party broke up, moving on to the trailer, and I walked to the ice cream social at the firehouse. There was a good crowd of people grouped under a tarp and at picnic tables, fanning themselves in the midday sun. When I had only a $20 bill or two singles to pay for my $2.50 hot dog, lemonade, and slice of apple pie, a woman knocked the change off with a smile. A bluegrass duo was playing on a stage in the parking lot, and donated six-packs of Coke and hunting knives were raffled off during their breaks. I chatted with the sheriff, deputy sheriff, and an elderly woman wearing a "Welcome Home Jessi" T-shirt who wanted to tell me about having shingles in her eyes. It was time for another trip to Palestine.

This time the What-Not Shop was open. I'd read about the store before, and the reason was clear: There was no place else to talk to the townspeople of Palestine, other than by finding them in Elizabeth or knocking on their doors at home. The owner of this store selling curio cabinets and panther figurines that roared when prodded gave the party line: "I'll talk to you but I don't have much to say." Two men, Clifford and Jack, sat in the store with him and asked me what kind of Coke I wanted (Coke being the generic term for soft drink). Clifford, who claimed to be the second-oldest person in Palestine, seemed to have been waiting for an audience and spent the next three hours regaling me with jokes of every sort: hillbilly (A hillbilly and a buckeye are on either side of the river. The buckeye calls out to the hillbilly and asks him how to get to the other side. The hillbilly answers, "What do you need to know that for? You're already there!"); blonde (Why doesn't anyone laugh at blonde jokes? Because blondes don't think they're funny and nobody else thinks they're jokes); and battle of the genders (The population of this town always stays the same; every time a baby is born, a man leaves town).

Jack mostly laughed at Clifford's jokes, and laughed at me laughing at Clifford's jokes, and then, when I mentioned I should head over to take another look at the Lynch home, handed me a CD as a parting gift. It was Miriah Duckworth's, and it included "Jessi's Song" written by Miriah's mother and, of course, "I'm Proud to Be an American." They were selling for $10 with $2 going to Jessi's fund, but Jack said he'd bought every copy he could find and was selling them for $15. I mentioned this later back at the trailer, and no one seemed surprised or perturbed; as Randall told me two days before, you made money however you could.

Clifford figured he'd ride along with me to make sure I found it (again), and he told me about the history of the region as we drove. He pointed out the "monstrosity" of a building—a general store—that had put both of Palestine's grocery stores out of business and then gone out itself. Now there was just the What-Not Shop, and the only food they sold was an assortment of Cokes. The monstrosity was a two-story white clapboard place, but it looked like it had been defunct for quite some time. "When exactly did all this happen?" I asked. It had been just after the war, he said, so a little over 50 years ago.

I parked in front of Jessi's house, fretting about blocking the road but not brash enough to pull into the driveway. Jessi's family was with her at the hospital in D.C., but unlike during my previous visit, there appeared to be people working on the premises. Afraid that Clifford, like Rob's *Register* lady ambush, might suggest I try to interview someone, I made a preemptive comment about the sign in the lawn that asked visitors to stay out. When I was little, I had been a miserable Girl Scout, selling cookies to my parents and one old woman down the street who looked forward to my annual visit. If people wanted cookies, I thought, why wouldn't they just buy some? Who wants someone rousing you in your own home to order cookies at twice the price that you won't be able to enjoy for months? I knew that the men sweating in this house had put in hours of manual labor (in addition to the work they did at their other paying jobs) to level the floor for Jessi's wheelchair and add bedrooms and a custom-fitted bathroom; it had already been reported. A car pulled up and a balding man in shorts got out. He and his wife had come from Charleston, he said, to see what the hubbub was about—just sightseers.

As I got out of the car to take a picture, Clifford gestured across the street to the trailer below. "That's the tobacco field that New York reporter was talking about. Pick me a couple leaves from down there while you're out," he chortled, absolutely gleeful to reference Jayson Blair's fabrications. I laughed, but the significance wasn't lost on me. Clifford directed me to the city-limit sign, recently moved to the other side of Mayberry Run Road despite the fact that Jessi's home was a few miles from the town proper, and pointed out Jessi's grandparents' former home, which was on the other side of a great ravine and accessible only by a swinging rope bridge. I'd probably found the best possible guide to Palestine, but it was too late. I was leaving in the morning. And besides, R.T. had told me that I'd shot the gun well, looked like a natural, and there'd been talk of a drive-in movie or late-night ridge-running after dinner.

And so there I was, my last evening in town, sitting in the trailer kitchen, eating leftover deviled eggs that were sweating almost as much as me. Rob's allergies were still bothering him, so Renee had gone to Parkersburg with her sister without him. R.T. refused to go to dinner as planned, which meant I had to decide between meeting up with only Renee or spending the evening in the trailer. Renee had shown an interest in my article and had been a great help in forcing others to give me ideas. I worried, though, that she would now want to know what I had accomplished and ask for the umpteenth time whether I had enough to write about. And so I decided to stay back.

Craig and Rob were discussing the infamous Pamela Anderson/Tommy Lee video, and the topic of Craig's two divorces came up (he was 24), which led, somehow, to a proposal. Craig told me that he had an uncle who was a minister, and we could have it done right then and there. "You think I'm joking?" he kept repeating. "I'm dead serious." I told him that I didn't know him well enough to tell if he was in fact joking, but either way, I imagined my boyfriend wouldn't be too happy about such an arrangement. He replied without a moment's hesitation, "Does he fancy an ass-whooping?" He had to work that night, but proclaimed he'd call in sick if I wanted to get married; I declined again, he shrugged, and we said goodbye.

Rob, R.T., and I drove out to pick up Levi, then settled in on the front porch. The night was wearing on and I had a long drive in the morning, but I hadn't resolved everything I needed to. Finally, I broke into the conversation. "I have two important questions I need to ask you," I said. "First, I know that you didn't have anything to say for my piece about Jessica Lynch. But I've spent a lot of time with you and I think I'd like to write about you anyway. I know I never really said that, so do I have your permission, and is there anything you've said around me that, had you known it might end up in an article, you wouldn't have said?" Rob looked unconcerned, and R.T. sighed. "I don't give a damn," he said.

"I just thought there were some things you probably wouldn't want me to include," I pressed. R.T. had refused to let me take any pictures of him, and he generally had, it was safe to say, definite opinions on most matters.

"I don't give a damn," he repeated.

"Certain things I might not even realize you didn't want me to talk about?" I said.

"Don't give a damn."

"Or things that I know make you upset, like mentioning your full name?"

He paused, and spoke slowly, shaking his head for emphasis. "I DON'T GIVE A DAMN." And then, of course, the caveat I'd been waiting for. "You can write any goddamned thing you want. If I don't like it, I'll just come to New York and shoot you."

I argued with him for a while that if he'd just clue me in ahead of time as to what he might not like, we could save him the trouble of hunting me down, but the more I pestered him, the more detailed his description of my death became. I moved on to my second question.

"I'm completely serious about this. I don't know the answer, and I want you to be honest," I said. "Why have you let me hang out with you all weekend? I'm a total stranger, and you don't know anything about me. Why have you been so nice to me?" The question was deeper than that. I didn't really understand the people I'd met in Wirt County that weekend, any of them. I'd been given gifts, meals, even offered a place to stay (so I wouldn't have to drive back to my hotel), but none of it was your average hospitality. The fact of the matter was that nobody seemed to pay much attention to me one way or the other.

I didn't flatter myself that what little attention I had received had anything to do with me specifically. Craig had asked me to marry him because, as he'd said, "It'd be something different." To Clifford, I was someone who hadn't heard his jokes before. Alone in a car with Renee that first night, I'd talked a little about where I was from and what I did; other than that, most people knew I was from New York and was writing something. Many people I'd tried to interview begged off completely or asked that I not use their name, some maybe because they had negative or contentious things to say, but most because they just didn't want the attention. They were not small-town rubes bowled over by fast-talking city folk; they'd had enough media in town over the past couple of months to have figured out how to exploit or shun me to suit their purposes.

When I'd asked an uncle of Jessi's who'd been pointed out to me in the supermarket why, as he said, he didn't know anything about it, he'd answered, "I work." He wasn't being flip or rude. He was giving me the genuine answer: He was busy. Like much of Wirt County in general, he was good-naturedly disinterested in the Jessica Lynch saga and in me.

All of this was wrapped up in my question. What I really wanted to ask, I suppose, was not why they were nice to me, but why they weren't nicer. Why did they act as if I were just one of the gang?

Rob thought for a moment, and R.T. watched to see what he'd answer. "Honestly?" he said.

"Yes," I answered, and waited to hear what I already knew.

"It's nothing personal. We treat everybody like this."

R.T. coughed. "Everybody," he said, "who we don't want to shoot."

I'm hoping that still includes me.

Contributors' Notes

Michael Arad is an Israeli American architect who is best known for being the designer of the National September 11 Memorial at the World Trade Center site. Arad, who is a partner at Handel Architects and whose current projects include the design of a memorial to the victims of the 2015 massacre at the Mother Emanuel AME Church in Charleston, South Carolina, earned a B.A. from Dartmouth College and a master of architecture degree at the Georgia Institute of Technology.

Larry Auerbach (1923–2014) directed the soap operas *All My Children*, *Another World*, *As the World Turns*, and *Love of Life* (for the entirety of the latter's 28-year run). Auerbach received a Daytime Emmy award in 1985 for his work on the ABC soap *One Life to Live* and was also the recipient of the Directors Guild of America's Robert B. Aldrich Service Award in 1991. In 2004, the DGA named him an honorary life member, a designation he shares with an elite group of filmmakers that includes Charlie Chaplin, Frank Capra, and Walt Disney.

Chantal Bizzini is a French poet, translator, photographer, and collage artist. Her published volumes of poetry include *Boulevard Magenta* (le bousquet-la barthe éditions, 2015) and *Disenchanted City* (Black Widow Press, 2015). Bizzini has translated into French the American poets Ezra Pound, Hart Crane, Adrienne Rich, Jorie Graham, and John Ashbery, among others, and she is currently working on a series of meditations on photo-illustrated books, including Walker Evans's *Many Are Called* and Brassaï's *Paris de nuit*.

Carter Burwell is an American composer of film scores who has frequently collaborated with the Coen brothers, having scored most of their films, including *Blood Simple*, *Raising Arizona*, *Fargo*, *The Big Lebowski*, and *The Ballad of Buster Scruggs*. Burwell has also worked often with directors Todd Haynes, Spike Jonze, and Martin McDonagh. He received Academy Award nominations for Best Original Score for both Haynes's *Carol* and McDonagh's *Three Billboards Outside Ebbing, Missouri*.

Anthony Cheung is a composer and pianist, an assistant professor of music at the University of Chicago, and the artistic director of the Talea Ensemble, which he cofounded in 2007. His music has been commissioned by the New York Philharmonic, Frankfurt Radio Symphony Orchestra, Ensemble Modern, and the French National Orchestras of Lille and Lorraine, among others. Cheung has received awards from the American Academy of Arts and Letters and ASCAP, and the Rome Prize from the American Academy in Rome.

Lesley Clayton studied English at the University of Texas and lives in Fort Worth, Texas.

John Conway (1937–2020) was an English mathematician active in the theory of finite groups, knot theory, number theory, algebra, geometry, combinatorial game theory, and coding theory. He also made contributions to many branches of recreational mathematics, most notably with the invention of the cellular automaton called the Game of Life. Conway was elected a fellow of the Royal Society in 1981 and was the John von Neumann Distinguished Professor at Princeton University from 1987 to 2013.

Julia Drake received her B.A. in Spanish from Williams College and her M.F.A. in creative writing from Columbia University, where she also taught writing to first-year students. She works as a book coach for aspiring writers and teaches creative writing classes for Writopia Lab, a nonprofit that fosters a love of writing in young adults. Her debut novel, *The Last True Poets of the Sea* (Little, Brown) won the 2019 New England Book Award for Young Adult Literature and was named a best book of 2019 by *Publishers Weekly*.

Jessica Rae Elsaesser, a Brooklyn-based poet and book artist living in Brooklyn, NY, was a 2013 Poets House Emerging Poets fellow. Her recent works have been included in *Looking for You* (Du-Good Press, 2021), *Thou Who Holds But Owns Not* (TLTRPreß, 2020), *Completely and Without Pause: Feminist Notes on Oppression and Expansion* (Print Experimentation Area, 2019), and *Daisyworld Magazine #2*. She collaborates with her sister, Lindsey Ann Elsaesser, on the self-publishing project Place of the Linden.

Stéphane Gerson is a professor of French, French studies, and history at New York University and is the director of the Institute of French Studies. Gerson is the author of *The Pride of Place: Local Memories and Political Culture in 19th-Century France* (Cornell University Press, 2003), which won the Jacques Barzun Prize in Cultural History and the Laurence Wylie Prize in French Cultural Studies, and *Nostradamus: How an Obscure French Doctor Became the Modern Prophet of Doom* (St. Martin's Press, 2012).

Ann Goldstein has translated works by, among others, Elena Ferrante, Primo Levi, Pier Paolo Pasolini, and Jhumpa Lahiri, and she is the editor of *The Complete Works of Primo Levi* in English. Goldstein, who was the head copy editor at *The New Yorker* for 30 years, is the recipient of a Guggenheim fellowship and awards from the Italian Ministry of Foreign Affairs and the American Academy of Arts and Letters. Her translation of Ferrante's *The Story of the Lost Child* was short-listed for the 2016 Man Booker International Prize.

Stephen Adly Guirgis is a playwright whose works include *Our Lady of 121st Street, Jesus Hopped the "A" Train, The Last Days of Judas Iscariot, The Motherf**ker with the Hat* (nominated for a 2011 Tony Award for Best Play), and *Between Riverside and Crazy*, which won the 2015 Pulitzer Prize in Drama. Guirgis is co-artistic director and a member of the LAByrinth Theater Company, and he has appeared as an actor in the films *Margaret, Synecdoche, New York*, and *Palindromes*, among others.

Upon his return from the Vietnam War, **Rick Holen** attended St. Cloud State University and received an M.A. in opera design from Indiana University. Holen and his wife, Anne, have worked as scenic and costume designers in film, television, opera, theater, and dance throughout the U.S.

Lonnie Holley is an artist and musician whose artwork has been the subject of numerous exhibitions, including *Thumbs Up for the Mother Ship* (with Dawn DeDeaux) at MASS MoCA, North Adams, Massachusetts (2017), and *Everything That Wasn't White: Lonnie Holley at the Elaine de Kooning House* at the Parrish Art Museum in Water Mill, New York (2021). Holley, who has collaborated musically with Dirty Projectors and Animal Collective, has released a number of albums, including *Keeping a Record of It* (Dust-to-Digital, 2013), *Mith* (Jagjaguwar, 2018), and *National Freedom* (Jagjaguwar, 2020).

Mitch Horowitz is a historian of alternative spirituality, mysticism, and the occult whose work, as described by the *Washington Post*, "treats esoteric ideas and movements with an even-handed intellectual studiousness that is too often lost in today's raised-voice discussions." Horowitz is a lecturer-in-residence at the Philosophical Research Society in Los Angeles, a writer-in-residence at the New York Public Library, and a PEN Award–winning author whose books include *Occult America* (Bantam, 2009) and *The Miracle Club* (Inner Traditions, 2018).

Pamela A. Ivinski (1963–2017) was an author, editor, and the senior research associate for the Mary Cassatt catalogue raisonné committee. Her articles appeared in *Print, Antiques and Fine Art*, and *publicsfear*, the arts zine she cofounded and edited with Tod Lippy from 1992 to 1994. Ivinski was the coauthor of *Women Impressionists: Berthe Morisot, Mary Cassatt, Eva Gonzalès, Marie Bracquemond* (Hatje Cantz, 2008).

Michael Patrick King began work in the entertainment industry performing stand-up before writing for a number of TV series, including *Murphy Brown* and *Will & Grace*. In 1998, he was hired as a writer on HBO's *Sex and the City*; King eventually directed a number of episodes and became co-executive producer of the series, which garnered him two Primetime Emmy Awards. King was also the writer, director, and producer of the feature films *Sex and the City* and *Sex and the City 2*.

Karl Ove Knausgaard is a writer, editor, and essayist best known for his critically acclaimed six-volume autobiographical novel *My Struggle [Min Kamp]*, published in Norway between 2009 and 2011 and since translated into 22 languages. Knausgaard's other books include *A Time for Everything* (Archipelago, 2004) and *The Morning Star* (Penguin Press, 2021). From 1999 to 2002, Knausgaard coedited *Vagant*, a Norwegian literary magazine, and in 2013 he published *The Soul's America: Writings 1996–2013*, a collection of essays. Knausgaard has also written for *The New Yorker* and *The New York Times*.

Lisa Kudrow began her career by performing with the improvisational-comedy troupe The Groundlings in Los Angeles. After taking on smaller roles in *Cheers* and *Mad About You*, she won the part of Phoebe Buffay on the NBC series *Friends*, ultimately winning a Primetime Emmy Award and a Screen Actors Guild Award. Kudrow has since acted in a number of films and television shows, including *Romy and Michele's High School Reunion*, *Analyze This*, *The Opposite of Sex*, and *Feel Good*. Kudrow was nominated for two Emmys for her portrayal of Valerie Cherish in *The Comeback* and was cowriter, coproducer, and star of the Showtime series *Web Therapy*.

Katherine J. Lee is a bicoastal writer and artist who has worked as a legal library filer, writing instructor, shop girl, textile artist, college prep tutor, memoir editor, artist's assistant, and gardener. Her work has been published in *Storychord*, *fwriction : review*, and *Cactus Heart*.

Kenneth Lonergan is a playwright and filmmaker whose plays include *Lobby Hero* (2001; winner of the Outer Critics Circle Best Play Award); *The Waverly Gallery* (2000; Pulitzer Prize finalist); and *This Is Our Youth* (1996; Drama Desk Best Play nominee). His first film, *You Can Count on Me*, was nominated for an Academy Award for best screenplay; his second, *Margaret*, was released in 2011 and proclaimed a "masterpiece" by *The New York Times*. Lonergan's 2016 film, *Manchester by the Sea*, won Lonergan an Academy Award for Best Original Screenplay and was nominated in multiple other categories.

Victory Matsui is an editor at One World, a publisher of works of fiction and nonfiction, including titles by Thi Bui, Anelise Chen, Mira Jacob, Riva Lehrer, Jordy Rosenberg, and Maurice Carlos Ruffin. Matsui cofacilitates the People of Color Sangha at the Brooklyn Zen Center and is a founding member of Yellow Brown Power Hour, a radical Asian American performance group and hot pot club.

Joe Mauro returned from the Vietnam War and pursued careers in several fields (none of them, to his regret, entertainment). Now retired, he lives in Lincoln, Rhode Island.

Edward McPherson is a Pushcart Prize–winning author of the books *Buster Keaton: Tempest in a Flat Hat* (Faber & Faber, 2004), *The Backwash Squeeze and Other Improbable Feats* (HarperCollins, 2009), and *The History of the Future: American Essays* (Coffee House Press, 2017). He has written for *The New York Times Magazine*, the *Paris Review*, and *Talk*, among other publications. A contributing editor of the *Common Reader*, McPherson teaches in the creative writing program at Washington University in St. Louis, Missouri.

Heather McPherson (née Larson) has published her nonfiction essays in *Time Out: New York* and *T: The New York Times Style Magazine* and has edited manuscripts for *Rolling Stone* and *Details*. She holds an M.F.A. in creative nonfiction from the University of Minnesota and is a lecturer in English at Washington University in St. Louis, Missouri.

Stuart Nadler, a recipient of the "5 Under 35" award from the National Book Foundation, is the author of two novels—*Wise Men* (Little, Brown, 2013) and *The Inseparables* (Little, Brown; chosen as a best book of 2016 by *Kirkus*)—and the short story collection *The Book of Life* (Little, Brown, 2011). He is a graduate of the Iowa Writers' Workshop, where he was a Truman Capote Fellow. Nadler teaches creative writing at Boston College and is also a faculty member of the Bennington Writing Seminars.

Daniel T. Neely is a musician and ethnomusicologist with specialties in the music of Ireland and Jamaica. He earned a Ph.D. in musicology from New York University, receiving a Fulbright Scholarship for his dissertation on Jamaican *mento* music. Neely has contributed essays to a number of books, including *Jamaica Jamaica!* (Philharmonie de Paris, 2017), *Victorian Jamaica* (Duke University Press, 2009), and *The Concise Garland Encyclopedia of*

World Music (2008); he writes a weekly column about traditional music for the *Irish Echo*.

After the Vietnam War, **John Nutt** studied film at Stanford University. He has since worked as either a sound or picture editor on more than 60 films, including *Munich* (2005), *Rushmore* (1998), *Blue Velvet* (1986), and *Apocalypse Now* (1979). Nutt won a BAFTA award for his sound editing on *Amadeus* (1984).

"Penelope" is the pseudonym of an Atlanta-based decor artist.

Chelli Riddiough received a B.A. from Williams College and an M.F.A. in writing from the University of Minnesota, where she has also taught in the English department. A freelance writer and editor, Riddiough is director of marketing and community engagement at a bicycle shop in Minneapolis.

Lev AC Rosen is an author whose books include *All Men of Genius* (Tor Books, 2011), *Depth* (Regan Arts, 2015), *Jack of Hearts (and Other Parts)* (Little, Brown, 2018), and the forthcoming *Lavender House*. His acclaimed young-adult novel *Camp* (Little, Brown, 2020) has been adapted for an HBO Max film to be directed by Billy Porter. Rosen lives in New York City with his husband and a very small cat.

Ethan Rutherford's fiction has appeared in *Tin House*, *Ploughshares*, *Conjunctions*, *BOMB*, and *The Best American Short Stories*. His first book, *The Peripatetic Coffin and Other Stories* (Ecco, 2013), was a finalist for the *Los Angeles Times* Art Seidenbaum Award for First Fiction and a finalist for the John Leo nard Prize. His second collection of stories, *Farthest South*, was published by A Strange Object in 2021. Rutherford teaches creative writing at Trinity College in Hartford, Connecticut.

Kelly Sandoval is a speculative fiction author whose stories have appeared in *Uncanny*, *Strange Horizons*, and *Best American Science Fiction and Fantasy*. The author of the interactive novel *Runt of the Litter* (Choice of Games, 2017), Sandoval is also one of the senior editors and publishers of *Liminal Stories*, an online literary magazine.

Nicole Sealey is the author of *Ordinary Beast* (2017), a finalist for the PEN Open Book Award and Hurston/Wright Legacy Award, and *The Animal After Whom Other Animals Are Named* (2016). She has been awarded a 2019 Rome Prize and a Stanley Kunitz Memorial Prize, as well as fellowships at the Bread Loaf Writers' Conference and the MacDowell Colony. Sealey has been a visiting professor at the City College of New York and Boston University and was a 2019–2020 Hodder Fellow at Princeton University.

Kansas City native **Bob Sevra** attended Stanford University as an undergraduate and was pursuing a master's degree in English at the University of Michigan when he was drafted for the Vietnam War. Upon his return, he began a career as an actor and writer. He lives in New York with his wife, actress Rita Gardner.

Vivien Shotwell is a Canadian-American author and mezzo-soprano whose first novel, *Vienna Nocturne* (Ballantine, 2014) has been translated into seven languages. Shotwell has performed with the Rai Symphony Orchestra in Turin, Italy, and the Los Angeles Opera, among others. She received a B.A. from William's College, an M.F.A. from the Iowa Writer's Workshop, and an artist diploma from the Yale School of Music, where she was awarded both the David L. Kasdon Memorial Prize and the Phyllis Curtin Career Entry Prize.

Danielle Spencer is the academic director of the Columbia University Narrative Medicine Program, author of *Metagnosis: Revelatory Narratives of Health and Identity* (Oxford University Press, 2021) and coauthor of the Perkins Prize–winning *The Principles and Practice of Narrative Medicine* (Oxford University Press, 2017). Her creative and scholarly work has appeared in diverse outlets ranging from *Ploughshares* to *The Lancet*. Spencer, who was formerly artist and musician David Byrne's art director, was a 2019 MacDowell Fellow and a 2021 Yaddo Fellow.

Rick Stinson received his B.A. in fiction from Bennington College and is the prepress editorial lead at Oxford University Press. Stinson, who has worked as a freelance writer and copy editor, was editor-in-chief of the music blog *The Little Black Egg*.

Jennifer Tipton is the recipient of two Bessie Awards and an Olivier Award for lighting dance, collaborating with artists who include Mikhail Baryshnikov, Jerome Robbins, and Twyla Tharp. Tipton's work for theater, for which she has been given two Tony Awards, an Obie, and two Drama Desk Awards, includes productions of *The Cherry Orchard*, *Waiting for Godot*, and the Wooster Group's *To You, the Birdie!* Her lighting for opera includes Robert Wilson's production of *Parsifal* (Houston Grand Opera) and Peter Sellars's staging of *Tannhäuser* (Chicago Light Opera). Tipton, who received a MacArthur "Genius Grant" in 2008, teaches at the Yale School of Drama.

Raphael van Lierop is the founder and creative director of Hinterland, an independent game studio based in North Vancouver Island that is responsible for the influential video game *The Long Dark*. Van Lierop has worked at such studios as Relic Entertainment and Ubisoft Montreal, and he has contributed to the award-winning titles *Company of Heroes* (the highest-rated real-time strategy game of all time), *Far Cry 3*, and *Warhammer 40,000: Space Marine*. Van Lierop has lectured internationally on subjects related to the development of original intellectual property and game-development methodology.

Maureen O'Leary Wanket is an author and teacher based in Sacramento, California. Her books include *How to Be Manly* (Giant Squid Books, 2014), *The Arrow* (Geminid Press, 2014), and *The Ghost Daughter* (Coffeetown Press, 2016). Her poetry and short stories have been published in *Prick of the Sprindle*, *Night Train Journal*, and *The Black Fork Review*, as well as in the Shade Mountain Press 2015 anthology *The Female Complaint: Tales of Unruly Women*.

Robert Warner is a collage artist, letterpress printer, optician, and eyewear designer based in New York City's Greenwich Village. In 2011, Warner staged the exhibition and event series *Ray and Bob Box*, which related to a yearslong correspondence between himself and the artist Ray Johnson, at Esopus Space in New York City; it subsequently traveled to venues including the University of California, Berkeley, Art Museum and the Valade Family Gallery at the College for Creative Studies in Detroit.

Originally a soloist with the New York City Ballet, **Christopher Wheeldon** was named the company's first resident choreographer in 2001. In 2007, he founded Morphoses/The Wheeldon Company and was appointed an associate artist for Sadler's Wells Theatre in London. Wheeldon has choreographed works for the Royal Ballet (where he is an artistic associate), the Metropolitan Opera, the Joffrey Ballet, and the Bolshoi Ballet, among many others. He received a 2014 Tony Award for Best Choreography for the Broadway revival of *An American in Paris* and was the director and choreographer of *MJ: The Musical* (2021).

Jody Williams is the chef and owner of Buvette in New York City's Greenwich Village and and, along with her wife, Rita Sodi, chef and owner of the restaurants Via Carota and The Commerce Inn in the same neighborhood. Williams opened a second location of Buvette in the South Pigalle neighborhood of Paris in 2013, followed by a third, Buvette Tokyo, in 2018. She is the author of *Buvette: The Pleasure of Good Food* (2014) and she was the recipient, with Sodi, of the James Beard Award for Best Chef: New York City in 2019.

Stephanie Adler Yuan is practicum coordinator and a lecturer in the Columbia University Narrative Medicine Program. A 2015 graduate of the program, Yuan has lectured widely about relationships of care and has led narrative medicine workshops for a variety of patient, student, and clinician groups at NYU Lutheran Medical Center, Memorial Sloan Kettering Cancer Center, Maimonides Medical Center, and other medical institutions.

Acknowledgments

Esopus was often described as a "one-man magazine," but the truth is it might not have existed, and it certainly never would have thrived, without the participation, support, and encouragement of many remarkable people.

Keriann Kohler, the Esopus Foundation administrator—and the only other employee of the foundation—joined me in a part-time position in 2007 after we received a capacity-building grant from the Andy Warhol Foundation for the Visual Arts. Over the past 15 years, she has seamlessly navigated the foundation through the choppy seas of grant writing and fundraising, subscriber fulfillment, event planning, accounting, and distribution. She has also been an invaluable sounding board and idea-generator for *Esopus*, not to mention a delightful partner to have in this whole enterprise.

The current members of the Esopus Foundation's Board of Trustees—Monroe Denton, John Melick, Kay Rosen, and Howie Seligman—have provided unwavering advocacy and guidance, and they never hesitate to embolden me to take on new projects (including this book). Emeritus members Martin Fox, a mentor of mine since I worked for him at *Print* magazine in the early '90s, and Barbara Turner (1936–2016), whose brilliant work as a screenwriter and generosity as a friend and colleague were a boundless source of inspiration, both offered indispensable feedback in the early days of the foundation's existence. Another former member of the board, Bradley Goldman, donated his time to shepherd us successfully through the labyrinthine legal process of applying for 501(c)(3) status.

So much of the material that ended up in *Esopus* was the direct result of advice, suggestions, and Rolodex-sharing by the magazine's vital advisory board: Joe Amrhein, Sara Bader, David Brendel, Mary Ellen Carroll, Daniel Clowes, Walter Donohue, Steven Heller, Pamela A. Ivinski, Gareth Jones, Julie Lasky, Alex Marvar, Louis Menand, Scott Menchin, Stephen Motika, Mike Powell, Jim Shepard, Chris Trela, Dean Wareham, Glen Weyl, and Joshua White.

Needless to say, an organization consisting of one full-time and one part-time staff member will never survive without a steady supply of able interns. All of the students who assisted us over the years did much more than errand-running. They wrote and edited copy; helped ensure our events ran smoothly; offered superb suggestions for content; installed exhibitions; and in general, made us feel a little bit younger with their endless enthusiasm and energy. Sincere thanks to Lily Arzt,

Moriah Askenaizer, Logan Beck, Margot Bowman, Jessica Butler, Marina Caron, Lisa Case, Cecilia Cholst, Court Conwell, Nathan Dixon, Penn Eastburn, Aaron Fowler, Andrew Daly Frank, Clément Gagliano, Leo Gertner, Hannah Gruendemann, Claire Taylor Hansen, Katie Heiserman, Alexander Iezzi, Moise J. Michel, Vicki Kim, Catherine Kirk, Anne Lai, Taylor Larson, Jacqueline Lash, Jamie Lerman, Christina Livelli, Eli Meixler, Andrew Menfi, Kelsey Mitchell, Katherine Oshman, Sun Kyoung Park, Maricarmen Perez, Nicholas Pierce, Phebe Pierson, Mike Powell, Marisa Prefer, Gracie Remington, Euan Rugg, Lev AC Rosen, Benjamin Santiago, Elana Schlenker, Thomas Seely, Daria Solomon, Lauren Stefaniak, Sam Sullivan, Melissa Tuckman, Aidan H. Weider, and Laura Williamson.

While it would easily fill another book to name the hundreds of individuals who have offered their financial or logistical support to the Esopus Foundation over the years, it's worth citing those whose substantial generosity has rarely wavered over nearly two decades: Meg Armstrong, Keith and Felicia Anzel, Lori and Tito Beveridge, Melva Bucksbaum, Georgia Cool, Mona Dinsmore, Philipp Engelhorn, Marli Higa, Karen Holtzman, George Kondogianis, Wynn Kramarsky, Jack Larson, Marjorie and T. Edward Lippy, Frank Rich and Alex Witchel, Hila and Saul Rosen, Ed Ruscha, Alison Simmons and Louis Menand, Robin and Geoff Strawbridge, Robert Taffera, Willard Taylor, John Travis, and Chris Young. Of course, we wouldn't have survived without considerable grants from many public and private institutions, including the American Center Foundation, the Andy Warhol Foundation for the Visual Arts, the Coby Foundation, the Dedalus Foundation, the Elizabeth Firestone Graham Foundation, the Fleishhacker Foundation, Foundation for Contemporary Art, the Greenwall Foundation, the Lily Auchincloss Foundation, the Mary Duke Biddle Foundation, the Milton and Sally Avery Arts Foundation, the Mondriaan Foundation, the National Endowment for the Arts, the New York City Department of Cultural Affairs, the New York Council for the Humanities, the New York State Council on the Arts, the Peter and Carmen Lucia Buck Foundation, the Puffin Foundation Ltd., the Stephen and Mary Birch Foundation, and the Strypemonde Foundation.

David Hariton not only offered his unconditional support of and counsel on *Esopus* at every step of the way; he convinced me to start the publication in the first place. None of this would have been possible—and none of it would have been remotely as rewarding—without this superlative human being by my side.

Finally, I offer my deep gratitude to the two groups I endeavored to bring together with this whole enterprise: our readers, whose enthusiasm and engagement over the years has made every effort worthwhile; and our contributors, whose creativity has never ceased to amaze, delight, and inspire me.